BY MEANS OF PERFORMANCE

The field of performance studies embraces performance behavior of all kinds and in all contexts, from everyday life to high ceremony. This volume investigates a wide range of performance behavior – dance, ritual, conflict solution, sports, story-telling, and display behavior – in a variety of circumstances and cultures. It considers such issues as the relationship between training and the finished performance; whether performance behavior is universal or culturally specific; and the relationships between ritual and aesthetics, popular entertainment and religion, and sports and theatre and dance.

The contributors to this volume discuss these and related subjects using the examples of initiation rites among the Mbuti of central Africa, the deer dancing of the Yaquis of the American Sonoran desert, Sri Lankan ritual, mainstream and experimental theatre and dance in Europe and America, Korean shamanism, Indian kathakali dance-theatre, Purim plays in Brooklyn, Protestant and Catholic church ceremony in the American south, Japanese noh theatre, and circus clown performances. Beneath this diverse panoply of subjects lies a singularity of approach, the underlying unity of which consists in treating all these events as performances – as actions rehearsed, prepared, and presented.

The volume brings together essays from leading anthropologists, artists, and performance theorists to provide a definitive introduction to the burgeoning field of performance studies. It will be of value for scholars, teachers, and students of anthropology, theatre, folklore, semiotics, and performance studies.

BY MEANS OF PERFORMANCE

Intercultural studies of
theatre and ritual

Edited by

RICHARD SCHECHNER AND WILLA APPEL

CAMBRIDGE
UNIVERSITY PRESS

Published by the Press Syndicate of the University of Cambridge
The Pitt Building, Trumpington Street, Cambridge CB2 1RP
40 West 20th Street, New York, NY 10011, USA
10 Stamford Road, Oakleigh, Melbourne 3166, Australia

First published 1990
Reprinted 1993

Printed in Great Britain at the Athenæum Press Ltd, Newcastle upon Tyne

British Library cataloguing in publication data

By means of performance: intercultural studies
of theatre and ritual.
1. Man. Social behaviour
I. Schechner, Richard II. Appel, Willa
302

Library of Congress cataloguing in publication data

By means of performance: intercultural studies of theatre and ritual
/ edited by Richard Schechner and Willa Appel.
p.   cm.
Bibliography
ISBN 0-521-32608-7. – ISBN 0-521-33915-4 (pbk)
1. Theater and society. 2. Performing arts – Philosophy. 3. Rites
and ceremonies. 4. Turner, Victor.   I. Schechner, Richard, 1934–
II. Appel, Willa.
PN2039.B9   1989
306'.484 – dc19   88-37458   CIP

To Victor Turner

Contents

Contents

Figures

The sources for the illustrations in this volume are as follows: Introduction, Richard Schechner; chapter 1, Victor Turner; chapter 2, figures 2.4 to 2.12, Phillip Zarrilli, figures 2.13 to 2.18, Paul Ekman and Wallace V. Friesen, *Pictures of Facial Affect*, 1976 (Palo Alto, CA: Consulting Psychologists Press), figure 2.19, Roland Fischer, all other figures, Richard Schechner; chapter 3, Colin Turnbull; chapter 4, figures 4.2 and 4.3, Richard Schechner, all other figures, Edith Turner; chapter 8, Phillip Zarrilli; chapter 9, Du-Hyun Lee; chapter 10, figures 10.3 and 10.9, Tanaka Masao, all other figures Monica Bethe.

Notes on contributors

Willa Appel is the Executive Director of the Citizens' Housing and Planning Council, an independent non-profit-making think tank concerned with New York City's housing and urban development issues. Author of *Cults in America* (1983), she has also published numerous articles on various subjects including power relations in southern Italy, urban housing problems in the U.S., and immigration to the U.S. in the early twentieth century. She has lectured in social anthropology and housing concerns, and was responsible for developing a series of international conferences on theatre and ritual for the Wenner-Gren Foundation.

Monica Bethe graduated from Radcliffe in 1967. She then became a student and practitioner of Noh, studying first mask making then song, dance and all the instruments. Performances include full noh of *Tadanori* (*shite*), *Kakitsubata* (hip drum), and *Kiyotsune* (flute), as well as the lead in *Crazy Jane* by David Crandall. She devised costumes for *Crazy Jane*, for Crandall's next play, *The Linden Tree*, and for Izumi Yoshio's *The Afternoon of the Faun*. Publications include *Noh as Performance* (1978), *Dance in the Noh Theater* (1982–3) (both with Karen Brazell), translations of *Bugaku Masks, Tsujigahana*, and articles in *Noh Costumes of the Ii Family, Kosode*, and *The Encyclopedia of Japan*.

Herbert Blau, currently Distinguished Professor of English at the University of Wisconsin – Milwaukee, has also had a long career in the theatre. Starting with The Actor's Workshop of San Francisco, of which he was cofounder, he later became codirector of The Repertory Theater at Lincoln Center in New York, and subsequently Artistic Director of the experimental group KRAKEN. Two recent books, *Take Up the Bodies: Theater at the Vanishing Point* (1982) and *Blooded Thought: Occasions of Theater* (1982), received the George Jean Nathan Award in Dramatic Criticism. He has just published *The Eye of Prey: Subversions of the Postmodern*, and recently finished another book entitled *The Audience*.

Paul Bouissac is a Professor of French and Linguistics at the University of Toronto (Victoria College). His principal research interests are nonverbal communication and the semiotics of the performing arts. Among his publications are *La Mesure des gestes: Prolégomènes à la sémiotique gestuelle* (1973), *Circus and Culture* (1976), *The Semiotics of Nonsense* (1977); he has co-edited *The Encyclopedic Dictionary of Semiotics* (1986) and *Iconicity: Essays on the Nature of Culture* (1986).

Karen Brazell is Professor of Japanese Literature at Cornell University. She is currently working on a book tentatively titled *The Ghosts of Warriors on Stage: Noh Plays by Zeami*, and editing two volumes: *Plays from the Noh and Kyōgen Theaters* to be published by the Cornell China-Japan Program, and *Traditional Japanese Theater: An Anthology* with Stanford University Press.

Barbara Kirshenblatt-Gimblett is Professor of Performance Studies in the Tisch School of the Arts at New York University, where she holds a secondary appointment as Professor of Hebrew and Judaic Studies. She is also Research Associate at the YIVO Institute for Jewish Research. Her essays on various aspects of Ashkenazic Jewish ritual and the artifacts associated with them, including weddings, childbirth amulets, Torah binders, ceremonial textiles, and food will appear in a volume to be published by Indiana University Press. Her publications include *Fabric of Jewish Life: Textiles from The Jewish Museum Collection* (1977) and *Image Before My Eyes: A Photographic History of Jewish Life in Poland, 1864–1939* (1977, with Lucjan Dobroszycki).

Du-Hyun Lee, born in 1924, graduated from Seoul National University majoring in Korean literature. His academic career began at the College of Education, Seoul National University, and he later went to Peabody College and Catholic University in the United States to study drama and Anthropology for a year. He received a Litt. D. degree from Seoul National University in 1968 and is now professor of Korean drama and folklore at its College of Education.

He was Visiting Professor at Tokyo University in 1968, at the Ruhr University Bochum, West Germany in 1975, and at the National museum of Ethnology, Japan in 1981. He is Director of Research Institute of Korean Mask-dance Drama (since 1969) and was president of Korean Society for Cultural Anthropology (1972–74) and Korean Society for Theatre Research (1975–77). He is a member of National Academy of Sciences, Republic of Korea (since 1982).

His publications include, among others, *A History of Modern Korean Drama* (1966), *Korean Mask-dance Drama* (1969), *A History of Korean Folk-life* (1973), *A History of Korean Theatre arts* (1973), *Introducing Korean Folklore* (1974) and *Essays on Korean Folklore* (1984).

Barbara Myerhoff, who died in 1985, was Professor of Anthropology in the Anthropology Department at the University of Southern California. Among her writings were *The Peyote Hunt* (1974) and *Number Our Days* (1978). The latter book was the basis for a documentary film which won an Academy Award.

Ranjini Obeyesekere taught for several years in the Department of Literature, University of Sri Lanka, Peradeniya, and at the University of California, San Diego. She is now lecturer in the Department of Anthropology, Princeton University. Her publications include *Sinhala Writing and the New Critics* (1974), articles on Sri Lankan literature and culture, and translations of Sinhala poetry and fiction. She was co-editor of *An Anthology of Modern Writing from Sri Lanka* (1981), and guest editor of *Writing from Sri Lanka* (1987). She also translates and directs for the Sinhala theatre: *Muhudu Yanno* (1966), (Synge's *Riders to the Sea*) and *Bernadage Sipirigeya* (1971) (Lorca's *The House of Bernada Alba*) which was recently revived (1986).

James Peacock holds a doctorate from Harvard in Social Anthropology and is Kenan Professor of Anthropology at the University of North Carolina at Chapel Hill. He has done fieldwork in Indonesia and Appalachia. His books include *Rites of Moderniz- ation: Symbolic and Social Aspects of Indonesian Proletarian Drama* (1968, reissued with an Afterword, 1988) and *The Anthropological Lens: Harsh Light, Soft Focus* (1986).

Miles Richardson is Professor of Anthropology in the Department of Geography and Anthropology at Louisiana State University. He has pursued the theme of how people in the American South and those in Spanish America use space in the construction of their lives in several authored or edited writings: *San Pedro, Colombia* (1970), *The Human Mirror* (1974), and *Place: Experience and Symbol* (1984). He is currently at work on a manuscript titled "Being-in-Christ and the Social Construction of Death in Spanish America and the American South: A Humanistic Portrayal." Similar themes appear in the fiction he has published in *The Southern Review, Louisiana Literature,* and *Amelia.* Richardson is editor of *The Anthropology and Humanism Quarterly,* the journal of the Society for Humanistic Anthropology.

Richard Schechner is Professor of Performance Studies at the Tisch School of the Arts, New York University. He is editor of *TDR*, a journal of performance studies, and he is a theatre director whose productions with The Performance Group include *Dionysus in 69, Mother Courage and Her Children, The Tooth of Crime, Oedipus,* and *The Balcony.* In New Delhi he directed Chekhov's *Cherry Orchard* (in Hindi) and in 1989 he directed Sun Huizhu's *Tomorrow He'll Be Out of the Mountains* (in Chinese) at the Shanghai People's Art Theatre. His books include *Environmental Theater, Essays on Performance Theory* (1977), revised as *Performance Theory* (1988), and *Between Theater and Anthropology* (1985). He is co-author of *The Engleburt Stories: North to the Tropics* (1987) which he wrote with his son, Samuel MacIntosh-Schechner.

Rosamond B. Spicer completed graduate studies in anthropology at the University of Chicago, and then in 1936 came with her husband, Edward H. Spicer, to make a community study of immigrant Yaqui Indians at Pascua Village, near Tucson, Arizona. In 1942 they did a similar study of Potam, in Rio Yaqui, Sonora, Mexico. Living in Tucson from 1946 on, they were much in contact with Yaquis, including the founding of the new village of Pascua Pueblo and the attaining of a reservation. The Spicers also worked with many other Southwestern Indian tribes and Mrs. Spicer conducted a community study of the Papago. For many years Mrs. Spicer taught modern dance and Dr. Spicer was professor of Anthropology at the University of Arizona.

Yi-Fu Tuan, born in China but educated in Australia, England, and the United States, has taught for many years at the University of Minnesota. He is now the J.K. Wright and Vilas Professor of Geography at the University of Wisconsin. His interests have shifted from desert landforms and cultural geography to history of ideas and the psychological dimensions of human reality. His books include *Space and Place* (1977), *Segmented Worlds and Self* (1982), *Dominance and Affection* (1984), and *The Good Life* (1986).

Colin M. Turnbull was born in 1924, educated at Westminster and Oxford, England; first pursued philosophy and music, doing post-graduate work for two years at Banaras Hindu University, then going into Anthropology with Africa as his major area of research. Currently Randolph Distinguished Visiting Professor of Anthropology at Vassar College, he formerly taught at George Washington University, and as a Visiting Adjunct Professor in the Department of Performance Studies at New York University.

Edith Turner is on the Faculty of the Department of Anthropology at the University of Virginia. She is author of *The Spirit and the Drum* (1988), co-author of *Image and Pilgrimage* (1978), and has published a number of articles on ritual and initiation. Her fieldwork has been wide ranging. For instance she has worked among the Ndembu of Africa, Mexican pilgrims, the Yaqui Indians of Arizona, and Civil War re-enactors. In 1985 she made a restudy of the Ndembu and has completed a full-length manuscript on their contemporary ritual entitled *The Tooth: Switching Realities in an African Healing Ritual.* She is at present in Northern Alaska following up an interest in the healing procedures in the Inupiat Eskimos.

Victor Turner (1920–83) was an anthropologist and comparative symbologist with a deep interest in ritual and theatre. He was a principal organizer of the series of conferences upon which this book is based. Turner's field research began in Africa among the Ndembu of Uganda. Later he traveled to India, Israel, Mexico, Ireland, and Japan. His academic career included posts at the University of Manchester and Cornell University. In 1977 he became William R. Kenan Professor of Anthropology and Religion at the University of Virginia, a chair he held until his death. His many books include *The Forest of Symbols* (1967), *The Drums of Affliction* (1968), *The Ritual Process* (1969), *From Ritual to Theatre* (1982), *On the Edge of the Bush* (1986), and *The Anthropology of Performance* (1986).

Anselmo Valencia, Yaqui Indian and U.S. citizen, has held a prominent place in Yaqui society since the 1950s. He was largely responsible for the founding of the new village, Pascua Pueblo, and led the campaign to grant Yaquis federal recognition as an American Indian tribe. Holding the positions of chairman of the Pascua Yaqui Association and later Community Manager, he has watched Pascua Pueblo grow from an idea to a village of several thousand Yaqui inhabitants. Through teaching and example he has fostered Yaqui culture in all its complex aspects, including language, law, religion, and ceremonial life. He is himself an eminent singer of the sacred Deer songs.

Heather Valencia is married to Anselmo Valencia, and is of mixed English and Cherokee Indian blood. She values the Indian way of life and sees that it comprehends her philosophical predilections. She is a medicine woman and oracle in her own right. She attends all the ceremonies and assists in the village in many capacities.

Phillip B. Zarrilli is Associate Professor of Asian Performance at the University of Wisconsin-Madison where he directs the Asian/Experimental Theatre Program. He studied *kathakali* in Kerala under M.P. Sankaran Namboodiri at the Kerala Kalamandalam, and *kalarippayattu* under Gurukkal Govindankutty Nair of the C.V.N. Kalari, Trivandrum. His books include *The Kathakali Complex: Actor, Performance, Structure* (1984) and (with Farley Richmond and Darius Swann) *Indian Theatre: Traditions of Performance* (1988). He is currently completing an ethnography of the process and experience of practicing *kalarippayattu*, *'Conquering Even the God of Death': Accomplishment and Power in a Traditional South Indian Martial Art.*

Concerning Victor Turner

This book, really, is a festschrift for Victor Turner who died in 1983 at the age of sixty-three. He, more than anyone, conceived and birthed the conferences after which this book comes. Turner's wide and generous mind and spirit housed an indefatigable will to connect, weave, link, contact, and interact. He wanted to form, furnish, and enjoy what he embraced in his very widely cast big net of energy.

I was happily drawn into Turner's net in the spring of 1977 when, one morning, Turner phoned me. He wanted me to participate in the 1977 Burg Wartenstein Symposium No. 76 on "Cultural Frames and Reflections, Ritual, Drama and Spectacle." The conferences of 1981 and 1982 that form the background to *By Means of Performance* flowed naturally from the 1977 Symposium.

During the years I knew him, Turner focused ever more carefully and passionately on the relationship between theatre and ritual. On a number of occasions he participated in the work of the Department of Performance Studies at NYU (where I am a professor). In the summer of 1979 Turner and I were joined at NYU by Barbara Myerhoff, Alexander Alland, Edith Turner, and (for two days) Erving Goffman for a two week workshop exploring the relationships among theatre, ritual, and performance in everyday life. This intense summer workshop was a place where not only discussions but practical exercises and experimental performances took place, where we deconstructed texts, played with on-site staging, and laid the groundwork for what Turner and his wife Edith called "performing ethnography." Sadly, Turner, Myerhoff, and Goffman are dead, all too early in their lives. I hope this book will help propel their worthy work forward.

Richard Schechner

Introduction

RICHARD SCHECHNER AND WILLA APPEL

By their performances shall ye know them

So began a short statement written by Victor Turner in December 1980 addressed to the planning committee for the upcoming series of conferences on ritual and theatre held in 1981 and 1982 in Arizona and New York. These conferences – one on the Yaqui deer dance, one on Japanese performance, and one on the interrelation of a number of genres viewed from a global perspective – were sponsored by the Wenner–Gren Foundation for Anthropological Research and supported by a consortium of organizations.[1]

By Means of Performance is a further step in the process of exploring some of the interweavings of ritual and theatre, a process Victor Turner and Richard Schechner had been exploring for some time. In 1980, Turner articulated very clearly what he saw as the goal of the 1981 and 1982 conferences

> Cultures are most fully expressed in and made conscious of themselves in their ritual and theatrical performances. [. . .] A performance is a dialectic of "flow," that is, spontaneous movement in which action and awareness are one, and "reflexivity," in which the central meanings, values and goals of a culture are seen "in action," as they shape and explain behavior. A performance is declarative of our shared humanity, yet it utters the uniqueness of particular cultures. We will know one another better by entering one another's performances and learning their grammars and vocabularies.

In his statement, Turner put forward not only his hopes for the conferences (which we were able to realize to a considerable degree) but his utopian vision of world community based on mutual respect and enjoyment of cultural differences, exchanges of feelings as well as of ideas, and the increasing ability of people to experience and re-experience each other's cultural identities.

Translating Turner's vision into workable conferences took the concerted and long term efforts of a dedicated group of planners: Lita Osmundsen, then the director of research of the Wenner-Gren Foundation; Richard Lanier, director of the Asian Cultural Council; Martha Coigney, president of the

1

International Theatre Institute; Jack Morrison, executive director of the American Theatre Association; Phillip Zarrilli, professor of theatre at the University of Wisconsin-Madison; and this book's co-editors Richard Schechner and Willa Appel. From time to time this core group called on others whose expertise we needed.

At first, we felt that we could pack everything into one big conference. Our ambitions were truly global – to bring together performers, scholars, directors, and choreographers from a wide cross-section of the world's cultures. We wanted these people to interact not just "academically," on the basis of prepared papers and formal responses, but through "lived experience." We intended not only to see finished performances, and fragments thereof, but methods of training, and to explore the various ways performances were received in different cultures and contexts. We wanted to consider not only "pure" performances – or idealized versions of traditional genres – but also tourist shows, hybrids, and genres in the midst of profound disturbance and/or transformation. We wanted contemporary Euro-American performance represented as well as genres from Asia, Africa, and other parts of the world. We attempted to include various kinds of performance – from sacred ritual to experimental theatre. And we wanted divergent scholarly approaches represented.

In November 1980 Schechner made a graph with three axes to show what we were aiming for (see figure 1). One axis extended from ritual through popular and folk genres on to commercial theatre; another axis led from genres with documented early origins (such as the Sanskrit kutiyattam theatre) through to very recent experimental performances; the third axis represented our desire for as wide a geographical-cultural distribution of cultures as possible.

The conferences were only partially successful in achieving these aims, just as this book is only partially successful in carrying forward the work of the conferences. If we were aiming for a "world conference," too large a proportion of the traditional forms came from Asia, and too many of the scholars from America. But we did bring together a wide range of genres and scholars from Asia, Africa, and native America.

At our planning meetings we covered walls and blackboards with charts showing how genres would possibly relate to each other. We were particularly interested in finding "link people" who could, in a sense, translate across cultural and scholarly boundaries. We struggled, for example, over how persons totally unfamiliar with India would be able to enter into a meaningful discussion of kutiyattam. We not only wanted the scholars to talk across disciplines and fields of concentration, we wanted to encourage interaction among performers from diverse cultures and genres.

We planned sessions where scholarly participants could try out training and performance techniques themselves, as a way of experiencing different genres in their bodies. We arranged for some sessions to be on site if not wholly in the

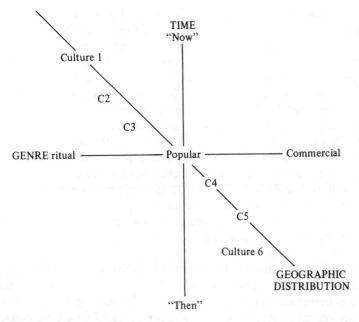

Figure 1 The three axis distributional model.
The 1980 graph with three axes drawn by Schechner to show the kinds of distribution –
scope the planners of the conferences were aiming for.

field. The conference on Yaqui deer dancing was held both at Pascua Pueblo
near Tucson and at the Oracle Conference Center. To initiate the August
Symposium, Kim Keum-Hwa, a Korean shaman, performed a "welcoming
ceremony" at the New York Korean Cultural Center. During the next twelve
days we met not only at the Asia Society, our principal venue where we held
many discussions and saw noh drama and kutiyattam, but also attended a
church service at the Institutional Church of God in Christ in Brooklyn, saw a
performance in the 23rd Street store front theatre of the experimental group
Squat, and went to Broadway for *A Chorus Line*.

   Our intellectual goal in the conferences, and in preparing this book, was to
approach the genres of theatre, dance, music, sports, and ritual as a single,
coherent group, *as performance*. The underlying question became whether or
not the same methodological tools and approaches could be used to
understand a noh drama, a football game, a Yaqui deer dance, a Broadway
musical, a Roman Catholic Mass, an Umbanda curing ritual, a Yoruba
masked dance, and a postmodern experimental performance? We knew that
very few people qualified as "comparative performatologists" and so the basic
question would have to be dealt with genre by genre, culture by culture. We
hoped that the conferences would lay the groundwork for proposing general
principles or, as Turner called them, "universals of performance." The
problem that engaged us was divided into six specific areas of interest.

1. *Transformation of being and /or consciousness.* Either permanently, as in initiation rites, or temporarily as in aesthetic theatre and trance dancing a performer – and sometimes spectators too – are changed by means of performance. How does this change come about? How is it made part of a performance? The deer dancer of the Yaqui is a man and a deer simultaneously – the mask he wears atop his head, like the noh mask which is too small to cover all of the *shite*'s face – does not erase the human being who has also become the deer. The white cloth separating the deer dancer's face from the deer's head, a cloth the dancer keeps adjusting, is the physicalization of an incomplete transformation, of the simultaneous presence of man and deer. In the performance itself, at this precise juncture of time and space, the problems of representation, imitation, and transformation converge.

2. *Intensity of performance.* While performing, a certain definite threshold is crossed – that moment when spectators and performers alike sense a "successful" performance is taking place. This intensity of performance has been called "flow," "concentration," and "presence." Performances seem to gather their energies almost as if time was a concrete manipulable thing. This gathering of intensity occurs even in performances which, like the steady whirling of dervishes, do not build to a climax. But these spinning dancers, in the steady repetitive simplicity of their movements, often lift themselves to ecstatic trance, sweeping spectators along with them. The uses of monotone and monorhythm can be as intense experientially as the varied melodies and rhythms of a Beethoven symphony. Understanding intensity of performance is finding out how performances build, how they draw spectators in (or intentionally keep them out), how space, scripts, sounds, movements – the whole *mise-en-scène* – are managed. In this regard, the work of the performers is only part of the story. The scope of the inquiry broadens to include directors, visual artists, scene designers, costumers, mask-makers, and musicians.

3. *Audience-performer interactions.* How does an audience provide the context for a performance? When a performance moves to a new place encountering new audiences (on tour, for example), even if everything is kept the same, the performance changes. The same happens when an audience is imported, as when tourists or anthropologists see "the real thing." Aside from these questions of context, there is a wide range of audience behavior from full participation as in many rituals and festivals to the sharp separation of stage from audience in the proscenium theatre. And what of genres that mix participation with observation? There have been a number of experiments in Asia, America, and Africa along that line. The reception of a performance varies according to how much individual spectators know about what's going on. In noh drama, an audience of connoisseurs is sought. On the other hand, some initiation rites depend on secrecy and surprise.

4. *The whole performance sequence.* Generally Western scholars have paid more attention to the "show" – what is most understandable in Western

aesthetic terms – than to training, rehearsals, ritual frames just before and just after the performance, and the aftermath following performances. But every performance event is part of a systematic sequence of occurrences. Performance includes six or seven phases: training, rehearsal (and/or workshop), warm-up, the performance, cool-down, and aftermath. Not all performances in all cultures include all these phases – but finding out what is emphasized and what is omitted is very instructive. For example, codified traditional performances – kutiyattam and noh, for example – demand extensive training but little or no rehearsal. This makes sense: If one plays the same role or role types over and over again, and if there is an orderly and predictable progression of roles to be played over the years, the need for preparing individual *mise-en-scènes* for each production diminishes. But where newness is prized, where performers are expected to be able to play a number of different kinds of roles, training is less important than intense *ad hoc* workshops and rehearsals to develop the idiosyncratic quality of each individual production. The cool-down and aftermath phases of performance are also very important. Aftermath can be a slow unfolding process involving how performances are evaluated, how the experience of performing is used by the community. Scholarly conferences and books are aftermath phenomena. Cool-down is more immediate, dealing with knitting the performers back into the fabric of ordinary life. In Bali, for example, rituals exist that take a person out of ritual trance – for it is as important to get someone out properly as it is to put her/him in. In America, many performers, after a strenuous show, will go out to eat, drink, and talk – often boisterously. Someone who doesn't know performers wonders at how much energy they have left. But these celebratory bouts are not really "after the theatre" but part of it – a way of cooling down, of reintegrating into ordinary social life.

5. *Transmission of performance knowledge.* Performance consists of mostly oral traditions. Even where there is written drama, the arts of performing (as distinct from the dramas performed) are passed down through direct oral transmission. Precisely how these traditions are passed on in various cultures and in different genres is of central importance. Some surprising parallels exist, for example, between the way athletes are trained and the way Asian performers master their crafts. Athletic coaches are often former players. They transmit their "secrets" to younger players. Former players – living and dead – are respected for their records, singular achievements which reflect their mastery of technique. Korea and Japan have a category of performer called "Living National Treasure" roughly analogous to being in baseball's or football's Hall of Fame. Asian performing arts are historically connected to martial arts, so it is not surprising that training for the stage and for (now archaic forms of) combat are very similar. But in much of Africa, performance knowledge is transmitted in a more informal manner – through imitation beginning in very early childhood. Mothers move the arms of infants in time with the drums; young children attempt the dance steps and are lovingly

encouraged. Slowly, over many years, skills are absorbed, practiced, and sharpened. The audience during a performance is vocal in its approval or disapproval. The question of transmission of performance knowledge is not limited to how one generation learns from another, but also includes how performers learn from each other.

6. *How are performances evaluated?* This is a very sticky problem because criteria vary from culture to culture, genre to genre. Are there any "universal," or at least general, principles to be used to determine whether performances are "good" or "bad"? Do we go by the standards applied inside a given culture and if so, do we use what performers have to say or what critics, scholars, and audiences say (recognizing that these opinions are often at odds)? Also, to whom are evaluations directed – to the performers, to would-be spectators, to scholars?

These six areas of interest guided both the planning of the conferences and the organization of the book. But this book was not envisioned as a record of the conferences. It would be impossible to compress into a book the multiplex interactions of the twenty-two days of meetings held in Arizona and New York.[2] Even attempting that would take a whole other kind of project involving the transcription of many of the very lively encounters that occurred. A complete record of the conferences is on soundtapes in the archives of the Wenner-Gren Foundation. The culminating conference, the International Symposium on Theatre and Ritual, was held in New York from 23 August to 1 September 1982. Forty-eight scholars and performers participated "full-time" in the Symposium and a number of others were invited to observe some of the demonstrations and discussions. Of course the public performances of noh and kutiyattam at the Asia Society, and other genres around New York, attracted many people.

Our goal in *By Means of Performance* (a title suggested by Herbert Blau) is to continue the work of the conferences, not summarize them. As Blau pointed out in a letter he wrote in November 1982

> The critical recurrence [. . .] in Oracle [Arizona] & New York, was the question of subjectivity, in perception & methodology. [. . .] The pathos of the anthropologist that must be talked about is in that subjective distance, in the very subject of desire, which is – and this may be the appropriate bridge back from East to West – the territory of apprehension which we know a good deal more about in our theatre, with the crucial difference there being, however, that between simpleminded psychologism & psychoanalytical knowledge, knowing how we change the subject by talking about it, yet getting closer in. Anyhow, if there were another conference, I'd want to make this perceptual problem central – facing up to the presumptions of methodology, and what is ideologically behind it.

This book is, to a certain degree, in lieu of that other conference.

But we realized that a book could not capture the quality of the face to face meetings – the formal and off the record interchanges that, in deep but fleeting ways, expressed links across cultures and genres, between and among performers and scholars. The book represents a scholarly approach, primarily articulated through analytical, formal essays. One contributor, Colin Turnbull, was unable to attend any of the conferences. Others revised their papers in light of the work of the conferences. Barbara Myerhoff was planning to do so, but cancer killed her. The book covers a wide scope and presents a healthy divergence of styles, opinions, and approaches. However, as principal conveners of the conferences and as co-editors of the book, we are sorry that there is less coming directly from the many fine practitioners who participated in the conferences. We do hear Yaqui ritual leader Anselmo Valencia, but not from members of the kutiyattam troupe, or from noh, the Korean shamans, or the Yoruba performers. Absent also is the Euro-American experimental cohort. The silence of all these practitioners is not due to their inability to articulate what they do. The absence is largely due to the very different media of communication used in live performance, the transmission of performance knowledge, the scholarship of oral traditions, and the written essay. How to overcome these gaps – even wondering if they can, or ought to be overcome – may be the emergent central question concerning anthropologists, artists, teachers, and performance scholars.

Thus this book is neither beginning nor end, but a continuation.

Notes

1 This consortium consisted of the Wenner-Gren Foundation, the Asia Society, the Asian Cultural Council, the International Theatre Institute, the American Theatre Association (now defunct), and the Tisch School of the Arts, New York University. Money for the conferences and for this book came from the National Endowment for the Humanities, the Wenner-Gren Foundation, and the Asian Cultural Council.
2 The first conference, 19–24 November 1981, took place in Arizona near Tucson at Pascua Peublo and at the Oracle Conference Center. The second conference on Japanese Theatre was held in New York at the Japan Society, 19–24 May 1982. This conference largely dealt with the work of experimental director Suzuki Tadashi whose group was performing in New York at that time. The third conference, the International Symposium on Theatre and Ritual, was held in New York 23 August–1 September 1982. See Appendix for a complete list of participants.

1

Are there universals of performance in myth, ritual, and drama?

VICTOR TURNER

In this essay I will discuss what I think is a characteristic developmental relationship from ritual to theatre, and I will lay out the relationship of both to social drama. The figures in this chapter express schematically some of these connections. I have argued that every major socioeconomic formation has its dominant form of cultural-aesthetic "mirror" in which it achieves a certain degree of self-reflexivity. Nonindustrial societies tend to stress immediate context-sensitive ritual; industrial pre-electronic societies tend to stress theatre, which assigns meaning to macroprocesses – economic, political, or generalized familial problems – but remains insensitive to localized, par-ticularized contexts. Yet both ritual and theatre crucially involve liminal events and processes and have an important aspect of social metacom-mentary. In many field situations I have observed in markedly different cultures, in my experience of Western social life, and in numerous historical documents, I have clearly seen a community's movement through time taking a shape which is obviously "dramatic." It has a proto-aesthetic form in its unfolding – a generic form like the general mammalian condition that we still have with us throughout all the global radiation of specific mammalian forms to fill special niches. As detailed in my earlier writings, in the first stage, Breach, a person or subgroup breaks a rule deliberately or by inward compulsion, in a public setting. In the stage of Crisis, conflicts between individuals, sections, and factions follow the original breach, revealing hidden clashes of character, interest, and ambition. These mount towards a crisis of the group's unity and its very continuity unless rapidly sealed off by redressive public action, consensually undertaken by the group's leaders, elders, or guardians. Redressive action is often ritualized, and may be undertaken in the name of law or religion. Judicial processes stress reason and evidence, religious processes emphasize ethical problems, hidden malice operating through witchcraft, or ancestral wrath against breaches or tabu or the impiety of the living towards the dead. If a social drama runs its full course, the outcome (or "consummation," as the philosopher John Dewey might have called it) – the fourth stage in my model – may be either (a) the restoration of

8

peace and "normality" among the participants, or (b) social recognition of irremediable or irreversible breach of schism. Of course, this mode, like all models, is subject to manifold manipulations. For example, redressive action may fail, in which case there is *reversion* to the phase of crisis. If law and/or religious values have lost their cultural efficacy, endemic continuous factionalism may infect public life for long periods. Or redressive failure in a local community may lead to appeal to a higher court at a more inclusive level of social organization – village to district to province to nation. Or the *ancien régime* may be rejected altogether and revolution ensue. There may a "transvaluation of values."

In that case the group itself may be radically restructured, including its redressive machinery. Culture obviously affects such aspects as the style and tempo of the social drama. Some cultures seek to retard the outbreak of open crisis by elaborate rules of etiquette. Others admit the use of organized ritualized violence (almost in the ethological sense) in crisis or redress, in such forms as the holmgang (island single-combat) of the Icelanders, the stick-fights of the Nuba of the Sudan, and the reciprocal head-hunting expeditions of the Ilongot hill peoples of Luzon in the Philippines. Simmel, Coser, Gluckman and others have pointed out how conflict, if brought under gradual control, stopping short of massacre and war, may actually enhance a group's "consciousness of kind," may enhance and revive its self-image. For conflict forces the antagonists to diagnose its source, and in so doing, to become fully aware of the principles that bond them beyond and above the issues that have temporarily divided them. As Durkheim said long ago, law needs crime, religion needs sin, to be fully dynamic systems, since without "doing," without the social friction that fires consciousness and self-consciousness, social life would be passive, even inert. These considerations, I think, led Barbara Myerhoff (1978: 22) to distinguish "definitional ceremonies" as a kind of collective "autobiography," a means by which a group creates its identity by telling itself a story about itself, in the course of which it brings to life "its Definite and Determinate Identity" (to cite William Blake). Here, meaning, in Wilhelm Dilthey's sense, is engendered by marrying present problems of the living present to a rich ethnic past, which is then infused into the "doings and undergoings" (to quote John Dewey) of the local community. Some social dramas may be more "definitional" than others, it is true, but most social dramas contain, if only implicitly, some means of *public reflexivity* in their redressive processes. For by their activation groups take stock of their own current situation: the nature and strength of their social ties, the power of their symbols, the effectiveness of their legal and moral controls, the sacredness and soundness of their religious traditions, and so forth. And this is the point I would make here: the world of theatre, as we know it both in Asia and America, and the immense variety of theatrical sub-genres derive not from imitation, conscious or unconscious, of the processual form of the complete or "satiated" social drama – breach, crisis, redress, reintegration, or schism – but

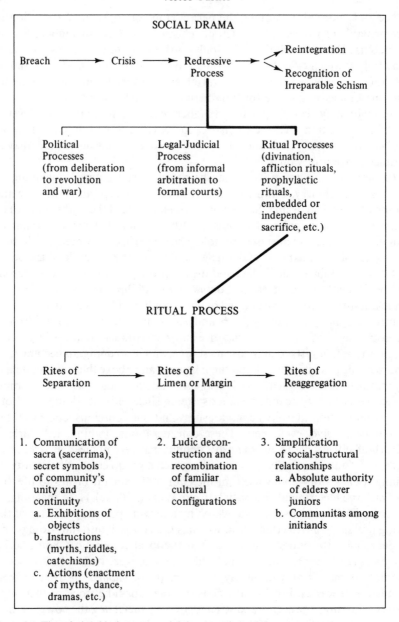

Figure 1.1 The relationship between social drama and ritual process.

specifically from its third phase, the one I call redress, especially from redress as *ritual* process, rather than *judicial, political*, or military process, important as these are for the study of political or revolutionary action. Redressive rituals include divination into the hidden causes of misfortune, personal and social conflict, and illness (all of which in tribal societies are intimately interconnected and thought to be caused by the invisible action of spirits, deities, witches, and sorcerers); they include curative ritual (which may often involve episodes of spirit-possession, shamanic trance mediumship, and trance states among the patients who are subjects of ritual); and initiatory rites connected with these "rituals of affliction." Moreover, many of those rites that we call "life-crisis ceremonies," particularly those of puberty, marriage, and death, themselves indicate a major, if not altogether unexpected breach in the orderly, customary running of group life, after which many relationships among its members must change drastically, involving much potential and even actual conflict and competition (for rights of inheritance and succession to office, for women, over the amount of bridewealth, over clan or lineage allegiance). Life-crisis rituals (and seasonal rituals, too, for that matter) may be called "prophylatic," while rituals of affliction are "therapeutic." Life-crisis rituals portray and symbolically resolve archetypal conflicts in abstraction from the milling, teeming social life which characteristically and periodically throws up such conflicts. Society is, therefore, better equipped to deal with them concretely, having portrayed them abstractly.

All these "third-phase" or "first-phase" (if we are talking about life-crisis) ritual processes contain within themselves what I have in several writings called a liminal phase, which provides a stage (and I used this term advisedly when thinking about theatre) for unique structures of experience (a translation of Dilthey's *Erlebnisse* "living-through"), in milieus detached from mundane life and characterized by the presence of ambiguous ideas, monstrous images, sacred symbols, ordeals, humiliations, esoteric and paradoxical instructions, the emergence of "symbolic types" represented by maskers and clowns, gender reversals, anonymity, and many other phenomena and processes which I have elsewhere described as liminal. The limen, or threshold, a term I took from van Gennep's second of three stages in rites of passage, is a no-man's-land betwixt-and-between the structural past and the structural future as anticipated by the society's normative control of biological development. It is ritualized in many ways, but very often symbols expressive of ambiguous identity are found cross-culturally: androgynes, at once male and female, theriomorphic figures, at once animals and men or women, angels, mermaids, centaurs, human-headed lions, and so forth, monstrous combinations of elements drawn from nature *and* culture. Some symbols represent both birth *and* death, womb *and* tomb, such as caverns or camps secluded from everyday eyes. I sometimes talk about the liminal phase being dominantly in the "subjunctive mood" of culture, the mood of maybe, might-be, as-if, hypothesis, fantasy, conjecture, desire, depending on which of the trinity, cognition, affect, and conation (thought, feeling, or intention) is situationally dominant. We might say, in terms of brain neurobiology, that here right-hemispheric and archaic brain functions are very much in evidence and probably culturally triggered by ritual action. "Ordinary" day-to-day life is in the indicative mood, where we expect the invariant operation of cause-and-effect, of rationality and commonsense. Liminality can perhaps be described as a fructile chaos, a fertile nothingness, a storehouse of possibilities, not by any means a random assemblage but a striving after new forms and structure, a gestation process, a fetation of modes appropriate to and anticipating postliminal existence. It is what goes on in nature in the fertilized egg, in the chrysalis, and even more richly and complexly in their cultural homologues.

Theatre is one of the many inheritors of that great multifaceted system of preindustrial ritual which embraces ideas and images of cosmos and chaos, interdigitates clowns and their foolery with gods and their solemnity, and uses all the sensory codes, to produce symphonies in more than music: the intertwining of dance, body languages of many kinds, song, chant, architectural forms (temples, amphitheaters), incense, burnt offerings, ritualized feasting and drinking, painting, body painting, body marking of many kinds, including circumcision and scarification, the application of lotions and drinking of potions, the enacting of mythic and heroic plots drawn from oral traditions. And so much more. Rapid advances in the scale and complexity of society, particularly after industrialization, have passed this unified liminal configuration through the analytical prism of the division of labor, with its specialization and professionalization, reducing each of these sensory domains to a set of entertainment genres flourishing in the leisure time of society, no longer in a central, driving place. The pronounced numinous supernatural character of archaic ritual has been greatly attenuated.

Nevertheless, there are today signs that the amputated specialized genres are seeking to rejoin and to recover something of the numinosity lost in their *sparagmos*, their dismemberment. Truly, as John Dewey has argued, the aesthetic form of theatre is inherent in sociocultural life itself, in what I call "social drama" and Kenneth Burke calls "dramas of living," but the reflexive and therapeutic character of *theatre*, as essentially a child of the redressive phase of social drama, has to draw on power sources often inhibited or at least constrained in the cultural life of society's "indicative" mood. The deliberate creation of a detached, still almost-sacred liminal space, allows a search for such sources. One source of this excessive "meta-" power is, clearly, the liberated and disciplined body itself, with its many untapped resources for pleasure, pain, and expression. Here, the experimental theatre of Jerzy Grotowski, Julian Beck and Judith Malina, Joseph Chaikin, Richard Schechner, Peter Brook, Suzuki Tadashi, and Squat Theater in New York City has its growing importance. Another source draws on unconscious processes, such as may be released in trance foreshadowed by some of

Antonin Artaud's theories. This is akin to what I have often seen in Africa, where thin, ill-nourished old ladies, with only occasional naps, dance, sing, and perform ritual activities for two or three days and nights together. I think that a rise in the level of social arousal, however produced, is capable of unlocking energy sources in individual participants. Then there is the work we have been considering on the neurobiology of the brain, summarized in *The Spectrum of Ritual* (d'Aquili *et al.* 1979; 146), which, among other things, shows how the "driving techniques of ritual (including sonic driving by, for example, percussion instruments) facilitate right hemisphere dominance, resulting in Gestalt, timeless non-verbal experiences, differentiated and unique when compared with left hemisphere functioning or hemisphere alternation" (Lex, 1979: 125). Conferences devoted to the neural substrate of mental and emotional phenomena in ritual and the role of ritual in human adaptation may help to throw further light on the organic and neurological correlates of ritual behaviors.

My argument has been that what I would like to call the anthropology of experience (abolishing the sharp distinction between the classical study of culture and sociobiology) finds in certain recurrent forms of social experience (notably social dramas) sources of aesthetic form, including stage drama and dance. But ritual and its progeny, the performance arts among them, derive from the subjunctive, liminal, reflexive, exploratory heart of the social drama, its third, redressive phase, where the contents of group experiences (*Erlebnisse*) are replicated, dismembered, remembered, refashioned, and mutely or vocally made meaningful (even when, as so often in declining cultures, the meaning is that there is no meaning as in some Existentialist theatre). True theatre is experience of "heightened vitality," to quote John Dewey again (McDermott 1981: 540). True theatre "at its height signifies complete interpenetration of self and the world of objects and events." When this happens in a performance, there may be produced in audience and actors alike what d'Aquili and Laughlin (1979: 177) call in reference both to ritual and meditation a "brief ecstatic state and sense of union (often lasting only a few seconds) and may often be described as no more than a shiver running down the back at a certain point." A sense of harmony with the universe is made evident, and the whole planet is felt to be communitas. This shiver has to be won, achieved, though, to be a consummation, after working through a tangle of conflicts and disharmonies. Theatre best of all exemplifies Thomas Hardy's dictum: "If a way to the better there be, it exacts a full look at the worst." Ritual or theatrical transformation can scarcely occur otherwise. Problems and obstacles (the "crisis" stage of social dramas) challenge our brain neurobiology into full arousal, and culture supplies that aroused activity with a store of preserved social experiences which can be "heated up" to supply the current hunger for meaning with reliable nutrients.

I have had to defend myself against such trenchant critics as my former teachers Sir Raymond Firth and the late Max Gluckman, who accused me of

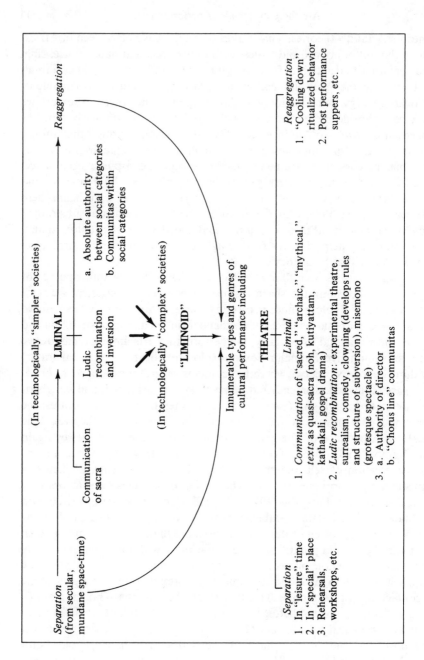

Figure 1.2 The evolution of cultural genres of performance: from "Liminal" to "Liminoid."

unwarrantably introducing a model drawn from literature (they did not say Western literature, but clearly they had the Aristotelian model of tragedy in mind) to throw light on *spontaneous* social processes, which are not authored or set in conventions, but arise from clashes of interest or incompatible social structural principles in the give and take of everyday life in a social group. Recently, I have taken heart from an article by Clifford Geertz, "Blurred Genres: The Refiguration of Social Thought," which not only suggests "that analogies drawn from the humanities are coming to play the kind of role in sociological understanding that analogies drawn from the crafts and technology have long played in physical understanding" (Geertz 1980: 196), but also gives qualified approval to the "drama analogy for social life" (Geertz 1980a: 172). Geertz numbers me among "proponents of the ritual theory of drama" – as against "the *symbolic action* approach" to drama which stresses "the affinities of theatre and rhetoric – drama as persuasion, the platform as stage" (Geertz 1980a: 172), associated with Kenneth Burke and developed by Erving Goffman. He writes: "For Turner, social dramas occur 'on all levels of social organization from state to family.' They arise out of conflict situations – a village falls into factions, a husband beats a wife, a region rises against the state – and proceed to their denouements through publicly performed conventionalized behavior. As the conflict swells to crisis and the excited fluidity of heightened emotion, where people feel at once more enclosed in a common mood and loosened from their moorings [a good description of "ergotropic" behavior], ritualized forms of authority – litigation, feud, sacrifice, prayer – are invoked to contain it and render it orderly [trophotropic response]. If they succeed, the breach is healed and the status quo, or something resembling it, is restored; if they do not, it is accepted as incapable of remedy and things fall apart into various sorts of unhappy endings: migrations, divorces, or murders in the cathedral. With differing degrees of strictness and detail, Turner and his followers have applied this schema to tribal passage rites, curing ceremonies, and judicial processes; to Mexican insurrections, Icelandic sagas, and Thomas Becket's difficulties with Henry II; to picaresque narrative, millenarian movements, Caribbean carnivals, and Indian peyote hunts; and to the political upheaval of the Sixties. A form for all seasons."

The last comment arises from Geertz's insistence in several of his writings that the social drama approach focuses too narrowly on "the *general* movement of things" (italics added) and neglects the multifarious cultural contents, the symbol systems which embody the ethos and eidos, the sentiments and values of *specific* cultures. He suggests that what he calls the "text analogy" (Geertz 1980a: 175) can remedy this, that is, textual analysis attends to "how the inscription of action is brought about, what its vehicles are and how they work, and on what the fixation of meaning from the flow of events – history from what happened, thought from thinking, culture from behavior – implies for sociological interpretation. To see social institutions, social customs, social changes as in some sense 'readable' is to alter our whole sense of what such interpretation is towards modes of thought rather more familiar to the translator, the exegete, or the iconographer than to the test giver, the factor analyst, or the pollster" (Geertz 1980a: 175–76). The inscriptions may be usefully subjected to structural analysis; but, in a sense, and often, they are like the shucked off husks of living process, tiderows left by the receding sea, useful signs, indicators, markers, pointers, readings, crystallizations. But their vitality has gone elsewhere – it is found in the *drama* process.

One answer I could make to Geertz would be simply to reiterate certain features of the social drama approach. He mentions "ritualized forms of authority – litigation, feud, sacrifice, prayer" that are used "to contain (crisis) and to render it orderly." Such forms may crystallize any culture's uniqueness; they are forms for particular seasons. They dominate the third stage of the social drama which can compass immense variabilities. For my part I have, indeed, often treated the ritual and juridical symbol systems of the Ndembu of Western Zambia as text analogues. But I have tried to locate these texts in *context* of *performance*, rather than to construe them from the first into abstract, dominantly cognitive systems. However, Geertz does, in fact, concede that many anthropologists today, including himself, use both textual and dramatistic approaches, according to problem and context. His book entitled *Negara* (1980b), on the drama of kingship in Bali, exemplifies his dual approach. Some of these misunderstandings and apparent contradictions can be resolved if we examine the relationship between the two modes of acting – in "real life" and "on stage" – as components of a dynamic system of interdependence between social dramas and cultural performances. Both dramatistic and textual analogies then fall into place.

Richard Schechner and I represented this relationship as a bisected figure eight laid on its side (see figure 1.3). The two semicircles above the horizontal dividing line represent the manifest, visible public realm. The left loop or circlet represents social drama, which could be divided into its four main phases: breach, crisis, redress, positive or negative denouement. The right loop represents a genre of cultural performance – in this case, a stage of "aesthetic" drama (though it would be better to say the total repertoire of types of cultural performance possessed by a society). Notice that the *manifest* social drama feeds into the latent realm of stage drama; its characteristic form in a given culture, at a given time and place, unconsciously, or perhaps preconsciously, influences not only the form but also the content of the stage drama of which it is the active or "magic" mirror. The stage drama, when it is meant to do more than entertain – though entertainment is always one of its vital aims – is a metacommentary, explicit or implicit, witting or unwitting, on the major social dramas of its social context (wars, revolutions, scandals, institutional changes). Not only that, but its message and its rhetoric feed back into the *latent* processual structure of the social drama and partly account for

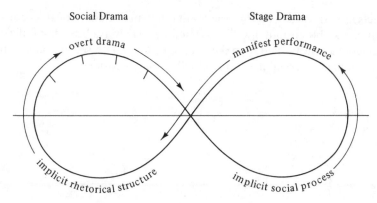

Figure 1.3 The interrelationship of social drama and stage drama.

its ready ritualization. Life itself now becomes a mirror held up to art, and the living now *perform* their lives, for the protagonists of a social drama, a "drama of living," have been equipped by aesthetic drama with some of their most salient opinions, imageries, tropes, and ideological perspectives. Neither mutual mirroring, life by art, art by life, is exact, for each is not a planar mirror but matricial mirror; at each exchange something new is added and something old is lost or discarded. Human beings learn through experience, though all too often they repress painful experience, and perhaps the deepest experience is through drama; not through social drama, or stage drama (or its equivalent) alone, but in the circulatory or oscillatory process of their mutual and incessant modification.

If one were to guess at origins, my conjecture would be that the genres of cultural performance, whether tribal rituals or TV specials, are not, as I have said, simply imitations of the overt form of the completed social drama. They are germinated in its *third*, redressive phase, the reflexive phase, the phase where society pulls meaning from that tangle of action, and, therefore, these performances are infinitely varied, like the result of passing light through a prism. The alternative versions of meaning that complex societies produce are innumerable. Within societies there are different classes, ethnicities, regions, neighborhoods, and people of different ages and sexes, and they each produce versions which try painfully to assign meaning to the particular crisis pattern of their own society. Each performance becomes a record, a means of explanation.

Finally, it should be noted that the interrelation of social drama to stage drama is not in an endless, cyclical, repetitive pattern; it is a spiraling one. The spiraling process is responsive to inventions and the changes in the mode of production in the given society. Individuals can make an enormous impact on the sensibility and understanding of members of society. Philosophers feed their work into the spiraling process; poets feed poems into it; politicians feed their acts into it; and so on. Thus the result is not an endless cyclical repetitive pattern or a stable cosmology. The cosmology has always been destabilized, and society has always had to make efforts, through both social dramas and esthetic dramas, to restabilize and actually *produce* cosmos.

2

Magnitudes of performance

RICHARD SCHECHNER

A figure for all genres

At the descriptive level there is no detail of performance that occurs everywhere under all circumstances. Nor is it easy to specify limitations on what is, or could be treated as, performance. Figure 2.1 is an exemplary but somewhat serendipitous panorama of just how diverse and extensive the performance world is. Criteria for inclusion in the chart were: (1) events called performances in this or that culture; (2) events treated "as performance" by scholars. I limited myself as much as possible to events that I have either seen or studied. I wanted to fight the tendency to seek "origins" or "sources" in performances below the horizons of fieldwork or reliable historical research. I took my cue from anthropological fieldwork: the evidence I sought was *in vivo*, close at hand, mostly from the practices of living people. I know that another person could make another time-space-event chart populated by different items. But I believe the outcome would be a similar riot of apparently disparate particulars. What hope is there of unifying such a figure?

If "universals" are wanted, they might be found in processual models explaining how one set of genres, ritual performances for example, become other sets. Does ritual "evolve" into dance, theatre, and sports, and if so how? This search for universals occupied Victor Turner during much of his life. Turner felt his "social drama/liminal-to-liminoid model[1] worked universally. In one of his last essays – "Are There Universals of Performance in Myth, Ritual, and Drama?" (chapter 1, this book) – he said as much:

Theatre is one of the many inheritors of that multifaceted system of preindustrial ritual which embraces ideas and images of cosmos and chaos, interdigitates clowns and their foolery with gods and their solemnity, and uses all the sensory codes to produce symphonies in more than music: the inter-twining of dance, body languages of many kinds, song, chant, architectural forms (temples, amphi-theaters), incense, burnt offerings, ritualized feasting and drinking, painting, body painting, body markings of many kinds, including circumcision and scarification, the application of lotions and drinking of potions, the enacting of mythic and heroic plots drawn from oral traditions. And so much more. Rapid advances in the scale and complexity of society, particularly after industrialization, have passed this unified liminal configuration through the analytical prism

19

Figure 2.1 Performance Event–Time–Space Chart

	AESTHETIC THEATRE	SACRED RITUAL	SECULAR RITUAL	SPORTS	SOCIAL DRAMA	MINUTES OR LESS	H
PRIVATE & RESTRICTED	Theatre on Chekhov Street[1]	Initiation rites	Executions in USA	Sports played at home	Election of Pope	Execution	Th Ch St
PRIVATE BUT OPEN	Happenings & Performance Art	Bar mitzvah	PH.D. Orals	Sandlot baseball	Murder trial	Puja at Hindu temple	Ha ba etc
LOCAL	Ordinary theatre & dance	Teyyam	Macy's Thanks-giving Day Parade	Big league baseball	Turnerian social drama	Stuart Sherman[4] street spectacle	O the da
GENERAL	National Network TV drama	Pilgrimage	Inaugura-tion of US President	Olympics	Hostage Crisis; wars	TV commer-cials	Fe fil
SACRED SPACE	B & P in St. John the Divine	Religious events Aborigine landscape	Town meeting in church	Aztec ballgame	Church where Pope is elected	Puja; eucharist	Or ch ser
SECULAR SPACE	Ordinary theatre & dance	Jewish cir-cumcision; home wedding	Macy's Parade; Olympics	Playing fields	Town square; legislative hall	Stuart Sherman; Jewish cir-cumcision	Or the da
FOUND SPACE	Rooftops, beaches, streets, galleries	Sacred trees, rocks, rivers	Parade routes	Sandlot ball	Wars; US Embassy during Hostage crisis	Some happenings	Pa sor hap
TRANSFORMED SPACE	Stage set; environmental theatre	Churches; Ramlila environments	Courtroom; execution chamber	Stadiums	Courtroom; throne-room	Execution	Or the dar
INDOOR SPACE	Theatres	Churches, temples	Courtroom; execution chamber	Field-houses[2]	Courtroom; legislative hall	Some happenings; execution	Or the da
OUTDOOR SPACE	Greek or Elizabethan theatre	Aborigine initiation grounds	Parade route; US inaugura-tion	Stadiums	Tiwi 'duel'[3]	Stuart Sherman	Gr Eli the
SINGLE SPACE	Ordinary theatre & dance	Church service	Courtroom	Stadiums fieldhouses	Courtroom; legislative hall	Execution	Or the dar
MULTISPACE	Many happenings; environmental theatre	Pilgrimage	Parades	Marathon running; Olympics	Hostage Crisis	Some happenings; some guerrilla th.	Sor hap

	MONTHS OR MORE	SINGLE TIME: ONCE ONLY	REPEATED	MULTI-TIME: SEGMENTED	CALENDRICAL CYCLE	EVENT-GENERATED TIME	SYMBOLIC TIME
n e	Some initiations	Execution	Theatre on Chekhov Street	Election of Pope	Some Aborigine performances	Election of Pope	Theatre on Chekhov Street
ings	Teching Hsieh 'Yearlong' performance[5]	Bar mitzvah	Some happenings	Some happenings	Puja at Hindu temple	Some happenings; sandlot baseball	Some happenings
a;	Orokolo cycle[6]	Some happenings	Ordinary theatre & dance	Ramlila; Yaqui Easter	Ramlila; Macy's Parade	Big league ball	Ordinary theatre & dance
cs	TV Soaps	Boxing title match	Feature films	Olympics	Olympics; World Series	World Series	Feature films
n e; ine nies	Pilgrimage	Bar mitzvah	Mass	Yaqui Easter; Ramlila	Yaqui Easter; Ramlila	Aztec ballgame	Ramlila; Yaqui Easter
's n[7]	Hostage Crisis	Wilson's *Ka Mtn*; Hostage Crisis	Ordinary theatre & dance	World Series; Olympics	World Series; Olympics	Baseball	Ordinary theatre & dance
's n	Brook's theatre in Africa[8]	Many happenings & Performance Art	Aborigine ceremonies	Aborigine ceremonies	Macy's Parade; Aborigine ceremonies	Sandlot baseball	Schechner's *Philoctetes* on beach[9]
r	Orokolo cycle; Pilgrimage	Some happenings	Ordinary theatre & dance	Ramlila; Yaqui Easter	Ramlila; Yaqui Easter	World Series	Ordinary theatre & dance
er	Teching Hsieh	Some happenings	Ordinary theatre & dance	Murder trial	Church services; folk Bugaku[10]	Indoor sports	Ordinary theatre & dance
n's rn	Orokolo cycle; Pilgrimage	Some happenings	Elizabethan theatre	Ramlila; Yaqui Easter	Ramlila; Yaqui Easter	Baseball	Elizabethan theatre
er	"Yenlong performance"	Boxing title match	Ordinary theatre & dance	Murder trial	Folk Bugaku	Indoor sports	Ordinary theatre & dance
ics; la;	Orokolo cycle; Hostage Crisis	Hostage Crisis	Ramlila; Yaqui Easter	Ramlila; Yaqui Easter	Ramlila; Yaqui Easter	World Series	Ramlila; Yaqui Easter

Notes to figure 2.1

General Note

The Chart lists examples anecdotally. That is, many more examples could be given for almost every category. At this level what the Chart shows is the great diversity of performative events in terms of genre and use of time and space; and it shows the interrelatedness of events–time–space.

The chart can be read as a grid. For example, a Ph.D. Oral Examination is an example of Private But Open Secular Ritual; a Town Meeting held in a church is an example of a Secular Ritual taking place in a Sacred Space; the Macy's Thanksgiving Day Parade is a Calendrical/Cyclical Event taking place in Found Space. And so on. All items can be located according to three axes: Event, Time, Space.

Not all items are so explained, but they can be. And some items, obviously, occur in more than one category. So, Ramlila is Multi-Time: Segmented plus Calendrical/ Cycle plus Symbolic Time plus Days in duration. But Ramlila is not so easy to locate in terms of whether or not it is Aesthetic Theatre or Sacred Ritual or Social Drama: it is all of these, and at some moments more one than the others. Thus the Chart's weakness: it categorizes whereas many performances transform from one category to another, or slip across categorical boundaries. Still I have found making the Chart helpful in organizing my thinking about performance; and I hope that it will be of use to others.

Specific Notes

1. The Theater on Chekhov Street was one of several in Moscow operating privately outside the control of censorship. A description of it, and other private performances, is found in *TDR*, 23: 4 (December 1979). Private restricted performances are common in places where public free expression is limited; it is also the mark of certain kinds of rituals that can be attended by certain people only.
2. Feildhouses, as the name suggests, are indoor spaces that attempt to bring the outdoors inside. Even more outfront in this intention are domed stadiums whose astroturf looks like grass.
3. The Tiwi settle certain disputes by using a ritual duel staged in the main village square. The duel is described by C. W. M. Hart and Arnold R. Pilling in *The Tiwi of North Australia* (New York: Holt, Rinehart and Winston, 1966). Using their account I discuss the Tiwi duel in 'Actuals: A Look Into Performance Theory' in *Essays on Performance Theory* (New York: Drama Book Specialists, 1977). The Tiw duel is a near-perfect example of Victor Turner's 'social drama'.
4. Stuart Sherman stages 'spectacles' on street corners, in theatre lobbies, in various other places not usually thought of as performances spaces. His spectacles are theatrically modest: a small table, an assembly of props all of which can fit in an attaché case, no dialogue; a total elapsed time of under 30 minutes. As he became more successful, Sherman began inside theatres, on stage, in more orthodox ways.
5. Teching Hsieh is a performance artist who specializes in 'one year performances'. According to Barry Kahn (*Live* 6/7, 1982, pp. 40–2): 'On 30 September 1978, Hsieh began a year of solitary confinement inside an 11′–6″ × 9′ × 8′ cell which he built within his studio. "I shall not converse, read, write, listen to the radio or watch television until I unseal myself." A friend, Cheng Wei Kwang, took charge of his food, clothing, and waste. At 5:00 p.m. on 11 April 1980, Hsieh punched

in on a standard industrial time clock he had installed in his studio, an act which he repeated every hour on the hour until 6:00 p.m. on 11 April 1981. And on Saturday 26 September 1981, Hsieh began his third one year performance: "I shall stay outdoors for one year, never go inside. I shall not go in to [sic] a building, subway, train, car, airplane, ship, cave, tent. I shall have a sleeping bag," his statement said.' During his one year performances Hsieh allows the public to view him at certain times. For the outdoor performance anyone who knows who he is can watch him.

6. The Orokolo of Papua-New Guinea used to perform a cycle play that took years to complete. It is described by F. E. Williams in *The Drama of the Orokolo* (London: Oxford University Press, 1940); and also discussed extensively by me in 'Actuals'. Extended performances – or connected cycles of performances – are not uncommon. A sports season can be thought of as a cycle of performances. Major League baseball is certainly this way – with several high points: opening games, All Star Game, 'important series' near the end of the season, 'traditional rivalries', playoffs, and World Series.

7. Robert Wilson staged a seven day performance as part of the Shiraz Festival in 1972. It involved 50 persons and took 168 hours. It was staged on a mountain, and took the form of a kind of ascent or pilgrimage. *Ka Mountain* is described in an article by Ossia Trilling in *TDR*, 17: 2 (June 1973), pp. 33–47.

8. From December 1972 through February 1973, Peter Brook and thirty actors, technicians, and support persons travelled by Land Rover through Africa from Algiers, across the Sahara, into Niger, Nigeria, Dahomey, Mali, and back to Algiers. During their trip they staged improvisations, exchanged theatrical (songs, dances, skits, techniques, etc.) items with Africans, and showed their own work. They played in many different situations. A uniting, and signalling, item was their 'peformance carpet'. 'We got out [of our vehicles],' said Brook, 'unrolled our carpet, sat down, and an audience assembled in no time. And there was something incredibly moving – because it was the total unknown, we didn't know what could be communicated, what couldn't. All we disccovered was that nothing had ever happened resembling this before on the market [at In-Salah, in Algeria]. Never had there been a strolling player or some little improvisation. There was no precedent for it. There was a feeling of simple and total attentiveness, total response and lightning appreciation, something that, perhaps in a second, changed every actor's sense of what a relation with an audience could be.' See 'Brook's Africa, An Interview by Michael Gibson', in *TDR*, 17: 3 (September 1973), pp. 37–51.

9. In 1960 I staged Sophocles' *Philoctetes* on the beach of Truro, Massachusetts (near Provincetown, where I was running a summer theatre). The audience had to walk over a mile of sand dune to reach the place where the performance took place. Philoctetes himself roamed the dunes; Neoptolemus and Odysseus arrived by boat (we had launched them about a half-mile further down the beach). The Truro dunes really conveyed the sense of desert island that the Sophocles play asked for.

10. In December 1979 I observed *dainichi-do* folk Bugaku in Northern Japan (Kazano City), at a Shinto Shrine. Peasants, wearing traditional masks, including a famous golden one said to possess great power, danced for about three hours on a makeshift square elevated stage – like a boxing ring without ropes – set up in the centre of the interior of the shrine. It was said that this same performance is done each year, and dates back many hundreds of years.

of the division of labor, with its specialization and professionalization, reducing each of these sensory domains to a set of entertainment genres flourishing in the leisure time of society, no longer in a central, driving place. The pronounced numinous supernatural character of archaic ritual has been greatly attenuated (p. 12).

Turner regrets what he calls the *"sparagmos"* of ritual, but he detects "signs that the amputated specialized genres are seeking to rejoin and to recover something of the numinosity lost in their [. . .] dismemberment." (p. 12). I pursued a similar theme in "From Ritual to Theatre and Back" (1977, 1988) where I suggested that the development of theatre from ritual was only one way of a two-way process, that rituals emerge from theatre (or other performative genres).

Turner's idea, contemporary as it is, also fits nicely into the approach of Jane Ellen Harrison, Gilbert Murray, Francis Cornford, *et al.* – the "Cambridge Anthropologists"[2] – who, during the first decades of the twentieth century followed the lead of J.G. Frazer. The Cambridge group thought they had discovered a "primal ritual," what Murray called a *"sacer ludus"* as the source of Greek tragedy and comedy. The problem with the Cambridge thesis, and with Turner's origin theory as well, is that it is neither verifiable nor falsifiable; nor is it supportable on the basis of common sense. The "origin" of the aesthetic genres – theatre, dance, music – could as well be themselves: these activities being co-existent with the human species; or, if one demands a functional origin, they could be rooted in healing, in fun-making, or teaching (as in story-telling and initiations[3]). To call all of these "rituals" is to beg the question.

Caveats taken, there are two meanings of "ritual" that can be applied to the study of performance, the ethological and the neurological. This last Turner was investigating in the months before his death (see his 1983 essay, "Body, Brain, and Culture")[4]. Ethologically, rituals are certain behavioral displacements, exaggerations, repetitions, and transformations that communicate and/or symbolize meanings not ordinarily associated with the behavior displayed. As Irenaus Eibl-Eibesfeldt writes, "ritualization is the process by which non-communicative behavior patterns evolve into signals [. . .] In a ritual expressive movements are integrated in a more complex event which is structured in a rule-governed way" (1979: 14, 10).

But let me back up.

Figure 2.1 lays out the time, space, and event parameters of performances without regard to culture or genres. I wanted to take an intergeneric, intercultural perspective and see what the "limits" of performance were. I tried to think of performances of different magnitudes, from the very longest lasting months or even years, to split-second events; from the longest cycle plays to the smallest "brain events' of conceptual art – performances making no spatial claims at all; from clear examples of theatre, dance, and music to what Clifford Geertz might lift his eyebrow at as the blurriest of genres: the Iranian Hostage Crisis of 1979–80, a bar mitzvah, famous murder trials (like those of Klaus von Bulow or Jean Harris), Hindu temple services, title boxing matches, TV soap operas, the Yaqui Easter Passion play, orthodox Euro-American theatre and dance, noh drama, ramlila . . . etc. etc. Some of these performances are one of a kind while others are generic; some are rituals, some entertainments; some take months, others are over in a matter of minutes or take no time at all. What figure 2.1 expresses is my triune thesis: 1. there is a unifiable realm of performance that includes ritual, theatre, dance, theatre, sports, play, social drama, and various popular entertainments; 2. certain patterns can be detected among these examples; 3. from these patterns theorists can develop consistent broad-based models that respect the immediacy, ephemerality, peculiarity, and ever-changingness of individual performances, runs, and genres.

In the essay that follows I will develop only a few aspects and consequences of the time-space-event chart. My aim is to indicate what the magnitudes of performances are and where each magnitude of performance takes place.

Insiders-Outsiders

Erving Goffman built his work on the basis that everyday life is framed and performed. Early in his investigations he wrote, "All the world is not, of course, a stage, but the crucial ways in which it isn't are not easy to specify" (1959: 72). Not easy because everyday life is suffused with interactions that are rule-bound, governed by conventions that are networks of reciprocal expectations and obligations.

> The legitimate performances of everyday life are not "acted" or "put on" in the sense that the performer knows in advance just what he is going to do, and does this solely because of the effect it is likely to have. The expressions it is felt he is giving off will be especially "inaccessible" to him. But as in the case of less legitimate performers, the incapacity of the ordinary individual to formulate in advance the movements of his eyes and body does not mean that he will not express himself through these devices in a way that is dramatized and pre-formed in his repertoire of actions. In short, we all act better than we know how (1959: 73–74).

Goffman goes on in this early, but decisive, enunciation of his core idea to say that in cultures where trance is practiced – such as Haiti (he could have added Korea and Bali, as well as certain African, Afro-American, and Euro-American religious sects) – the entranced person will

> be able to provide a correct portrayal of the god that has entertained him [because of all the contextual knowledge and memories available; that] the person possessed will be in just the right social relation to those who are watching; that

possession occurs at just the right moment in the ceremonial undertaking, the possessed one carrying out his ritual obligations to the point of participating in a kind of skit with persons possessed at the time with other spirits (1959: 74).

Goffman emphasized that his observations are usually not shared by the possessed people. "Participants in the cult believe that possession is a real thing and that persons are possessed at random by gods whom they cannot select" (1959: 74).

This break between the experience of the observer and that of the participant is one of the most interesting things about trance possession from the point of view of performance theory. This break is on a continuum with the less radical but still distinctly observable breaks between the experiences of performers and audiences in all kinds of performances. In terms of trance a very few examples must suffice as indicators of a general tendency.

Insiders. Shakers of St. Vincent: "Power is a breeze descended that comes as a rushing wind into the heart. When It leaves, you feel something leaving you" (Henney, 1974: 59).

Outsiders: Shakers of St. Vincent: Three "levels" of trance are perceived. "The first external sign of dissociation may be a convulsive jerk of one or both arms, of one or both shoulders, or of the head. It may be a shudder, shiver, or trembling; a sudden shout, sob, hiss, or series of unintelligible sounds [. . .] As more and more individuals throughout the church become involved in the random symptoms of the first level [. . .], a subtle change of behavior characteristic of the second level takes place. [. . .] Idiosyncratic movements and sounds, and breathing peculiarities become less conspicuous because of the concerted attention persons in possession trance give to the same rhythm pattern. [. . .] Sooner or later the second level of possession trance changes. The smoothly patterned phenomenon in which each individual submits to the group-impressed rhythmic beat is disrupted as the dissociated persons emit loud sighs and yells, and breathe with complete disregard for the previous regular timing. [. . .] All movements and sounds again become individualistic. [. . .] That the Shakers themselves are aware of differences in possession-trance levels came to my attention when I played for them some of the tapes I had made" (Henney 1974: 61–63).

Insiders, Balinese *sanghyang* trance: "GM [Jane Belo's Balinese assistant]: What is the feeling like when you are beginning to be smoked [put into trance]? Soekani: When I am just being smoked my ears are stopped up, hearing the song. After that I immediately lose consciousness, I feel as if I were all alone. When I am about to come to myself suddenly I know where I am. [. . .] Darja: When I've gone in trance, my thoughts are delicious, but I do not remember them. What's more, my whole body is very hot. And then, if I am touched with holy water, my thoughts are like a crazy person's. [. . .] Darma: When I'm a *sanghyang* snake, suddenly my thoughts are delicious. [. . .] When my body is like that, as a snake, my feeling is of going through the woods, and I am pleased. GM: And if you're a *sanghyang* broom, what's it like, and where do you feel? Darma: Like sweeping filth in the middle of the ground. Like sweeping filth in the street, in the village, I feel I am being carried off by the broom, led on to sweep" (Belo 1976: 156–58).

Outsiders: "The hypnotic threshold, the selective awareness of certain stimuli and imperviousness to others irrelevant to the situation, well-known in hypnosis experiments, is illustrated in the players' remarks about hearing the song, but not hearing people talking of other things, not seeing the singers, but trampling upon them when angered. The feeling of lowness, which Darma described as delightful, fits in with the whole constellation of ideas about being mounted, being sat on, and so forth, wherein the pleasurable quality of the trance experience is connected with the surrendering of the self-impulses. This is one aspect of the trance state which seems to have reverberations in the trance vocabulary in whatever country these phenomena appear – and the aspect which is perhaps the hardest for non-trancers to grasp" (Belo 1976: 158–59).

Even further outside are analyses like Chapple's (1970) and Lex's (1979)

Chapple: "Voodoo drums, the regular and driving rhythms of revivalistic ceremonies, the incessant beat of jazz or its teenage variants in rock and roll, must synchronize the rhythms of muscular activity centered in the brain and nervous system. Combined with the dance or with other rhythmic forms of synchronized mass movement – stamping the feet or clapping the hands over and over again – the sound and action of responding as the tempo speeds up clearly "possess" and control the participant. The external rhythm becomes the synchronizer to set the internal clocks of these fast rhythms" (1970: 38, quoted in Lex 1979: 122).

  Lex: "The *raison d'etre* for rituals is the readjustment of dyphasic biological and social rhythms by manipulations of neurophysiological structures under con-trolled conditions. Rituals properly executed promote a feeling of well-being and relief, not only because prolonged or intense stresses are alleviated, but also because the driving techniques employed in rituals are designed to sensitize or "tune" the nervous system and thereby lessen inhibition of the right [cerebral] hemisphere and permit temporary right-hemisphere domination, as well as mixed trophotropic-ergotropic excitation, to achieve synchronization of cortical rhythms in both hemispheres and evoke trophotropic rebound.[7] Furthermore, it is difficult to separate the impact of repetitive behaviors on the brain from their influence on the rest of the nervous system because the various driving techniques simultaneously excite numerous neural centers. In a given ritual one specific practice alone may be sufficient to establish a state of trance; that several techniques are engaged concomitantly or sequentially indicates redundancy, to guarantee reliability, potentially affecting the entire group of participants. In other words, manifold driving techniques accommodate individual differences in experience and genetic makeup. However, any complete interpretation of ritual trance also recognizes the symbolic qualities of human behavior [. . .] (144–45).

These differences are not just exercises in the "emic/etic" pitfalls of fieldwork. The great big gap between what a performance is to people inside from what it is to people outside conditions all the thinking about performance. These differences can be as great within a single culture as they are across cultural boundaries. In fact, in my own experience, performers from different cultures are more likely to understand each other – and be able to exchange techniques, anecdotes, information – than they can understand, and be understood, by people within their own culture who have not themselves either been performers or have gone out of their way to understand what performers experience. Performance experience – unlike eating, housing, speaking-listening, etc. – is something the outsider has to specifically go out of her/his way to get from the inside. This curiosity concerning performed experience prompted the Turners to experiment with "performing ethnography."[8]

The situation of the "professional performer" – a person who reflexively masters the techniques of performance (whether or not s/he gets paid for it) – is very different from the "Goffman performer" who is likely to be unaware of her/his own performance.[9] The theorist in Goffman's world is always an outsider because the theorist exposes precisely what the Goffman performer conceals or is unaware of: the very fact that s/he is performing. There are actually two kinds of Goffman performers: the ones who conceal, as conmen do; and the ones who don't know they are performing. Of this second type there are two subdivisions: ordinary people playing their "life roles" as waitresses, doctors, teachers, street people, etc. and those whose particular actions have been framed as a performance in documentary film, shows like Candid Camera, or on the 6 o'clock TV news. The woman whose children have perished in a fire in Brooklyn pours out her grief and bewilderment in front of and for whom? For the cameras, and behind them, invisible but present, the "public." Perhaps, even, for herself as later she watches replays of her own grieving. A person in a similar plight who does not "make the news" has not become a performer. There are real-life consequences: the woman on TV is likely to have offered to her the assistance of viewers moved by her circumstances, while an unbroadcast person in a similar fix will have to depend on her own resources and official aid only.[10]

Clearly, there are several bands of participation and reception, and these define what kind of performance is going on. The comparisons among framed-as performers, Goffman performers, and professional performers is depicted in figure 2.2. Using figures 2.1 and 2.2 together, one can situate performances of different cultures and genres. The main question one asks is whether a performance generates its own frame, that is, is reflexive (self-conscious, conscious of its audience, the audience conscious of the performer being conscious of being a performer, etc.); or whether the frame is imposed from the outside, as when TV crews arrive at the scene of a "tragedy." In between these extremes are many gradations of purposeful concealment or information sharing – even what the U.S. Government calls "disinformation" (what the Nazis called propaganda, what Madison Avenue calls a "campaign"). Concomitantly there are degrees of publicly articulated performance conventions, staging, and training.

Birdwhistell and Ekman

Ray Birdwhistell locates the sources of some of what Goffman observed in very minute behavior observable only by studying human interactions as they

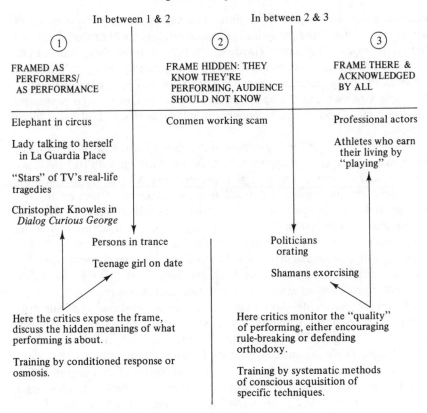

Figure 2.2 Frames of peformance.

are recorded and therefore susceptible to being slowed down, stopped, and repeated on film and tape.[11] Can we call the facial gestures that Birdwhistell says happen in milliseconds – such as eyebrow flashes, the turn of the lips that characterize certain smiles, tongue flicks, etc. – "performances"? Birdwhistell says these "kinemes" are culture-specific. There is an American way of flashing the eyebrows – or, perhaps it is more accurate to say, an American cultural context within which brow flashes communicate culture-specific meanings. But kinemes are not under anyone's conscious control – unless, that is, you study them in slow motion, learn what muscles are involved, and train yourself to execute the gestures, as Birdwhistell himself has done (and as, I would suppose, have many actors at least from the days of Delsarte onward[12]). Birdwhistell is an animated lecturer precisely because he can demonstrate in terms of facial displays a midwestern American teenage female's mode of greeting as distinct from that of a teenager from the deep south. As Birdwhistell points out there is a difference between understanding kinemes as expressing meaning and situating those kinemes in the various cultural settings that give them distinct social meanings. The number of kinemes is limited: "the [American] kinemic catalogue will probably contain between fifty and sixty items" (Birdwhistell 1970: 27). But these items can be combined with each other in various social contexts to yield the full range of "American" body languages. Birdwhistell's work has been used in conjunction with Goffman's as the basis of many workshops in body language and management of expressive behavior – what Arlie Hochschild calls "deep acting."[13]

Maybe the "deepest" acting goes on at the neurological level. Paul Ekman's work in this area, though apparently inimical to Birdwhistell's (the two have debated each other), actually meshes productively with it. Ekman believes that there are universally recognized facial displays of "target emotions." Ekman and his colleagues are currently detailing relationships between the autonomic nervous system (ANS) and acting. Here I mean acting as done by professional stage actors, though I do not doubt that similar results would be obtained using Goffman performers. In fact, the evidence is accumulating that the only difference between "ordinary behavior" and "acting" is one of reflexivity: professional actors are aware that they are acting.[14]

Ekman's experiments show that the six "target emotions" of surprise, disgust, sadness, anger, fear, and happiness elicit "emotion-specific activity in the ANS" (see figure 2.3). He got these data in two ways, using actors from San Francisco's American Conservatory Theatre. In one, subjects "were told precisely which muscles to contract [. . .]" constructing facial prototypes of emotion muscle by muscle;" in the other, "subjects were asked to experience each of the six emotions [. . .] by reliving a past emotional experience for 30 seconds" (1983: 1208–09). This reliving a past emotional experience is the classic acting exercise from the turn-of-the-century, called "emotion memory" or "affective memory" by the Russian theatre director Konstantin Stanislavski (see note 13). Stanislavski developed this exercise to help actors actually live on stage the emotional lives of the characters they were portraying. The same exercise, with modifications, is practiced today by many actors following the "Method" of Lee Strasberg and his Actors' Studio in New York.[15] In fact, Ekman wrote, "The idea of studying actors was suggested to me by Lee Strasberg some years ago. Although I never met Strasberg, we corresponded at some length about how our research might be used to explore the nature of the physiological changes that can occur when the 'method' is used" (1983: personal communication).

The actors who made Ekman's faces were not aware of what emotions they were constructing; rather they were coached muscle by muscle as they looked at themselves in mirrors.[16] Their work was a flagrant demonstration of "mechanical acting" – the kind despised by most American performers, but exactly what is learned by young Indian boys beginning their studies as performers in kathakali dance-theatre. There a most rigorous system of body and facial training is followed, one that more or less adheres to the ancient

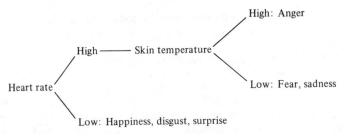

Figure 2.3 Emotions Ekman (1983: 1209) distinguishes on the basis of heart rate and skin temperature differences.

Sanskrit text on theatre, the *Natyasastra*, which I will discuss below in connection with Ekman's work. What should be noted now, is that the facial and body displays practiced by students of kathakali are not "natural" but exaggerated, wholly composed "deconstructions/reconstructions" of human behavior (see Schechner 1985: 213–60 and Zarrilli 1984a). If the kathakali displays also elicit changes in the ANS, might this not indicate the human neurological system accepts a very deep emotional learning? That is, human "fixed action patterns" or "ethological rituals" might be specifically transformable – a Batesonian play-frame built into the brain.

As noted, reliving emotions from past experiences is an exercise familiar to anyone who has studied acting in America. It is so common, in fact, that many people working in experimental theatre eschew it, detesting its cliches, lack of spontaneity, and underlying mechanistic approach to human feelings: the performer is drawn away from the actual present circumstances onstage concentrating instead on a "there and then" experience bootlegged into the present. On the other hand, such powerfully relived feelings generate performances in many ways similar to trance.

What is truly surprising about Ekman's experiment is not that emotional recall works, but that "producing the emotion-prototypic patterns of facial muscle action resulted in autonomic changes of large magnitude that were more clear-cut than those produced by reliving emotions" (1983: 1210). That is, mechanical acting worked better than getting the actor to feel. This is absolutely contrary to the Stanislavski–Strasberg canon. It also suggests that Hochschild's "deep acting" exists at the ANS level. And it asks for Birdwhistell's kinemes to be tested: do culture-specific facial displays also affect the ANS? Just how labile are humans, and to what level of the nervous system? Acting – professional and/or Goffman types – may be more than a neocortical event; acting may engage the old-mammalian and reptilian brains.

Ekman's experiment adds a new dimension to a growing body of evidence that suggests:

1. There are universal signals that not only repeat signifiers but signifieds: a "universal language," if you will, of "basic emotions" (see especially Eibl-Eibesfeldt 1979).

2.   This "language of emotions" is nonverbal and consists mostly of facial displays, vocal cries, body postures (freezes) and movements (stamping, rushing, crouching).
3.   There is a corresponding universal system in nerve and brain process – and this system probably underlies what anthropologists have called ritual (see Turner 1983 and d'Aquili, Laughlin, and McManus 1979).
4.   The culture-specific kinemes that Birdwhistell finds are built *on top of* the "universal language of emotions." That is, the universal language is neither static nor fixed but transformable – the more so, the more conscious individuals are of it. Professional performers – from shamans to actors on soap operas – skillfully manipulate the relationships between the two corresponding systems, the universal and the culture-specific.

Thus performances "take place" all along the continuum from brain events to public events of great spatial and temporal magnitude.

Ekman's findings do not invalidate what Birdwhistell and like-minded researchers have been saying: that each culture has its own way of encoding, using, contexting, and making-into-art the multi-channeled systems of nonverbal and paraverbal expressions. I want to go further. Each human group – family, circle of friends, workgroup, ensemble – develops its own dialect of movement. Artists are particularly adept at constructing variations of basic codes. This is what "style" is all about. What a theatre work is – not all it is, but the core of its "originality" – is how far a work can speak its own language without becoming unintelligible. Works called avant-garde or experimental sometimes go beyond this boundary, are rejected, only to be later incorporated into the canon as mainstream codes catch up with the avant-garde and critics and public learn what the previously rejected work is "about." That is, they learn to context the works, relocating the boundaries of accepted conventions to include works that were previously out of bounds. If this doesn't happen, the works are forgotten.

The Natyasastra

The *Natyasastra*, compiled in India between the second century B.C.E. and the second century C.E., describes in great detail various facial and bodily poses and expressions needed to perform the "eight basic emotions" of classical Indian dance-theatre: love, happiness, sadness (or grief), anger, energy, fear, disgust, and surprise. A ninth emotion, peace or sublime tranquility (*shanta*) was added later (see figures 2.4–2.12). Humankind has countless gods, but I would be very surprised if there were not some agreement concerning the "basic emotions." Love, energy, and peace are not on Ekman's list, possibly because he considers them to be "mixed" or composite emotions.

Compare one of Ekman's muscle-by-muscle descriptions with what the *Natyasastra* instructs the actor to do. Ekman (1983: 1208) says the fear-face is made by raising the eyebrows and pulling them together, raising the upper eyelids, and then stretching the lips horizontally back toward the ears (for the six basic emotions according to Ekman see figures 2.13 to 2.18). The *Natyasastra* deals with several kinds of fear and different classes of characters each of whom reacts differently to being afraid. But there are some possible generalizations. In Ghosh's (1967: 144) translation: "Fear is to be represented on stage by [. . .] shaking of the narrow limbs, body tremors, paralysis, goose pimples, speaking with a choked voice." Regarding the eyes and surrounding musculature, of which Ekman makes so much, the *Natyasastra* states: "[. . .] the eyelids are drawn up and fixed, and the eyeballs are gleaming and turned up" (155); and "the eyes are widely opened, the eyeballs are mobile in fear and are away from the center [of each eye]" (157). Also, "the glance in which the eyelids are drawn up in fear, the eyeballs are trembling, and the middle of the eye is full blown due to panic is called *Trasta* [frightened]" (159). But the *Natyasastra* is not entirely consistent. Its authors are always quoting *slokas* (sacred couplets). Sometimes these say that fear is to be represented by half-closed eyes. The *Natyasastra* is not a scientific study but a compilation of the stage experience by many actors over a span of centuries. A wide variety of emotions is conveyed by specific facial and bodily gestures for the eyes, eyelids, eyebrows, nose, cheeks, lower lip, chin, mouth, and neck; there are also sixty-seven gestures for the hands and many gestures for other parts of the body.

No one knows exactly how, in its day, the *Natyasastra* was put into action. Most probably it was a text like Stanislavski's books or Jerzy Grotowski's *Towards a Poor Theatre* (1968) collecting examples of what proved successful on stage. As such the *Natyasastra* serves as a node or transfer point linking previous practice with future practice. A hiatus of several centuries divides the Sanskrit theatre of the *Natyasastra* with even the oldest of the still-performed Indian dance-theatre, the kutiyattam of Kerala. But in kutiyattam, as in its sister genre, kathakali, a rigorous training continues the tradition of the *Natyasastra*. In kathakali there are numerous exercises for the eyes and facial mask (see figures 2.4 to 2.12).

In these exercises the forehead, eyebrows, eyelids, cheeks, and lips are all manipulated independently to gain individual control of the muscles like that demanded of the eyes. The eyebrows are exercised up and down while the eyes remain fixed on one point. While keeping the eyebrows raised and the eyes open and fixed on a point, the eyelids are independently articulated and fluttered. The lips and cheeks are exercised by practicing a closed-lip smile [. . .]. Similarly the muscles must be exercised to gain the pliability to give a broad frown. [. . .] While the facial mask is exercised, the young student must also learn the nine basic facial expressions which correspond to the nine permanent *bhavas* [feelings] and the corresponding *rasas* [emotions aroused in performer and spectator]. At first each facial expression is taught in purely technical terms (Zarrilli 1984: 133).

In the hands of a kathakali master these disciplines are not constraints, but the means to precise and spontaneous performances.

Richard Schechner

The nine *rasas*.

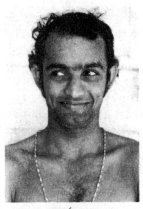

Figure 2.4 Śringāra: love, erotic, pleasure.

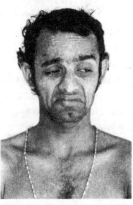

Figure 2.5 Hāsya: mirth, comic, but also impudence and lethargy.

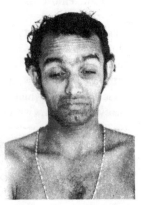

Figure 2.6 Karuṇa: sadness, pathetic.

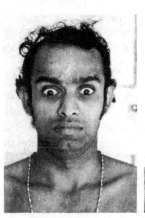

Figure 2.7 Raudra: anger, violence.

Figure 2.8 Vīra: vigor, heroic.

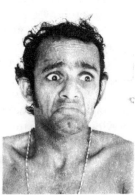

Figure 2.9 Bhayānaka: fear, guilt.

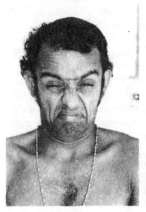

Figure 2.10 Bībhasta: disgust, repulsive.

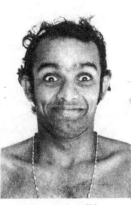

Figue 2.11 Adbhuta: surprise, excitement.

Figure 2.12 Śanta: peace, meditative mood.

The six basic emotions according to Paul Ekman and Wallace V. Freisen.

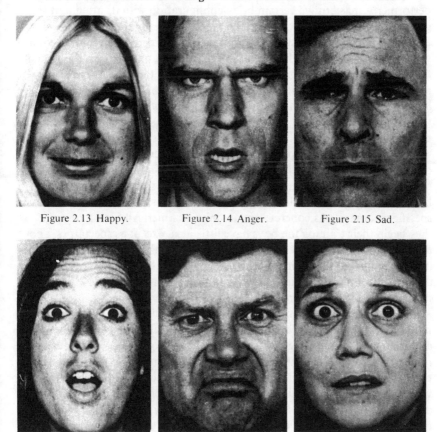

Figure 2.13 Happy.   Figure 2.14 Anger.   Figure 2.15 Sad.

Figure 2.16 Surprise.   Figure 2.17 Disgust.   Figure 2.18 Fear.

The *Natyasastra* – and the arts based on it – insist on what Ekman's experiments show: there are links between "mechanical acting" and feelings; the causal chain can go in both directions: feelings can lead to stage action while the practice of specific stage exercises can arouse feelings in the actor. In a definable way the performer can be moved by her/his own performance. Thus the performance – the psycho-physical score of a scene, dance, piece of music, etc. – occupies a space *between* the performer who is doing the action and the spectator who is receiving it. The performer performing can be the "objective correlative" T.S. Eliot finds in the enunciable literary text.[17] Reading the *Natyasastra* and studying the dance-theatre forms using it reveals that *abhinaya* – acting – is not only the means by which the audience gets the performance but also the way in which the actors get it – the "it" being not only gestures but feelings as well, feelings which are aroused by the practice of the proper gestures.

Take kathakali, for example.[18] The basis for becoming a kathakali performer is mastering a certain body configuration with its attendant steps, gestures of the hands, feet, torso, and face – especially the mouth, forehead, eyebrows, and eyes – in what to an American appears to be a very mechanical way. Boys begin training between the ages of eight and sixteen, the younger the better. They train for six or more years as their bodies are literally massaged and danced into shapes suited to kathakali. Even as they are learning the stories – taken mostly from the *Ramayana*, the *Mahabharata*, and the *Puranas* – their faces, feet, hands, and backs are learning by rote the sequences that add up to the finished performances. These sequences do not "make sense" by themselves; they equivocate concerning Ekman's assertions of universals. But these sequences can be thought of as aesthetic ritualizations of already ethologically ritualized "natural" displays. To a person educated in kathakali's face and hand language, the dancing makes sense, gestures convey specific meanings – as concrete and definite as American Sign Language. As they begin their training the boys have little idea, except as spectators, about these finished performances. But somewhere along the way the training "goes into the body" (as the Balinese, who use similar methods of training, say). An illumination of sorts occurs as what is being written in the bodies of the dancers is read *from the inside* by each of them.

What was rote movement, even painful body realignment, becomes second nature – a full language capable of conveying detailed and subtle meanings and feelings. The maturing performer now begins to internally experience his role with a force every bit as powerful as what an American Stanislavski-trained actor might experience. I believe that if such a kathakali performer were tested for ANS variation the results from the composed, performed facial displays would not be less pronounced or in any way markedly different from the muscle-by-muscle enactment of the "natural" emotions tested by Ekman. Aesthetic acting, learned from the outside, "composed" and culturally determined, penetrates deep into the brain. What was at the start of training an external effect becomes during the course of training an internal cause. As Padmanathan Nair, one of the best kathakali actors, told me in 1976: "A good actor is the one who understands the character very well, thus becoming the character itself. [. . . But] we should not forget ourselves while acting. While acting, half of the actor is the role he does and half will be himself." Bertolt Brecht, so affected by Chinese acting, would have been very pleased with Nair's answer. The "half actor" who is the role is the one who has internalized the fixed gesture patterns of kathakali; the "half actor" who is himself is the one observing, manipulating, and enjoying the actions of the other half. To achieve this kind of acting it is necessary to assimilate into the body the precise second-by-second details of performing. In kathakali, at least, this kind of mastery begins mechanically, à la Ekman; "feeling" at the experiential and/or ANS level comes later.

Lying and the performer's three halves

A depiction not merely of emotions, but of emotions that can easily be recognized, that can be composed and communicated – the raw material of theatre wherever it is found – is also the stuff lies are made of. As Ekman points out the face is not only a truth-teller but a liar without peer. And lying, as much as truth-telling, is the stock-in-trade of theatre.

> The face appears to be the most skilled nonverbal communicator and perhaps for that reason the best "nonverbal liar," capable not only of withholding inform-ation but of simulating the facial behavior associated with a feeling which the person is in no way experiencing (Ekman 1972: 23).

Here the Ekman of 1972 does not yet know what the Ekman of 1983 found out: that the "mechanical" construction of a face in the configuration of a "target emotion" elicits an ANS response, i.e., an "experience." Thus lying is a very complicated business in which the skilled liar – a person who can make a convincing face – *knows* he is lying but *feels* he is telling the truth. Exactly Nair's (and Brecht's) response. The half actor who "does not forget" himself is the knower, the half who "becomes the character itself" is the feeler. Exactly how this works neurologically remains to be investigated. Possibly there is a right-brain left-brain operation going on. This would suggest, even, that a skilled performer has "three halves." Both the ergotropic and trophotropic systems are aroused, while the "center" of the performer, the "I," stands outside observing and to some degree controlling. Clearly a complex operation engages both the cognitive and the affective systems simul-taneously, without either one washing out the other. A similar "triple state" accompanies some kinds of trance, while in other kinds of trance the feelings may be so powerful as to blot out entirely the "knowing half" of the performer.

Actor training in many cultures is largely about manipulating, controlling, manifesting, and communicating exact gestures, sounds, and other behaviors that elicit in the spectators particular *rasas* or feelings. It is not always expected that the actor experience the *rasa* s/he is producing. Of course, in some systems, both in the West and elsewhere, "authentic" feelings are asked of the performer.

The degrees of authenticity required by varying genres of behavior (you see, I am going beyond "theatre" and into "life") gets back to figure 2.2. Sometimes there is a mix of contexts and manipulations where ambivalence and ambiguity are delighted in. For example, animals at the circus are not aware of the varying human social and cognitive contexts of their behaviors. But it is these contexts that make the show enjoyable to the human spectators. The elephant bowing at the end of "his" act is not saying "thank you" although the spectators receive the elephant's behavior as such and applaud even louder accordingly. But how is what the elephant does different from what Laurence Olivier did when, in blackface, as Othello, raging, "Down, strumpet!" he takes up the pillow to murder Desdemona? The difference is that Olivier's knowing-half knows he is just acting and as such controls his gestures so that he does not injure the actress playing Desdemona. Even more, Olivier feels and does not feel rage against that actress. Olivier is absorbed in the task of "performing-the-actions-that-communicate-to-himself-and-to-his-audience-the-emotions-required." The whole bundle is necessary in order to understand this kind of acting. The Balinese dancer in trance is in a middle position. She might not know at the time that she has been dancing, that the *dedari* (gods) have possessed her. But before and after dancing she knows what trance is (in her culture), what the proper gestures are, what behavior is acceptable *while in trance* (even how far "out of control" to get). The trancer's situation is very different from that of the crazy lady shouting to the wind on La Guardia Place in Manhattan. The crazy lady is talking so convincingly to an absent Other that around her has gathered an absorbed, amused crowd. She may be performing the gestures of a great monologist, but prompted by some interior cue she is no better off than the circus elephant. Worse, even, because no trainer can get her to stop "acting," no shout of "Fire!" will make her quit the stage for a safe exit.

Or take Christopher Knowles, the "brain-damaged" or "non-ordinary" or "specially creative" boy (depending on one's point of view regarding the ancient and widespread tradition of using such people as entertainers) who worked with Robert Wilson in the 1970s. They did a two person show, *Dialog Curious George* where Knowles was – like the circus elephant or the lady in La Guardia Place – just "being himself." Wilson contexted his interactions with Knowles as a performance for the public who paid fancy prices to witness and admire it. Sometimes Knowles' responses – his way of re-telling the children's story, and Wilson's questions to Knowles, were very funny, wise, ironic, appropriate: one of those Simpleton Saints. Saint or not, Knowles was an elephant bowing at the circus – whatever his remarks meant to members of the audience they meant, or were, something else to Knowles.[19] Because Knowles couldn't lie, he couldn't be an actor – he could only be *situated and displayed as if he were an actor* inside Wilson's show.

Brain lateralization and performance

But how can one specify the differences between performances that are so only contextually and those that the performer is conscious of manufacturing? Could the difference be in how the brain is used? D'Aquili (1979) and his colleagues note that the left side of the brain is ergotropic and the right side trophotropic. They say that

> there is something about the repetitive or rhythmic emanation of signals from a conspecific that generates a high degree of limbic arousal. [. . .] There is

something about repetitive rhythmic stimuli that may, under proper conditions, bring about the unusual neural state of simultaneous high discharge of both [the sympathetic and parasympathetic] autonomic subsystems. [. . . The excited ANS] supersaturates the ergotropic or energy-expending system [. . .] to the point that the trophotropic system not only is simultaneously excited by a kind of spillover but also on rare occasions may be maximally stimulated, so that, briefly at least, both systems are intensely stimulated (1979: 157, 175).

Such maximal stimulation gives that feeling of the inexpressible which sometimes accompanies not only religious rituals and solitary meditation but large and small gatherings of many different kinds – from football games to Samuel Beckett's plays, from Nazi rallies to the soft rhythmic panting-chanting I teach as part of a theatre workshop.

In 1971 Roland Fischer devised what he called "a cartography of the ecstatic and meditative states" (figure 2.21) wherein the spectrum of arousal is outlined from trophotropic (hypoaroused) states such as Yogic samadhi and Zen meditation through the normal "I" states of daily routine, on to ergotropic (hyperaroused) states such as schizophrenia and mystical ecstasy. Fischer, like d'Aquili, speaks of a "rebound" from one extreme to another.

In spite of the mutually exclusive relation between the ergotropic and tropho-tropic systems, however, there is a phenomenon called "rebound to superactivity" or trophotropic rebound, which occurs in response to intense sympathetic excitation, that is, at ecstasy, the peak of ergotropic arousal. A rebound into samadhi at this point can be conceived of as a physiological protective mechanism. [. . .] Meaning is "meaningful" only at that level of arousal at which it is experienced, and every experience has its state-bound meaning. During the "Self"-state of highest levels of hyper or hypoarousal, this meaning can no longer be expressed in dualistic terms, since the experience of unity is born from the integration of interpretive (cortical) and interpreted (subcortical) structures. Since this intense meaning is devoid of specificities, the only way to communicate its intensity is the metaphor; hence, only through the transformation of objective sign into subjective symbol in art, literature, and religion can the increasing integration of cortical and subcortical activity be communicated (1971: 902).

Theatrical performance – from trance to Olivier to kathakali – seems to be a peculiar human activity in which there is high arousal of both ergotropic and trophotropic systems while some of the center – the "normal I" – is held back as an observing-controlling self. Performance training is the development of a number of communicative skills *plus* learning how to arouse the two extremes of brain activity without cancelling out the center "I" self; the theatrical performer never wholly loses self-control. Precisely how this is done in terms of neurobiology remains to be discovered, though I believe Ekman's work on the relation between the ANS and facial muscular control is a big step in the right direction. Strong theatrical performances are thus dangerous – on the edges – and yet playful; they are examples of psychophysical "deep play."[20]

Trance performances are on or even over the edge: self-control is reduced to

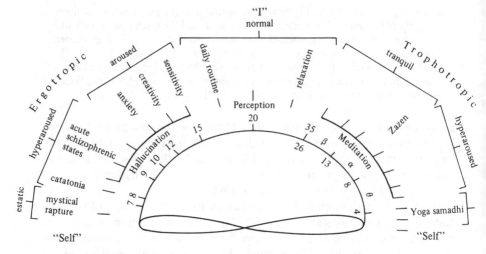

Figure 2.19 Fischer's (1971: 898) "cartography of the ecstatic and meditative states." He explains: "Varieties of conscious states [are] mapped on a perception-hallucination continuum of inceasing trophotropic arousal (*left*) and a perception-mediation continuum of increasing trophotropic arousal (*right*). These levels of hyper-and hypoarousal are interpreted by man as normal, creative, psychotic, and ecstatic states (*left*) and Zazen and samadhi (*right*). The loop connecting ecstasy and samadhi represents the rebound from ecstasy to samadhi, which is observed in response to intense ergotropic excitation. The numbers 35 to 7 on the perception-hallucination continuum are Goldstein's coefficient of variation . . ., specifying the decrease in variability of the EEG amplitude with increasing ergotropic arousal. The numbers 26 to 4 on the perception-mediation continuum, on the other hand, refer to those beta, alpha, and theta EEG waves (measured in hertz) that predominate during, but are not specific to, these states."

a minimum or absent, thus the necessity for helpers – people who stay out of trance specifically to aid those who are in trance, preventing injuries, assisting the trancers as they come out of trance. The crazy lady in La Guardia Place is not in trance because she has no way out. She has surrendered to, or been taken over by, schizophrenia. The normal "I" self has been permanently abolished. Christopher Knowles and the circus elephant have a "damaged" or non-existent "I."

Performing artists are forever playing around – not only with the codes, frames, and metaframes of communication – but with their own internal brain-states. Although artistic and scientific creativity have long been thought to be similar, there is this decisive difference: scientists focus their work on external phenomena; even a neurobiologist works on somebody else's brain. Performing artists – and, I would say, meditators, shamans, and trancers too – work on themselves, trying to induce deep psychophysical transformations either of a temporary or permanent kind. The external art work – the performance the spectators see – is the visible result of a trialogue among: (1) the conventions or givens of a genre, (2) the stretching, distorting, or invention of new conventions, and (3) brain-centered psychophysical transformations of self.

Performativity, theatricality, and narrativity

In other writings (Schechner 1985) I have described in detail the deconstruction/reconstruction process that performers use to effect transformations of self. This process, present in different cultures and genres under various names, is the "ritual process' van Gennep first specified and Turner explicated. D'Aquili, Lex, and Fischer investigate the same process from a neurological perspective. From a theatrical perspective what happens is that a person enters training or workshop as a "fixed" or "finished" or "already made" being. The training consists of specific methods of "breaking down" the neophyte, of rendering her/him psychophysically malleable. Quite literally the performer-in-training (or workshop) is taken apart, deconstructed into bits. The "bit" is not only computer jargon but a venerable theatre term meaning the smallest repeatable strip of action. Bits are as important to commedia dell'arte as they are to naturalistic or even formalistic acting; a bit is a molecule of action. The boys learning kathakali repeat the same bits over and over. Directors are always telling actors to "take that bit again" because it is at the bit-level that acting can be "worked on" from the outside. Stanislavski, co-founder of the Moscow Art Theatre and progenitor of the first and still the most influential school of modern acting and directing, broke down the scores of his *mises-en-scènes* into bits (sometimes translated into English as "beats"[21]).

Once bits are freed from their attachment to larger schemes of action, they can be rearranged – almost as the frames of a film being edited are rearranged – to make new action. This rearranging is not mechanical, for it is accompanied by varying degrees of self-conscious, reflexive reconstruction. How these rearrangements are accomplished in different cultures and genres varies. Sometimes the methods are kept secret as in noh theatre or in some initiation rites. Sometimes there is the opposite tendency – even a passion to spread the techniques as with many who make a career out of training actors and dancers. The devices of performer training go beyond the physical into realms of simulation, feigning, pretending, playing around with – all kinds of "as if-ing." Every performer knows that this kind of playing around is a dangerous game verging on self-deception-accepted-as-truth.[22]

Human communications systems are not reducible to the static model of "sender–channel–receiver," or any variation thereof, that assumes the existence of discrete parts. The human system is an extremely subtle multiplex-feedback one in which the originator of feelings is also affected by the emotions s/he is expressing – *even if these emotions are a lie*. That is what Ekman's experiment, and good acting, are saying: the doing of the action of a feeling is enough to arouse the feeling both in the doer and in the receiver.

Olivier need not work himself into a jealous rage against the actress playing Desdemona; but neither is he devoid of feelings; performing the actions of Othello will arouse Olivier. The so-called surface of emotion – the look on the face, the tone of the skin, the tilt of the body, the placement and moves of muscles – is also the emotion's "depth." Cortical and subcortical routines are linked and can be mutually trained.

Ekman's work and the instructions of the *Natyasastra* should caution scholars against depending on linguistic models when it comes to figuring out what's going on during performances. There are no universals of spoken or written language – no phonemes or graphemes that mean the same thing everywhere. Nor are there performance details at the level of artistic expression that are the same everywhere. But there are certain looks, sounds, and movements – certain facial displays, screams, laughs, sobs, crouches, stamps, and arm movements – which, if not universally understood, come close to conveying the same *feelings* everywhere. Nor are these feelings trivial: they constitute the very heart of human performing art and ritual as well as individual human experience. What I'm saying is that performances of theatre, dance, music, ritual by the very nature of their existence as behavior – as things done – give us our best examples for the intercultural study of human communication.

In a clumsy but ironically accurate way governments recognize this: from the most simple to the most sophisticated when one group wants to communicate to another across various boundaries (linguistic, political, cultural, geographical) the main initial signal is an exchange of performances, a mutual display of rituals. There is something about dance, music, theatre, and ritual that needs no translating – even as there is very much that is so culturally specific that it takes a lifetime of study to understand the performances of a culture not one's own. What jumps borders are the "rasas," the "universal target emotions" and what is so very culturally specific are the definite "texts" – the particular minute weaves of interaction made when these universal target emotions are combined with cognitive materials, masked, displaced, and played with in every imaginable way.

In figure 2.1 I offered examples of performances of varying magnitudes from the point of view of *mise-en-scène*, the various ways of organizing time, space, and events. But existing within these *mises-en-scènes* are Ekman universals. If Ekman is correct and there are certain facial expressions recognized universally, and if his work could be extended to include "target" gestures, moves, and sounds all studied from an ethological perspective, then we might be able to find out how performances use these universals. Do they build up from Ekman universals to Birdwhistell kinemes to specific genres to individual variations (the artist's "originality")? Or is context the determining factor – so that performances actually "build down" from larger meaningful units to smaller and smaller meaningless "performables." Brain events, microbits, and bits (see below for an explanation of this terminology) are not themselves units of meaning – they are like phonemes and words that acquire meaning only as used in sentences or bigger semantic units. Thus performances of small magnitudes gather meaning from their contexts. Or perhaps it is more complicated. Meanings may be generated and transformed up and down the various magnitudes.

Studies by Victor Turner, Fred Turner (1985), Melvin Konner (1982), d'Aquili *et al.* (1979) signal a convergence of anthropological, biological, and aesthetic theory. The focus of this convergence is ritual. Ritual studies are turning from looking at the "finished product" toward examining the "whole performance sequence": training, workshop, rehearsal, warmup, performance, cooldown, and aftermath. When this whole sequence is considered, it becomes clear that the ritual process is identical to what I call "restored behavior," "twice behaved behavior," behavior that can be repeated, that is, rehearsed (see Schechner 1985). Ritual process is performance.

From this perspective, performance magnitudes are not only about time and space but also about extensions across various cultural and personal boundaries. Thinking this way raises provocative questions: When is a performance a performance? How long does a strip of behavior have to be before it can be said to be performable in the ritual or aesthetic sense? When strips of behavior are taken from one context and played in another is it a different kind of performance if, in the replaying, the strip means something entirely different from what it meant "originally"? These transformations of meaning are inevitable if context determines meaning. But it's not so simple, because every strip, no matter how small, brings some of its former meanings into its new context. That kind of "memory" is what makes ritual and artistic recombinations so powerful.

To jump still farther ahead, it seems to me that the human community taken as a whole is entering a postmodern phase where the construction of intercultural aesthetics and ritual is both inevitable and essential. This ethnopoetics[23] occurs on three levels simultaneously: at the panhuman Ekman level where research might lead to the confirmation of the existence of some kind of behavioral version of Jungian archetypes; at the sociocultural level of diverse, particular performances: what anthropologists and performance theorists have until now focussed on; at an emerging post-humanist, postmodern level of the exchange of information through multiplex channels – a kind of intercultural reflexivity.[24]

Stay with me a bit longer. Are we to call the facial gestures Ekman describes "performances"? Why not? Can't they be brought under conscious control? So, too, we can call the vast social dramas that Turner describes "performances" – even though they may involve whole societies for years. Surely the events in Lebanon over how many decades make a well-knit Turnerian social drama, one that can never get beyond crisis and failed redressive action. Media encourages these large scale dramas to be viewed with varying degrees of anxiety and amusement by hundreds of millions of people. A "Rashomon effect"[25] occurs where the same data is woven into many different narratives according to cultural bias, editing, and individual interpretation – and these become parts of a Geertzian interpretation of cultures *by* different cultures.

The work for performance theorists now is to correlate a number of performance magnitudes identifying the transformational systems operating among them. Let me suggest seven "performance magnitudes" or levels whose interconnectedness ought to be explored.

1. Brain event: the neurological processes linking cortical to subcortical actions; ANS; the ergotropic-trophotropic system. Ekman's recent work, the speculations of d'Aquili and Lex. Turner's last investigations concerned these processes. "Deep acting" works on this level as well as on levels 2 and 3.

2. Microbit: seen only with the help of the slow-motion or stop-action camera. What Birdwhistell says delimits the kinemic vocabularies of discrete cultures.

3. Bit: the smallest unit of repeatable behavior. Ekman composes his subjects' faces bit-by-bit in order to test if their ANS is affected. Theatre directors and choreographers often work bit-by-bit, especially if they wish to compose images without interference by the performers' conscious intentions.

4. Sign: composed of one or more bits and readable, a piece of discrete information. Ekman claims that certain facial displays are universal signs. Ordinarily theatre and dance deal with events at the sign, scene, or drama levels. It is at these levels that spectators consciously receive performances.

5. Scene: a sequence of one or more signs that make up a whole unit of interaction. Goffman studied these. Narrative structures are visible at this level.

6. Drama: a complex, multiplex system of scenes ranging from aesthetic dramas to Balinese cockfights to initiations to long cycle plays such as the ramlila or the Yaqui Easter passion play. Geertz and Turner have analyzed these from a narrative point of view.

7. Macrodrama: large-scale social actions viewed performatively – what Turner calls "social drama" where whole communities act through their collective crises.

As we understand the relationships among these seven magnitudes – how, especially, the smaller are elicited, manipulated, and then composed into the larger and how the larger deport meanings down to the smaller – I think theorists will be able to better distinguish "performativity" from its close relations, "theatricality" and "narrativity." Performativity is present in all seven magnitudes but most decisively at levels 1, 2, and 3: the brain event, microbit, and bit. Theatricality begins with level 3, the bit, and is dominant at levels 4 and 5, the sign and the scene. Theatricality is absorbed *as scene* into levels 6 and 7, dramas and macrodramas. Narrativity begins at level 5, the scene, and is dominant at levels 6 and 7, the drama and macrodrama.

Ekman's work centers on performativity. Birdwhistell focuses on the area between performativity and theatricality. Goffman deals with theatricality. Turner, during most of his life, was concerned with narrativity – his theory of social drama can best be understood as a theory of performed narrative. Toward the end of his life, Turner became more and more interested in performativity, thus his speculations in "Body, Brain, and Culture."

Performativity – or, commonly, "performance" – is *everywhere* in life, from ordinary gestures to macrodramas. But theatricality and narrativity are more limited, if only slightly so. Differences in degree of magnitude do lead to differences in kind. Aesthetic genres – theatre, dance, music – are framed theatrically signalling the intentions of their composers to their publics. Other genres are frequently not so clearly marked – but this does not make them any less performative. And although performativity permeates all seven magnitudes, it doesn't work the other way round. There is no narrativity in a brain event, nor any theatricality either. Performer training begins below the level of theatricality or narrativity; workshops and rehearsals also often deal at these sub-theatrical, sub-narrative levels. Scholars who want to understand these formative processes must not focus on shows put on for the public – even Goffmanian performances of everyday life – but must attend to the brain events, microbits, and bits that pre-exist performances of larger magnitudes.

There is a continuity of performance magnitudes, from interior brain events to bits of training – the deconstruction/reconstruction process of workshops and rehearsals – on to public performances of varying scales – the end point being performances of worldwide dimensions, such as the Olympics, and the shooting down of KAL 007 and its aftermath. Some of these are media events, some social dramas. We have entered the epoch where a performance can be *both* a social drama and a media event, for example, the Iranian Hostage Crisis of 1980. However limited their magnitude at their points and moments of origin – a lone 747 trailed by a single fighter, an artist conceiving an art work – they soon catch a larger audience. Some net hundreds of millions of people in narrative and symbolic macrodramas unique to our own times and technologies. Others, like Allan Kaprow's recent private happenings,[26] remain intimate, almost dimensionless both spatially and temporally.

To what degree does our very survival as a species depend on how peoples and their leaders "act," not only in the sense of comportment but also in the theatrical sense? Exactly how a crisis is "handled" – played out, performed – becomes a matter of extreme importance. This brings me back to a basic paradox: humans are able to absorb and learn behavior so thoroughly that the new "performed" behavior knits seamlessly into ongoing "spontaneous" action. Performance magnitude means not only size and duration but also extension across cultural boundaries and penetration to the deepest strata of historical, personal, and neurological experience.

Notes

1. See Turner 1969, 1974, 1982a, 1986a, 1986b. For a discussion of why it might be better to apply not one but several performance theory templates in intercultural studies see Schechner 1985: 3–34.
2. The Cambridge Anthropologists were not fieldworkers. They were classical scholars who believed that a "primal ritual," a *"Sacer Ludus,"* was the root of Greek theatre. They claimed to have discovered vestiges of this primal ritual in existing Greek plays, especially Euripides' *The Bacchae.* See Cornford 1914,

Harrison 1912, 1913, and Murray 1912a, 1912b, 1925, 1961. Their approach has been much criticized, but their ideas are still widely taught. For a discussion of the Cambridge school as it bears on performance theory, see Schechner 1966, 1988.

3. Evolutionary progressions applied to performance make me very uncomfortable. Why ought theatre, dance, and professional and/or recreational sports "come from" ritual – as if ritual were the great unitarian artwork of prehistory shattered into the multiple genres of classical, modern, and postmodern societies? Rather, ritual *as a genre* exists side by side with the other performative genres. As far as the *ritual process* is concerned, I've discussed elsewhere how ritual process = performance-making process; therefore the ritual process was always part of performance, as much at the beginning as now (see Schechner 1985: 35–116, 261–94).

4. For a detailed discussion of Turner's essay, see Schechner 1986a.

5. From 1967 until 1980 I was artistic director of The Performance Group, a leading experimental theatre. I directed many plays and workshops with TPG, including *Dionysus in 69, Commune, Mother Courage and Her Children, The Tooth of Crime,* and *The Balcony.* After leaving TPG I have continued to direct, including *Richard's Lear, Cherry Orchard* (in Hindi with the professional Repertory Company of the National School of Drama, New Delhi, India), *The Prometheus Project,* and *Don Juan.* Most of these productions were developed during workshops.

6. For a recent discussion of the complex relationship between anthropologists and the cultures they study see Marcus and Fischer 1986. For a particular example of what happened in Kerala, India, when a team of scholars and filmmakers studied *agnicayana,* a "vedic ritual," see my review of Frits Staal's *Agni,* Staal's response to my review, and my response to Staal's response (Schechner 1986b, Staal 1987, Schechner 1987).

7. According to Lex, "*Ergotropic* response consists of augmented sympathetic discharges, increased muscle tonus, and excitation in the cerebral cortex manifested as 'dysynchronized' resting rhythms; the *trophotropic* pattern includes heightened parasymathetic discharges, relaxed skeletal muscles, and synchronized cortical rhythms" (1979: 135). The ergotropic/trophotropic responses are related to the distinct functions of the two hemispheres of the frontal cortex. Brain studies show that the two hemispheres are each specialized, though not as absolutely as the popular literature suggests. The right hemisphere is visual-spatial while the left is verbal and mathematical; trophotropic responses are associated with the right hemisphere, ergotropic with the left.

8. For Turner's discussion of "performing ethnography" see Turner 1986b: 139–55.

9. See Goffman's extensive writing on this subject: 1959, 1963, 1969a, 1969b, 1971, 1974. As people become aware of performing techniques, they begin to manipulate them. Many workshops now teach how to do it; ordinary people are becoming more and more like professional performers. It goes without saying that media skills – and the professional staff to exploit them – are necessary to every politician's career. The classic people ought to study is not Aristotle's *Poetics,* but his *Rhetoric.*

10. See my "News, Sex, and Performance Theory" in Schechner 1985: 295–324.

11. See Birdwhistell 1964, 1970 and Scheflen 1973.

12. According to theatre historian Marvin Carlson (1984) Francois Delsarte (1811–71) "began his *Cours d'esthetique applique* in 1839. The unfinished work, handed down in sometimes contradictory forms by his disciples, gained a

reputation quite the opposite of what its originator intended. Delsarte, reacting against the mechanical and formalized actor training of his time, attempted to return to nature by carefully observing and recording those expressions and gestures produced not by art but by instinct and emotion. But when these were codified for his students, the result was yet another mechanical system, the formal details of which were so rigorously taught by Delsarte's disciples for the remainder of the century that even today his system is almost a synonym for mechanical, arbitrary expressions and gestures, the very thing it was created to prevent" (218). There is a lesson here. Human activity – both physical and mental – is so labile that whenever a system appears that is "based on nature" it invariably finally discloses itself as being a cultural construct. The so-called "natural system" develops sclerosis as its adherents defend it against inevitable cultural change. They think they are opposing nature to culture when no such opposition exists. At most, there is a continuous oscillation between genetic tendencies and cultural systems that rewrite these tendencies over and over again, each time somewhat differently. For an American interpretation of Delsarte's system – including many exercises – see Stebbins 1902, reprinted, 1977.

13. As defined by Hochschild (1983), "deep acting" in acting done by a person with a trained imagination." Using the work of Stanislavski as her guide, Hochschild discusses emotion memory, the particularly powerful exercise of Stanislavski's whereby a person imagines all the "given circumstances" of an event – for example, the room, the temperature, the people present, the time of day, the smells, and so on – and soon the emotions of the event are "spontaneously" relived in all of their original force. The parallels with Freud's "abreaction" are obvious. Hochschild shows how deep acting is used in everyday situations. "In our daily lives, offstage as it were, we also develop feeling for the parts we play; and along with the workaday props of the kitchen table or office restroom mirror we also use deep acting, emotion memory, and the sense of 'as if this were true' in the course of trying to feel what we sense we ought to feel or want to feel" (1983: 43). She then goes on to show how techniques of deep acting are used by corporations and other "emotion managers" who wish their employees – mostly people in service jobs – to actually feel what those managing the institution thinks the job requires them to feel if they are to be effective in their work. In such a setting, airline stewardesses and stewards are taught to enjoy being helpful, ambulance paramedics to remain cool and efficient in the face of life-and-death crisis, etc. Deep acting persists, even when the learned affect and behavior might be inappropriate. For example, when airline stewardesses sueing United Airlines which fired them because either they had married or turned thirty-two, appeared on the stand they "behave[d] more like hostesses than litigants. When the lawyer who is challenging their testimony stands up and says, 'I am Mark Bigelow, representing United Airlines,' the witness is as likely as not to lean forward with a big smile and say, 'Hi!' " (Lewin 1984: D1). Hochschild contrasts deep acting with "surface acting" where "the expression on my face or the posture of my body feels 'put on'" (1983: 36). Paul Ekman's experiment with "put on" faces, discussed below, shows that a put on expression may affect the ANS every bit as much as a feeling deeply acted.

14. In Indian and Japanese dance-theatre – kathakali and kabuki, for examples – nonordinary body techniques are employed. Every gesture, look of the face, and move is codified. There is an extreme difference between the way each of these genres looks, but is there a corresponding interior difference? That is, were kathakali and kabuki actors portraying their stylized codified displays of emotion

tested, would their ANS show any, or as much, a reaction as the actors Ekman tested? Is it only "natural emotional displays" that yield ANS reactions; or will culturally composed displays do the same? My guess is that the culturally composed displays will affect the ANS.

15. For a discussion of the Method and other American variations of Stanislavski's system of actor training see two special issues of TDR devoted to "Stanislavski in America," vol. 9, 1 and 2 (1964) and Christine Edwards' *The Stanislavski Heritage* (1965).

16. Ekman told me that he had repeated the experiment without mirrors and obtained the same results. This, he says, shows that the subjects were not responding to seeing their own faces, but only to the muscle-by-muscle "making" of the faces.

17. Eliot in his essay on *Hamlet* states: "The only way of expressing emotion in the form of art is by finding an 'objective correlative'; in other words, a set of objects, a situation, a chain of events which shall be the formula of that *particular* emotion; such that when the external facts, which must terminate in sensory experience, are given, the emotion is immediately evoked" (1953: 145). This is precisely Stanislavski's "emotion memory" exercise.

18. For detailed descriptions and analyses of the training techniques in kathakali as practiced at the Kathakali Kalamandalam, India's premiere kathakali school, see Schechner 1985 and Zarrilli 1984a.

19. Wilson's workshop techniques, from which he developed several theatrical spectacles during the period of time he was working with Knowles and the deaf boy Raymond Andrews (the late 1960s to late 1970s), were drawn from his prior experience as a therapist. Wilson asked members of his performance workshops to follow the lead of Knowles or Andrews – to replicate and validate by means of imitation their experience, their view of the world. Thus the "small world" of the workshop expressed Knowles' and Andrews' otherwise inaccessible feelings and grasp of things. Members of the workshop did not try to "understand" how Knowles and Andrews felt – they tried to "behave like" and directly experience these feelings, to enter into their worlds. These worlds of extremely slow movement and silence constituted one of the bases of Wilson's theatrical work during that period.

20. See Geertz 1973: 412–53.

21. The Russian emigrees – Richard Boleslavsky, Maria Ouspenskaya, Michael Chekhov – who first taught Stanislavski's system in America spoke with a heavy accent. When they said "bit" their students heard "beat." Beat seemed an appropriate musical metaphor, and so the new pronunciation stuck. But Stanislavski meant "bit," a term familiar to vaudeville entertainers as well as actors on the legitimate stage.

22. A classic example of this in the anthropological literature is Levi-Strauss' (1963: 167–85) account of Quesalid, the Kwakiutl who set out to expose the fakery of shamanism but ended up as a renowned shaman in his own right defending the very techniques he had intended to debunk.

23. Jerome Rothenberg used the term "ethnopoetics" at least as early as 1975 when he and his co-editor Dennis Tedlock put out the first issue of *Alcheringa/Ethnopoetics*. In 1983, starting his "Pre-Face" to *Symposium of the Whole: A Range of Discourse Toward an Ethnopoetics*, Rothenberg said: "The word 'ethnopoetics' suggested itself, almost too easily, on the basis of such earlier terms as ethnohistory, ethnomusicology, ethnolinguistics, ethnopharmacology, and so on. As such it refers to a redefinition of poetry in terms of cultural specifics, with an emphasis on

those alternative traditions to which the West gave names like 'pagan,' 'gentile,' 'tribal,' 'oral,' and 'ethnic.' In its developed form, it moves towards an exploration of creativity over the fullest human range, pursued with a regard for particularized practice as much as unified theory [. . .]" (Rothenberg 1983: xi).

24. Efforts in this direction are visible both artistically and in terms of scholarship. The series of three conferences in 1981 and 1982 upon which this book is based is a prime example in terms of scholarship. In the artistic sphere, a powerful "fusion movement" combines Asian with Western performance. This has resulted in a number of interesting productions and even a few new genres, such as Japanese butoh. And one must not forget the extremely active tourist promotion of performances. Most tourist performances are sub-genres sharing qualities of condensation, simplification, and playing to audiences who want to be entertained. Some tourist shows, however, blur, into a kind of fieldwork, with qualified anthropologists and other experts setting up the programs. In all cases, there is a double pressure: to be "authentic" (a rotten term impossible to define), to modify what happens to suit the needs of the visiting group. Finally, many performing groups leave their home territories to bring their arts to strangers. This is not only a matter of Western impresarios and organizations importing "native arts." Aboriginal Australian groups hold festivals where they can see each others' dances and exchange techniques. Once every four years an all-Pacific festival is held. Similar exchanges are increasing all around the world.

25. The "Rashomon Effect" is when several contradictory accounts of the same event are presented with no account being privileged over any other.

26. Kaprow distinguishes between what he calls "artlike art" and "lifelike art." Artlike art is familiar to people – galleries, theatres, opera houses, etc.: art that *is* art. Lifelike art is often indistinguishable from ordinary living. For example, "For each day of a week, around 3 p.m. when the wind rose on the dunes, a woman took a walk and watched her tracks blow away behind her. Every evening she wrote an account of her walk in her journal. To begin each successive day, she read her journal story and then tried to repeat exactly what had happened. She described this experience, in turn, as faithfully as possible, until the week elapsed. Half in jest, she wrote in one passage, 'I wanted to see if I could stop change' " (Kaprow 1983: 100). And then there are "conceptual performances" where events never happen at all: the thought process is enough.

3

Liminality: a synthesis of subjective and objective experience

COLIN TURNBULL

Subjectivity and objectivity in 'participation'

In his book *From Ritual to Theatre: The Human Seriousness of Play* (1982) Victor Turner said that he was "frankly in the exploratory phase just now," and it is a great loss to anthropology that he did not have time to continue that exploration. I cannot pretend that the direction I propose to take is one that he would have taken, but it is something that we discussed the last time we met and we shared at least the mutual conviction that the liminal state or condition is of major importance for our understanding of human society, just as we shared the closely related conviction that anthropology and theatre have much to offer each other.

In that same book Turner is often openly subjective. He writes as much as an artist as from the more conventional viewpoint of the anthropologist. He writes with feeling and of feeling; he is plainly aware of the importance of his own subjective experience in the field, but cannot quite break with his intellectual rational, objective tradition for long enough to explore this further. This has perhaps always been the major stumbling block for any of us who have concerned ourselves with liminal phenomena, for too often we have insisted that it is something that can and should be *studied*, just as we have made the absurd assumption that our much vaunted "participant observation" technique provides us with a corrective insight to counterbalance our otherwise totally external view of culture. But we do not even bother to train ourselves for "participation," which we too often reduce to childish role-playing, ignoring the rigorous preparation and training readily available through the disciplines of theatre.

Victor Turner sensed this need to go beyond "the village of the sociologically known, proven, tried and tested"; he said our understanding of liminal and liminoid phenomena necessitated "studying symbols in social action . . . studying all domains of expressive culture . . . *total* social phenomena" (1982: 55). Yet he continued to insist on the process of *study*, which is necessarily objective, even though he clearly recognized that if we are

50

to understand *total* social phenomena, then something more than objective study is required. What is needed is a great deal more than amateur role-playing; what is needed is a technique of participation that demands *total involvement* of our whole being. Indeed it is perhaps only when we truly and fully participate in this way that we find this essentially subjective approach to be in no way incompatible with the more conventional rational, objective, scientific approach. On the contrary, they complement each other and that complementarity is an absolute requirement if we are to come to any full understanding of the social process. The criticism leveled against anthropology by third world scholars and laymen alike has much to do with our failure to be fully human and to use our full human potential when we make the attempt to understand others, treating them as though they were indeed not full human beings themselves but as things that could be satisfactorily examined and explained through the artifice of reason alone. This is perhaps the worst form of intellectual arrogance. What we need is a new technique that will at least get us closer to that central subjective essence that lies deep within any culture. We cannot dismiss the human element by claiming to be concerned only with social systems.

In the process of losing touch with our humanistic potential we have lost the very something that provides us with the key to that fundamentally simple condition of liminality, which with all his mastery of words Turner found such difficulty in defining to his own satisfaction. It is that something without which fieldwork and its published results become a mere exercise in ethnocentric intellectual gymnastics. What we have lost is the awareness that our ability to participate fully, to become emotionally as well as intellectually involved in another culture, in no way detracts from our objective, rational, intellectual analytical ability. On the contrary it provides a wealth of data that could never be acquired by any other means, which of course is our very argument for entering the field in the first place. It has become a major weakness of anthropology that we do not enter the field fully enough, and the superficiality of our understanding of other cultures (as of our own) is directly proportional to the superficiality of our participation in that culture.

The fieldworker's background: a personal example

This was something I discovered for myself not by any astute rational process, but by the sheer accident of being plunged into a number of different cultural contexts long before I had even heard of anthropology. The point of the personal example is to suggest the importance of turning to advantage any personal attributes, skills, inadequacies, qualities ("good" or "bad") as well as any accidental situations. It should also serve as a caution against over-rigorous planning and preparation, practical and theoretical. My initial brush with subjective experience was entirely involuntary; in no way did I consider it a "technique" of learning. In both India and Africa I found myself living in contexts that compelled the fullest possible participation and which made structural allowances for such participation by outsiders. When I first found myself in the Ituri Forest it was on my way back to Oxford from two years in India. I had not even heard of anthropology let alone become dedicated to any of its propositions, and I found myself comfortable in this exotic setting because on the one hand there was a structure that made allowances for my presence, and on the other I was under no constraints of any kind, other than physiological, that prevented my full participation in the life into which I had again accidentally stumbled. On that first trip to the Ituri I not only witnessed two dramatic, vitally important, central rituals, I experienced one of them in particular as a fully participating (however foreign and temporary) member of that society. In this state of academic ignorance, while one experience was emotionally stimulating long before it aroused any intellectual curiosity, with the other it was the reverse, a reversal that both tests and confirms my belief in the practicality and vital importance of total, subjective participation at some stage in the field experience. But a professional anthropologist can not of course justify his position as such if he places his personal emotional satisfaction above his professional competence, so we have to ask whether the academic results of this untutored experience of ritual were of merit. The answer is an unequivocal affirmative, for it provided insights that would have been impossible to come by had intellectual curiosity been my prime motivation, as it is for most fieldworkers.

The two rituals were the *molimo* of the Mbuti hunter/gatherers, a ritual that can be occasioned by any crisis, but particularly by death, and the *nkumbi* initiation of boys, a ritual of the neighboring horticultural Bira and Ndaka peoples, that takes place throughout the forest once every three years. There is no room here to describe the field experience of both rituals, so I shall confine myself to the *molimo* and, in the manner of the old fashioned ethnographic description (a straightforward presentation of the facts, the value of which has somehow fallen into disfavor in the pseudo-scientific shuffle), follow that experience in chronological order, as fully as space allows. It is hoped that a fuller account of the experience of both rituals will be published later in monograph form.

On my first visit to the Ituri, in 1951, I was present when a *molimo* was occasioned by a death, although it was not the death of anyone I knew. I was already enough of a participant through my intensive involvement with the music of the people, for the experience of being present at part of a *molimo* to fill my whole being, to satisfy it by transforming an emotional state of some anguish into one of contentment. At the same time that transformation negated the necessity for asking questions of any kind; whatever problems the death caused were resolved without any discussion or other intellectual activity of any kind. What discussions I witnessed later seemed like afterthoughts, performed rather as a technical chore.

While this first brief, fragmentary experience of the *molimo* in no way

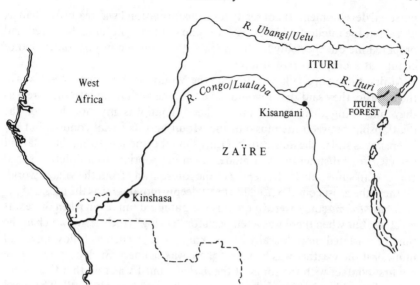

Figure 3.1 Location of the Ituri Forest.

provided me with the "hard data" expected of a trained observer spending much longer in the field, it did provide me with something I might well have missed with such an objective, academic approach. The experience is worth examining here precisely because it was so entirely subjective, and because the *molimo* is typical of the rites of passage that occupied so much of Turner's attention, involving the liminal condition that we are trying here to reexamine. We shall in this way be looking at what was in fact a liminal phenomenon, as perceived firstly by direct, immediate experience, through full, total involvement, then on a subsequent occasion (1954) as perceived by an intellectually curious mind housed in a body that was already familiar with the experience, but a mind whose curiosity was in things other than ritual. And thirdly we shall see the *molimo* as perceived (in 1957/58) by an intellectually curious mind filled with all the usual anthropological theories of the day.

Involuntary subjectivity: molimo 1, arrival in the Ituri

When I first reached the Ituri Forest, what made me decide to stay was not any interest in the "culture," but interest in the music which was far richer and more complex than anything I had yet heard in Africa, and which gave me an opportunity to pursue a lifelong involvement with European music and two years of study of the very different musical traditions of India. From the outset, then, I recognized the field experience as involving, even compelling, personal development. If not ready for transformation I was ready for change, at least at the intellectual level. My two years of living in India, however, had prepared me unexpectedly for the possibility of a much more radical kind of change at a deeply personal level.

At first I lived in a village, but when the Mbuti saw how interested I was in their music, they said that I would have to come with them into the forest as they only sang their "real" music there. That was my first hint of the relationship between the music of the Mbuti and its social context, but my interest was still in the music itself. Other than the one solo form, the lullaby, I detected four distinct musical modes, each appropriate to a different social context, all sung only in the depths of the forest, away from the village world. Of these the most complex, and the most deeply moving,[1] was the music of the *molimo*. *Molimo* songs were frequently sung at night time even when there was no crisis, but when there was a felt need for "curing" (their term, which at the time I translated more literally as "making good"), such as following a bad hunt, or if the weather was bad, or if there was sickness. Such occasions were my first contact with the songs of the *molimo*, but I was told that there were things I would only hear if the *molimo* itself was "brought out". The word referred not only to a form of music, and a crisis situation, and a curative practice, but also specifically to a long wooden trumpet used on certain special occasions, occasions I would now call ritual occasions.

This much I picked up during my first stay in a forest hunting camp, not in response to any formal academic inquiry into social organization, but rather as result of a deep personal fascination with and emotional reaction to the various kinds of song, the different singing techniques, the absence of the musical instruments that were such a dominant characteristic of village music, and so forth. I quickly found sound, in general, to be a vital factor in distinguishing the two worlds and in providing each with its own highly distinctive identity. Under no academic constraints I felt perfectly free to voice personal value judgments in terms of what I liked and what I did not like, and to make highly ethnocentric critical comments about the quality of the singing which at times seemed as abysmal as at others it appeared to be superb. This frankly ethnocentric, egocentric, judgmental stance is not what is recommended to students preparing for the field. In fact it is about as close to the opposite of the prescribed non-judgmental, relativistic stance as one could come. Two things resulted. The first was that I was quickly seen as being partial, and won friends and made enemies accordingly. While my judgments made for uneasy relations with the villagers, by the same token they gave me much greater access to the Mbuti who shared not only my equally judgmental opinions about the relative inferiority of village music but also my conviction as to the greater security, comfort, and health of forest life in general. Had I chosen to work with the villagers (as I did on a much later visit) this would have been a serious disadvantage (as indeed it was), but it would have been an equal disadvantage for working with either population had I not declared myself at all.

The second consequence of my open partisanship was that emotional reactions, which could hardly be avoided, were consistent with my declared self. Had I made a pretence of being other than I was, of holding different opinions, or of holding no opinions at all, the pretence would have been quickly perceived, and would have been as detrimental to my relations with the people I was living with as it would have been harmful to my own perceptions of them, their way of life and thought, and the world in which they lived. But far from restricting me to a narrowly enthnocentric viewpoint this initial freedom to be myself was exactly what gave me the freedom, and the ready ability, to move into being something else, and into being someone else making different judgments and having different opinions, and having very different emotional responses to the world around me. This was accepted as being perfectly natural by the Mbuti, who felt as free to disagree with me or to criticize me as I felt to do the same with them. There was no expectation on either side that I ever was or ever would be one of them, or even particularly like them, but whatever points of coincidence there were gained in importance by being completely uncalculated, coming from those incontrovertible (because they are non rational) gut feelings and judgments as to what was right or wrong, what was good or bad, and from the freedom with which they were expressed. In retrospect, and with reference to the conjunction that both Turner and I saw between anthropology and theatre, it could be said that this vastly improved the quality of my "performance" as a field worker, involving me immediately and personally in two basic elements of any ritual, transition and transformation, of which only the former has really been given serious consideration by anthropologists whereas the latter is essential to our full understanding of liminality. Richard Schechner has developed this point cogently from a slightly different perspective in his book *Between Theater and Anthropology* (1985).

First experience of hearing the molimo

Keeping in mind the overall importance of *all* sound in this initial field experience, here we have to restrict our focus to music. My responses to the first *molimo* song I heard were immediate. It was sung at night, partly for my benefit, partly because my presence in a forest hunting camp was something of a crisis in itself, and partly because the hunting had not been good. But clearly there was a felt need for what I later discovered to be thought of as the curing power of the song, for it was sung from the very outset with great intensity, all the more intense because to begin with it was so quiet. The technique involved hoquetting,[2] and that together with the structural complexity of the song form (involving both canon and counterpoint) demanded considerable effort, as accomplished as the Mbuti were as singers. I was aware of this, and it made me concentrate all the harder on what I was hearing. However, in sharp contrast their body positions were as relaxed as were their movements when, at will, they got up and moved around, perhaps just to get away from the smoke of the central fire, perhaps to stretch cramped legs, sometimes to perform a few impromptu dance steps before sitting down again. I myself felt a strange mixture of relaxation and intense concentration, and I could not put the two together, they seemed incongruent. So I moved from the one mood to the other, each seemed equally right for the occasion, but something was missing in my perception of what was taking place.

I mentioned this the next day, when I was asked what I thought of my first real *molimo* song. The answer I got, as near as I could translate it, was that it was all the same: it was all dance, it was all song, it was all work, and it was all play. Not yet being proficient in the language, nor yet academically interested, I was content to leave it at that . . . it somehow matched my own mood and thinking, just as it matched the modality of the music. Then when on another night I chose to watch the singers rather than listen to them, it was the song that sounded relaxed while their movements seemed intense and tightly controlled. Once again they seemed to be two different, almost opposed states of being. On the third occasion, no longer afraid that I was going to miss anything, and no longer looking for any explanation, just intent on enjoying myself, I closed my eyes (Why do we, true to the cliché, feel a need to "close our eyes in ecstasy," if not to dismiss the objective appearance of things that somehow obscures an inner reality?); I felt free to let my own body move as though, not being able to see myself nobody else would be able to see me. And by the same illogic I felt free to join in the singing. And in an instant it all came together: there was no longer any lack of congruence, and it seemed as though the song was being sung by a single singer, the dance danced by a single dancer. Then I made the mistake of opening my eyes and saw that while all the others had their eyes open too, their gaze was vacant . . . there were so many bodies sitting around, singing away, but I was the only person there, the only individual consciousness; all the other bodies were empty. Something had been added to the importance of sound, another mode of perception that, while it in no way negated the aural or visual modes of observation, none the less went far beyond them.

Then, not long before it was time for me to continue my journey back to England, when I was back down in the village, the Mbuti came to my house one night and told me to come up to their camp at the edge of the village, where they had been spending a few days. This time there was no question about the feeling of tension, it was stronger than I had yet felt it; but it was only later I heard that there had been a death. The *molimo* singing began, but it seemed at first only to increase the tension, it lacked the comfort and gently curative quality I had sensed in the forest. I remember feeling physical discomfort; the sound was unbearably loud. The body movements of the dancers seemed aggressive, directed at me, as if challenging me to join the dance. I felt real pain as I hunched down on a small stool, although I was usually able to sit this way for hours without any discomfort. The pain was so great that I was about to leave when I heard a new sound, a sound I had never heard before, but which plainly belonged to the *molimo*. At times it sounded like a voice singing, at times like an animal. Although it never diminished the intensity of the singing or dancing, this new sound appeared to have a power of its own, and a kind of antiphony developed in which it seemed that the singers were pleading to share the intensity of their own involvement. It was as though the singers were not in control of themselves and were as uncomfortable as I was, and sought comfort in the antiphony even though the *molimo* trumpet, for such it was, seemed merely to assert its own power without compromise. It was over quickly, for the sound brought out some villagers, and as soon as they appeared the trumpet stopped singing and, I was told, went back to the forest.

Lessons already learned

The Mbuti left the next day to follow the *molimo*, but I did not go with them. I had not even seen the *molimo* trumpet, I had only heard it on that one occasion, and what I had been told in words was so general that it did not even encourage further speculation. Yet there were some things that I already knew with absolute certainty:

1. While the mood of the *molimo* varied from one set of extremes to another, it was always "right and fitting;" it was "good," which I later discovered also to mean, in Mbuti usage, "curative."

2. It was emotionally stimulating while at the same time it was emotionally satisfying, i.e. it was dynamic rather than static. Having said that I can more safely put it in other terms generally avoided by anthropologists: it was spiritually fulfilling to a degree I had seldom experienced, except perhaps on special occasions, in company with others, during my studies in India; and during rare moments of solitude elsewhere. I deliberately introduce those personal reflections here for two reasons: a) because we need to deal with the concept of Spirit, the failure to do so has been one of the greatest weaknesses of contemporary anthropology, and b) because I believe that personal development is an essential and integral part of the field experience and is in itself valid ethnographic data as well as being essential for our proper evaluation of such fieldwork.

3. The state of satisfaction was as all pervasive as the state of stimulation, despite the extreme variation in the mood of the *molimo* even during the course of one evening of song.

4. These variations ranged between the following extremes, listed exactly as they occurred to me at the time of writing:

passive	active
submissive	dominant
friendly	hostile
receptive	donative
inclusive	exclusive
sacrificial	acquisitive
selfless	selfish

tentative	presumptive
trusting	mistrustful
open	closed
playful	serious
serene	disturbed
exhuberant	solemn
private	public
isolating	communalizing
happy	sad
exalting	depressing
invigorating	ennervating
gentle	rough
carefree	cautious
spontaneous	premeditated
informal	formal
introversive	extraversive

In very general terms the music itself was similarly characterized by obvious extremes:

slow	fast
quiet	loud
simple	complex
melodic	harmonic
concordant	discordant
precise (in rhythm and pitch)	imprecise
unstructured	structured

Similar terms again could be applied to the dance that I saw at this time.

But there was no ambivalence about the moods; they were as clear as they were contradictory. The *molimo* seemed to incorporate all the elements I have described; the totality of the present, including the singers, dancers, listeners, as well as the central fire, the trumpet, the camp itself, the clearing in which the camp is built, and the forest in which the clearing stands, and whatever if anything, contains the forest, and it very definitely includes whatever is implied by such equally ambivalent terms (as seen by some) as God and Spirit.

Questions already raised

On the basis of these subjective feelings that amounted to convictions, certain crucial intellectual questions inevitably present themselves, particularly given the dominant characteristic of coexistent opposites. Yet all of the above is derived from untutored observation over a relatively short period of time. Conventional anthropological criticism would replace "untutored" with "superficial". But in fact if we look at it in light of later research, we find all the key elements there, clear and unmistakable signs of the essential significance and reality of the *molimo*.

However, between this almost exclusively subjective, unprepared, un-
trained, initial experience, and the other extreme of exclusively objective
observation, and perhaps overpreparation and over-training, there is an
intermediate approach, which I inadvertently followed on my second visit to
the Ituri. On that occasion I was better prepared by virtue of my previous
experience, and while I was ready for the same highly subjective, personally
satisfying, emotional involvement, I also had a more specific academic goal,
which was to document the villager *nkumbi* initiation, of which I had seen
something on my first visit. Although this intellectual focus was on a totally
different ritual, it spilled over into my second experience of the *molimo* for at
the heart of both rituals was the liminal state, my understanding of which was
greatly intensified on this second visit.

Voluntary objectivity: molimo 2, objective documentation: preparation

The second experience of the *molimo* was in some respects more profitable and
more instructive than the first time, partly because of a new intellectual
curiosity that, however, was firmly attached to a conscious readiness to open
myself as before to an intense, full, unfettered subjective experience.

My primary conscious objective on this second visit to the Ituri, still with no
academic training in anthropology, was to film the *nkumbi* and record the
associated music as well as the rest of the rich musical tradition of the villagers,
and of course the very different musical tradition of the Mbuti. While it was
possible to plan for the former, it was quite impossible to plan for the latter, so
my attention was at first exclusively on the *nkumbi*. It is significant that
following months spent entirely in the village and its initiation camp I did not
think of the return to the forest specifically with reference to the *molimo*, but in
the much more all-embracing terms of returning to a forest of sounds and
smells and movement. For me the forest and the *molimo* had become identified
with each other.

The return to the forest

I recall the physical return to the forest, following the initiation, with extreme
clarity. The path led northwards through the village, and then through the
squalid temporary camp built by the Mbuti on the edge of the village for
somewhere to stay when they came in from the forest to barter. It was
particularly dirty at this time because so many Mbuti had been using it while
the boys were in the initiation camp; but now it was empty, every house had
been abandoned and the boys/men and their "fathers" shouted with pleasure
as we half ran through its emptiness. We shouted *"tsu kidi, tsu kidi; ema ndura
tsu kidi to"* . . . we are coming, mother forest, we are coming . . .

The forest rose almost sheer at the edge of the Mbuti village camp; the
villagers had not cut any plantations on that side so it was literally just a
matter of a few steps from the hot, hard, arid village path to the cool, soft,

Figure 3.2 The Ituri Forest.

moist, shady trail that ran through the forest to the distant hunting camp. I think of those few yards, now, as a physical counterpart of the liminal condition we are trying to understand. Those medial yards belonged simultaneously and equally to both worlds, the forest and the village; to some extent they belonged to whichever world whoever was treading them belonged to at that moment, which in turn depended to some extent on who they were and in which direction they were going. To that extent, plainly, those different states of being were necessarily coexistent in both time and space. And it was somewhere along those few medial yards that the young Mbuti who had just become village-initiated men became Mbuti children again: and it was somewhere along that same medial stretch of firm ground that the village world became obliterated and the forest became the sole, entire, exclusive

Figure 3.3 Mirror imagery in the Ituri Forest. The mirror reality is a constant phenomenon in the Mbuti forest world, taken by them to represent the co-existence of the sacred and the profane.

universe. And speaking for myself, it was on that liminal ground that the forest and the *molimo* became merged – as I entered the one I entered the other.

Filming and recording: gains and losses

On arrival in the hunting camp the boys/men reassumed their status as children, sitting on the laps of their mothers to make this quite plain. The fact that the Mbuti kept the two worlds, village and forest, systematically apart, each with its own code of values and behavior, its own language and its own music, could not have been made more plain. By now my own status in the forest was that of youth, and since youth among the Mbuti is a time when innovation is expected, my proposal to do some filming and recording caused

Figure 3.4 Deep in the Ituri Forest.

no undue surprise and no concern. I began with filming everyday life. By today's standards the equipment was unbelievably clumsy and cumbersome. Its very obvious presence, however, and the necessity for making constantly sure that all was in order, did not predispose me to look for any ecstatic, other-worldly experience any more than did my conscious, rational, academic objectives. But I did not yet recognize the nature or power of the liminal state, nor of the *molimo*.

Sometimes in the evening a few *molimo* songs were sung; aesthetically there were occasional moments of exquisite beauty, but not always. And when there were not, when the songs began to fizzle out due to lack of concentration or

Figue 3.5 A Mbuti young man.

effort, or whatever, the failure was met with joking obscenities and all of a sudden, as if by the very distance this profane behavior created, some sacred power made itself *felt* and the singing stopped abruptly. I made numerous recordings of various kinds of song, including those snatches of *molimo* songs that were sung for no particular reason other than general dissatisfaction with the weather, the hunt, or the "noisy" (disputatious) camp. But these turned out to be a special manifestation of the *molimo* known as the *molimo madé* over which the youths had control. It involved the singing of the same songs, but these would be interrupted by wild forays of youths rushing back and forth, shouting as if to try and drown out the song, while at the same time beating on the leaf huts with their fists, and generally turning the camp upside down. It seemed the very antithesis of the *molimo* I had thought I knew.

Figure 3.6 Consecrating the village at the opening of the three month *nkumbi* initiation of boys.

Personal transformation

When the time came for me to leave, all the filming and recording being finished in both village and forest, the Mbuti did not want me to leave. They said I *could* not leave, I had heard too much. This was not said as a threat, merely as a statement of fact. They were puzzled that I should even think of leaving. Was it to do with the fact that I was not married? They cut the marks of eligibility into my forehead. It was done very seriously, and I felt nothing but a mild discomfort. But when I returned to the camp and the women saw the marks and burst into laughter, ridiculing me, I felt something very strongly . . . not so much embarrassment as the touch of power . . . an awareness that something had happened to me, and that departure was now that much more difficult. Yet I could not or would not give up my plans to return to the world I thought I still belonged to, and continue with my life as I saw it. So I insisted that I was still going to leave. Then they cut some slits in the flesh of my right hand and wrist, and rubbed in a dark paste that one of them produced from an antelope horn. There was none of the seriousness of the first cutting, it was all clearly a joke. A small crowd stood by and laughed as it was done. With all the laughter I felt that power again, and knew that some transformation had taken place and that indeed they had tricked me and I never would be able to leave the forest, that I had lost a certain kind of personal, individual power and freedom while gaining another, infinitely greater.

It was then that the Mbuti seemed to accept that I *would* leave, and began singing the *molimo* so that I *could* leave, "curing" my departure. The trumpet

Figure 3.7 Women's *maipe* ritual dance, an essential part of the *nkumbi*.

did not make any appearance, but I was told this was a *molimo mangbo*, a "great" *molimo*, and that it would make it possible for me to leave safely, just as by being in the flesh of my wrist and hand it would keep me safe and bring me back . . . because really I was not leaving at all . . . I could never really leave. It is difficult to follow the Mbuti when they talk like this; they tend to use only the present tense, and the sense lies not so much in the words as in the inflexion of the voice and the facial and body gestures that accompany the voice. When they have anything important to say it is sung and danced. My response was a simple one . . . I cried. And that made the Mbuti happier than ever. "You see? We told you! The *molimo* is the most powerful animal in the forest. You can never leave us now . . . the forest is part of you, and it will (even) bring your body back . . . your spirit will always be here, because it belongs to the forest . . . it has heard the *molimo* and knows how to sing to the forest . . ." and at that moment I suddenly realized why they make so much use of the echo in their singing, and antiphony itself took on a deeper meaning.

By allowing myself the freedom to feel I had allowed myself to be touched by some power, but by trying to insist so much on the attempt to capture it on film and tape, and on trying to constrain it into an intellectual framework of rational understanding, I made impossible that total sacrifice, that moment (for it needs a mere millisecond) of utter abandon in which the power and the self are one and all questioning is resolved. Perhaps I was involved more in a series of temporary transitions than in an enduring transformation. But if I had failed to touch that power, it had not failed to touch me, and it may be that the transformation had already taken place; I just did not know it.

I was only to learn something of the art of consciously using both modes of awareness, feeling and intellect, during my third and most intensive experience of the *molimo*, three more years in the future, as we see it. By that time I was to have had my anthropological training, a training which then sat easily but firmly on a solid bedrock of subjective experience, and on the certain knowledge of the worth of that experience. Without denying the importance of that formal training or belittling it in any way, it has always seemed secondary in importance, adding a lot to the business of observation and the objective gathering of data, and of course to the subsequent task of proper analysis. But it adds nothing to the equally important gathering of a whole other body of data directly and only accessible through total immersion in subjective experience, something comparable to a sacrifice of self, or at least of external self.

A total field experience: molimo 3, analytical objectives rooted in subjective experience

When in 1957 I arrived back in the Ituri after yet another three year absence I had completed my studies of anthropology at Oxford and now had the conscious objective of gathering material for my doctoral dissertation. Yet so powerful was the influence of my two earlier visits that while not abandoning all that I had been taught about the merits of objectivity and detachment, I stepped right back to feeling the way I felt when I was there before. I found myself making the same subjective judgments, particularly those that opposed the village world to the forest world. To me the forest was a much more beautiful world, and filled with something that in turn filled me. The Mbuti expressed it easily for me, again using that word that translated my "it makes me feel good" into "it cures me." And with the very first song that I heard back in the forest I was immediately plunged back into that familiar sense of opposition and incongruity. The opposition worried me even less than it had before; I still did not understand it but just as each opposite extreme seemed right and proper, so did the opposition itself. However, perhaps because of the intervening training in anthropology, I was still bothered by apparent incongruities of mood, behavior and thought.

Here plainly ethnocentricism was at work: the incongruities were things that should have "worked" together in my own cultural context, whereas here there seemed to be almost a battle between them, as though they did not belong to each other and demanded to be separate as well as different. The mood of song could vary from one extreme to another without it bothering me, but song and dance together was outright conflict. It was not surprising then, to hear the Mbuti refer to it as "war." When dance warred with song, it

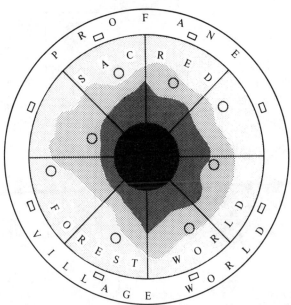

Figue 3.8 The most sacred area is at the center deep in the forest, the most profane area is on the periphery where the villages are. Hunting groups tend to stay equidistant between center and periphery.

was as likely to be as wild as the song was gentle, or as delicate and graceful as the song was rough and clumsy. And in so far as all song forms were corporate, so dance was usually solo, and again it bore no mark of being ritual performance; it appeared more to be individual improvisation. So also with male/female. In certain songs they both participated, with varying degrees of structural opposition, from hoquet to harmony, but with an incongruous element of conflict; and in some songs one or other gender was excluded completely; it was the same with different age levels. But no exclusion seemed as clear cut as the exclusion of the village from all forest song. All it needed was for one solitary villager making his way through the forest to come near the camp, and all singing would stop, or change into the form of song used by the Mbuti exclusively when they are down in the village world. It was not that the sacred had been profaned, but rather as if that which was holy had been replaced, or even become, that which was unholy yet still totally acceptable as such.

The other incongruities less easily defined at the time, though strongly felt, were those involving time and space. It was almost as though by drawing a small branch across the path leading from the village, that this was more than a symbolic exclusion of the village: by that act the village simply ceased to exist. So when certain songs were sung, the whole outside world, other than the forest surrounding that one hunting camp, ceased to exist. And similarly

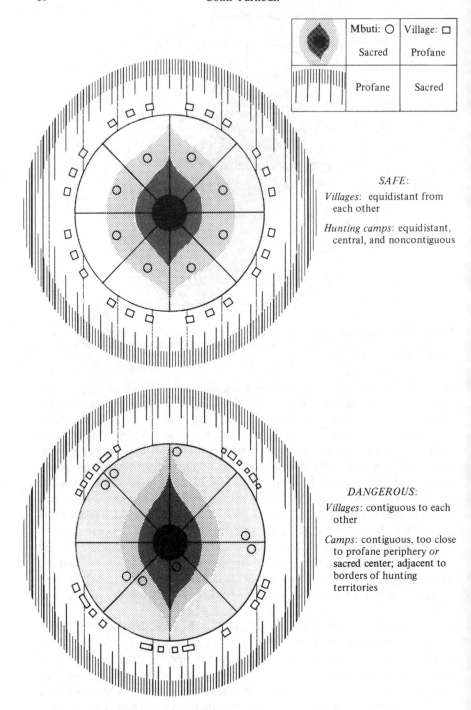

Mbuti: O	Village: □
Sacred	Profane
Profane	Sacred

SAFE:

Villages: equidistant from each other

Hunting camps: equidistant, central, and noncontiguous

DANGEROUS:

Villages: contiguous to each other

Camps: contiguous, too close to profane periphery *or* sacred center; adjacent to borders of hunting territories

Figure 3.9 The sacred and the profane: two world views .

with time, anything that was in the past or the future simply did not exist. But again, when it came to song, there was a moment in the song when just as the outside spatial world ceased to exist, so did the outside temporal world . . . all past and all future were annihilated. Our one solitary, tiny hunting camp, of maybe a couple of dozen families, sometimes much less, was the total extent of all humanity, and our universe was the forest that surrounded the here and now of our microscopic little circle of huts in that vast, womb-like primal forest.

Death: emotional participation, when and when not to reason

But then, one day when the band was down in the village, bartering forest produce for village goods, old Balekimito took sick and died. She probably died in my arms; who knows when whatever we call "death" really takes place? One hand held tightly onto mine long after the other stopped fluttering around, as if talking. It was not the clutch of fear, it was no clinging to life; it certainly was not taking life from me. Just the contrary: old Balekimito was giving life to me, pouring it out of her tired old body. I did not know until then that she even liked me, but she gave me that final gift, and when her hand finally slipped from mine and, as the Mbuti say, she began to die completely, absolutely, and for ever, I felt not so much sad or empty as utterly lost, as a blind person must feel being guided through a strange place and suddenly finding the guide was no longer there.

Plainly such a feeling was highly specific to my still being a stranger among the Mbuti, looking to the elders for guidance and getting it. There is no way of demonstrating to what extent, if any, this feeling was in any way shared by others standing around Balekimito, or huddled on the ground as close as they could get to the old lady as she died. But when that moment came their behavior changed in an instant, just as did my feelings. I can best describe what I felt by saying that while Balekimito was dying I felt sad at the impending loss, but at the moment of her death that was quickly replaced by a feeling of blind anger . . . blind because there was no direction to my anger, there was nowhere that it could be sent, so it remained within. The younger people rushed out of the little house, and when I followed them I felt a part of what they were doing, but did not know how to participate myself. They too were angry, but instead of keeping that anger inside they let it out, sending it in any and every direction, at things they picked up and destroyed, and at people whom they attacked with a ferocity I had never seen at any other time among the Mbuti. And the movements of these normally graceful people were sharp and uncoordinated: just as there was no music in the sounds they made, so there was no rhythm in their motion.

Yet, as with their dance and their song, with their moments of extremity, so this extremity of behavior somehow seemed right and proper, and whatever objectivity I had merely observed that my body was not in the melée with the rest of them, and that I wished it was . . . I would have felt less lost, in the middle of that seeming anarchy.

The turmoil went on, dying down then flaring up again, until someone, old Moké, I think, stepped into the middle of the camp and said that we should all get ready to go back to the forest and take out the *molimo* to "rejoice" and put an end to all this "noise." The satisfaction that gave me, as I both remember it and reason it, was because I knew that the *molimo* would solve all my problems, put an end to the sadness, the frustration, the anger, and that terrible sense not of loss but of being lost. In the *molimo* I felt certain I would find myself, and even as we moved from the village, the next day, and took those first steps into the shade of that immense forest, I felt an additional excitement because I then also knew that the self I would retrieve would be a new self, at least new to me. And as soon as we took those first steps into the forest shade, still within earshot of the village, the Mbuti began shouting and singing, each in his own way and his own time, but all the sounds blending with each other so as to make a single declaration of faith, faith that all would be well.

Throughout the weeks that followed, I was aware that every single action, however serious or however slight, was seen as being "work." That awareness was all that was necessary for my own actions to be in keeping with those of others. And it was here more than ever that total participation paid off, in terms of both what was observed and what was felt. The ideal was not to sleep at all, and in point of fact since the men and male youths sang from dusk to dawn and were strictly forbidden to sleep during this time, there was only about an hour or so of real sleep possible before the day's hunt got under way, and then perhaps a couple of hours could be snatched in the afternoon if the hunt was quickly successful. But if the fatigue was real, so was the stimulation we received from all this work; it was as though the harder we worked the more energy we were given, and the most energy-giving work of all was the nightly singing. And that was when the curing really took place. That was when I felt clean and whole, free of all doubt and worry. It was not that any questions were answered, it was simply that they were removed; at first, at the conscious level, they just became insignificant and inconsequential, then they simply vanished. And that of course was a far more powerful way of getting rid of any problem than the most rational of explanations or answers, for reason can always be made to turn on itself, it is the handmaiden of doubt and suspicion. Here we were safely far beyond the reach of mere reason and that rational form of religious experience known as "belief." Here we were in the realm of "faith" and that is why it is so vitally important to distinguish the two, something most anthropologists have neglected sadly, resulting in their often trite and trivial rational, objective "explanations" of other religious systems. Among the Mbuti there was no room for such ethnocentrism, it too vanished, and was replaced by an egocentricism the center of which, however, was not the individual ego, but a greater self.

Something else that vanished during the month-long celebration of the *molimo* was the recognition of the many oppositions and incongruities that I had experienced on my last two trips. The same actions were performed, the same contrasts of extremities were there, more so than ever, but in the framework of all action being "work," work that had a curative end even if we did not know what that end was. There was no opposition and no conflict. Different actions all contributed to the same end, achieving different, lesser ends along the way. Thus the thievery of young Pepei was as functional (the anthropologist would say) as his generosity; and old Sau's ill humor was just as much an instance of that feisty old lady working hard for the good ("cure") of society as was her boundless love and caring for all her children (just about the entire camp). The most serious criticism leveled against anyone was if they did not put all the energy they had into the singing. It did not seem to matter in the least whether or not one sang well or badly, for as they said, the music is only really good (curative) when it is work; and since the work of the *molimo* on this occasion was to "cure" the death of Balekimito, who was so immensely old and immensely good, the cure could only come if we worked immensely hard at it. And "work" was plainly the effective quality, not perfection of pitch or rhythm.

And so with all those other seeming contradictions that I had both seen and sensed before, as between male and female, young and old, village and forest. Now they were manifest daily, but in increasingly conscious, even choreographed performance which for the moment we might call ritual, for as I use the word it has essentially religious connotations, and the essence of religion is Spirit; that which is supra-rational, beyond definition and therefore beyond description. Yet it is real, just as real as the material world that for many of us seems to be the only reality. The Mbuti would say that those who do not recognize Spirit have merely forgotten (or never knew) how to reach it: "they do not know how to sing." Other cultures have other ways of making contact with Spirit, but for the Mbuti their prime, supreme way, is song.

The rational process in place

The *molimo* managed to make consistent those things that seemed inconsistent, reconciling the otherwise irreconcilable. Even the most ordinary actions of the Mbuti changed subtly. I could not say if the changes were consciously contrived or were unconsciously compelled, in either case they matched the mood of the moment with action that was consistent with it, expressing it so forcefully that it was ultimately expelled. With the expulsion there was no void, for it made room for another mood, one that more often than not was the very opposite of what had gone before. This again was expressed by performance in such a way as to expel it. This process seemed endless, as endless as the quest for the perfect (effective) sound that it was said would bring the *molimo* to life, a quest that went on night after night. And when ultimately the perfect sound was discovered it coincided with the discovery of the perfect mood: all disharmony, social, spiritual, mental, physical, musical . . . all inconsistency . . . all incongruity . . . vanished and for a brief moment the Mbuti ideal of *ekimi* reigned, "making good" everything, for, in their own words, whatever *is*, when that moment is reached, is good, otherwise it would not, could not, *be.*

These were among the many highly subjective judgments I was making, truths I was feeling with absolute conviction about actions that I now think of as performances; it is at such a point in the field experience that more consciously considered observation and rational analysis becomes more profitable. For example:

Firstly there were informal, seemingly spontaneous performances by individuals. These were more than "actions" in that, while they were in keeping with the normal personality of the individual, none the less they were special. Sometimes they seemed almost contrived, and often contrived so as to be particularly offensive by being unmistakable, open, and deliberate. So young Pepei, always a strangely solitary youth given to helping himself unobtrusively to whatever anyone else had that he wanted, began repeatedly stealing food from an old lady, Sau, openly and in broad daylight.

And old Sau herself, whom the villagers claimed to be a sorceress but who in fact was one of the most saintly of people, always willing to help others, began to act like a nasty mean old woman but not in any way, it seemed, as a result of Pepei's thievery. In fact towards him she remained more like her old, gentle, kind self.

It was the same when old Cephu, who was always a trouble-maker, now became more troublesome than ever, arguing about the hunt and interfering with it, as though he deliberately wanted to ruin it and make us all go hungry.

And my closest friend, an unmarried youth called Kengé, who was well known for being one of the most active and knowledgeable Mbuti in the whole forest but also for being somewhat unpredictable and moody, became lazy and almost totally uncooperative, pretending not to know how to do the simplest of tasks, or else deliberately doing them badly.

But even performance initiated by individuals was essentially communal. It always involved the communal center of the camp to some extent, and elders dominated that center, commanding communal attention. These old people, like the children, who played blissfully through performances of all kinds, seemed almost in a world apart. Without a conscious effort at objective observation and analysis, being classified as a youth myself it would have been easy to see only from that perspective, as that was the only perspective from which I was able to experience performance. It was we youths and adults that were caught up in the world of oppositions and conflict. And so it was we who engaged in the even more obviously ritual, communal performances which seemed to be mandatory rather than spontaneous. And these were clearly related to that primary opposition that divides any human society into two major segments according to gender.

One of these formal, communal performances appeared in the guise of a pastime, and as such was from an outside perspective merely enjoyable: for a participant however, it was "work." Sometimes when the call for a tug of war was raised Mbuti even complained: "we have done enough work today." It took the form of a ritual rather than of a game, however, in that the rules negated competition by requiring that if one side was winning, a member of the other side should change sides and, in so doing, adopt the gender of the losing side. Not only was any latent individual feeling of superiority expressed, more importantly all latent sexual ambivalence was thoroughly explored, and for some the crossing over was clearly closer to transformation than mere transition. And this was equally true of the other "reversal" ritual, *ekokomea*, in which adults and youths (again) explored even more thoroughly any latent hostilities by engaging in overt ridicule of the opposite gender, yet with the same almost nervous ambivalence.

It was the very act of total participation and awareness of my personal feelings at that moment and in that place that led, later, to the most valuable speculations, and to awareness that through such performance a transformation takes place, not a mere transition, and this has everything to do with our understanding of liminality and, I believe, calls for a rethinking of what we mean by that term. And it was no accident that toward the end of the *molimo* another ritual began, one which continued after the *molimo* had ended. That was the *elima*, which celebrates the first menstrual period of a girl, her flowering into the full potentiality of womanhood as one who has the power to give birth to life itself. But any description and explanation of this ritual that ignored the transformative elements of the individual and communal performances, informal and formal, as discovered through total participation, would be lacking.

Plainly the fieldworker needs to prepare for performance, in this light, rather than for superficial role-playing. But participation is probably best not planned let alone thought of as "acting." If considered as a technique it should be more in the nature of the best theatrical traditions of improvisation. On my first visit to the Ituri my shyness, prudery, sense of privacy, and probably a whole lot of other ethnocentric characteristics, led me to refrain from too much overt behavioral participation. I felt strongly, and was emotionally deeply moved by both song and dance, but barely participated physically in either. On this occasion, however, there was no hesitation and not a moment of embarrassment. I was too filled with feeling, to even think about what I was or was not going to do. I did not plan or contrive my participation, it arose directly from personal and/or academic (i.e. total) needs. I once found myself getting up from the group of singers, sitting around the central fire (the *kuma-molimo*), and just walking to the edge of the camp, slowly circling around the others, listening to them and listening to the forest as it echoed their voices, it seemed, back from its furthest depths. That is what I thought I was doing, but the very first time I did it some Mbuti told me afterwards that they were so glad to see me "dance," for it was "our" work to dance as well as to sing. But even with that encouragement I never planned on "dancing"; either it happened or

Figure 3.10 While *molimo* always takes place at night, *elima* dances celebrating the first
menstrual period of a young woman happen during the day. *Elima* dances are always
circular, often around an older woman with a hoop.

it did not. But the more it happened the more other things happened. Not only
did seemingly incontrovertible oppositions disappear, such as joy and grief,
noise and quietness, masculinity and femininity; but somehow the differentiation between my senses seemed to disappear and I began touching
moonlight, smelling the sound of the songs, hearing the scent of the various
kinds of wood blazing away at the *kuma-molimo*, and seeing the truth, even if I
could not understand what I saw.

Now this kind of experience is easily enough dismissed as romantic, if the
critic is being kind, or as unmitigated mystical trash, if the critic really feels
threatened. But unless we learn to deal with the concept of Spirit we are going
to continue misunderstanding and misrepresenting the phenomena of religious belief and practice that we analyze to death in other cultures, as though
the mystical concept of Spirit was irrelevant to such analysis. And similarly
with the condition of liminality, I think we are going to have to face the reality
of Spirit and spiritual phenomena, for they are real, every bit as real as those
fantasies academics are wont to call theories, and possibly more so. Whether
the reality is empirical or conceptual is secondary.

The merits of total participation

I have necessarily had to limit myself to one aspect (performance) of my own
field experience, but have tried to show within those confines the merits of a

judicious combination of what amounts almost to total abandon and conscious, rational investigation. It has been my experience that it was in those moments of abandon that the most significant discoveries were made which provided a basis for the most fruitful subsequent investigation. After all, ethnographic description has to precede analysis, and I am doing no more than suggesting the necessity for including description at another level, using all our faculties, not merely our minds.

In the same way that informal, individual, even private performances were of immediate significance and meaning without any intellectual process, their truth being self evident and felt rather than reasoned, so it was with the formal, public performances described, such as the tug-of-war and *ekokomea*. Through objective study we are tempted to focus too much on the more obvious message in such rituals of reversal or rebellion, messages that are indeed of vital importance, but do not constitute the total import of the ritual. In just the same way that Pepei's individual predeliction for helping himself to whatever he wanted became a reminder to the rest of us of our own potential for laziness, covetousness, or whatever, thus bringing us together to the extent that we all saw something of ourselves in Pepei's performance, so it was with the ritual performances such as the tug-of-war and *ekokomea*. We all recognized our potential for competition, for female or male chauvinism, as well as coming to the recognition the performance gave, as its message, that both competition and chauvinism are dysfunctional. But we also recognized our potential for being something else, that despite the physiological limitations of our bodies there was in each of us something of the other gender. Men too had a potentiality for motherhood, they too were nourishers, life givers, just as women had the potential of the male hunters, not so much in terms of dominance (though that was part of it in this hunting society), but more essentially as takers of life. Through acts of reversal and ridicule we tested that other potential and reinforced our conscious satisfaction with (or perhaps just acceptance of) what we were, and reaffirmed our equally conscious determination, by reverting to our original state once the ritual of reversal was over, to be what we had, thus, *chosen* to be. Even something as fundamentally and irrevocably determined by our physiology as gender became a matter of choice, of feeling; a subjective state rather than an objective reality. And far beyond the immediate influence of such rituals, gender (as only one example) was still a subjective state, though then it was also, secondarily, an objective reality.

Conclusions: perception, transformation, and liminality

There are many points of correspondence between the anthropological process and the theatrical process, particularly with respect to performance. For one thing the fieldworker is almost constantly engaged in performance of one kind or another. At one moment he is an actor, acting out a role he has been ascribed by the society he is working with; at another he is "performing" in order to achieve specific goals; in other (almost all) instances he is a spectator and thus an integral part of a wider performance. And in a more subtle sense he is always a performer while in an exotic field context because that very context compels him to modify his personal behavior so that it becomes different, special, with different and special significance for others. I have been suggesting that in order to understand liminality, whether we are in the field or in our studies, we have to be willing to accept such changes, to utilize them, and to become more than merely different, to become something else. The work of a performer demands, among other things, 1) intense discipline and concentration, 2) a clearly defined goal, or perhaps 3) in some instances the negation of all goals, which amounts to a sacrifice of inner self and the willingness to become something else. The anthropologist is usually in agreement with the first two demands, but when overly preoccupied with an objective, exclusively rational approach is consequently unable (and/or unwilling) to sacrifice his academic objectives and innermost values, beliefs and personal identity. A willingness to make a temporary suspension of belief and practice is not enough for the total participation required, particularly in our study of religious phenomena. The field experience could in itself almost be considered as a liminal condition and as such, to be fully explored. Sacrifice and transformation are an integral and necessary part of it.

If the liminal state is to be experienced rather than studied, this demands total participation, total sacrifice of the academic as well as the individual self, and it is only then that the subjectivity and emotional involvement are no longer incompatible with objectivity and reason. Such participation rather provides insights that could not be had by other means, as well as providing "hard data" that might well not be otherwise readily accessible. I have tried to indicate the potential from a very limited number of examples from one single field. In his 1982 book Turner seemed to be on the verge of making a plea for greater subjectivity, but it was as if he was restricted by his own concept of transition and moved from moments of subjective insight to another realm of objective analysis, without allowing the one fully to inform the other. Perhaps this accounts for the clarity with which he recognized a truth about liminality and the enormous difficulty he had in expressing it in words, as witnessed by the many semantic struggles of his own and of his colleagues.

But our comprehension of liminality has to deal with another problem that, with its counterpart in the world of theatre, has to do with the modes of perception and communication that we employ. The anthropologist, dedicated to objectivity and intellect, is not only unlikely to abandon even temporarily his objective and intellectual self and become truly immersed in another culture, on the grounds that he would then no longer be an anthropologist, but he is going to be restricted to what he observes, which is largely what he sees with his eyes and hears with his ears. And of all the vast array of sounds that he hears with his ears he is likely to focus mainly, if not exclusively, on sounds that he can translate into words, if not just on words themselves. Yet there are many other modes of communication just as there are many other modes of perception. Few of us, for instance, pay nearly enough attention to the use of the senses of smell, taste, and touch, or to non-verbal sound. Yet these, particularly sound, are often key elements in ritual and other religious behavior. Sound alone provides a royal road to the liminal condition, and the feelings it evokes can become highly significant for the fieldworker if he allows them, if not the sound itself, to move him both physically and emotionally, instead of confining himself to an exclusively conscious, rational framework.

Time and space perception are also modes of awareness that we far too infrequently grapple with. In the rites of passage that so much occupied Turner's attention, following up on van Gennep's purely rational analysis, we habitually talk of transition. Yet transition is a concept of special validity within a linear framework of time and space, whereas for some cultures time is seen as cyclical, and in others it is something else. The Mbuti, for instance, have a spherical concept of time and space, with spheres enclosing spheres. They are well aware of the problem of the space that exists between two adjacent spheres in their conceptual model: but that is not liminal space for them, its nature is merely unknown. It may be entered by moving in what the anthropologist would recognize as an anti-social manner, or as the Mbuti say "too fast," "with too much noise" or "like an elephant" (i.e. too destruct-ively), reaching the wall of the sphere before it has had time to catch up as it should be allowed to do, keeping the individual safely in the center. The individual then passes through into that space, or into another sphere if one happens to be contiguous at that moment. When that happens your "other self" (a kind of mirror image) is likely to replace you, a look-alike that can only be detected by its *wazi-wazi* (unusual, aberrant) behavior. Such movement is perhaps closer to the notion of transition. However, the movement from one condition, call it the normal, material, mundane, or secular condition, to the liminal, other worldly, or sacred condition, is more a movement of the spheres than of the individuals, though individuals or groups of individuals (more easily) can cause such movement to take place (as through ritual performance, for example the *molimo*). This concept is much better translated by the word "transformation" than by "transition," and the distinction is of major significance. However, the liminal state is not only reached by ritual, and ritual in itself does not have the power to induce it in ritual participants.

This all tells me that our notion of a rite of passage as involving mere transition from one status to another is as overly simplistic as our notion of liminality as a medial state. "Transition" may be an accurate description of what takes place from a purely objective, material, rational point of view, and it may well describe what takes place at certain stages of such rites, but that does not mean that it in any way describes the overall process as it is

Colin Turnbull

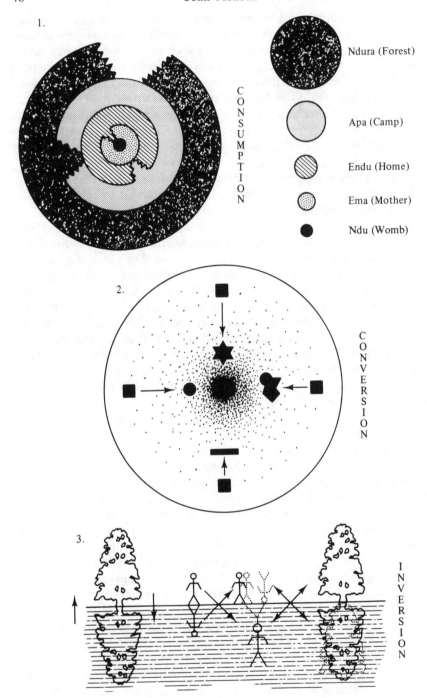

Figure 3.11 Three Mbuti analogies for "transformation."

experienced by the individuals concerned. Their experience is one of transformation. In the *nkumbi* initiation of the villagers, which closely resembles that of the Ndembu initiation studied by Turner, the villagers agree with the Mbuti that the crux of such rites is that one becomes something or someone else. Whether that transformation is reversible or not is another issue; it would seem that in some cultures at least there is a technique of reversal that can be learned, or may be inherited. As far as I could understand it from the Bira and the Mbuti, and from my own limited experience, in one sense for them it is irreversible, unless by further subsequent transformation. However, a rather different form of change of state is possible and is theoretically a matter of choice, though for individual initiates the ritual prescribes that initially they shall outwardly revert to the normal, mundane plane. Thereafter they may revert again to their liminal condition whenever they wish, either by an act of volition, or through ritual performance (in which case it may be involuntary) or when "called" (i.e. compelled) to do so by the ancestors in times of crisis. Ritual priests and prophets tend to remain in the liminal state, which, the Bira say, accounts for their odd behavior as well as their extreme perceptivity. The Mbuti are less concerned with individual abilities, perceptual or otherwise, and see the liminal state as being one that is coexistent at all times with the normal state of being, and which can be brought into play, usually for the entire community rather than for an individual, again either by ritual performance or at the will of "the forest." In discussing what takes place they suggest several analogies: it may be a matter of exchanging one sphere for another, such as the exchange that takes place when an Mbuti steps into his reflection in the water, each taking the other's place; or it may be what happens when one sphere "eats" another; or perhaps a sphere simply turns into something else, like the chameleon, or the toad that (they say) can suddenly become a snake.

Transformation of this kind is what they see as taking place in what we call the medial state; liminality itself is then the process of transformation at work. The technique of consciously achieving transformation is the process of entering the liminal state. The two problems, subjectivity and modes of perception, are similarly related, for subjectivity is a mode of perception. The use of subjectivity, of total (including emotional, spiritual) participation, of other modes of perception and communication, is not at all unlike use of the rational process by which we recognize without any discomfort that things are seldom, if ever, what they seem to be, and set about arriving at a more accurate, more complete knowledge of what they are by reconsidering them in light of other information, from different perspectives, and so forth. Anthropologists go to exceptional lengths, in fact, *not* to accept things for what they seem to be, but those lengths generally are entirely intellectual and, all too often, spectacularly acrobatic but ultimately meaningless.

Used unconsciously, we often dismiss subjective modes of awareness as intuition, that uncomfortable ability that some people seem to have of perceiving the answer almost before the question is asked. Our unwillingness to accept this alternative mode of awareness is just another of our many ethnocentricisms, and is easily seen in our long standing fascination with and misunderstanding of rites of passage and liminality.

What I am suggesting then is that the liminal state is an "other" condition of being that is coexistent with the state of being of which we are normally conscious (the material state of being susceptible to rational awareness and sensory perception). But we can not be aware of it, know it or understand it as long as we restrict ourselves to the rational, objective, analytical approach of contemporary anthropology. In initiations that I have witnessed it is stated as clearly as can be stated not that the initiate moves from one stage to another, but rather that he becomes something else. And the process by which this transformation is achieved is not so much by the invocation of spiritual presence, though in some societies it could be put that way and seen in that way, but rather by painstaking preparation and purification. But as long as we insist on taking liminality to imply a transitory in-between state of being, we are far from the truth. In our own terms it would be better seen as a timeless state of being, of "holiness," that lies parallel to our "normal" state of being, or is perhaps superimposed upon it, or somehow coincides and coexists with it. It may be seen as essentially spiritual whereas "this" plane is essentially material. Liminality is a subjective experience of the external world in which "thisness" becomes "thatness." It is integrative of all experience; in the liminal state disorder is ordered, doubts and problems removed, the "right" course of action made clear with a rightness that is both moral and structural since the inevitable discrepancies between belief and practice in the external world are among the many problems ordered and removed in the liminal state. It thus provides a charter for individual behavior and, by extension, for communal, social, behavior. The importance of this liminal state in societies that are aware of it, and have developed techniques for moving in and out of it, or of invoking it, is enormous. It provides the perfectly integrated point of view that enables those who can move freely in and out of the liminal state with the ability to make rational judgments that seem infinitely wise because they are so infinitely effective and functional. It is indeed well perceived as holy, as a timeless state of grace.

The connection between ritual, drama, and entertainment, all of which are key elements of any rite of passage, and hence of the liminal state to which such rites may lead, has frequently been mentioned by anthropologists though seldom examined systematically. Yet it is a connection that is both explored and exploited expertly and rigorously at almost every stage of the theatrical process, which may well be why Turner was increasingly turning his attention to theatre. The concepts of transformation, of penetration (a form of possession?), of making visible that which is invisible, are familiar in the world of theatre. They are not easily dealt with there, any more than they are in anthropology, but they are not ignored for that reason, for they are recognized as being central to the theatrical process, just as liminality (if some manner of transformative phenomenon is what we mean by the term) is central to the social process. And just as theatre becomes empty and barren without this recognition, so ultimately does any anthropological study of society.

Notes

1. The word "moving" is not used lightly. The music compelled a physical reaction, whether the movement was perceptible only to the performer or whether it erupted into ecstatic dance. I believe this compulsion, to "movement" of many kinds, to be an essential part of the liminal state.
2. In hoquet the individual notes of any melodic line are ascribed to individual singers, so that no one singer carries the entire melody but each carries an essential part of it and all are therefore equally necessary.

4.

The Yaqui deer dance at Pascua Pueblo, Arizona

EDITH TURNER

20 November 1981: the day of Anselmo Valencia's talk

The talk took place in the ramada, a plain brick shelter open to the south (see figure 4.1). The members of the Wenner-Gren conference sat on one side, while Anselmo Valencia stood on the other, on the dancing ground of the deer – sacred ground, as he explained to us. To his left lay a blanket, on which we saw the deer dance regalia set out: the deer's head, rasps, and water drum. At a board rising in a nearly 90° angle at the sacred side of the entrance were set a flat drum and a flute.

Valencia began by introducing the dancers – deer and pascola. Then he turned to his listeners and reminded them that they were Anglos, anthropologists, and that he had had a lot of trouble from anthropologists. Their incessant questions made it very difficult for the Yaquis. There must be no photographs, there had been too much of that sort of thing. (For that reason, I could not bring out my notebook and take down everything he said, contenting myself with writing down afterwards what Victor Turner and I remembered.)

Valencia strode up and down a little, getting indignant. "What is this word, 'savage'?" he asked – a word that Anglos and Mexicans used about the Yaquis. He asked various people in his audience what the word meant. Victor Turner replied that he never used the word but it meant the people of the wilds, the woods, the heath. Victor Turner's own people, the Scots, he explained to Valencia, had been considered savages. Savages were people who sometimes fell prey to their impulses. Other definitions, including Edward Spicer's, were similar. Valencia laughed and said we were getting around the issue. (Though he had indeed succeeded in shaming some of us, whether guilty or not.) This atmosphere pervaded much of Valencia's talking during the conference. He went on to give the definition he had heard from Anglos, that savages were murderous before anything else.

He picked up the flat drum and described how it had been invented by a "savage" Yaqui. In the beginning, the Yaquis did not have to work, they lived

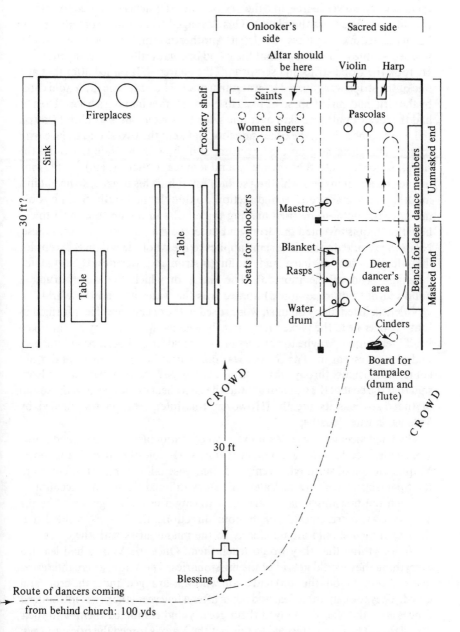

Figure 4.1 Ground plan of Pascua ramada.

off the natural food of the land, they had plenty of time on their hands. One of them saw a palo verde tree, like the one out there (Valencia pointed to a wispy tree fifty yards across the plaza). This "savage" tried doing something – he burnt the tree in a few places, then left it. Another day this "savage" – he was idle, you see – came by and found that the wood had naturally come away in strips. He took the wood strips and scraped off the charcoal. It rained after that and one of the strips was covered by water in a pool. The next time the Yaqui came by the strip had curled up, so he fixed its ends together making a hoop. Then he had the idea of putting a skin over one side of the ring, but it wouldn't stay on so he put some skin on the other side too, and kept the two skins in place with thongs. (Valencia held up the flat drum and showed the thongs around the sides.) As for the flute, the "savage" found some cane one day. He tried blowing in one end and it made a whistling sound. But it hurt his tongue, so he put in a mouthpiece. He added a second section, to double the length. Still he could not alter the note, so he tried making three holes in the bottom. And this is how the Yaquis invented the drum and flute; the Anglos did not invent these. No savage could do this. The same applies to the whole deer dance, except for the Mexican-derived harp and violin (instruments positioned at the far "upstage" end of the ramada). The water in which the water drum (a hollowed-out upturned gourd) floated was the water around the world.

Valencia listed many Spanish words used in the deer dance. He informed us that the deer head (he picked it up and showed us) was made by a "shrunken head" technique. Maybe the antlers of another deer had been been attached, and glass eyes put in. The regalia was constructed empirically, and did not come into existence through mystical means. Felipe Molina, Valencia's godson, said that the beat of the water drum was the heart beat of the deer and the sound of the rasps was its breath. (However, this interpretation was denied by Valencia's wife, Heather.

Then Valencia gave us a Yaqui version of Yaqui history. He related it in a story-teller's style rather than an academic's. He told the story of the oldest Yaquis, the small statured Surem, and their wise talking tree. He went on to the Spanish invaders – and Valencia's story differed from other accounts.

When the first missionaries arrived carrying a cross, a sign very like the Yaquis' own representation of the four directions, the Yaquis decided that their own men should attend closely to the missionaries with the cross and learn everything that they would teach them. Once the Yaquis had learned everything they would get rid of the missionaries. The Yaquis were interested in the idea that God (the sun) had a son who was dragged under the cross and killed. They took up that idea, and when after a few years the priest introduced processions the Yaquis enjoyed them greatly and combined them with their deer dance. The priest objected to this but the Yaquis forced the priest to keep the Yaqui customs, threatening to get rid of him if he refused. This is how it was, said Valencia, not the other way around.

Valencia gave another addition concerning the period just before the coming of the missionaries that I do not remember seeing in Anglo or Spanish histories. He said that the Yaquis sought the peace treaty of 1610 with the Mexicans because although the Yaquis had militarily beaten the Mexicans they too had suffered greatly. The Yaquis felt that if the wars continued they would be altogether destroyed. Anselmo told how the Yaquis had won the great battle of 1610 defeating Diego de Hurdaide's forces. When the Yaquis saw they were losing, they sent a group of drummers up a hill into hiding under instructions to drum loudly as if they were another large force coming to help the Yaquis. When the Mexicanized Yaquis fighting on Hurdaide's side heard the drums they were terrified, knowing they would be slaughtered if the Yaquis succeeded in surrounding them. So they influenced their leaders to yield to the Yaquis.

Then Valencia described briefly something of the deer dance itself.

When teaching the dance, care should be taken to keep the rattles in time with the rasps and drums, while the feet keep time with the rhythm of the song. The head of the dancer moves in accordance with the plot of the story.

At question time Alan Lomax asked what were the important things a dancer had to do. Valencia pointed to Peter Acuna – his Yaqui name means "Fallen Fields" – who is to dance tomorrow. "This dancer is too young, he may conclude too late. The step to end the dance with must be right."

> Question: Is there any Yaqui ritual that includes women?
> Valencia: Yes, we are reviving one. It is like the Sadie Hawkins Day Race where the girls race after the boys hoping to catch the one they want to marry. But in our version the boys will catch the girls.
> Once a woman wanted to dance the deer dance. She did so for a while and gave up later. [At this the pascolas, the elders, and the junior deer dancer smiled broadly. Someone on our side said, "She would have to be naked above the waist."]
> Question: Do you sing any newly-composed songs at the deer dance?
> Valencia: No. But old songs that are very little known may be revived. There are no new songs, even at funerals. New songs sound wrong, they are too modern.
> Question: Who makes the regalia – deer's head, rattles, belt, and so on?
> Valencia: Each dancer usually makes his own.
> Question: Do you use any hallucinogens?
> Valencia: No, they are not allowed here. We have an objection to alcoholism too. Drunks cause trouble in our night dances.

Valencia complained about the priest of the Pascua church, Father Macarthy. It was Valencia who persuaded him in the first place to come to Pascua. Father Macarthy helped the Yaquis obtain baseball equipment. But since then he has tried to rule the way the Yaquis run their festivals, and he wants to abolish the "pagan" elements of the regalia.

During the morning talk, the violinist and the harpist sat quietly at their instruments, while an old but able-bodied man stood in front of them, along with a younger man and a boy. These two later sat down on the bench opposite, but the older man kept standing all morning. In the afternoon, he too sat.

21 November 1981: the day of the deer dance

Preliminary discussion

Valencia said that Father Macarthy had not spoken to him in five years. The priest had insisted on having a new house in the village. He wanted Valencia to ask permission every time he wanted to use the church. Valencia objected to this.

Spicer: The sacred dancers go inside the church – that is, the chapayekas go in on Ash Wednesday and during Holy Week. The Catholic Church here is a grasping institution, always happy with a Knights-of-Columbus-sponsored church, aggressive, dominating the deer dance organization, making it marginal. The sacraments are not given every week.

Richard Schechner: Are they given more often in Tucson's Old Pascua or out here in New Pascua?

Answer: More in New Pascua.

Spicer: Father Macarthy at first said Mass weekly but now does not do so. At Old Pascua the priest at the Church of the Holy Family, half a mile away, is not against the people. He is a supporter of the Salvadoran peasants, he is helpful to the people, he does not interfere with their autonomy. He is an easy-going guy. The church is an increasing presence. At Old Pascua they are training young Yaquis as priests. One of these younger Yaquis pushes priest domination in a very Yaqui way. There is tension, but not like Father Macarthy's tension. In Old Pascua the priest steers clear of government organization as in the eight towns of Yaqui Sonora in Mexico. At Easter the priest is in an administrative role. The Yaqui maestro [Yaqui non-ordained priest] living at Potam in Sonora has now been made a priest.

Richard Haefer: At Guadalupe Pueblo at Phoenix the priest dances with the matachinis.

Spicer: I'm suspicious about that. Let's find out more. Guadalupe people say that Old Pascua is a "barrio loco," a "crazy town," because professional photographers photograph parts of the ceremony and pascolas are let out on Palm Sunday when they should not be.

Schechner: Which of the pueblos has the best reputation?

Spicer: Old Pascua says that Guadalupe has no right to be an authority. I go to all three pueblos when I can. New Pascua lets the pascolas perform at the Gloria (Sabado de Gloria, Holy Saturday). Old Pascua is more crowded. At the Old Pascua church there are fourteen statues, the number corresponding to the fourteen stations of the cross, and the seven things the deer wears.

Valencia points out the Yaqui dancing instruments, describing them.

Then he says: When the deer dancer should end, I give him a nod. We will sing three songs, then the deer will be led out. We are cutting an hour-and-a-half out of the songs to get everything in today. It should be a night ceremony; doing it in the daytime does make it different.

(Before the dancing started, a few men dug a hole about thirty feet away, outside the ramada, and planted in it a white painted cross.)

Valencia continues: There will be a sermon. Those people sitting in cars a hundred yards away [he points to Yaquis in cars] are invited to the sermon for spiritual benefits and sacrifices.

Someone asks about training.

Valencia answers: Yes, there is training at home. I am out of coordination but I know the steps and teach them. What we do here is for the spiritual benefit of the world – and is not a superstition. I love what I'm doing. Feel free to ask questions. You can take a few pictures. Don't forget that we love the thing so much that we don't want it misused.

The pascolas

Now the violin and harp begin a jigging, liquid tune – like Scottish music, Victor Turner said. Valencia works a tape recorder which is placed on the blanket beside the regalia. It is playing the same violin and harp music, in time with what we are hearing. Rattles are heard, and we all look around. Way out in the plaza three pascolas, holding poles between each other, are being led in like blind men by the maestro. They are like babies, we are told, and need to be led. By the end of the day they and the deer dancer (a "fawn" at first) will be mature. The pascolas are bare to the waist, wearing bright-colored blankets peculiarly wrapped around their legs like trousers, with bells around the waist. Stuck in the back of the felt is a sistrum – a hand rattle with moving metal discs.

They are masked – the masks look like prognathous beasts, all hair. The pascolas pause at the white cross and bless themselves three times with the sign of the cross. Then they proceed to the ramada. They make a murmuring sound, hooting and hooing, a kind of laughing sound, not loud. The maestro leads them in very solemnly, right up to the harp at the inner end of the ramada. The noise they make isn't a song but an animal noise, a hollow low-sounding hooing sound, "Ooooh, mutter, mutter, hooh, mutter, mutter." The pascolas never sing. Now they place the ends of their canes in touch with the harp, each one in order of precedence. They are the same older man, young man, and boy as yesterday. They are "charged up" by the music, through their canes. Now they touch their hands to their feet, and then they take off their sandals. Fred Eggan observes that all the dancers have very projecting heels, and low-slung ankles. It seems to me that the noses of the dancers resemble the fine muzzles of deer.

We turn at the sound of the tampaleo (drummer-flutist) sitting against his board, beating some arresting blows on it. The three pascolas come forward six paces, then turn, all the time tapping the pulse with their bare flat feet and rattling. They end with laughter – a "Hur-hur-hur" – rapidly, and finally a slower, groaning chant. They turn around again with comic jigs, striding taps, and the comic "hoo" sound. Then the flute and drum begin. The pascolas now advance halfway down the ramada, carrying their sticks horizontally, beating their sistrums, now held in their hands, against the stick in the other hand. The flute is lively, like Mexican Volador music in rhythm. The pascolas dance a phrase on one foot, then shift to the other, like conchero dancers outside the shrine of Guadalupe, Tepeyac, near Mexico City. The end of this part of the dance comes in a couple of loud beats. The pascolas withdraw to the harp end of the ramada and discuss something or other with Anselmo, still using their odd voices. The elder pokes his stick "by mistake" into the ceiling rafters where it "gets stuck." All the Yaquis laugh. (We heard later that our lack of laughter was difficult for them – they like to have dialogue with the spectators in Yaqui and Spanish.) They stop and put their masks to the backs of their heads.

The maestro sweeps the dirt floor – fine ashes have been spread on it, and it is very smooth, soft. Dust flies, you can smell the ashes.

The oldest pascola adjusts a triangular yellow waistcloth. He strides, placing his foot here and there. The boy is placed by the others between them. He makes foot signs to the north, east, south, and west, which interests me, for this quincunx sign – four sides and a center – is so important in Indian culture (see Hunt 1977: 177). Then he does a heel-tap dance, bending a little at the waist – flick, flick, with his feet seeming to roll. Victor Turner observes that in a Scottish dance the legs would be going right up, lifted strongly from the hip. One can hear the rattle sound, out of time generally, the feet flicking forward to jig to the music fiddled out on the violin. The second, slightly obese dancer now faces the harp and does a less rapid but careful dance, more in time to the music: the rolling of his rattles is somewhat in time. The eldest dancer walks up and makes the quincunx sign on the ground; then he performs the same dance delicately; the rolling of the rattles has even more detail than the jig of the violin. The elder ceases, and ties up the binding on his leg which has come loose. Victor Turner observes that they all wear something like a priest's stole, very narrow, coming from the center of the waist to the thighs, tied around there, with long fringed ends hanging down.

The boy moves his mask to cover his face and goes to the drum end of the ramada, the open end. Taking his sistrum in hand he dances to the drum "like African hunters dancing," comments Turner. There is very rapid wild music, with loud flicking high notes up and down on the flute. The step: he turns his foot out at alternate treads. The middle pascola adjusts his mask and performs in the same way, and then the eldest. The eldest seems to be looking for something on his left. They end together, on a high note of laughter – "ee-e-ee."

The eldest now talks in Yaqui, in a sad voice, poetic and musical. So it is not Valencia alone who owns this style. It is sad, but also a matter of smiling and laughing. Yaqui listeners gather outside the entrance to the ramada.

Figure 4.2 Yaqui deer dancer.

The eldest pascola smokes. Offering cigarettes and smoking is an important part of the ritual – tobacco is a woman, there are legends about her. We are all waiting while this "interlude" continues. The violin and harp play quietly, back in the shadows, exploringly; they start on a little water jig which turns into bright fiddle music. The boy starts out dancing again at the back end of the ramada, his mask worn on the side of his head, not covering his face. He repeats the same dance as at first, his face solemn, his hands loose – they could be deer forelegs. Then the second Pascola, his head bent, the face watching the feet, detached, as if there were two halves to his body.

Figure 4.3 Yaqui pascolas and deer dancer.

The drummer beats his drum, then the flute and drum start a staccato piece. The flute sounds like a sharp flower above, while the drum hammers down at its root. The boy, now masked, dances to the drum; the second dances, ending with an "e-e-e-e" (like a soft mocking comment). The eldest does the same searching dance as before.

> Valencia: The seniors sat facing east since ancient times, in the place where you anthropologists are sitting now. The holy images come into the ramada at the right, from the south. The deer dancer faces east, as do the deer singers. The deer dancer sits facing east. The Yaquis present should learn this.

The deer dance

A tiny boy sits at the center post by the blanket on which is the sacred deer regalia. With Valencia leading, the rasps begin, and the water drum, which has a liquid sound. Three singers sit on the blanket, facing east. Now suddenly we see the deer dancer himself approaching at the right, looking and jerking left and right, then cautiously entering. He shuts his eyes at the drums, he treads high, he greets the pascolas. He crouches forward, and gives a terrific shake to his rattles (for a full description of his regalia see Evers 1981: 8).

The pascolas stand up facing the drum (see figure 4.2). The deer dancer is still a little bowed, the pascolas straight up. The deer dancer's nose is seen breathing, the nostrils flaring; the eyes of the deer's head above him seem satisfied – it has arrived home, one feels. Peter Acuna as the deer dancer looks

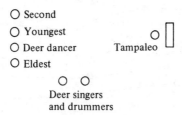

Figure 4.4 The spatial arrangement showing the relative positions of pascola dancers, deer singers, and tampaleo player.

fiercer than the deer. The deer face looks calm, the life of the deer having descended into the nostrils of the dancer. Walens says that when the animal face is depicted above the human, not hiding it, the meaning is transformation – either the animal is turning into a human or the human is turning into an animal (1982: 184, 187).

The eldest pascola sermonizes.

He says, in brief, "We ask the Lord for grace for all present, men, women, and children; may the Lord give us endurance and grace to continue our duties which are the inheritance of the Yaqui people."

Now all the Yaquis stand. The eldest pascola smokes, and the deer dancer takes off the deer head. He is still somewhat bowed forward.

> Valencia: The name Yaqui was derived from the Spaniards' question, "What is your country?" and they answered, "Y-aqui," "Here." (It was also said to mean "obstinate" in Yaqui.) The sticks were placed on the harp because the pascolas are newborn, they have to get the spirit from the harp. Then when they get the stick stuck in the rafters it is time for all sorts of clowning, in much more detail than is shown in the dance today.

The dance begins again. The pascolas put their masks on in front and dance to the drum. The deer dancer wipes his hands on his thighs, adjusts the white headcloth, tying it on more tightly, bends and takes one rattle with the thong over his wrist, with his head down, then the other rattle, puts the first rattle down, then puts on the deer head and ties it on, takes up the other rattle quickly, and immediately "jumps" into the deer role with a terrific shaking of the rattles. The drummer and raspers sing deafeningly, a big sound.

The deer dancer moves with a swaying, wringing gesture of the hands bearing the rattles. His eyes are closed, but he is very awake. Acuna's human nose is running like a wet deer muzzle. I notice sequin crosses sewn onto the red flower scarf ends that bind the deer's antlers, they must have been especially sewn on. The flowers on the scarf are green. The deer takes a red kerchief and mops his face and fans it. The church bell rings three times, then three more, then three more again, and then many times.

The boy pascola now does his dance at the harp end, with his mask at the

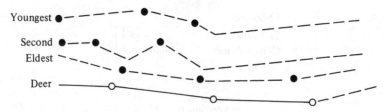

Figue 4.5 The three pascolas perform behind the deer dancer – the dance suggests that they are stalking the deer.

side. Valencia says that he volunteered to perform, he likes it very much. Three or four boys volunteer from time to time.

The drum starts. The pascolas utter a chant rapidly, a quiet, wild chant. The eldest's eyes are glaring.

The boy puts his mask on in front and does the sistrum dance. The deer dancer, now without his head-dress, arranges his belt, then puts the head-dress on as before, tying it by means of a loop under his chin. Immediately he's off, rattles going, and he's all deer again. The eldest comes up behind – it is hunting music, pursuit music, rapid, rapid, this way, that way (see figure 4.3). The deer dances with one leg in the air, flicking in time to the music, then he jumps with both legs, then one again, stamping with the foot "running" but not getting anywhere, fleet yet static.

Victor Turner: "the controlled nervosity of a deer, a circumscribed velocity."

A pause, and a new session. The boy is put forward with his mask on, in front of the deer dancer who hasn't put the head on yet. Acuna is very graceful in his blue rebozo breachclout, his legs and thighs flow when moving. Now he puts the head on again, puts his tongue out while trying to adjust the head. The notes sound like the bounding of the deer and again, the "e-e-e-e" noises sound along with the drums. Now the song begins, the group really shouts the song. The music reminds me of the humping bounding of the deer, then its swift run, followed by more bounds, then running. The dancer stays in one place, static, yet full of flight.

The boy suddenly attacks the deer.

"Whooop!" is his cry.

They've got him, tears come to my eyes. The maestro beckons the boy (his mask is off) to surround the deer, along with the second pascola, who comes up by the drums, his mask not covering his face, his head held proudly, right back, dominant. The deer is sweating, bent over; they are all circling, first the deer dancer, then the pascolas, boy, second, and eldest in that order. The pascolas clown.

In a flash the deer is down, he leaned right over backwards, recovered, and was back again. The boy goes down backwards in the same way, helpless. The second pascola clowns it, the same collapse. The eldest examines his thighs.

The second clowns around with his tongue out, poking it here and there, on each side of the entrance post: the Yaqui kids who are watching laugh. The eldest parodies the collapse, and at once the second and the boy surround him, lift him up onto one of his legs, then the other. They take his head and turn it this way and that.

It's tragi-comic, I shudder and laugh. Up they all come and fool around – all except the deer dancer, who is still solemn. The second pascola charges right out into the crowd – pandemonium. The second roars aggressively, and everybody laughs. The boy faces the deer – he and the deer point their feet at each other. The deer dancer does not smile, but everybody else does.

Afternoon session

They begin at the harp end. First the boy, then the deer dancer for the first time is at the harp end, then the second, then the eldest, who has the lightest feet of all. The deer dancer meanwhile fixes the boy's mask for him, very kindly. The deer dancer goes to the drum end and puts on his deer head-dress with the same set procedure. (In his dancing I notice how Acuna has a different style of shaking each rattle.)

He lifts his leg and he's off! Flare of the rattles – and the sharp stopping of his head after this, as before. Singing breaks loose – a plunging forward of rattles in an aggressive shake. The right hand circulates, the left hand goes up and down. Turner comments that the dancer's center of gravity is in the abdomen. We can see the deer head above coming alive like the doll Virgin of Zapopan carried into Guadalajara, at the mercy of human prelates, yet commanding them.

The second pascola is huge, "he struts," says Turner, "like the wrestler Black Jack Mulligan." One can judge the accurate time-keeping of the deer dancer by his knees, his feet go too quickly to catch the beat. Acuna has perfect steady balance around a low center of gravity, thus there is no stumbling. His legs go out, then back to the center at once. The left foot is more often firmly planted than the right. He wipes sweat from his hands on to his rebozo breachclout.

> Turner comments: The deer dancer and the first pascola are together but in separate worlds, this is unlike the kufukujila "agreeing" dance of the Ndembu of Zambia where two dancers confront one another directly.

The singers sing in perfect unison, in a minor key; it seems to be a hunting theme, with the last note prolonged plangently. Then there is a sudden stop.

In the next dance the deer rubs his antlers on "trees," that is, halfway down the two posts at the end of the ramada. Then he goes on all fours. I happen to glance at the Yaqui women who are watching. Their faces look somewhat sad, in the usual Yaqui style. (Heather Valencia told me that Valencia has eleven children of his own, has raised twenty-two, and has adopted two. Ten of his children were by one wife, and one by another – none were Heather's. She has a son somewhere else in the United States.) The singers begin the Song of the Iguana and the pascolas pretend to climb up posts, arching their backs, with their hands and legs out. Heather Valencia says this is a "happy song." The deer dancer is tying on his headband, and his arms and back muscles seem to form a cross – the cross metaphor comes to mind easily.

All the dancers seem to stop perfectly in concert without signals that I could see. Afterwards, Schechner, who had gone around behind the tampaleo, reported that Valencia gave a signal, just as he said he would do.

While Acuna takes a break and smiles, his canine teeth show over his lower lip like an animal's.

> Valencia: Next they will perform the Dance of the Animals and the blessing of the four winds.

He explains that if the deer dancer wore the traditional skin breachclout instead of the blue rebozo, that would now be regarded as "artificial."

Acuna is tired. He and the pascolas line up and the eldest gives a sermon. For this the very old men whom we have seen collecting on the bench opposite take off their hats, putting them on again after the sermon. The very wizened man who we are told is 102 years old was in the Coyote Society. He was a pascola in 1936, says Heather Valencia. She wishes they could have a Coyote Society now, as the Yaquis in Mexico do. Valencia has tried to form one, but there weren't enough Yaqui interested. She says that last year in Sonora the Yaquis and the Mexican peasants banded together to resist further land seizure. They tried to stop the building of a road and one person was killed.

> Victor Turner: The black pascola mask is like the mask of Harlequin in commedia dell'arte and also like Javanese black-face clowns.
> Lomax: The flute and drum unit is from the shepherds in Catalonia, Spain. They used it to divert themselves when they were lonely – a one-man band.
> Valencia: The maestro is the chief story-teller of the community. He tells serious myths and folktales. There should be saints' statues at the harp end of the ramada.

The deer dancer slows. The singing stops while the drums continue. The deer dancer hesitates, then a crescendo from the singers and the pascolas dance again. Now the tampaleo leaves his post, and as the deer dancer approaches Valencia on the blanket everything stops. The drummer is leaving. Everyone except Acuna goes to the cross outside. Acuna is inside, looking out. The tampaleo is outside. Then out comes the deer dancer and a row forms (see figure 4.6). They go back and forth to the cross, and past it, and then they go behind the church. There, we are told, they bury the deer regalia – "La Muerte del Venado."

For a while a boy of about twelve practices the deer dance. He is praised by his mother and by the crowd.

Figure 4.6 The pascolas, tampaleo, and deer dancer leave the ramada and form a straight line from which they approach the cross. Then they go behind the church where the deer regalia is buried.

Finally, the metal bowl of water for the water drum, which had been buried in the ground up to its rim, is taken up and the water thrown out near the cross – some say, in the form of a cross.

> Heather Valencia: In the days of the Surem the deer did not have to be hunted. If one deer was named, it would come to the men and they would shoot it painlessly in the heart. It sacrificed itself for the people.

Keith Basso's eye witness account of natural deer behavior
Apache Indians often observe a strange performance by deer and once Basso saw it himself.

It occurs at night just before the deer mating season in a clearing close to a stream up in the San Carlos mountains on the Apache reservation.

Four or five does come within 500 yards of the stream. The bucks go down to the stream and drink, and afterwards the does drink. At some signal, the bucks stand up on their hind legs. The does don't, but the bucks do it again and again. At last the does rear up too, and they all do it. They keep falling back because they can't keep their balance. The animals accompany their actions by a low noise – "u-u-u-u-wheeze; e-e-e-e." After this performance but before the actual mating, the males battle antlers-to-antlers, pairing off against each other in competition for the does.

At another time of year when the deer are about to lose their antlers, they make a noise by rubbing their antlers against the ponderosa pines which have a rough corrugated bark. This rubbing sounds like an irregular rasping, and can be heard a long way off. Apache hunters go into the field with antlers and rub them against the trees as the deer do. The bucks actually come, Keith does not know why.

5.

A Yaqui point of view: on Yaqui ceremonies and anthropologists

ANSELMO VALENCIA, HEATHER VALENCIA,
AND ROSAMOND B. SPICER

Participating

Anselmo Valencia: Ever since I can remember I have thought that the spectators came and in some way participated just because they were there. They made numbers, they made a crowd. I was told when I was about six or seven that, whether or not people came, non-Yaquis, that this was not for the benefit of the public only, but really for the benefit of us, with the mandas[1] and all that. But the old maestro[2] – you remember the old maestro? – he said that anybody that came close, even out of curiosity, believer or non-believer, was sent by a being superior to us, by somebody superior to anything else, that we don't know, that we haven't seen a picture of or anything. Without planning to think it, I know that the people who are there, they are participating in some way and that they are somehow sent there.

Now that I deer-sing – which I understand better than most Yaquis – I know that it's a call from a superior being. I know that a person that's there, whether they believe or not, gets intensely involved with the action of the deer dancer. They are not seeking healing, but I know that they are going to go away with a good feeling. Regardless of why they are there, watching it gets their minds so deeply involved in it that, whether they go there with a headache or depression or ache somewhere in the body, they forget their pain, and to me that is healing. Those are the powers of the deer dancer or the deer singer.

Heather Valencia: It's like watching a good performance from Shakespeare. It's something alive that happens on the creative level, and it's more than that, it's spiritual. Many people want to come to it, they sense something they would like to touch, but they never make it there. Other people make it there not ever knowing what's happening. There is a right moment.

Anselmo Valencia: Out of curiosity I asked each of the people at that conference[3] "What did you see? What did you think it did for you?" And it surprised me a lot when they said what I would have expected from my people, the Yaquis, to feel when they leave a deer dance. As old as I am I was still surprised by this group, because I'd always said that this belongs to the Yaquis, nobody else. But as the years go by I'm realizing that all the benefits – the spiritual benefits, obviously – do not only belong to the Yaquis but to whomever comes near it.

People may be wandering around, but as soon as the drummer starts tamping his drum, they rush over to the ramada. It is a call for them to take part in a very, very – to me – in a very spiritual, sacred ceremony. A few minutes of the deer dance, about three minutes, that is enough to bring them a light, a divine light. And I think they feel it because, especially the non-Yaquis – I see them tapping or dancing. The Yaquis don't do that because they have a tremendous amount of control – they want to do it, but then somebody might laugh at them. In fact, in here, inside them, they really feel it.

Heather Valencia: When Anselmo gives the sermon he says that this is for the whole world, to change things in the etheric realm for the whole planet.

Anselmo Valencia: Yes, that's how I see it, how the old men see it. The old men want to talk about it, but the young people don't want to listen – because there is the radio, there's the TV, and there's a little game-playing, and others say "Yeah, that's a nice story, superstition, you know." But I always figured, it's funda-mental, this stuff. I'm always telling the younger people what we believe it is, and how to get more spiritual well-being out of these performances. So, curiously enough, it surprised me a lot when these scholars, these learned people, saw what I know is there.

I didn't think they would see it because I thought this was for Yaquis only. In a way I think that, but then it is not. That's why I have begun to invite people in there during, for instance, the Sabado de Gloria.[4] I tell them, "Come in and take part in it with us." In talking about the Gloria, at that moment, without realizing it, many people unite spiritually, whether their god is Jehovah, Muhamed, Buddha, or Jesus – whatever name you call your god, it's the same. They feel something – at the first run, the second, and the third. They get chills, goose bumps, or something, everybody does. I watch a lot of Yaquis, they'll blow their nose or wipe their eyes or something. Something comes on them, a warmth. At that moment we are one with God, with the Creator. And curiously enough, at that moment I don't think of Jesus or the Virgin Mary. Something greater, something tremendous, something connected to us. The Yaquis call it the Divine Light. We couldn't draw a picture of it.

A brief history by Rosamond B. Spicer

It has always been a subject for discussion, and possibly an insoluble puzzle, about what in Yaqui culture as we now know it are the elements which have been retained from aboriginal times and what elements were brought to the Yaquis by the Jesuits and the Spanish Conquistadors and settlers. Although the Yaquis had been hearing of the Spanish as they advanced up the west coast of what is now Mexico, there was no actual contact until Diego de Guzmán reached the Yaqui River in the present-day state of Sonora in 1533 and was turned back by a Yaqui fighting force, which, a Spaniard who was in the battle reported, showed the greatest fighting ability of any natives of New Spain. It was not until 1617 that the Jesuits actually entered the Yaqui country and embarked on their missionization program. There followed a relatively peaceful and cooperative period under Jesuit domination until about the middle of the eighteenth century when, in 1767, the Jesuits were withdrawn from all of New Spain. From that time on the Yaquis were to a large extent left on their own in the religious realm, although in the political realm there was ever-increasing turmoil. The Yaquis' riverine-rich land was some of the most fertile in all Mexico and there were continual efforts at encroachment by the Spanish and then the Mexicans. The Yaquis defended their homeland with vigor and intelligence but were finally defeated by superior forces, resulting in forced deportations to the Yucatan and a Yaqui diaspora into the United States. After the 1910 Revolution, many Yaquis returned to their Eight Towns along the Yaqui River and there the economic struggle for retention of some autonomy continues to this day. However, most of those who had fled to Arizona from extreme persecution remained and established several Yaqui villages. There, in the midst of an alien – but largely friendly – culture they revived their distinctive ceremonies, maintaining their identity to such an extent that in 1978 they became recognized by the Congress of the United States as an American Indian tribe, the Yaqui Tribe, with headquarters and a tiny 220 acre reservation at New Pascua, or Pascua Pueblo, near Tucson, Arizona.

The Yaquis were converted to Catholicism by the Jesuits and remain Catholics, but it is definitely a Yaqui type of Catholicism in which the maestro (lay priest) conducts the church services and a number of ceremonial societies take part. There are also special dancers, such as the pascola and deer dancer, of which Anselmo Valencia speaks. There are many ceremonies or fiestas, both calendrical and non-calendrical, which occur throughout the year. The most widely known of these are the Easter ceremonies, which start on Ash Wednesday and continue throughout Lent, or Cuaresma, and Holy Week until the climax on Sabado de Gloria and the finale on Easter Sunday. The pascolas and the deer dancer take part in many of these yearly ceremonies, the fariseos and the masked chapayekas are active only during the Cuaresma.

Probably the majority of Yaquis simply accept their Yaqui type of Catholicism, hardly noting the gradual changes that have taken place over time. Others, however, like some of the maestros and the "old men," and persons like Anselmo Valencia, are continually pondering about what there is still of the ancient and what it might have been like.

"More Yaqui than Catholic"

Rosamond B. Spicer: There is a belief among some of the older people that Jesus was born in the Yaqui country . . .

Anselmo Valencia: Yes, I get into big discussions with the maestros. They say that Jesus was here and our Virgin Mary gave us this and He gave us that. But before the Jesuits I am sure that the Yaquis had never heard of Jesus or the Virgin Mary.[5] Some old people, men and women, they say that before we had the Cuaresma we adored the sun, we danced three times to the sun and there were no santos or Jesus or Virgin Mary. These old people were not believed because of the good work that the Jesuits did – too good a job on the minds of the Yaquis.

One of the old maestros used to tell me that he saw the modern world, he saw the ancient world in the astral sense of the word. I have seen the old world, I have seen the new world, I see the world that's coming – as far as the Yaquis go. I have proved to some very old people some of these things and they say, "How do you know?" and I say "Because I have talked to the spirits." I tell the young people, "You do it, you have the power, but you do not know, you do not practice it, you do not know what you're supposed to do, say, or feel." And I do believe that everybody has the power. So this power flows out, in our performances, to the non-Yaqui, to the non-believer, whether the person is sober or drunk, it flows out to them, and therefore a healing process takes place at that moment.

I don't think we could be hired if someone was sick to go and sing and dance for them. But how do I know that this isn't one of the commands that we had been given. I don't know. It's never been done, except before Christianity. Back then they used to do it like the Navajos still do it, the sand painting and the gourd singing, and the people get well. Why? I'm very curious to find out why. There was a Yaqui man, and some superior being, an old man, gray-haired with a beard – not a long beard, but Yaqui-style – came to him while he was awake. Our old people used to do that. I don't know at what point it started beginning. Was it when the Good Book was brought? The old people embraced Catholicism with so much need, so much want, and so much hunger. The same thing would have happened whether they were Assembly of God, Jewish, or Mormon. But we still have the deer dancer, the pascola, and possibly the chapayekas, because the chapayekas we had before, before the Spanish came, but not in formation.[6] Christianity from the Holy Book was interwoven with Yaqui belief to where, before we start a ceremony now, we say a prayer, "Our Father" and the rest of the prayers, and make the Sign of the Cross.

Before we had this modern Sign of the Cross we did it on the heart, the lips, and the head. It means "From my heart, permit me not to criticize my brother, and may the Divine Light shine upon us." Some of the older pascolas and matachinis still do it. I would like to bring some of these old things forward again. My deer songs come from the old time. Some of the old dances have died out, but I would like to return to some of that old drama. In the last two or three years the young people have become very interested. The problem with us is that we're going too modern too fast. We do not care to learn the songs for those dances.

Heather Valencia: The first Easter, when I first experienced the deer dance, I didn't have any reference to what it was about. I was shocked when they said they were walking the path of the cross, because all I saw was Indian. I saw the chapayekas, I saw the deer dance, and I saw the pascolas, and nothing else. I never even saw the matachinis. I didn't know what they were, but when Anselmo told me I had a lot of respect for that. I didn't observe anything in connection with the church. It was as though, to me, they didn't exist. I didn't know what they were. I brought offerings to honor the different societies I had observed and I didn't observe anything in connection with the church. And when other Indians come, they don't get the connection with Catholicism either, they just see the Indian part. They just see the chapayekas as representing the forces of evil and the sun coming to power. The other Indian friends who come to participate with us, like my Lakota friends, and my Ute friends, and different Indians, they don't get the Catholic part, but they just love the Indian part and that's what they see. People go, "This is Catholic?" And I say, "This is Yaqui Catholic." And then the people say, "More Yaqui than Catholic."

The deer singer[7]

Anselmo Valencia: I see the new adopted religion, but I feel more of the old, old. That's because I was confirmed as the capitan at the age of five, in 1926. Then I couldn't run around all the time, playing with the kids. I had to be in the circle or at bonfire or in any gathering. It's been my life, it's really been my life. You probably remember my drinking days, when I used to be an alcoholic. During Lent I would not drink because I would not permit myself to pollute my thinking. And it's hard for a drinker to be on the wagon for seven weeks, very very hard, very extremely hard.

I've known these deer songs since I was a little boy because I used to dance, and all that. But there were so many deer singers and I had other duties to perform, so I didn't come out until lately with it. When I did, people said, "How did you learn?" and I said, "Oh, I've always known them." Those songs that I didn't know, they just come to me. Sometimes I wake up at 1 o'clock, 2, or 3 a.m., and write it down. I know practically 215, 220 different songs. In one night, now, we usually sing about five songs, so if I sing night after night I could probably not repeat if I didn't want to even one song on all those nights. When the other singers say, "How does it go, I never heard it before," and I know that they haven't heard it before, except the real old people. I don't like that because I feel that I may not be singing for too long, because of my age.[8]

The powers of the deer dancer or the deer singer is what I am describing in my book, the deer dance ritual. It's almost finished, I also want to write the story of the history of the culture. These lines are going to try to prove more to my own people than to anybody else, because non-Yaquis would not understand what I mean. The Yaquis are really excited that that should be done, especially the maestros. I have accepted the Book, of course, but I don't want to lose the history of our culture. I don't want the kids to lose it, at least as a story.

Being of service – the anthropologists

Rosamond B. Spicer: When we lived in Pascua in 1936–37 we saw articles in the newspapers about the Yaqui Easter ceremonies and they were so wrong, had such misinterpretations in them. So Ned [Edward H. Spicer] for quite a number of years would write the articles for the papers, explaining what was really happening. There were also some pamphlets which we helped with that were sold at the Easter ceremonies. Do you think doing that helped the general public, the people of Tucson, to understand?

Anselmo Valencia: I think it's very well understood. My grandfather in 1926 came out with a little old pamphlet. He wanted to give the sense of the Yaqui ceremonies, to explain to the non-Yaquis that we were not doing anything pagan, that we were worshipping a common god. I suppose he was very much criticized.

Rosamond B. Spicer: There was also a little book by Phebe Bogan. She really felt with the Yaquis, she was trying to understand, but there are errors in that, too. Then there's that book which Muriel Thayer Painter,[9] "Budge," wrote about the Easter ceremonies. It is now being prepared to be published by the University of Arizona Press. But you have read it . . .

Anselmo Valencia: Yes, I read most of her books before they were printed.

Rosamond B. Spicer: Do you think that Ned's work has been of any meaning to the Yaquis?

Anselmo Valencia: I always recommend Dr. Spicer's work to people who want to learn something about the Yaquis and other Indians, his *Cycles of Conquest*. I read it once in a while for my own thoughts or when I make a speech for Pima College, because it has that certain thing that brings out a clear understanding – the change of life from one era to another, from one sort of fashion to another. To me he says the same things, anybody agrees, and should understand exactly. They understand it like I do, the Yaquis, as well as the Papago. It's very clear. The other book[10] also can be of benefit to people, except that the terminology in that is anthropology terminology. It's clearer, though, than a lot of anthropology I have read. Yaquis have been very proud, you know, that he wrote those stories about them. You know me, I was always on the borderline whether to believe or not to believe – whether to approve or not to approve is the better way of putting it. And I'm like that with everybody, with everything. I have to – I'm not from Missouri but I have to be shown! And then I have my own ways of thinking about Yaqui things, or Indian. And I like to explain, express my thoughts out loud and in no uncertain manner.

As far as the culture goes, Dr. Spicer did bring out a very clear understanding or explanation of what we are doing, what the Yaquis are doing, and I suppose that the other Indians could say the same things for them.

The non-Yaqui reading it would understand the Yaqui as strictly a religious group, a religious entity, a religious nature. We do things other than things in the religious way. But it brings out the fact that we are absolutely connected with the non-Yaqui Catholic religion, except that we dramatize it. He brings that out so that is an understanding.

A group came down from Phoenix, maybe last year [1984], a lot of them. They caught me, as is normal for me, going all over the place, in the midst of everything. They told me they had read the text. And I told them, "If you have read the book you understand everything and you don't need to ask questions and you know what's happening, right?" And they said. "Yeah." And I said, "Well, excuse me. I'll be right back." "Well," they said, "we know that you are very busy, we have been watching you for the last two or three hours. But we just want to tell you that we know what you are doing."

I've stood in formation many many years, and people standing there, non-Yaquis, they come out with the wildest ideas of what we are doing. Oh, man! It is really funny – and everybody looks so serious. "Oh, yes, a good friend of mine, he told me this and he told me that." But after that I could write a book about those things that the people believe we are doing. And a person who is not going to research with the Yaqui could not hope to write a book about the Yaqui because he would be putting out his own ideas. But however sincere non-Yaquis are, they have their own way of explaining a thing that is not exactly the way I would explain it, or some other Yaqui would explain that – the inner feeling. Because to the learned person there has to be a word in certain terminology that would explain things to them, but not to another Yaqui or to another Indian.

Heather Valencia: Indians learn through feelings and symbols. And they express their religion through feelings and symbols.

Anselmo Valencia: And some of them believe uttered words or actions. There is not a word yet in English for them to explain it. There may be words close to it, but they cannot find a word because it's not in the dictionary, because it has not been invented. It's hard because the interpretation goes in-between the Yaqui and the non-Yaqui and it gets off somewhere.

Rosamond B. Spicer: But is there a usefulness in trying to explain as much as possible?

Anselmo Valencia: I don't know. Something I've thought of: is it absolutely necessary that we really try to explain our feelings to someone else?

Rosamond B. Spicer: It would be much better to try and explain them yourself. And Yaquis will be doing that. You'll be doing it, there'll be others who will do it. But up to this point, or fairly recently, there has been no one, no Yaqui, I mean.

Heather Valencia: When a mystery is totally exposed to the light there is no more mystery and it dissolves into the ether. That's what the trouble is. I'm half white with the white point of view; we have to expose everything to the light. That's what our mind teaches us, and all I see is that that's what life's all about, that's what creation is all about. The white race and the dark race as lovers, and they have a union and something else new grows. There's value in that, the something new growing. But too much of one is no good, and too much of either one is no good.

Rosamond B. Spicer: When we lived in Pascua the people didn't know much English and there were many things that they needed. They needed help in going to "las oficinas" downtown, they needed help in transportation, they needed help in sickness, they needed help in all kinds of ways. They used to say to Ned, "You are like a kovanao [head or governor]."

Anselmo Valencia: Yes.

Rosamond B. Spicer: And they wanted him to become a kovanao.

Heather Valencia: He would have been a good one.

Rosamond B. Spicer: He knew very well that he could not assume that kind of position.

Heather Valencia: Well, what it means, Anselmo told me, is that you're a queen now and what that means is that you do everything for everybody. You are the one who does all the giving, that's what it means.

Rosamond B. Spicer: There were many many things that the people needed and he – and when you are able to do it you just do it.

Anselmo Valencia: That's so, and you just better help.

Rosamond B. Spicer: And I think that, over the years, was what Ned's point of view was. He tried very hard, in every way he could, to help, both through his writing and in working with you in establishing New Pascua, Pascua Pueblo.

Heather Valencia: It wouldn't surprise me at all if your husband returned in a form more akin to the culture he loved.

Anselmo Valencia: We believe in that, we believe it happens. That's what I tell the people, that there are non-Yaquis, whatever color they may be, in appearance, but their souls are really Yaqui. And it can be said that they must have come back from somewhere to being an Indian, some sort of Indian, Yaqui or otherwise.

Rosamond B. Spicer: Do you remember Juana, the cantora? She was a wonderful person and I was quite close to her. One time when I went over to visit her she took my arm and held it next to hers, and she said, "The skin is a different color, but underneath it's the same."

Anselmo Valencia: That's what we feel at Sabado de Gloria. You feel we're all children of the sun, you feel how we're all the same. At Sabado de Gloria that's what everyone who is there feels. They feel the beauty of humility, how none of us are greater or lesser, how we're all one. That's what we all feel then, when it's so magic.

And that's what keeps surprising me at the Conference we had over the deer, the deer dance. We all sat around that big table and when I first asked that scholar, I don't remember his name, he didn't give the answer I wanted to hear. After I went all around the table asking all the others I knew that the other people had enjoyed it, so then I came back to him and I said, "Do you think all these other people are mistaken and they don't know?" And he said, "No, they saw right." What did he see there? I don't know where it comes from, but then I realized.

Rosamond B. Spicer: I wonder if Ned in trying to understand the Yaquis, and writing about them, has made any difference to the Yaqui young people – that a scholar feels that the Yaqui culture is something to be studied and written about and understood.

Anselmo Valencia: Well, it probably brings something out to them, to their benefit – if they read it. But if they have the book, they wouldn't read it because it would seem a little out of their realm to read – reports and stories about anthropology, archeology, and whatever 'ologies. If it is not easy to read then I think it does not have that call to them.

Heather Valencia: Nevertheless, the books have a value – they help the Yaquis.

Anselmo Valencia: Oh, yes.

Heather Valencia: And in a serious way, and in a very mysterious way, your husband's writings have helped the people, because all that attention on the Yaqui nation helps draw thinking white intelligentsia, voting intelligentsia, to the Nation. He was a force in helping the Yaquis secure their position and their land. It's all in the etheric realm, it's nothing you can define precisely. He was a focal point. He was a bridge between the two worlds. But the Yaquis didn't understand exactly what he was saying. He helped them. They have been written about by someone important.

Anselmo Valencia: There is a reason why so many Yaqui people will not read Dr. Spicer's writings. Our idea is that Dr. Spicer wrote it for the benefit of the non-Yaqui so they could understand the Yaqui. And therefore the Yaquis don't know if they have to read it because the Yaquis think they understand the Yaquis. And then, if they don't see pictures of the dancers, and all that, it doesn't have the call. And then because the way the book is written, it's a little bit technical, like lawyer talk. But the young people going to the University, I tell them if they want to understand the Yaquis they should go to the anthropological library and get all that Dr. Spicer and Mrs. Painter have done. And I say that I don't know of two other people who have done a damn good job that you could name. We don't have any conflict, because I am still with the idea that he discovered how to educate the non-Indian, the non-Yaqui, to what the Yaquis are made of, believe in, worship, and all that.

Heather Valencia: And he told what the Yaquis have accomplished.

Anselmo Valencia: Oh, yes, of course, there's no doubt there, of course.

Heather Valencia: Your husband was very honored among the people, he always had been. You both were recognized when you first came among those people as somebody very special to them. And he loved the Yaqui nation.

Anselmo Valencia: Oh, yes.

Heather Valencia: And what he writes inspires others to love them also.

Anselmo Valencia: There are young Yaquis now who are brilliant. And their minds go that way . . .

Explanation
Rosamond B. Spicer

This article derives from a conversation between the authors, Anselmo Valencia, his wife Heather, and myself. The conversation was requested by Richard Schechner who had suggested the subjects which he wanted us to discuss for this book in honor of Victor Turner. The Valencias came to the Spicer home specifically for this purpose on Sunday afternoon, 3 February 1985. Anselmo led the discussion, saying the things that were on his mind and about which he had thought much. The two hours of talk were taped and thereafter transcribed. The order of the conversation given here is much as it happened, although in some instances two or more statements on the same subject are included as one statement. The words used are direct quotations, with but minor editing.

Notes

1. When a child is ill, his parents, and possibly others concerned with his welfare, frequently make a promise (manda) to either the Virgin Mary or Jesus that the sick one will serve that deity in some ceremonial capacity and thus regain and maintain his or her health. It is through these mandas that the personnel of the ceremonial societies is maintained. The pascolas and deer dancers receive their call in other ways, such as through dreams.
2. The early Jesuits taught the Yaquis the prayers and rituals of the Catholic Church. After the Jesuits were expelled from New Spain in 1767 there were few, if any, priests to serve the Yaquis and, in order to carry on the ceremonies, lay priests or maestros (Spanish for teacher) assumed the duties. They do not perform the sacraments nor wear robes, but without them the Yaqui ceremonies and rituals could not be carried out. The maestros have also become repositories of the deep knowledge of Yaqui ways and the Yaqui past and through their sermons teach Yaqui values and morals.
3. Conference on Ritual and Performance, held at New Pascua and Oracle, Arizona, November 1981. Organized by Richard Schechner and Victor Turner and sponsored by the Wenner-Gren Foundation for Anthropological Research. The subject of this conference, one of the series on which this book is based, was the Yaqui.
4. On the Sabado de Gloria (Holy Saturday, the day before Easter) the forces of evil (the fariseos or Pharisees) challenge the forces of good (the church group, the matachin dancers, the deer and pascola dancers) and are defeated. This is dramatically enacted by the fariseos furiously running at the church and twice being beaten back by the child angels and the throwing of flowers. On the third run, devoid of all paraphernalia, the evil beings are completely defeated and they enter the church to be rebaptized as men.
5. Anselmo is saying here that he does not think, as do some of the old people, that Jesus was born of Mary *in the Yaqui country*, but the people were prepared through the myth of the Talking Tree to receive Christianity when it was brought to them.
6. For a full explanation of the various kinds of ceremonial participants mentioned in this interview see any of the Painter or Spicer publications listed in the references.

7. Translations of a number of the deer songs were made by Carleton S. Wilder. Three examples of songs are given here, with the Yaqui words, an interlinear translation, and a free translation. The words, seemingly simple, have deep meanings.

Introductory Song

SONG ONE

Basic stanza (sung five times)

1.   séwa   malíci   yé. usuwéyekai   ?ímsu
     (flower)   (fawn)   (you are about to come out) (this)

2.   séwabá.mpo   yéyewe
                     (in the flower water)   (you play)

Concluding stanza

3.   ?iyimínsu   séye wáilo   séwatebácipo
     (yonder)   (place name)   (in the flower patio)

4.   séwabá.mpo   yéyewe
                     (in the flower water)   (you play)

5.   séwa   malíci   yé. usuwéyekai   ?ímsu
     (flower)   (fawn)   (you are about to come out) (this)

6.   séwabá.mpo   yéyewe
                     (in the flower water)   (you play)

   Little flower deer
      You are about to come out
   To play in this flower water.

   Yonder in the home of the deer
      In the flower patio
   You are playing in the flower water.
   Flower fawn, you are about to come out to play
      In the flower water.

(Wilder 1963: 176)

SONG SEVEN

Basic stanza (sung six times)

1.   jíta   júya   séwa   só?ila   má.ci
     (what)   (tree)   (flowers)   (is bent)   (obviously)

2.   seyá   kúta   séwa   só?ila   má.ci
     (flower)   (stick)   (flowers)   (is bent)   (obviously)

3.   jíta   júya   séwa   só?ila   má.ci
     (what)   (tree)   (flowers)   (is bent)   (obviously)

4.   seyá   kúta   séwa   só?ila   má.ci
     (flower)   (stick)   (flowers)   (is bent)   (obviously)

Concluding stanza

5.	?yimínsu (yonder)	séye wáilo (place name)	se wáilo (place name)	sániluápo (in the sagebush)	
6.	náisukuni (midst)	wóto bóli (flower name)	séwa (flowers)	só?ila (is bent)	má.ci (obviously)
7.	seyá (flower)	kúta (stick)	séwa (flowers)	só?ila (is bent)	má.ci (obviously)

> What tree is so bent over
> Burdened with flowers?
> The flower stick is clearly bent over
> With many flowers.
>
> Yonder in the home of the deer
> In the midst of the sage brush
> The wóto bóli is bending down
> With flowers.
> Flower stick is clearly
> Burdened with flowers.

wóto bóli is the name of a flower
flower stick = rasp

(Wilder 1963: 183)

SONG NINE

Basic stanza (sung four times)

1.		?ábwe (well)		sáila (little brother)	?ini.kún (so here you are)
2.		séya (flower)	yoleme (deer)	sáila (little brother)	?áwasum (antlers)
3.		líolíotamyó.wa (move and shake)		sáila (little brother)	?áwasum (antlers)
4.		líolíotamyó.wa (move and shake)		sáila (little brother)	

Concluding stanza

5.	kátikun (why not)	seyá (flower)	yoléme (deer)	sutu (hoof)	púliem (cleaned-out)
6.	líolíotamyó.wa (move and shake)		sáila (little brother)		kátikun (why not)
7.	seyá (flower)	yoléme (deer)	tenebólim (téneboim)		sí.osí.otamyó.wa (move and rustle)
8.	sáila (little brother)		?awasum (antlers)		líolíotamyó.wa (move and shake)
9.	sáila (little brother)				

> Well, little brother, so here you are,
>   Flower deer.
> Shake your antlers, little brother
>   Shake your antlers, little brother.
>
> Why don't you shake your belt of deer-hoof rattles,
>   Flower deer?
> Why don't you rustle your cocoon ankle rattles,
>   Little brother, flower deer?
> Shake your antlers, little brother.

(Wilder 1963: 184)

As examples of the type of music to which these songs are sung, three musical notations are here given as recorded and transcribed by Frances Densmore. For each poem there is a different tune, usually using a five-tone scale. As accompaniment two or three of the singers rapidly stroke hardwood rasps which rest on half gourds; another singer beats a water drum, which is a larger half gourd floater in a pan of water.

No. 87. The Deer Are At Play (Catalogue No. 1277)
Recorded by Juan Ariwares

Free Translation
Away in the brush they (the deer) are playing.

Analysis. – The character of this melody is playful in accordance with the words. The first thirteen measures were sung four times, these renditions being separated by a break in the time, which varied from approximately two to four counts. The ascending major sixth in the seventh measure is interesting, as well as the triple measure that follows it. The song has a compass of an octave and is based on the fourth five-tone scale. Almost half the intervals are in descending progression (Densmore, 1932: 159).

No. 88. The Deer and the Flower (Catalogue No. 1278)
Recorded by Juan Ariwares

Free Translation
The deer looks at a flower.

Analysis. – The first performance of this song comprised three renditions of the repeated portion with a break in the time between each. The latter part of the song followed after a brief pause. The meolody contains little interest, and it is noted that the idea expressed in the words is simple. The song has a range of five tones and contains the major triad and second. More than half the intervals are whole tones and occur only in descending progression (Densmore, 1932: 160).

The following song was sung after midnight: No. 89. The Summer Rains (Catalogue No. 1279)
Recorded by Juan Ariwares

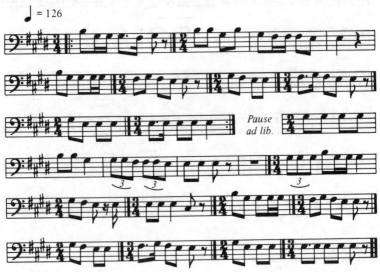

Free Translation
In summer the rains come and the grass comes up.
That is the time that the deer has new horns.

Analysis. – Although rhythmic in character this song contains no rhythmic unit. The first portion was sung three times with a break in the time between the repetitions. The intonation on the repetitions of a tone was not steadily held, the pitch being lower on the last tones of the series (Densmore, 1932: 161).

8. In 1985 Valencia was 64 years old.   9. Bogan 1925; Painter 1986.
10. Valencia is referring to Spicer's *The Yaquis: A Cultural History*, 1980.

6.

Performance of precepts/precepts of performance: Hasidic celebrations of Purim in Brooklyn

BARBARA KIRSHENBLATT-GIMBLETT

The life of an observant Jew is shaped by the performance of hundreds of precepts. Through ritual elaboration, small and large, the most commonplace acts become deliberate and conscious activities. Special benedictions are recited upon rising, before sleeping, before and after eating, when hearing bad or good news, when seeing lightning or hearing thunder. The createdness of the universe is brought to consciousness again and again, with each ritual acknowledgment of the Almighty and that which he has made, or has made to happen. The performance of precepts thus ritualizes and invests with meaning activities that would otherwise be habituated, taken for granted, or considered trivial.

The performance of precepts also creates events of its own. Each week, month, year, and lifetime, there are special days which acquire their peculiar character through observance of an additional set of precepts prohibiting profane work and enjoining sacred work of specific kinds. About one out of every three or four days in the Jewish calendar is a special day. The variations and contrasts created during special days refreshes the performance of precepts in everyday life.

Hasidism arose in Eastern Europe during the eighteenth century, in part as a reaction against the scholasticism of traditional orthodoxy. As a popular, pietistic, and mystical movement, Hasidism emphasized the expression of devotion through ecstatic prayer, dance, song, narrative, and other means. Organized in the form of dynastic courts and guided by charismatic leaders, Hasidim evolved an elaborate "festival code," the central feature of which is the *rebes tish* (literally: the Hasidic rabbi's table), as described below. The festival code of the Hasidim of Bobov, a town in southern Poland, has been studied in detail by Epstein (1979).

The holiday of Purim as celebrated now among Hasidim in Brooklyn provides an especially rich case for examining the performance of precepts in

109

relation to the precepts of performance. In the fifth century B.C.E., the Jews of Persia were saved from a plot to murder them. Their deliverance, narrated in the Scroll of Esther, is celebrated each year on the holiday of Purim in the Jewish month of Adar (February/March). The major obligation on Purim is to make merry. In contrast with other holidays, Purim is subject to relatively few precepts, whether injunctions or prohibitions. As a result, there is considerable freedom in realizing the major prescription, which is to express joy.

Several activities are required by religious law – the fast of Esther on the day before Purim, the ritual reading of the story of Purim from a scroll, the exchanging of gifts, the gathering of alms, and the preparation of feasts. Other activities have evolved as local customs over long and short periods of time – for example, the folk drama which Yiddish-speaking Jews have performed since at least the sixteenth century (see Kirshenblatt-Gimblett 1980 for descriptions of Purim play performances in Eastern Europe), or the more recent custom of an American-style Purim parade. What is particularly noteworthy about the Purim celebrations among Hasidic groups in Brooklyn today is the broad range of forms they take, from masquerade to communal feast. In these activities, distinctly Hasidic precepts of performance may be discerned.

Purim celebrations take place in the home, in the *bes medresh*, and on the street, as well as in schools and other public spaces. The home, the female domain, is where the family gathers for the festival meal. The *bes medresh*, the male preserve, is the place where the *rebe* and his court assemble. The street is where men, women, and children of various Hasidic courts as well as other people mingle, as they shop, stroll, and go about their business. The central paradigm for celebrations in both domestic and public ritual spheres is the table: since the destruction of the Temple in Jerusalem two millenia ago, the home and *bes medresh* or synagogue have functioned as the sanctuary, the table as the altar, and the food upon it as offerings. The distinctive genre of Hasidic performance is the *tish*, or literally the "table," an event in the *bes medresh* where the *rebe* presides over his male followers around a table, at a communal and largely symbolic meal. The Purim entertainments – parodies, music, plays – are extensions of the *tish*. In contrast, the street is a public space that is heterogeneous, loosely structured, and often rather spontaneous; it is in the street that political protests and parades reach out to the larger neighborhood and borough, rather than to the family or Hasidic court, and it is in the street where the juxtaposition of familiar and festival is most strident. Performances by children, who often engage in miniaturized and temporally displaced celebrations of the holiday in school settings, and by women, who are essentially excluded from the *tish* but who may produce their own plays for a female audience, are also an important part of the holiday.

Adar 5742 (1982)/Brooklyn

During the two days of Purim, the streets of Williamsburg and Boro Park are transformed by the promenading of costumed figures and adults in festive clothing. Bobover men wear a *bekeshe* (kaftan made of a dressy silk or brocade), slipper-like shoes without laces, and calf-length pants tucked into white stockings. The women dress in stylish outfits, wigs, and hats. Small but revealing differences in dress distinguish the members of various Hasidic courts, and mark age, marital status, and stringency of adherence to Hasidic ideals. Children and young men dress up in costumes and masks.

Cars cruise blaring music and carrying costumed figures on their hoods or trunks. Shops are open, and many normal activities continue even as bears, clowns, walking alms boxes, and royalty stroll informally up and down the main streets of the community. The easy mix of normal holiday dress and fantastic masquerade allows the carnivalesque to permeate and "festivalize" the commonplace world of the street.

The costumes, worn only on Purim, intensify the hilarity of the occasion and allow children to act out the aspect of disguise in the Purim story itself – Esther succeeded in saving the Jews by disguising herself, and her Jewish identity in particular. As Epstein has noted, the Hasidic folk etymology for the name of Esther is the Hebrew root *hester*, which means "hidden." The costumes, assembled from Halloween supplies available at the local hardware stores and supplemented with homemade elements, articulate cultural categories through hyperbole and inversion. Children appear as heroes from history, as symbols of authority, or simply as adults. They appear also as the opposite of what it means to be *human*, *Jewish*, and *Hasidic*. Androgynous clowns, beasts, monsters, inanimate objects, non-Jews (such as cowboys with over-sized stetson hats, Blacks, Indians, Arabs, hippies, and bums), and non-Hasidim (such as seductive women and boys wearing denim jeans and tee-shirts) define core cultural categories by stating their opposite. The inversions reveal the careful and detailed observations which Hasidic children make of the world around them and provide a controlled opportunity for a vicarious experience of "otherness," an otherness which is a source both of attraction and repulsion.

The undirected wanderings of masked figures is coupled with the house visit. In keeping with a requirement of the holiday to exchange portions – that is, ready-to-eat food – children and men (the women are usually busy at home) hand deliver fruit, baked goods, nuts, candy, and wine. The foods may be placed in Easter baskets, special boxes, or on platters, and wrapped with colored cellophane. *Shalakh mones*, as the exchange of gifts is called, is an example of symmetrical reciprocity. Unlike the ideal of asymmetrical giving that governs the rest of Jewish life, giving on Purim is directly reciprocated. As Shuman (1982) points out, *shalakh mones* is, however, particularly complex. Since the foods that arrive as gifts are redistributed and since many of the foods were prepared in someone's kitchen, the kosherness of these foods depends upon knowing and trusting the purity of their source. Subtleties of social relations are played out in the course of the exchange, and much of the cooked food ends up in places of work following the holiday, where indiscriminate eaters may feast.

The wanderings and visits are punctuated during the afternoon of the first day of Purim by a political demonstration. In 1982, grotesquely costumed figures in Williamsburg beat cars with sticks to force them to stop. Having cleared a key intersection and in the midst of interested crowds, these figures created a street performance to protest the formation of a Jewish state before the arrival of the Messiah. Several ultra-conservative Hasidic men proceeded to hoist and ignite the Israeli flag to the mixed response of onlookers, many of whom were taken by surprise. Intoxication, a required part of the holiday, helped increase the intensity of singing and dancing that culminated the demonstration. As the flames died down, the crowds dispersed, and the informal wandering resumed. In 1977, a Jewish Defense League protest against President Gerald Ford's Middle East policy was expressed in Boro Park during Purim by burning Secretary of State Henry Kissinger in effigy – a highly appropriate Purim performance, since it has long been customary to substitute local and contemporary villains for Haman, the evil plotter in the Purim story, and to find symbolic means of destroying them. Dobkin (1979) describes how in a displaced persons center after World War II, Hitler was burnt in effigy as part of the Purim festivities.

Complementing this street activity are the formal rituals that take place in the *yeshive* (school), the *bes medresh* (house of study and prayer), and the home. On the eve and the morning of Purim, the scroll of Esther, or Megillah, is read aloud in public, before no less than ten adult males. Because Esther, the hero of the saga, is a female, women are required to hear every word of the story. The ritualized reading of the Megillah is a performance in its own right. Not only is a special kind of cantillation used, but also the text is to some degree dramatized. When the name of the villain Haman is mentioned, the sound of his name is killed by the noise of stomping feet which carry Haman's name in chalk on their soles, or by ratcheted *gragers* or other noisemakers. When the villains in the story are killed, the phrase stating this fact is uttered in one breath. In contrast, when good falls on the Jews, the congregation repeats the phrase. Short melodies may be inserted into the reading, and particular words are stressed. Those who cannot get to the *bes medresh* to hear the reading can conduct their own reading at home.

By far the most elaborated performance event, and this is unique to Hasidim, is the collective and symbolic feast, called the *tish* (literally "table"). Since the destruction of the Temple in Jerusalem, the Jewish home and synagogue (and by extension the *bes medresh*, especially for Hasidim) have become the sanctuary. The table is the altar. Food and prayer are the offerings. There are required domestic feasts, which in the Old Country were the occasion for folk dramas by wandering players. In addition, among Hasidim such as the Bobover, there are five "royal feasts" or *sudes melukhim*. Thousands of men crowd the *bes medresh*, which in contrast with a synagogue is a place where food, drink, and merriment are allowed. Segregated in their own section, women scramble to see the goings on in the men's area. The *rebe*, a charismatic religious leader, presides. Food is served in "golden" vessels, and the *rebe*, after a mere taste, passes the remnants, or *shirayim*, to his followers, for whom food touched by the *rebe* has been trans-valued and is sacred. Food is but a very small part of the feast, however, since everyone eats a meal prior to the *tish* and partakes of the *shirayim* not out of hunger, but out of the symbolic value of sharing the *rebe*'s leavings.

The most elaborated of the five Bobover *tishn* is the one that occurs at the end of the first day of Purim, and that extends into the morning of the second day, which is called Shushan Purim. This *tish* is a complex event extending over a ten-hour period from about seven in the evening until five the next morning. Consistent with Hasidic styles of worship and celebration, much time is given to warming up, and accordingly, among the Bobover, the activities are scheduled to take place late into the night. The first five hours or so consist of informal gathering, prayer, alms collecting, and later on, instrumental music. Susceptibility to intense religious experiences is enhanced by the fatigue, alcohol, the mesmerizing repetitiveness of song and dance, and the gradual build up of intensity.

Though the *tish* held during the night and early morning of Shushan Purim is distinguished by the performance of a folk drama, which itself lasts about four or five hours, the play occupies less than half of the total time and precedes the true peak of intensity which occurs after it is done. Following the play, the *rebe* distributes food, makes contact with individuals seeking his counsel and blessing, and leads singing and dancing. The moment the *rebe* prepares to leave, which happens suddenly, the event quickly winds down and the congregants return home.

The performance of a Purim-*shpil* is an old and continuous tradition among the Bobover Hasidim. The repertory consists of plays on Biblical themes, as well as plays based on stories of post-Biblical Jewish heroes, or Hasidic saints. In recent years, the Bobover have performed the Binding of Isaac, the story of Daniel and the fiery furnace, and the Golem of Prague, for example. The plays invariably work out of a consistent paradigm – there is a threat to Jewish survival. The Jews' faith is challenged. They are pressed to convert or assimilate, or they are threatened with physical annihilation. Through faith in God or through a divine miracle, the Jews are saved.

Shifra Epstein (1979) studied two such plays in the late 1970s. According to her account, young men in the community begin preparing the production about seven to ten days before the performance. There are four rehearsals. The script is assembled by committee, and may be old or new. *Yeshive* students do the necessary research for the script, finding appropriate materials. About a week before the performance, the script is typed, mimeographed, and distributed. The play is directed by a more experienced middle-aged man. During the afternoon of the performance, the stage is set up. It consists of a platform of tables, set in front of the Torah ark. The stage is about 12 feet by 6 feet in size. Backdrops are painted on kraft paper and rolled on dowels. The curtain consists of a sheet supported by tubing which is suspended from the ceiling. In recent years, electrical sound amplification and videotaping have been introduced.

During the afternoon of the performance, the *bes medresh* is prepared for the appearance of the *rebe* and performance of the Purim-*shpil*. The furniture is portable, makeshift, and easily shifted around to accommodate different needs as they arise. Rough hewn benches and tables are arranged to form bleachers for the men to stand on, provide tables for the *rebe* and his followers, and a stage for the players. The informality and robustness of the Bobover attitude to the *bes medresh* and its furnishings are consistent with a more general Hasidic value on sincerity and enthusiasm over formality and virtuosity. The *bes medresh*, free of many of the constraints of the synagogue, is thus the preferred setting for Hasidic worship, and preciousness or superficial aestheticism of any kind is generally eschewed, whether in architecture and furnishings or in the conduct of worship and celebration.

The physical arrangement provides important clues to the nature and meaning of the event. Just as the Purim-*shpil* is an extension of the communal meal, so too is the stage literally an extension of the table. Furthermore, the stage is positioned so that the players directly face the *rebe*. Whereas the *rebe* has the best view of the play, which is performed for his delight (*misameyakh zayn dem rebn*), congregants with the choicest seats have the best view of the *rebe*. This arrangement makes clear that the audience for the play is the *rebe*, whereas the performance for the congregants is, in the first instance, the *rebe's* response. Men seated close to the *rebe* include his sons and sons-in-law to his left, and the oldest men to his right. Unmarried men are seated or stand on the periphery. Women occupy their own section, behind a wall separating them from the men. Once, when crushed among hundreds of women struggling to catch a glimpse of the action in the men's section, I asked an older woman beside me if she could see the *rebe*. She answered, "From the expressions on the men's faces, I can see the reflection of the *rebe*." As a charismatic leader, the *rebe* is at the very center of Hasidic life: charismatic leadership is a hallmark of Hasidism. This is the source of the focus on him and his response to the Purim play.

The Purim performances during Adar 5742 (1982) were unusual and especially interesting. In an effort to raise money for charity, several Hasidim, many of them from Bobov, organized a large-scale Purim play performance, *The Golem of Prague*. To accommodate a large crowd, they rented the Felt Forum at Madison Square Garden. Because of the effort required for this event, the Bobover Hasidim did not produce a formal play in the *bes medresh* in 1982, but rather a series of skits, Purim *toyres* (parodies of sacred and liturgical texts), and music. The evening in the *bes medresh* was convened by the Bobover *badkhn* (folk jester), who filled the role of Purim *rov*, the parodic Purim rabbi for the day. He was dressed in a striped kaftan and tall white hat. After the skits, the tables were shoved to the side and the customary singing and dancing followed.

The Sunday after Purim, four to five thousand Hasidim filled Felt Forum to see *The Golem of Prague*, a folk drama unrelated to the classic play in the Yiddish theatre repertoire by H. Leivick. Drawing upon traditional legends, the play tells of how the Rabbi of Prague, who lived in the sixteenth century, saved the Jews from a blood libel – the Jews had been accused of killing Christian children and using their blood to make Passover matzas (unleavened bread). The Rabbi's method was to create a homunculous, a Frankenstein, called Yosele Golem. The live band usually found in the *bes medresh* was replaced in Felt Forum with a synthesizer that imitated orchestral instruments. The usual painted sets on brown paper were replaced with elaborately painted cloth drops. The usual white sheet hung from an improvized aluminium pipe was replaced by a red velvet curtain. But the structure of the play, the costuming of the characters, the declamatory acting style, the rhyming couplets, the preponderance of singing, the loose and slow pace, the informality of the audience (they talked, walked about, ate food they had brought with them), were quite consistent with performances I have seen in the *bes medresh* over the last ten years. We thus had an opportunity to see the small-scale Purim-*shpil* adapted to a formal theatrical context. As Brooks McNamara has pointed out, this occasion revealed Hasidic knowledge of nineteenth-century popular staging techniques and a complex layering of multiple performance traditions.

Though Hasidim have a long history of folk theatre, they have avoided contact with modern American television, film, and professional theatre. They are quite willing, however, to rent drops and costumes from a supplier to the trade, including masks from Star Wars, which appear in *The Golem of Prague* for supernatural figures, and to utilize sophisticated sound, lighting, and video technology. Many Hasidim are in the electronics business, a factor which may explain the use of an elaborate synthesizer for the music of *The Golem of Prague*, the rumor that the actors were prompted by means of walkie talkies, since they didn't have the time to learn their lines properly, and the number of spectators recording the event on videotape, film, and sound cassettes. Cassette recordings of Purim plays may be purchased in local groceries and book and record stores.

In other ways, the production at Felt Forum is closer to popular European and American staging during the late nineteenth and early twentieth centuries than to what is done in the theatre today: for example, the use of stock scenery, in particular painted scenic drops, and the mixture of rented and homemade costumes and properties. Practical solutions take precedence over stylistic consistency and historical precision: in the late 1970s, royalty in ancient times were dressed in costumes from the period of the American Revolution, apparently because such costumes were plentiful and inexpensive after the bicentennial celebrations. In *The Golem of Prague*, Jewish children in period dress are chased by "gentile" children in blue jeans, tee-shirts, and thick curly hair, the epitome of what is not Hasidic at the present time. Hasidic boys normally dress in white shirts and dark jackets and trousers, and wear their hair closely cropped. The result is a stylized and general, rather than historically accurate, sense of the period of the play: such eclecticism and anachronism are not simply a failure to achieve consistency, but rather serve to underscore the timeless and paradigmatic significance of the story. (See Epstein 1979 for a fuller discussion of this point.)

Stock characters do traditional bits of comic business, especially slapstick – a man takes a broom to bed, tries to sweep with it upside down, sweeps his feet, falls, breaks eggs, makes a mess and tries to clean it up. Actors deliver their rhyming couplets in a declamatory style, facing out to the audience, even though they are miked – some have large microphones strapped to their chests – and could be heard in a less frontal stance. The story is well known, and special pleasure is taken in the singing. Indeed, Hasidic Purim plays, and *The Golem of Prague* in particular, are more like operettas than dramas.[1]

The production at the Felt Forum was staged to raise money for charity. However, removed from the traditional context of the *tish* and situated in a building where men and women could not be as strictly separated as in the *bes medresh*, it was a source of some controversy in the community. It also stands in contrast to the plays produced by women to raise money for charity. In 1982 the women performed *My Fair Lady* and *Alice in Wonderland*, among others. On a proscenium stage in a school auditorium, girls and young women produce these amateur theatricals for a female audience, and unlike the men, they select their material from non-Jewish sources.

Hasidic precepts of performance

Among Hasidim, particularly as seen in Bobover Purim celebrations, an aesthetic of invocation takes precedence over an aesthetic of virtuosity, to utilize Armstrong's (1981) distinction. In traditions where virtuosity matters, the emphasis is upon *howness*, upon excellence within an autonomous internal system and upon mastery of execution. Where invocation is valued, the focus is on *whatness*, on investment by external power and enrichment through prayer and tribute. Consistent with the aesthetics of invocation, the Purim-*shpil* is not an end in itself; it is performed to gladden the heart of the *rebe*. As noted above, the audience for the play is the *rebe*, whereas the performance for the congregants is the *rebe*'s response. Accordingly, the play is dedicated not to the validation of itself, but to the validation of the social and cosmic order of the congregants; the effort is communal, rather than individualistic. What we see in Hasidic precepts of performance is a studied effort to suppress the aesthetics of virtuosity. (Hasidim reject the professional cantor and the formal concert-style service found in other Jewish communities, for example. They prefer a more participatory style of worship.) Actors are not trained. Less than two weeks are allowed for preparation. Old material is presented, reworked, or incorporated into new plays. Aspects of the performance itself may be unpolished. The mechanics of the production may not be fully under control – occasionally a performer will read directly from a script; the sound and lighting may malfunction; backstage activity may be heard or seen; considerable time may elapse between scenes. The audience is also informal – people walk around, chat, eat, drink, and smoke. There is much scrambling for space, and most people stand precariously on benches, crowded together for hours in the hot *bes medresh*.

To an outsider accustomed to the production values of contemporary professional theatre, the Hasidic efforts appear amateurish. However, the looseness of the Hasidic performances, which does not stop the crowd from thoroughly enjoying events, is not a failure to meet professional standards, but rather an expression of different performance values. Sincerity, enthusiasm, and depth of feeling are more important than artistic excellence. There is virtuosity within their aesthetic of invocation, but it is a virtuosity of cultural knowledge transposed from contexts of study and discourse, rather than a virtuosity of theatrical polish.

The power of Purim performance among Hasidim resides in the invocation of their paradigmatic quality, rather than in their virtuosic aspect. These are truly cultural performances, in the sense suggested by Singer (1972: 67–80), where the community invokes, hyperbolizes, and inverts categories and values through a multiplicity of performance modes. While Purim masqueraders display to the community who they are by articulating who they are not, the folk plays present repeated instances of the paradigm of survival in the face of physical and spiritual threat. Each large-scale communal meal, a hyperbolization of the family feast, invokes and affirms the idea that the community is a large family, and is testimony to its continuity. These themes are vibrant in the lives of people who, as survivors of the Holocaust, have met the greatest test of their faith.

Notes
1. For documentation of three different productions of *The Golem of Prague* mounted in New York City during the spring of 1982, including the Hasidic one at Felt Forum, see Ashley 1982.

7.

The significance of performance for its audience: an analysis of three Sri Lankan rituals

RANJINI OBEYESEKERE

Performances of Theravada Buddhist Sri Lanka cover a spectrum ranging from ritual to theatre, usually associated with different levels and stages of social organization (tribal, agrarian, industrial). All, however, are performed in present day Sri Lanka and it is not uncommon for the same individual to participate in all of them. An analysis of these three types of performances and their interrelationships may provide insights into the nature of their significance for their audience/participants and help extend present definitions of such relationships. The three performances are: a *pirit* ceremony; a *Sanni Yakuma ritual*; and a theatre piece called *Maname*.

A pirit ceremony

This is a Theravada Buddhist ritual, one of the few major ritual performances associated with the "higher" religion (as distinct from the folk Buddhist rituals) and where the performers are Buddhist monks. The ceremony consists of monks reciting specific Buddhist texts in Pali, as protection against sickness, disease, demonic afflictions, and evil planetary influences. The magical transference occurs by an "act of truth" or *satyakriya*. The truth of the statements uttered by the monks is believed to generate a power that has a beneficial, protective, prophylactic effect. The performance is serious, sacred, largely non-dramatic and has very little element of play in it.

In his study of the Sinhala theatre, Sarachchandra (1966) claims that Buddhism (he is here referring to the Sri Lankan brand), because it was anti-ritualistic, largely non-congregational, and had hardly any prescribed ritual for lay life, gave little scope for the growth of theatre. Painting and sculpture, by contrast, attained great heights of sophistication in Buddhist Sri Lanka and this he attributes to the fact that they were essentially individual and private, not social arts. Early Buddhist missionaries realizing the mass need for external or supernatural supports to cope with the vicissitudes of daily life, allowed folk rituals to exist side by side with Buddhism. Over time, a large number of Hindu gods and Hindu practices were incorporated into these rituals. Many underwent varying degrees of transformation under the impact of Buddhism but all were integrated over time, into an elaborately formulated, Buddhist framework. Gods and demons thus became part of a highly structured pantheon in which they were made subservient to the Buddha and derived whatever power they wielded from him, through a system of *varan* (warrants) (G. Obeyesekere 1963).

Thus while it was quite acceptable for a Sinhala Buddhist to practise or participate in any form of *deva* worship or demon propitiation, there was an equally fundamental assumption that a Buddhist's path to salvation, the achievement of Nirvana, had nothing to do with all this. For that reason a Buddhist monk, the symbol of that other-worldly quest, was expected to keep aloof from such magical or exorcistic practices and involvements.

It is when seen against this background that the *pirit* ceremony becomes significant. *Pirit* is perhaps the only Buddhist ritual, magical in its function, which is officially performed by Buddhist monks. It is also accepted by both monks and laymen as an integral part of Thervada Buddhist practice. Participating in a *pirit* ceremony is clearly seen as an "act of merit" a *punya karma*. No other folk ritual or exorcistic ceremony, however integrated into the Buddhist framework, is seen in these terms. All such other ceremonies and rituals are seen as being performed to achieve cures, personal advancement, or for succour in the day-to-day crises of living. They are not "merit-bearing."

The Sinhala word *pirit* comes from the Pali word *paritta* meaning protection, originally a broadly generic term denoting protective charms, palliatives or amulets. Thus a *paritta valika* referred to sand worn as an amulet on the head and a *paritta suttaka* was a magical thread worn for protection (Rhys Davids and Stede 1923). In early Buddhism, certain texts became associated with a similar function and came to be known as *parittas*, and were recited for protection against sickness and demonic plagues. There are six such *parittas* referred to in a first century Buddhist text *The Milinda Prasna*, which indicates that the practice of reciting Buddhist texts (suttas) as *parittas* was prevalent among Buddhists as far back as then. Those six texts together with several others, are now recited by monks in a special ritual performance called a *pirit* ceremony.

In the words of Rhys Davids (1921), Buddhism seems to have been "Compelled to adopt and then adapt, in the *parittas* the *raksha mantras* (demon exorcistic formulas) dear to its converts." Rhys Davids adds, however, that "These guarding runes are not alien to Buddhist doctrine [. . .] the agencies whose power to harm are deprecated, are not, as in other cults, cursed and anathematised, but are blessed with good wishes and suffused with outgoing love" (1921: 186). J.J. Jones (1949) similarly in a note on a reference to *pirit* in his translation of the *Mahavastu* (a Buddhist Sanskrit text), claims that they were not "formules d'exorcisme" but rather that their intention was to confute popular belief in the worth of omens, spells, and charms. Jones refers to the *Mahamangala Jataka* in which the Bodhisatta is asked to define what constitutes things of good omen and replies, contradicting the popular notions of good luck, by giving instead a list of moral qualities the possession of which alone can confer blessings on men.

While it is true of the content of the texts, there is definitely another level at which participants in a *pirit* ceremony regard *pirit* as having a magical, protective, prophylactic, if not curative power. It is interesting that the very earliest reference to *pirit* which occurs in the Milinda Prasna, focuses squarely on this fundamental contradiction between the tenets of Buddhism, as a religion of individual salvation achieved through one's own actions (karma), and the magical protective power of *pirit*. The Bactrian King Milinda (Menander) questions the elder Nagasena thus:

> If, Nagasena, a man can escape death's snare neither by going to heaven, nor by going to the summits of lofty palaces, nor to the caves or grottos or declevities or clefts or holes in the mountains, then is the *pirit* ceremony useless. But if by it there is a way of escape from death, then the statement in the verse I quoted is false.

Nagasena replies:

> The Blessed One, O King, said the verse you have quoted and he sanctioned *pirit*. But that is only meant for those who have some portion of their life yet to run, who are full of life and restrain themselves from the evils of *kamma*. There is no ceremony or artificial means for prolonging the life of one whose alloted span of existence has come to an end. . . .

Nagasena goes on to compare it with medicine given to a sick, not a dying man. When the King asks whether *pirit* is a protection for everybody, he replies "To some not others" and concludes with the remark, "*Pirit* which is a protection to beings, loses its protecting power by acts done by those beings themselves" (Milinda Prasna IV: 2, 19). Nagasena thus frames it firmly within the orthodox Buddhist doctrine of responsibility for one's own salvation. We know from this early reference in a much venerated and oft quoted text, that historically, *pirit* has long been an accepted part of Buddhist practice.

The origin myth of *pirit* clearly stresses the magical and protective properties of the ritual. The city of Vaisali was devastated by demonic plagues and pestilences. The Liccavis, a powerful tribal group, whose capital it was, went to the Buddha and requested that he visit Vaisali and rid it of its plague. The *Mahavastu* version states that "When the Exalted One had crossed the Ganges he came to the frontiers of Vaisali and caused the demons of the plague to flee" (Jones 1949: 224). In other versions he is supposed to have circumambulated the city, reciting the *Ratana Sutta*, a text which exalts the Buddha, the Dhamma (the Doctrine) and the Sangha (the Order), and exhorts all beings, gods, and demons, to show love to humans. In yet others he is said to have sent his disciple Ananda to recite the *Ratana Sutta* and lustrate the city with holy water.

The present day *pirit* ceremony consists of the recital of the *parittas* or selected texts that have a protective power, the distributing of holy water at the end of the ceremony to the participants and the tying of a *pirit nul* or protective thread on the arm of the participants.

One of the *paritta* texts, the *Atanatiya Sutta*, has a fascinating content. In it the demon king Vessamuni, accompanied by his hosts, comes up to the Buddha and tells him that, since there are demons and evil spirits who do not look kindly on him and his teachings, and since his disciples often inhabit lonely places far from human habitation, they are likely to be subjected to harassment by demons and evil spirits. He thus suggests that the Buddha should teach his disciples a protective *mantra*, to be recited in a loud tone. The Buddha makes no comment. Vessamuni, interpreting the Buddha's silence as acquiesence, goes on to recite the *mantra* which is, interestingly enough, no more than a recapitulation of the names and the powers of the many past Buddhas. The Buddha in turn recounts the entire incident to his disciples, including the *mantra* recited by Vessamuni. This is the content of the *Atanatiya paritta*. However, since most lay Buddhists do not understand Pali, the popular belief is that this text is about "driving away demons." The belief is further strengthened by the fact that this particular text is recited with a great deal of rhetorical flourish and volume. It is the only point at which the *pirit* ceremony becomes even mildly dramatic.

The occasion for a *pirit* ceremony can be any event or crisis in the life of the individual or of a group. Paul Wirz, writing in 1954, says "A *pirit* ceremony may be performed for all kinds of reasons: on account of an illness, at a wedding, when one has built a new house, when a *dagoba* or temple is erected, when a baby takes his first solid food and on any other occasion." The scale, too, varies from the simple ceremony in a village home, with three or four monks, to the large scale performances held today in institutions like banks, schools, government departments. What is important, however, is that while it is a sacred, religious ritual, it is not obligatory as are the cyclical agrarian, and tribal initiation rituals. *Pirit* is completely optional, both in terms of timing and in terms of the choice of occasion.

Often in the case of rituals associated with the agrarian cycle, or exorcistic rituals against demonic effects, not performing the ritual is believed to bring dire evil consequences. This is not so in the case of *pirit*. Its power is only protective. Thus, while its performance can be beneficial, not performing it does not necessarily aggravate the present illness or misfortune as is the case with exorcistic rites. At least this is how the participants perceive it. Perhaps this non-obligatory aspect of the ritual is yet another reflection of the Buddhist Theravada doctrinal position that rituals – even a ritual like *pirit* which has had such longstanding sanction – are fundamentally extraneous to the individual's quest for salvation.

The *pirit* ceremony is simple and non-dramatic. Several monks (the number varies with the scale of the performance) are led in a procession from the nearest temple to where the ceremony is to be held. When the procession arrives the monks enter a specially prepared area called a *pirit kotuva* (protected square). This area could be a room in the house or a specially constructed space enclosed on three sides, lined with white cloth and decorated with coconut and areca flowers. The monks seat themselves on the three sides within the protected area facing the audience/participants who sit immediately outside it. A white three-ply thread, one end of which is tied to the relic casket, is threaded around the sacred area, passed to the seated monks who each hold a section of it, then extended outside and passed from hand to hand among the participants. The outermost end of it is held by the patient or the chief lay sponsor of the ceremony. The monks begin chanting the *suttas* (texts) and go on for about an hour. Then all except four monks, or sometimes two, leave the sacred area. From this point till dawn, four monks at a time, take turns to chant the *parittas*. Around 6 a.m. the full contingent of monks gather once again in the sacred area for the final chanting. When the ceremony is over, holy water (water which has been placed in a clay pot within the protected area for the duration of the chanting) is given to the participants to drink, and the sacred thread is broken up into small pieces and tied around the hands or necks of the participants.

While the *pirit* ceremony is a "sacred" ritual performance, it is not a "rite de passage." Even if one were to extend the definition to this ceremony by claiming that it does have the elements of separation, inclusion, and the change in ritual status that characterize such rituals there is definitely no transitional phase. The liminal, in-between period so crucial to "rites de passage," involving ludic events, ambiguity, disorder, inversion, reversal, or bizarre behavior described by Victor Turner (1982), is completely absent in the *pirit* performance.

In *pirit* the participant audience does move from an exposed to a protected state, but not by passing through a transitional liminal stage. It is as if the monk performers, separated into a sacred space and time, by the cumulative effect of their continuous chanting, create a kind of magical envélope or sheath that emanates out of the sacred space and extends to the outer area of lay participants, incorporating both into a new, protected, blessed state. Even evil and demonic forces in the environment are included into this "blessed" state, and their malignancy thereby countered. Perhaps the elimination of the transitional phase in the *pirit* ceremony is made possible because the kind of transformation that takes place in the movement from one status to another is not an internal individual transformation, but an external, one might almost say environmental, one. The power of the utterance causes the transformation of the environment, the world around the individual, and consequently, the individual or the group. In that sense the transformation is the result of a force outside the individual. The liminal phase, I believe, is essential in rituals where the movement from one state to another involves an internal, psychological, transformation in the individual or group.

Let us now turn again to the fundamental contradiction that lies at the heart of the Buddhist ritual of *pirit*. The Buddha on the one hand, in specific texts such as the *Brahmajala Sutta*, categorically rejected the use of charms, spells, magic, astrology, etc. Yet it is claimed by no less an authority than Nagasena, that he "sanctioned" the use of *pirit* to ward off disease, evil spirits, or evil planetary influences.

An interesting comparison can be made with the Sherpa offering rituals which Sherry Ortner describes (1978). Ortner sees offering rituals as an attempt to deal with a fundamental contradiction between Sherpa religion which stresses other-worldly goals and ultimate salvation, and the Sherpa social values which stress mutual cooperation and the efficacy of hospitality in eliciting this cooperation. Ortner suggests that the offering rituals resolve the dilemma by integrating gods into the social pattern of hospitality, and associates these patterns with the accomplishment of cosmic religious ends.

The same resolution is suggested by the performance of *pirit*. Human beings feel a need for external support at times of crisis, a need satisfied by using Buddhist texts to perform a quasi-magical protective function. However, since the content of the texts is a statement of Buddhist values, the performance of the ritual then becomes more than a mere magical perform- ance. It becomes an "act of merit," a *punya karma*, which takes the performer a step further along the path to salvation. Participation in a *pirit* ceremony provides protection and blessings in terms of "this worldly" goals, and by the accumulation of "merit" aids the individual in his quest for salvation. Just as the Sherpa offering rituals help, according to Ortner, "redifine the other- worldly religion in terms of human social values and sanctify social values of hospitality normally condemned by the religion," so the *pirit* ceremony sanctifies a type of protective ritual otherwise condemned, and integrates it with the religious goal of individual salvation. The compromise is not between religious and social values as in the Sherpa case, but between religious values that clearly put the burden of salvation on the individual, and a pragmatic recognition of the human, psychological need for external or supernatural support in times of crisis.

Hanson (1981), in a critique of Ortner, claims that her analysis of the relation between ritual and social life as being "consequential," is a functional analysis, commonly made but incorrect. He argues that if rituals solve problems, then at some point the problem would cease to exist and the ritual become unnecessary. Therefore, Hanson suggests, the relation between ritual and social life is "semiotic," not consequential. He describes semiotic relationships as one of the ways in which cultural constructions of reality are communicated to people, enabling them to understand their world and hence operate in it.

This is certainly so in the case of *pirit* which is a cultural construct, a performance that reconciles the psychological needs of the masses with the Buddhist doctrinal position. There are, however, limits placed even on such attempted reconciliations. Nagasena's statement that, "*Pirit*, which is a protection to beings, loses its protecting power by acts done by those beings themselves," (1963: 218) clearly defines those limits. Such limitations are revealed also in the Sinhala Buddhist's attitude towards *pirit*. While performances of *pirit* are very popular and often performed, and Sri Lankan Buddhists all believe in its protective power and beneficial effects in general, they rarely expect it to achieve magical cures or immediate solutions to specific problems. If a Sri Lankan Buddhist were to perform a ritual to god Kataragama or an exorcistic ceremony to the *Sanni* demons, he would expect, and in fact claim to have obtained, specific results and solutions to problems. There is a difference in his perception of the efficacy of *pirit*. What the ceremony does achieve is that it generates a certain sense of security and reconciles a psychological need with the doctrinal position. I would therefore agree with Hanson that such a ritual solution is "not a cause before which the problem retreats as a consequence, but a message which declares that in some contexts at least, the problem is not a problem at all" (Hanson 1981: 178). However, in so far as the ritual itself is a symbolic construct created in order to take cognizance of, and give expression to, the need for such a reconcilation, it might also be termed functional.

A Sanni Yakuma

This is an exorcistic ritual that propitiates and drives out the *Sanni* demons. As G. Obeyesekere has pointed out, like all other exorcistic and propitiatory rituals in Sri Lanka, they are considered definitely a part of "folk" or "Sinhalese" Buddhism (1963), and are clearly distinguished from performances such as *pirit* which is associated with the higher religion. The performers of exorcistic rituals are lay priests or shamans. The performance is colorful, dramatic, with a strong element of the comic and ludic. Buddhist monks neither perform nor participate in such rituals. The *Sanni Yakuma* is in many ways similar to exorcistic rituals that have been studied cross-culturally by anthropologists. Both the shaman performers and the patient, and the participant/audience, see them as having a specific curative as well as protective function.

There are several detailed descriptions of this ritual in the ethnographic literature (Wirz 1954; Sarachchandra 1966; Obeyesekere 1969; Kapferer 1975, 1979, 1983). Its three part structure of separation, transitional liminality, and inclusion or reaggregation, has been analyzed in structural functional terms by Obeyesekere and Kapferer.

The first part, or the performances of the evening watch, consist of rituals that sanctify and demarcate the ritual arena; sanctify and consecrate the priests or shamans; and by means of invocations bring the gods and demons into the sacred area to accept the offerings of humans.

The second or liminal stage of the performance occurs when, during the rituals of the midnight watch, the *Sanni* demons make a dramatic appearance in masks and costumes and dance in a frenzy to the accompaniment of drums. Towards the early hours of the morning or the dawn watch, comic ritual enactments take place. The terrifying demon apparitions that danced frenziedly in the sacred area are now presented as comic figures, ridiculed, humiliated, forced to cajole, coax and bribe the guardian deities who bar them from entering the city. This second stage of the performance thus has all the elements associated with liminality – reversals, transformations, topsy-turvy transitional states, and the comic ludic performances of sacred play.

During the final stage of the ritual, a chastened *Kola Sanniya* (originally a non-Buddhist, non-believing, alien demon) obtains permission from the Buddha, agrees to accept the offerings made by humans and desist from troubling them, and is allowed to enter the city. The comic drama enacts the symbolic inclusion of *Kola Sanniya* in the formal Buddhist pantheon where he is given a status (though lowly) in the hierarchical system (G. Obeyesekere 1969).

The *Sanni Yakuma* has been brilliantly analyzed by Kapferer (1979) in terms of the "dynamic of the transformation of the participant or patient," (1979: 128) and the processes relating to the "construction, negation, and reconstruction of the Self" (1979: 127). Kapferer sees the rituals of the first part as a "re-representation" of the negation of the patients social Self, where the patient, the victim of demonic attack "is separated from the "Other" and absorbed into a demonic reality as this is understood to be conceived by the patient" (1979: 124). The patient thus becomes isolated and consumed in a demonic hell, as manifested in trance-like behavior and lapses of consciousness. In the heightened sequences of music and dance of the midnight watch, Kapferer sees the participant audience, hitherto only marginally involved in the ritual performance, now focus directly on the action and become drawn into the patient's world.

In the later sequences of dramatic enactment, mime and comic dialogue, Kapferer sees a reversal of this process leading to a movement towards a reconstruction of the Self in culturally typified terms. "The comic treatment of the demons, the ridicule, humiliation and insults they are subjected to, reduce them to their legitimate position as subordinate to deities and to human beings." This is how they are seen by the "normal healthy Other" and how they should be conceived of by the patient. The patients participation in the comic laughter Kapferer sees as an indication that the patient has "entered in a We-relationship with the audience and effectively taken on the attitude of the Other, which is part of being himself" (1979: 127).

While this analysis offers insights into the process of transformation taking place in the patient, Kapferer's identification of the rest of the ritual audience as the "Other" tends to imply to it a homogenity that is not warranted. The audience in a *Sanni Yakuma* is in fact composed of participants whose degree of involvement or participation varies greatly. The patient is completely involved, though sometimes involuntarily, in the ritual performance. Similarly, the immediate family and kin group comprise an equally involved participant audience. There is another category of visitors, outsiders, sometimes even passersby, however, for whom the performance is a spectacle, to be enjoyed as entertainment.

Whether the *Sanni Yakuma* is analyzed as a "rite de passage" in which a transformation of status and identity occurs and an alien supernatural is included in a Buddhist framework or whether it is analyzed in terms of the dynamic of transformation of the patient's perception of the Self, what is interesting is that such transformations occur through rituals that involve performances of an essentially liminal nature. In the case of the *pirit* performance, however, the transformation of status of the participant/audience from an unprotected to a protected state, takes place without the mediation of transitional, liminal rituals. In *pirit* this liminal, transitional stage is not developed, and one might even say it is suppressed. What heightens the contrast is that the origin myth of the *pirit* and the origin myth of the *Sanni Yaka* deal basically with the same set of mythic events. The contrasting ways in which the two rituals *perform* that myth are therefore illuminating.

In the origin myth of the demon *Kola Sanniya*, he is the son of the King and the Queen of the Liccavis who rule the city of Vaisala. The king suspects his wife of adultery and orders her tortured and killed, At the moment of execution she gives birth, and her offspring, *Kola Sanniya* grows up "feeding on his mother's corpse." He vows vengeance on his father and sets about destroying the city of Vaisala with the help of eighteen demons he creates. One text describes it as follows:

> "Thousands daily they killed and ate
> The stench of the corpses spread far and wide
> Hosts of *pretas* invaded the city of Visal
> Pestilence spread."

The Liccavis came to the Buddha for help.

> "The Lord of the World compassionately
> Summoned his disciples and told them
> 'When you take *pirit* water to Visal
> The power of the demons will be quelled.' "

The text ends with a specific reference to the
  pirit ritual.

> "The people conducted them (The Buddha and his
>   disciples) with great pomp
> To the city of Visal;

Pirit was recited from the Jewelled Sutta (the
    Ratana Sutta)
Fear struck the minds of the demons.
Today too by the power of the *pirit*
We'll banish demons, the diseases of the
    patient
We'll banish from their roots.
We'll give him long life, protection,
Power and youthfulness."

(G. Obeyesekere 1963).

Thus, although both *Pirit* and the *Sanni Yakuma* set out to achieve the same ends – protection against demonic influences and the cure for such illnesses, their performances differ radically.

In the *pirit* performance the monks recreate the incident of the cleansing of the city of Vaisala of demonic plague, by *reciting* the texts supposedly chanted by the Buddha on that occasion. They do not retell or reenact the myth. In fact, anything that might lend itself to a dramatic presentation or even a dramatized reading seems to be submerged by the monotonous manner in which the text is rendered. Chanting diffuses any inherent dramatic quality in the text; in that dialogue, commentary, and descriptions are made totally indistinguishable and are in no way marked even by tonal variations. The *Atanatiya Sutta* is the only text that is rendered rhetorically, in loud tones. But here, too, the entire text is chanted without distinction between passages of commentary and dialogue. In consequence, any intrinsic dramatic possibilities do not surface.

Paul Wirz, in his description of a *pirit* ceremony (1954), makes a fascinating reference to the recital of what he terms the *Atmidima Sutta* by

Four monks who distribute the following roles among themselves: 1. Buddhu hamuduruvo (Gautama Buddha); 2. Mahasut Hamuduruvo (Buddha's cousin and deputy) 3. Ananda mahaterun vahanse (Buddha's disciple); 4. Vessamuni rajjuruvo (the Buddha's antagonist).

Wirz goes on to say

The four persons enter into a dispute in which the first named ones try to conquer and defeat Vessamuni rajjuruvo. But the demon offers strenuous resistance. The argument grows more and more passionate, each one tries to convince the other and to prove his tenent against that of the opponent. Towards daybreak the discussion reaches its climax but it of course terminates in a complete victory for Buddha and his dogma while his adversary is beaten and makes his retreat. (1954: 193)

What is interesting about this account is that Wirz is obviously quoting a lay informant's account of what *he perceived* to be happening during the recital of the *Atanatiya Sutta* at the climax of the *pirit* ceremony. It is not an accurate version of the content of the Pali text that is recited. Four monks do chant alternate lines but the text nowhere refers to four characters, nor do the monks take on "roles" as Wirz describes. Vessamuni, the demon king, does appear in the text, but the passionate confrontation with the Buddha that Wirz describes is entirely an imaginative construct, conjured up in the mind of the listener, who, like most lay Buddhists, is ignorant of Pali. It is also likely that Wirz's informant, familiar with the folk ritual enactment of the confrontation between the demon king and the guardian deities, performed in the *Sanni Yakuma*, assumed that in the rhetorical rendering of the *Atanatiya Sutta*, such a confrontation was in fact taking place. The simple fact is that there is no Pali sutta called the *Atmidima Sutta* in the *Book of Pirit* (Pirit Pota). *Atmidima* is a Sinhala not a Pali word. Wirz's informant's interpretation is not surprising or unusual because even today many lay Buddhists (I, too, until I read the Pali in translation during the course of writing this paper) believe that the *Atanatiya Sutta* which is recited at the climax of the *pirit* ceremony, is a confrontation and victory over the demon forces. The Pali text, however, merely recounts a somewhat amicable encounter between the Buddha and the demon king!

Wirz's description is particularly interesting in that it both suggests the dramatic possibilities inherent in the *pirit* performance, as well as the lay audiences *perception* of such dramatic qualities even where they do not exist. We are also made aware of the degree to which the *pirit* performance has in fact eschewed all such dramatic possibilities. This is further emphasized when contrasted with the demon exorcistic rituals where, in the performances of the liminal phase when the demons appear in the ritual arena, normal operations of the ordered universe are temporarily suspended, controls are lifted, reversals occur, excess is legitimized, and comedy, obscenity, and sensuality are given full play. Any such liminal performance in a *pirit* ceremony would completely undermine Theravada Buddhist doctrine, which advocates awareness, vigilance, and control of the senses. Therefore, while the practice of a protective ritual developed and was accepted as an orthodox Buddhist ritual, the dramatic, ludic, liminal aspects of the performance seem to have been kept to a minimum.

Had the ritual developed according to the inner dynamics of the liminal phase, the inherent contradiction between "magical" practices and Buddhist doctrine which is now resolved through the present manner of the performance would have been exacerbated. This is perhaps why the central core of the performance has remained for over a thousand years, a recital of texts, without developing any performative aspects. It is also perhaps the reason why Theravada Buddhist monks can still officially "perform" a *pirit* ceremony as a part of their religious functions.

Exorcistic rituals like the *Sanni Yakuma* must have had their roots in pre-Buddhist cults. Early Buddhism either absorbed and incorporated such beliefs as Mahayanism did, or integrated them through a strictly defined hierarchical machinery into the Buddhist framework as the Theravadins in Sri Lanka did. The origin myth of the *Kola Sanniya* which links it to the Buddhist story of the cleansing of the city of Vaisala, was no doubt such an attempt at inclusion. In the ritual performance of the *Sanni Yakuma* the myth is given "a local habitation and a name" and its dramatic potential fully exploited.

Richard Schechner, in his *Essays on Performance Theory* (1977), suggests that the basic opposition is not between ritual and theatre but between "efficacy and entertainment." He sees theatre history as a continual oscillation in which these oppositions of efficacy and entertainment interweave, coming together and drawing apart at different points in time. Ritual tends towards efficacy and theatre towards entertainment, but innumerable combinations of the two also occur in different types of theatre performances. The two performances we have compared suggest that this is also true of ritual. However, the assumed correlation between the degree of seriousness or sacredness of a ritual and its degree of efficacy, is not always correct. The *pirit* performance is a very serious, sacred, ritual with hardly an element of entertainment. But its efficacy too is limited. By contrast, the exorcistic ceremonies of the *Sanni Yakuma* are both highly effective and very entertaining.

Maname

This is a modern theatrical performance written and produced by E. R. Sarachchandra and intended purely as a form of secular entertainment. Its plot, however, is based on a story that is part of popular Buddhist culture. Techniques and movements drawn from exorcistic ritual performances are used and the dialogue is sung or chanted by the characters. It was perhaps no accident that the chief drummer who collaborated with Sarachchandra in training the actors for the original performance, was in fact a very famous shaman from the South of Sri Lanka.

Sarachchandra succeeded in synthesizing these elements into the creation of a modern theatre piece. *Maname* was instantly successful. It has been playing now for over twenty-five years and still draws capacity crowds of urbanites, villagers, professionals, businessmen, and students. Its wide appeal is no doubt because of its closeness to the familiar ritual performances. Perhaps also the fact that exorcistic rituals, especially the elaborately developed (and therefore more entertaining) kinds, are becoming inordinately expensive, hard to organize, and less frequently performed makes the spectator element that we recognized in the ritual audience, turn increasingly to the modern Sinhala theatre. This I think accounts for the increasing popularity of such "liminoid" genres such as *Maname* in present day Sri Lanka.

In analyzing ritual performances, we tend to assume that all ritual audiences are necessarily also "participant" audiences. This is often so in the case of obligatory rituals such as tribal initiation rites or agrarian fertility rituals. From the rituals discussed we have seen that it is not an assumption one can make about all ritual audiences. In a *Sanni Yakuma*, for example, there are not only the two categories of performer and participant but different kinds of participants and different degrees of participation. The shaman and his assistants are the performers. The patient for whom the ritual is being performed is one category of participant and s/he may in the course of the ritual become also a performer. The immediate family of the patient, kinsmen, and helpers are yet another category, whose involvement is in some instances even more intense than that of the patient, since its effectiveness is crucially important to them. Unlike the patient they do not actively perform in the ritual arena, but their back-stage participation and emotional involvement is great. For them the ritual is a serious/sacred performance, entirely obligatory. There is in addition a third category of "visitors" and onlookers who are spectators very much in the sense of theatre audiences. They come to enjoy the performance, sit around, gossip, laugh, are involved in the dramatic action as theatre audiences are, and often leave when they have had enough. They are not participants in the sense in which members of a Catholic congregation are participants in a mass, or even in the sense of being a participant in a *pirit* ceremony. They are indeed spectators, no different from the audience who see Sarachchandra's plays.

Thus, just as performances can be analyzed in terms of efficacy and entertainment and varying combinations of these oppositions can occur in performances ranging from ritual to theatre, so audiences can also range between the categories of participant and spectator. Any performance can call forth one or the other, or varying combinations of these two categories. We would define participants as those involved chiefly in the efficacy of the performance, spectators as those interested in the entertainment aspects. The *pirit* ceremony thus has participants and no spectators, a play like *Maname* has only spectators. Exorcistic rituals which have highly complex and elaborately liminal performances, which are entertaining as well as efficacious, have categories of both participants and spectators, for whom the significance and meaning of the performance must necessarily be different. This is perhaps why present day Sri Lankans can, without any feelings of disjunction, be participants/spectators in any one or all of the different types of performances discussed.

8.

What does it mean to "become the character": power, presence, and transcendence in Asian in-body disciplines of practice

PHILLIP B. ZARRILLI

Hearing an Asian actor say that in performance he "becomes the character" is a response very like what a Western actor might say. But in spite of the similarity, I've long been bothered by the fact that there has been little discussion in the literature of exactly what the Asian actor means. For the Indian kathakali or Japanese noh actor, "becoming the character" is a statement which epitomizes (1) the lifelong process of training and (2) the immediate psychophysical process of engaging in performing (doing) the acts which constitute a performance on any given occasion. The entire disciplined path is a gradual interweaving of external techniques and internal processes.

Over the past seven years I have been studying, practicing, and researching various "in-body" disciplines of Asian meditational, martial, and performing arts. These disciplines share many assumptions, principles, and details of practice.[1] Primary is the fact that daily repetition of physical exercises and/or performance techniques encodes the techniques *in the body*. By daily practice all physical and mental obstacles in the way of correct practice are gradually eliminated. The goal of all such virtuosic systems is reaching a state of "accomplishment" (Skt., *siddhi*) in which the doer and done are one. Through such actualized practice comes both control and transcendence of "self."

Most Westerners, in their initial encounter with Asian masters of in-body disciplines are so overwhelmed by the sheer virtuosity of technique, the fluidity of practice, and the powerful presence of the performer that both "what" that virtuosity is and "how" the performer achieves that state is left unexplored. For example, when I first saw a practitioner of Kerala, India's martial art, kalarippayattu, leap twelve feet into the air in a jumping kick and strike a ball suspended from the ceiling, the impressive "gymnastic" virtuosity hid the fact that the act itself is much much more than a virtuosic display. The world of gymnastics assumes as its ideal a "ten" which is devoid of overt cosmological, religious, ethical, and/or social assumptions. However, for the traditional practitioner of kalarippayattu or other Asian martial arts, each act in each moment resonates with psychospiritual implications in personal, social, and cosmological spheres of being.

The same is true for many traditional performing arts and artists. A kathakali actor for example says, *"Natan kathapathravumayi tadatmyam prapikanam,"* or "The actor becomes one with the character." Similarly the noh actor is engaged in a process of "becoming" as well (Masakazu 1984: xli–xlv). While from these statements it may appear that the Asian actor is simply "playing a character," it soon becomes clear that the act of performance itself is often highly charged with a pregnant set of assumptions. If one is persistent in questioning the practitioner about what it is that he "does" when practicing his art, what it means "to become," he is likely to respond that he is absorbed in performing (doing) psychophysical acts which totally engage his body, mind, and spirit. For both martial and performing artist trained in disciplines of practice there is nothing except each particular moment of concentrated action in the present. "What," I ask, "is the process of interiority which explains this total absorption? This "becoming?"

Any comprehensive approach to performance must take into account both the difficult to express affective state of the performer and the training process used to achieve this state. As M.P. Sankaran Namboodiri, master teacher and performer of kathakali said: "First, perfection of the body is most important." It is only when the fundamental techniques of practice which constitute the given discipline have been so well embedded into the neophyte's body that such techniques are a part of his body-consciousness, ready-at-hand to be used at any moment, that the student is ready for higher stages of development. Kathakali and kalarippayattu begin this encoding process by taking the student through an extended process of preliminary physical training which renders the body ready to receive the imprint of more difficult particular techniques. Other genres like the noh launch the student's formal training directly with performance techniques.

The encoding of body-consciousness is viewed as a long-term process, part of a "path" or "way." Without romanticizing the daily drudgery involved, it is assumed that such a path must be followed if one is to approach mastery. The training regime encompasses the entire life, from youth through mastery and into old-age. Success is not guaranteed – accomplishment in any discipline is an open question. The "path" is not a "course of study," but a totally absorbing way of life. In the past, a person's place in the social hierarchy set by birth determined if he would or would not take up such a path. Unlike the renunciant or practitioner of some meditational disciplines, the neophyte in the martial or performing arts usually did not "choose" such a path, but was born into it.

A common assumption of these disciplines is that each is a psychophysical means to effecting a fundamental transformation in the individual: the martial arts effected an actual transformation from a raw, unknowledgeable, inexperienced, unconcentrated, unskilled youth to seasoned, "knowledgeable," experienced, concentrated, integrated, skilled warrior capable of "conquering even the god of death."[2] Such a transformation is characteristic of all Asian in-body disciplines. Each phase of transformation is marked by rituals. In kalarippayattu for example, rituals punctuate every aspect of training: initiation into the process of training, entry into the *kalari* (place of training), in the exercise process, as part of taking up a weapon, exit from the *kalari*, calendrical marking of training seasons, advancement to learning a new weapon, and, at least in the past, entry into the status of warrior.[3] In kathakali, even at the Westernized Kerala Kalamandalam, the process is punctuated by rituals that mark the training, from entry into the training place to the annual honoring and remembrance of teachers marking the onset of a new season of practice and performance, to taking into one's mind the master(s) before a performance. The training process in such Asian disciplines is not simply like ritual process, it is a ritual process. The result may be just as radical and effective a transformation of the individual as what occurs in healing or life-cycle rituals.

The process of transmission of performance knowledge in such disciplines is one of constant repetition where the neophyte literally mimicks the master. Day after day the student repeats over and over again the techniques of the system under the watchful eye of the master. In genres like kathakali, odissi, kathak, or bharatanatyam the entire whole-cloth of performance is deconstructed, broken down into its smallest units – the independent articulation of individual sets of musculature.[4] Knowing how to articulate such muscles is necessary in such highly codified forms in order for the student to reach even a minimally acceptable level of expressivity and competence. Forms such as noh do not require such exhaustive independent articulation of muscles, nor do they have as part of training such deconstructed sets of preliminary techniques. However, in all cases the constant repetition of set exercises, and/or forms (Japanese *kata*) eventually leads to a level of ability beyond empty, vacuous, presence-less, and powerless mimicry. The student passes from sheer repetition to a reconstruction enlivened by proficiency.

What is the result of this deconstruction? The basic units of the art are objectified. For the seven or ten year old going through training, there is nothing romantic or exciting about the process. There is nothing "personal" in the training. In fact, the neophyte's "personality" has no place in that process; if it showed itself much, it would intrude, blocking the way of the exercises at hand. The forms that are gradually encoded into the student's body through such drill are simply there as part of his performative, permanent body-consciousness, ready-at-hand to be used "unthinkingly."

This process is the same in the performing, the martial, and the meditative arts. After conforming to behavioral restrictions, the practitioner of classical yoga begins his formal path by first mastering poses (*āsanas*) and breathing (*prāṇāyāma*). Only when these have become habitualized in-body processes is the practitioner ready to begin higher stages of meditation. But even in these preliminary practices, the yogi is beginning to free himself from the flux of the body's agitation, and from the flux of the normal, everyday psychomental stream of consciousness. Similarly for the martial artist and many performing artists, the in-body work begins the process of freeing the individual from the very form he is learning – from the necessity of consciously having to remember the form. Although the martial and performing arts movements are much more dynamic than yoga or *zazen* (sitting meditation), nevertheless, the individual eventually achieves a state of stillness in motion. In essence, mastery of in-body form, when combined with the ability to fix and focus both gaze and mind, frees the martial or performing artist from "consciousness about," preparing him for a state of "concentratedness." The yogi is freed for meditation; the martial artist is freed to fight; the performer is freed to perform. All three are dynamic sets of actions – doings in the now moment.

What is assumed, but often unarticulated in such disciplines, is the fundamental psychophysical nature of the techniques.[5] Below the surface of external control is a subtle interior psychophysical process which transforms neophyte into master. Behind the virtuosity of the kathakali performer as he manipulates the musculature of his face to create the external configuration of a particular emotive content, behind the surface quietude of the noh actor gliding across the floor or kneeling in pregnant readiness are those psychophysical cultural assumptions which account for the interiority through which he "becomes the character."

As a first example I will cite the practice of kalarippayattu. What I want to unfold is how the Indian practitioners themselves explain accomplished doing: the release of full *śakti* (power) in a basic kalarippayattu pose, the "lion pose" (*simhavaḍivu*) as taught at the C.V.N. Kalari, Trivandrum, Kerala. Figures 8.1 through 8.7 illustrate the sequence of movements which collectively are called *simhavaḍivu*. *Vaḍivu* or "pose" is a term for this general class of movements. *Vaḍivu* are the fundamental building blocks of kalarippayattu technique. There are eight such poses, each named for an animal whose movements are embodied in the forms: elephant, lion, horse, wild boar, serpent, cat, cock, and fish. These poses are not static. They are dynamic sets of movements to which and from which the practitioner moves in delivering offensive or defensive blows, cuts, and thrusts, with weapons or in empty hand combat. Correct practice of each pose may take years of practice, for the full power of a pose will be tapped only when three aspects of practice are combined: (1) external realization of form (as seen in the accompanying figures), (2) repetition and achievement of accomplishment (*siddhi*) in a *mantra* associated with practice of a pose, and (3) correct breathing associated with a particular pose.

The sequence of external moves of the lion pose can be seen in figures 8.1–8.7. Notice how firm and natural the spinal posture is as it follows the

The lion pose – *simhavaḍivu*.

Figure 8.1 With hands/arms crossed over the chest and "ready," the movement originates in the "center" at the *nabi mula*: the leg is kicked up, energy flows from the center out through the knee and through the foot as it extends up . . .

Figure 8.2 to forehead level with the big toe extended.

Figue 8.3 The leg descends along the line of the body, the energy flow returning to the center as the leg descends.

Figue 8.4 The natural extension of the descent of the leg is a forward step in which the foot is firmly planted.

Figure 8.5 The firmly planted foot provides the base for a jump, executed off the forward foot, as the hands extend behind the body, thus making the jump a total body movement, again originating from the center.

Figure 8.6 Landing from the jump the energy is recycled and drawn into the center as . . .

Figure 8.7 The final position in the complete sequence is assumed, hands placed in front of the chest.

normal alignment of the spine. This is even true of the initial high kick. A common mistake among beginners is to try so hard to kick the foot up that correct spinal alignment is lost, the abdomen collapses inward as the spine assumes a concave form. The result is to cut off the flow of breath.[6]

Proper centering eventually leads from psychophysical integration to the release of *śakti* or power. Centering in kalarippayattu is literally originating movement from the "center" located below the navel known as the *nābhi mūla* ("root of the navel"). When impulses originate from the *nābhi mūla*, one observes a very different quality of movement. Movements are "grounded," "centred," "integrated," "filled out," "dynamic." The *nābhi mūla* of kalarippayattu is identical to the *svādhiṣṭhānam* of classical yoga. Its location is two finger widths above the anus and two finger widths below the root of the navel. It is at this center that both breath and impetus for movement into and out of forms originate. The psychophysical importance of the *nābhi mūla* to the practice of kalarippayattu cannot be overstressed. When performed correctly, there is a natural "gripping" (*piḍuttam*) in the *nābhi mūla* as the practitioner assumes the final position of the pose (see figure 8.7). A description from one family palm leaf manuscipt (*grandam*) describing correct practice of the pose reads:

> When doing the action stay firmly in the *vaḍivu*, planting the foot in this position, holding the breath firmly in the *nābhi mūla*, [thus] raising to life [your] strength (*balam*).

It is in the gripping of the *nābhi mūla* while simultaneously controlling the breath that the psychophysical base is laid for releasing full power into any form.

Many practitioners of kalaripayattu believe that all parts of the body are controlled through the active cycling and coursing of *prāṇa* ("the breath of life, breath, respiration, spirit, vitality," Monier-Williams, 1984: 705) through the body. Masters often equate *prāṇa* with *jīvaṅ* (life) itself. In kalarippayattu practice *prāṇa* originates in the *nābhi mūla*, and streams out from this center to "energize" the body. In doing the lion pose, there is a constant cycling of movement and breath/energy out from the center into the initial kick; back to the center as the leg descends from the kick; out from the center as the leg continues its descent into the step-jump; back to the center landing from the jump; and out from the center in the final pose (summarized in figure 8.8). The power and strength of the final pose may be seen in the dynamic quality of oppositional energy of the ultimate pose (see figure 8.9). As the practitioner moves into this final position, the gripping in the *nābhi mūla* creates an oppositional set of forces, outward and forward from the center along the line of the spinal column, and on out through the arms/hands and eyes. The body forms a solid triangle (see figure 8.9): the base of the triangle (B) is the ground point of downward opposition and energy; the tip (A) of the triangle is the

1–7 correspond to previous figures.

– – indicates the flow of energy beyond the body – such that extended
energy would constitute an offensive move (the kick with the big toe
at the peak of 1/2); or a defensive posture of strength (the final figure
in 7), which in turn is poised for an ongoing offensive attack

→ indicates the flow of energy from and back to the center

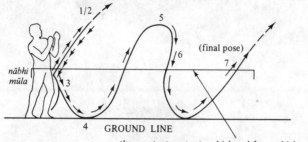

the constant center to which and from which movement
and energy returns and originates

Figure 8.8 The flow of energy and movement in the lion pose: a summary of figures 8.1 to
8.7. (The numbers indicate which photo is referred to; the arrows indicate the the direction
in which the energy is flowing.)

point of outward energy; the spinal column is the central axis and line of the
triangle (A–B).[7]

Once the exterior form can correctly be physically assumed, once the correct
breathing is a part of the form as executed, then it is possible that the
"energized life force" (*prāṇa vāyu*) will naturally course through the body-as-
vehicle. The forms that the body is now capable of assuming become the
conduit for the release of the energized life-force. Directed control of that
force becomes manifest as one part of the realization of full *śakti* or power,
and *balam* (strength) in the forms of the discipline. The quality of movement
observable as the characteristic "dynamic power" of a master comes only in
this highest level of practice.

Achieving correct practice, even in this one pose, is not isolated from other
aspects of the ongoing process of in-body training. Indeed, all of the exercises,
combined with special preliminary breathing techniques and a system of full-
body seasonal massage, collectively constitute the proper embodied discovery
of the center, and the psycho-physical energy released into the forms. Space
does not permit a fuller account of all other factors which contribute to
achieving the highest level of practice: daily, calendrical, and occasion-specific
ritual practices; ethical teaching; behavior modelled after the master; and the
development of mental power (*mana śakti*) through *mantra siddhi*. One
example will suffice. The full power of a single pose depends upon the
additional accomplishment of the *mantra* associated with that pose. These
secret techniques are only given to the most advanced and trusted disciples
who have achieved accomplishment of form. Achieving accomplishment
(*siddhi*) in a *mantra* is possible only by receiving the syllables which constitute

Figure 8.9 The oppositional flow of energy in the final position of the lion
pose (figure 8.7). The arrows indicate the direction in which the energy is
flowing. This opposition creates the triangle which is the lion pose's solid base
and source of strength. Note also that the central axis of the spine follows the
long line of the triangle. The spinal column and the interior "subtle channel"
of the body is thought to be the central axis through which the *prāna* is
channelled.

the *mantra* directly from the master, and, after daily purification, recitation of
the *mantra* the required number of times. Once *mantra siddhi* (accomplishment in the mantra) is reached, taking the *mantra* in mind at the moment of
execution of the *vaḍivu* will release its additional power into the form.

In kathakali, which is directly related to kalarippayaṭṭu, *prāna vāyu* is
understood to be the energized life-force which is most evident as the breath.
Control of the breath is one of the most important means to creating the
"power of presence" in the performance. Energy is first experienced and then
controlled through correct use of the breath. As one teacher said

> The *vāyu* is spread all over the body. It is how to control that that is [an implicit]
> part of the training.

Through the daily repetition of exercises *vāyu* is controlled. In both
kalarippayaṭṭu and kathakali, students from their earliest days of training are
instructed to breath through the nose, and not the mouth – a simple

instruction which, when adhered to in conjunction with correct spinal alignment in performing the sets of exercises, develops breathing which naturally originates in the *nābhi mūla*. Correct instruction also comes from the hands-on manipulation of the student's body by the teacher.

> Without a verbal word of instruction the teacher may, by pointing to or pressing certain parts of the body, make the student understand where the breath/energy (*vāyu*) should be held or released.

In taking the basic position characteristic of kathakali (see figures 8.10–8.11), the same basic principle of "gripping" in the *nābhi mūla* produces the same set of oppositional forces in the stance which gives kathakali its fundamental stylistic quality of grounded strength – certainly a direct link between the martial and performing art.

This centered groundedness extends to other aspects of performance, including the gesture language (*mudrās*). When performing *mudrās* correctly, each articulation of the hands/arms is "energized" from the *nābhi mūla* by the manipulation of the breath. Thus, the performance of any given set of hand gestures originates in the region of the *nābhi mūla*. After the initial release from the center, the breath/energy becomes a controlling force, shaping the qualitative dramatic and narrative dimensions of release into the gestures. Again, as in kalarippayattu, the manipulation of the breath – by holding/gripping, releasing, or constant flow – makes possible the release and control of internal energy. This enables the actor to "become the character."

Breath control and its consequent energy release is also necessary for the accomplished realization of the emotive content of the nine basic facial expressions (*navarasas*) of kathakali. The correct manipulation and control of the breath in performing the facial expressions is not taught in an overt manner, but rather by the usual process of demonstration, imitation, and gradual correction. For example, performing the erotic sentiment (*rati bhāva*) (see figure 8.12) the external manipulation of the facial mask executes the following basic moves, which are closely coordinated with the breathing pattern

> Beginning with a long, slow and sustained in-breath, the eyebrows move slowly up and down. The eyelids are held open half-way on a quick catch breath, and when the object of pleasure or love is seen (a lotus flower, or one's lover), the eyelids quickly open wide on an in-breath, as the corners of the mouth are pulled up and back, responding to the object of pleasure.

The breathing is deep and connected to the *nābhi mūla*; it is never shallow chest breathing. The characteristic breath pattern associated with the erotic sentiment is slow, long, sustained in-breaths with which the object of love or pleasure is literally "taken in," i.e., breathing in the aroma, sight, etc. of the lotus or the beloved.

Figure 8.10 The basic kathakali pose: feet planted formly apart, toes gripping the earth.

Figure 8.11 The oppositional forces of kathakali's basic stance.

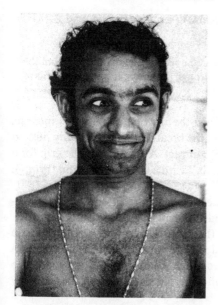

Figure 8.12 The erotic *bhāva: rati.*

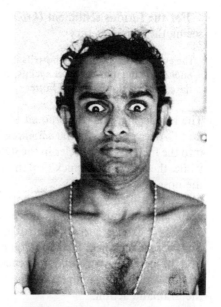

Figure 8.13 The furious *bhāva: krodha.*

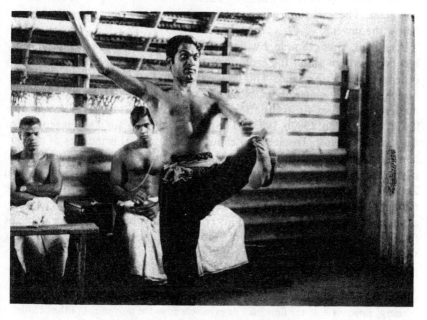

Figure 8.14 Fully embodied fury.

For the furious sentiment (*krodha bhāva*) (see figures 8.13 and 8.14), on seeing the object of fury

the eyes are open wide, the nostrils flare and the *vāyu* is literally pushed from the *nābhi mūla* out into the lower eyelids, and through the nose, causing the nostrils to flare, and the lower lids to flutter.

The teacher may tell the student to "push the *vāyu* from the navel into the face." After gripping in the *nābhi* region, the breath/energy is literally pushed into the face, as the muscles in the *nābhi* contract. After holding the grip for a while, there may be a quick "catch breath," with a slight exhalation through the nose.

The breath/energy release in both these cases is a release into a configuration of facial muscles in which is encoded the message, "pleasure/erotic" or "fury." It is the correct control of the breath/energy that makes these otherwise mechanical facial configurations live with presence. The conjunction of breath/energy and muscular configurations enables the actor to literally embody the manifestations of the internal state (*bhāva*) demanded by the dramatic action.[8]

When the breath, life-force, is controlled, when the actor has the ability to spontaneously release his energy into the embodiment of character, he is able to "become the character." Becoming the character in kathakali means that the life-force within the actor becomes the energy filling out the external physical forms (bodily, gesturally, facially) which collectively constitute the character. The kathakali actor and the character he becomes coincide just below the navel.[9]

As a final, brief example, I will draw upon the noh theatre of Japan. More has been written about the esoteric interior process of noh acting than any other genre of performance. This is largely due to the existence of a substantial body of primary material discussing the actor's work – Zeami's (1363–1443) numerous treatises (in translation, Rimer and Yamazaki [1984], Nearman [1978, 1980, 1982a, 1982b, 1983]). The goal of the noh actor is similar to that of the kathakali actor. Discussing Zeami's "fundamental principles of acting" contained in his treatise, *Kakyō*, Mark Nearman articulates the internal psychophysical process assumed by Zeami. Nearman makes clear that in Zeami's conceptual world there exists an "activating force" (*ki*, from the Chinese *ch'i*) which is a "person's creative energy" (1982a: 346). Nearman explains that Zeami has assumed his reader (a member of the inner circle of family charged with instruction of future generations of actors) is familiar with the phenomenon of such a personal *ch'i*.

Awareness of personal *ch'i* may be achieved through application of any of several methods for breath control designed to make the student conscious of a sense of energy flow. At first, the flow may be experienced as the movement of the breath, but later is experienced as an energy flow capable of being directed independently of the physical process of breathing. To "center" this energy prior to directing it to some purpose, the student learns to concentrate on a point called the *tanden*, located in the belly approximately two inches below the navel. The *tanden* functions as the point from which the performer feels his vocal thrust arise to produce a sound analogous to what is called in Western systems "a projected or supported vocal tone." This point will also operate as his center of gravity when using his *ch'i* to produce body movement (1982a: 346–47).

Nearman points out that the psychophysical exercises alluded to in Zeami's treatises lead to an "arousal" of the actor's *ch'i*, which is "part of the actor's inner, psychological preparation for performing" (1982a: 349). The actor engaged in his total being in a psychophysical process where his internal energy, aroused in his vital center below the navel (*hara*), then directed into and through the embodied forms of external gesture (body and voice) is of course fundamentally the same as the interior process of the kathakali actor. This despite the fact that the exterior manifestation of the internal process is different.[10]

The physiological result of noh's interior process is fundamentally the same as that of kathakali. As Junko Sakaba Berberich recently pointed out regarding noh's basic posture and movement

> In the basic posture and during movement as well . . . energy pulls the body in all directions, and the pelvis stays in the center of this dynamic balancing of the overall body. The energy pulling the body outward is counterbalanced by the energy drawing it inward toward the pelvis (1984: 210).

Berberich comments that the characteristic three dimensionality of noh movement results from the fact that energy carried in one direction is simultaneously counterbalanced (1984: 215–16). This oppositional internal tension and energy, creates the potential for "dramatic" manifestation and manipulation by the performer. Again, the actor's engagement of the internal *ki*/*ch'i* makes possible an objectified "becoming."

While the process of internal release and control of the life-force is similar in noh and kathakali, the expressive forms are very different. In noh breath control is most evident in total body movement and the expressive use of the fan and voice. In kathakali manipulation of breath and release of energy is manifest in strength and facility of footwork, use of gesture language, and facial expression. The deepest shadings of expressivity come for noh in the voice and in sustaining gesture and for kathakali in the face and hands. But in both cases it is the use of *prāṇa vāyu* or *ki* which creates and modulates the expression.

The true "drama" of such forms is fundamentally created in each moment of expressivity, in the actor's engagement in each psychophysical act in the ongoing score of performance, and in the relationship between this particular moment, its overall resonances and relationship to the shaping, form, and feeling tone of the next moment. For the noh actor, there is the lingering vocal extension and/or movement as he tests the limits of the expressive moment, using *jo, ha, kyū* in the "controlled release" of energy in time and space.[11] For the kathakali actor there is the lingering tension in gripping and pushing the breath into the lower lids to express fury. In all such precise psychophysical moments, the "character" is being created – not in the personality of the actor but as an embodied and projected/energized/living form between actor and audience. These Asian forms assume no "suspension of disbelief," rather the actor and spectator co-create the figure embodied in the actor as "other." The "power of presence" manifest in this stage other, while embodied in this particular actor in this particular moment, is not limited to that ego. That dynamic figure exists between audience and actor, transcending both, pointing beyond itself.[12]

The emotion of the actor in performance is not equated with the actor's own emotional life or personality. The release of energy/life-force constituting the "presence" of the performer is something objective and (ideally) separate from the ego-bound personality. To experience the directed flow of *prāṇa vāyu* or *ki* through kathakali, noh, or other similar forms is not an act of self-aggrandizement, but humility in the face of such larger forces. In such moments of release the performer is transparent, the medium for the other. His life-force is but one infinitesimal manifestation of the macrocosm. This is what Zeami was referring to in his *Kyūi* when he discussed the highest level of attainment

> The performing of an actor who attains Level One is beyond a matter of critical analysis and judgment . . . it transcends even praise . . . Its external mark is No-Mark . . . For the actor on the First Level, within every action and at every instant, the Absolute is ever-shining, and although not seen by the eye, can be perceived directly by the perceiving Mind. Actor, art, technique, beauty, meaning are no longer discernible because they are no longer separable. Only the particular and the ineffable remain. (Nearman 1978: 324–25).

There is still something more – some affective and qualitative difference between this kind of performance and performance in the West. What an Asian means by "self" is not the same as what a Westerner means. As Clifford Geertz points out

> The Western concept of the person as a bounded, unique, more or less integrated motivational and cognitive universe; a dynamic center of awareness, emotion, judgement and action organized into a distinctive whole and set contrastively both against other such wholes and against a social and natural background is, however incorrigible it may seem to us, a rather peculiar idea within the context of the world's cultures . . . [We need to] set that conception aside and view their experience within the framework of their own idea of what selfhood is. (1983: 59).

While space does not permit a full delineation of the Japanese and Indian understandings of the self, some suggestions about the Indian understanding will clarify the point. A fundamental assumption of Indian thought is the Upanishadic statement, *tat tvam asi*, "you are that." (*Chāndogya Upaniṣad* 6.1 6: 12–13.) *Tat tvam asi* is a giant philosophical/cosmological backdrop on which Indian life both ordinary and esoteric is projected. "You are that" asserts a fundamental identity between microcosm and macrocosm, the individual self and the universe: a person can become one-with and join-with; there is no object set over against a subject. (See also Singer 1984).

This joining-with suffuses daily life. A Hindu from childhood takes the deity into herself/himself in the act of *darśan* – seeing the deity (Eck 1981). Amidst the cacophany and turmoil characteristic of temple life, the individual in getting even a glimpse of the deity takes the deity fully within. The kathakali performer's act of "seeing" is the same. "Seeing" the lotus of the text in performance is not projecting something onto the mind's screen, but joining with the image as it emerges from the energy streaming from the *ñahbi mūla*, controlled through the breath, filling out the gestural patterns shaped by the hands, and coursing upward through the facial muscles and eyes. The immediate sensuality of the Hindu world, the ease with which daily life offers such joinings, provides a cultural context for the performer's psychophysical process. This correspondence between the microcosm (self), and macrocosm (universe), creates a fundamental "resonance" between acts/states of being in the human sphere and the all-embracing macrocosm. Present actions, doings, are understood to have at least the potential to resonate beyond themselves and thus serve as a means to altering both microcosm and macrocosm.

Let me turn to the highly suggestive language used by A.C. Scott in discussing the affective dimension of Asian performance

> It is in words used as sound and incantation invoking visual imagery by acoustic stress, rhyme, melody and repetition, rather than literary communication, by which the power to make present the absent is invoked in stage practice. (1975: 209).

In saying that even secular performances are "a calling forth or out," Scott was emphasizing the underlying similarity of ritual and non-ritual genres. The in-body performances of Asia are not far removed historically and experientially from their origins. The vocalizing of Sanskrit in the kutiyattam style is based upon modes of Vedic chanting; kathakali's original vocal style, *sōpānam*, was based upon a form of devotional temple singing; noh recitation is close to Buddhist incantation; Indian *mudrās* resonate with the *mudrās* of temple priests performing daily rituals; the psychophysical basis of kathakali is derived from its martial-ritual precursor.[13]

The disjuncture between ritual and entertainment in the West is more radical than in Asia. The internal connection of the performer to the performed, the doer to the done, resonates deeply within Asian performance genres since they are so close to the connectedness of the sources of their embodied gestures. This does not mean that our Western contemporary genres are devoid of such resonance, but rather that it is much more difficult to identify, verify, authenticate, and ultimately experience.

The Western separation of the arts into distinct traditions, the public perception of the various arts as distinct and separate, and the surrounding assumptions which we possess about such arts, their practice, and the type of praxis or action resulting from their performance have all been factors which have precluded a clear perception of the fundamental nature of Asian disciplines of performance. The pervading presence of the assumed main-stream Western approach to acting, characterization, and performance in which "mimesis" and "persona" play such an important part, has contributed to Western confusion over performance in non-Western cultures where different sets of assumptions exist about the "self" of the performer, what constitutes "a character," and what the relationship is between the performer (doer) and performed (done).

Asian performance is founded on the assumption that the world constituted in performance is not separate from the world outside the performance. As James Brandon points out

> The [Asian] performing arts are not viewed as being different from some real world; they are one manifestation of the one world which encompasses all . . . [Thus] Coleridge's "willing suspension of disbelief" only makes sense if you begin from the view that art is pretending to be what it is not (it is not "real") (1982: 2–3).

It is this fundamental psychophysical unity in the act of doing that many contemporary practitioners of theatre have tried to find – Grotowski, and even Stanislavski. Eugenio Barba's recent research in "theatre anthropology" exemplifies this search for the fundamental principles of performance (1982). My own practical theatre work is similar. There is in all this work a striving toward that sense of ineffable presence which the accomplished Asian actor embodies when he "becomes the character." There, at that moment, through the interior psychophysical process, he *is* that character.

Notes

1. The approach and inspiration for this discussion of the phenomenon of performance is informed by the work of Merleau-Ponty 1962, Scott 1975, and Blacking 1977. Merleau-Ponty pointed the way when he stated:

   > Our view of man will remain superficial so long as we fail to go back to that origin, so long as we fail to find, beneath the chatter of words, the primordial silence, and as long as we do not *describe the action* which breaks this silence. The spoken word is a gesture, and it means, a world. (1962: 184; my italics.)

2. The ultimate goal of the Indian martial artist was to "conquer even the god of death," through psychophysical practices leading to a "steadying" of the vision of both the "inner" and "outer" eyes (M.N. Dutt, ed. and trans., *Agni Purān*, Vol. 2.

Calcutta: Elyseum Press, 1904: 898–99). Conquering the god of death means conquering oneself, i.e., overcoming all obstacles in the way of entering the battlefield and confronting the enemy without fear.

3. For specifics see Zarrilli 1978.
4. A complete description with photographs of the deconstructed set of exercises and process is found in Zarrilli 1984a, chapter 4.
5. In practice most Asian disciplines of practice are non-reflexive. In many traditions there exist technical manuals, i.e. shorthand notations or compilations of techniques and/or "secrets" of the tradition. Even in traditions where there is no overt or written tradition of reflexivity, there still exist principles and assumptions about what is or is not correct practice. Some teachers are more prone than others simply by personal disposition to reflexive speculation on the principles of practice.
6. The descriptive comments made here are based on interviews and observations in the field, as well as on extended personal practice of the forms. The use of certain principles and terms, like "centering," are my own and are consciously used as a means of descriptive explanation of emic categories. While the use of the word "centering" is my own, it has been chosen since it best describes the observable result of correct practice resulting from instructions given in situ. Instructions and corrections, of course, never refer to such a "center," but emphasize "centering" through mimetic illustration and example: "Do this (the instructor shows); not that (he shows the mistake)."
7. For a fuller explanation and detailed ethnographic report on the full process see Zarrilli forthcoming, "*Conquering Even the God of Death: Paradigms of Accomplishment and Power in a Traditional South Indian Martial Art.*
8. In the area of emotional affect, the research of Paul Ekman is significant in providing quantitative data. In a recent article Ekman summarizes research in which subjects were instructed to "voluntarily move particular patterns of facial movement, hypothesizing that such deliberate performances of facial actions would turn on the autonomic nervous system [. . .] we told them particular muscles to move on their face" for fear, anger, surprise, disgust, sadness and happiness. Ekman achieves significant results in changes in the Autonomic Nervous System. (See Paul Ekman, "Expression and the Nature of Emotion," in *Approaches to Emotion*, eds., Klaus R. Scherer and Paul Ekman. Hillsdale, N.J.: Lawrence Erlbaum Associates, 1984: 319–43. See also Richard Schechner's discussion of these data in chapter 2 of this book.
9. In my earlier writing on kathakali (1984a), for lack of the fuller understanding articulated here and based on an analysis of emic concepts, I misguidedly suggested that this process of filling out the form was "passive."
10. A concern with the specific dynamics and practical phenomenon of performance is evidenced throughout Zeami's writings. For example, in the *Kakyō*, Zeami begins the treatise with a discussion of the relationship between pitch, breath, and vocal production. His description of correct practice is enlightening and revealing

Correct pitch is based on sustaining the proper breath. While listening carefully to the pitch of the accompanying instruments [flute, etc.] that precede him, the actor must align the increasing intensity of the pressure of air in his chest to this pitch, close his eyes, and draw in his breath, so that, when he projects his voice, his first sounds will automatically be produced at the proper pitch (Rimer and Yamazaki 1984: 74).

Having observed how the actor correctly prepared for vocalization, Zeami immediately discussed the problems encountered

> If he merely listens to the pitch but does not align himself with it [by preparing the proper amount of air in his chest], then when he produces his first sounds he will by no means find it simple to enter on the proper pitch level. Because proper pitch is regulated by the intensity of the pressure of air used to produce the voice, it can be said that the proper order involves, first, determining the pitch, second, preparing the breath, and third, producing the voice. (Rimer and Yamazaki 1984: 74).

According to Kavalam Panikkar (interview, 1985), a similar process is followed in traditional Indian forms of vocalization where the "dynamics" of control are also based on the "intensity" of release from the center into the pitch. The origin of the "vocalized sound" is, like the origin of movement, in the *nābhi mūla*. Modulating the effective energy release allows the vocalizer to "shape" the sound in a manner similar to that described here by Zeami. As Nearman points out, Zeami's understanding of the nature of sound is based on a theory of vibration originating in Indian philosophy (1982a: 364) – another common psychophysical assumption shared by these performance traditions.

11. The configuration *jo, ha, kyū* is a fundamental progression which informs all aspects of noh performance and may roughly be summarized as moving from "an introduction, slow, simple, dignified" (*jo*), to "development" (*ha*), to "short, fast finish (*kyū*) – exciting, but leading back at the end to the introductory *jo*" (Bethe and Brazell 1978: 6).

12. The creation of the figure between audience and actor is a foundation of the *rasa* aesthetic theory of India. See Schechner (1985: 117–50).

13. The potential *rigor mortis* of meaning and affect should be remembered in this context. The "model" or "ideal" of practice always exists as "model" and "ideal," i.e., that toward which the best and most self-conscious practitioner moves. In most martial traditions like kalarippayattu today, the wrenching of the discipline from its traditional socio-religious context is producing variations in practice which atrophy meaning and affect, effectively changing the form from a discipline of psychophysical practice into one of physical practice more akin to modern sports or hard street fighting devoid of the ethical restraints on use of deadly techniques.

9.

Korean shamans: role playing through trance possession

DU-HYUN LEE

Korean shamans can be roughly divided into two types: possessed, or charismatic shamans and hereditary shamans. The former, most of whom are female, called *naerim mudang*, are typically found in the northern half of the Korean peninsula. After suffering from *sinbyŏng*,[1] an illness which is generally interpreted as a sign of a shamanistic calling, a potential *naerim mudang* apprentices herself to an established shaman from whom she acquires the knowledge and skills appropriate to her new occupation. The two women establish a "spirit mother" – "spirit daughter" relationship, the spirit mother later conducting the initiation rite which transforms her apprentice into a full-fledged shaman.[2] In the course of their rites, these shamans not only become possessed and experience ecstatic trance states themselves but may also induce their clients to do the same.

The hereditary shamans, both male and female, called *tangol mudang*, are found in the southern half of the Korean peninsula. They are recruited not through possession sickness but simply by being born into a shaman's family. This type of shaman does not personally undergo trance possession but may cause other persons to become possessed in the course of a rite.

Types of trance possession

There are at least three different types of trance possession in Korean shamanism, *chinogwi-kut*, *sumangogu-kut*, and *mugam* dancing. The first, performed by the *naerim mudang*, can be seen in the rite performed to guide the spirit of a deceased person to the other-world. In this rite, known as a *chinogwi-kut*, the shaman plays the role of the deceased. She talks, cries, and otherwise communicates with the dead person's family. Details of the *chinogwi-kut* will be expounded in the following paragraphs through a careful description of an actual *kut*.

This *chinogwi-kut* was held in mid-August 1981, for Yun-jin Noh, an ordinary citizen who had lived the uncomplicated life of a small-town florist.

A month before the *kut*, he died of hypertension at the age of sixty-two. In compliance with the wishes of his widow, an old shaman named Yŏng-ja Jo came to take charge of the ritual service. The shaman, aged seventy-four, had been blind for ten years. Her reputation was well known among the people of her province. Not only did she have several spirit daughters but she also had her own shaman altar in Yuyang-ri, Yangju-gun of Kyŏnggi-do, where many *kuts* had been performed.

When the day of the *kut* came and all the preparations for the rite had been completed, the shaman held the ritual with the help of her three spirit daughters, Kyŏng-ae Kim (aged 42), Yong-rae Park (45), and Soonie Lee (57). The widow and younger sister of Mr. Noh, three daughters-in-law, and two wives of his nephews attended the shaman. It should be noted that all the participants were women, except for the eldest son of the deceased.

The *kut* was divided into a natural progression of sixteen rites. The order of the first nine was as follows:

1. *Pujŏng-gŏri*, purifying the alter, the opening ceremony
2. *Sangsan-gŏri*, prayer to the mountain of god for protection
3. *Pyŏlsang-gŏri*, prayer to the Spirit of Smallpox for expulsion of diseases
4. *Obangsin-jang-gŏri*, prayer to the Warrior Official spirits of the Five Directions for protection
5. *Sangsantaekam-gŏri*, prayer to the Low-Level Spirit-Official for protection
6. *Ponhyang-gŏri*, prayer to the guardian spirits of the village for protection
7. *Chosang-gŏri*, prayer to the spirits of ancestors for protection
8. *Sŏngju-gŏri*, prayer to the household god for happiness
9. *Chángbu-gŏri*, prayer to the deity of dead actors for protection from accidents.

The opening nine rites, which are also basic to the Family Ritual for Happiness, were performed on the veranda of the house, in front of the altar erected there.

The remaining seven rites (10–16), the main parts of the *chinogwi-kut* for the dead, were held in front of another altar erected for the dead man in the yard of the house.

One of the spirit daughters, Kyŏng-ae Kim, performed the following two seances (10–11): *arin-kamang-gŏri* (invocation of mournful gods) and *chungditaewang-gŏri* (prayer to the Ten Kings of the underworld for the repose of the departed soul). Then, the shaman, wearing a yellow robe and a hemp cloth tied around her head with a straw cord, came into the yard through the front gate. She had a stick in her right hand, a shaman's brass bells in her left hand, and a dried fish wrapped with white paper (symbolizing the abode of the departed spirit) on her back. She then began the twelfth seance, the *saje-gŏri*.

The *saje-gŏri* involves the acting out of a melodrama between the family of the dead man and the shaman herself who becomes a greedy messenger from hell (see figure 9.1). The shaman says, "The deceased told me 'we are so rich

Figure 9.1 *Saje-gŏri* from *chinogwi-kut*. Here shaman Kyŏng-ae Kim enters the yard through the front gate. She will perform a "greedy messenger from hell."

that we can afford to give you a huge feast.' But what poor treatment! Your goddamned dead husband made a fool of me." The messenger (the shaman), in a rage, comes to throw away the abode of the departed spirit (the dried fish on her back). Then the members of the family, apologizing for their lack of hospitality, give the messenger some money. (This also means that the family has asked the messenger not to take the deceased to hell.) After receiving the money, the messenger sings *"Saje t'aryŏng"* ("The Messenger's Song," sung by the shaman) while holding the dried fish in her left hand and shaking the brass bells with her right hand. Here is an abstract of the *"Saje t'aryŏng"*:

When the florist died of hypertension, the messenger came to take him to be judged. They journey to the gate of the other-world, where the Ten Kings will give him judgment. The shaman (the messenger) asks these judges to allow the dead man to live on the lotus blossom peak in paradise, despite the fact that the dead

man was not noted for his acts of charity. The shaman informs the Ten Kings that
if the dead man ever lives on earth again he will be extremely kind, considerate,
and charitable.

When *saje-gŏri* ends, Yŏng-ja Jo, wearing a red robe and a big wig
decorated with a crown, continues with the thirteenth rite. It is called *malmi-gŏri* (recitation of the myth of Princess Pari) (see figure 9.2). In this seance, the
invocation is addressed to the founding-spirit of the shamans, *Pari-kongju* (lit.
"Rejected Princess"). This title refers to the guiding of the deceased's soul to
the other-world by Pari-kongju.

Pari-kongju, the seventh and last daughter of a king, was rejected by her
parents who wanted a prince to be born. She was abandoned and endured
many hardships. When her parents fell sick and died, she obtained medicinal
water from another world. With this she brought her parents back to life.
Thereupon she herself becomes a deity, the foundress-spirit of shamans,
endowed with the gift to guide the deceased to the other-world.

The shaman recited *pari-kongju*, a long shaman epic song taking more than
an hour, shaking the brass bells in her left hand and beating a *changgo*
(hourglass-shaped drum) with a *changgo* stick in her right hand. At several
points during this performance, Pari-kongju does succeed in taking the dead
to a better world. Also, the family shows their concern by wailing continuously throughout this part of the ceremony.

This seance contains two ideas which seem worthy of deeper consideration.
First, after suffering, Pari-kongju is given a medicine, which brings her
deceased parents back to life. This becomes the reason why during this rite she
is asked to lead the soul of the deceased to a better world. Second, after her
return in triumph she chooses to renounce royal ways and becomes the
benefactor of the despised shamans. She calls herself *Inwi-wang* ("King of the
Despised"). This may symbolize a refusal to compromise with the tradition of
"Man first" in her society.

After blind Yŏng-ja Jo finished reciting the long epic song, she allowed
Yong-rae Park, her spirit daughter, to perform the fourteenth rite, *toryŏng-gŏri* (circumambulation) in her place. With a fan and a shaman's knife in her
hand, the spirit daughter puts on a red robe and a big wig. Shaking her brass
bells, the shaman proceeds to go around the dead man's altar three times. She
moves erratically, going three steps forward and then two steps backward to
the beat of shamanistic music. The members of the dead man's family follow
the shaman, weeping. The widow carries a portrait of the deceased, and her
two daughters-in-law hold a new robe for the dead, incense, and candles. This
circling around the altar symbolizes the journey of the dead man from this
world to the gates of the other-world.

After this circling is completed, the shaman holds in one hand a fan which
she opens and closes continuously above her head. In her other hand, she
twists a knife in the air, twice to the left above her head, and then throws the

Figure 9.2 *Malmi-gŏri* from *chinogwi-kut*. Shaman Yŏng-ja
Jo recites the myth of the Rejected Princess.

knife to her assistant on the opposite side of the altar. The assistant catches the
knife and returns it to the shaman again. This process symbolizes the
purification of the area around the altar by the act of circling. Then the
shaman dances a unique kind of dance, involving various hops, skips, and/or
jumps. And then she sings a song for the dead. This song will hopefully
guarantee the dead man's entrance into paradise.

Next the shaman performs the fifteenth rite, *chungdi-garŭm-gŏri* (divided
cloth bridge rite) (see figure 9.3). This rite needs a *siwang-po* in order to be
performed. The *siwang-po* is made of two different kinds of cloth, hemp and
cotton, each of which is seven *Cha* (7 × 12 inches = 84 inches) long. Six cloth
bridges are prepared for three people: the deceased, his mother, and his
brother who had been killed in the Korean War (two bridges for each person).
The moment four members lift one of the cloth bridges up over their heads,
pulling its four edges, the shaman, beating the cymbal, goes under the bridge.
After turning left and right two times, she proceeds through the cloth bridge

Figure 9.3 *Chungdi-garŭm-gŏri* – the divided cloth bridge rite
– from *chinogwi-kut* as performed by Yong-rae Park.

(*siwang-po*) with her breast, thereby splitting each of the cloth bridges in half.
This ceremonial action is considered to have opened the way to paradise for
the dead by smoothing the road to the world beyond. There are also two other
reasons why the cloth bridges are used. First, the hemp cloth, which is called
"unclean bridge" or "siwang bridge," opens the way to the Ten Kings of Hell.
Second, the cotton cloth, called the "clean bridge" or "Buddhist bridge,"
opens the way to Buddha or paradise. As the shaman marches through the
cloth bridge, the family of the deceased hurriedly put down money on the split
cloth. This act symbolizes their best wishes for the dead.[3]

In splitting the cloth, the shaman demonstrates an extreme state of emotion,
in other words, a compressed, determined attempt to cut off the attachment
between the living and the dead. In this way the act of splitting the cloth not
only opens the way to the world beyond for the dead, but it also splits the dead
from the living.

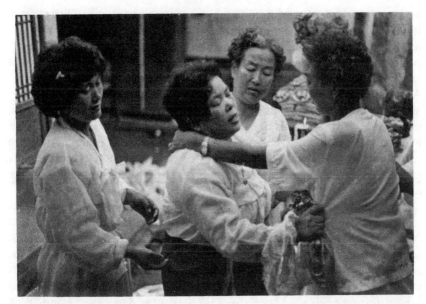

Figure 9.4 *Nŏkchŏngbae-gŏri* –the invocation of spirits – from *chinogwi-kut*. Here Yong-rae Park, possessed by the spirit of the deceased husband, grabs his wife (widow).

The split *siwang-po* is then brought in and out of a thorny gate three times. This is a kind of prayer for the dead, expressing the hope that he will not be entrapped in the gate when entering the world beyond. When the *kut* ceremony ends, the *siwang-po*, along with the paper image of the spirit and the clothes of the dead, is set on fire before the front gate of the house. Next, before the invocation of the spirit seance, the shamans and members of the family set up an offering table in front of the altar of the deceased; and they perform a memorial ceremony for the deceased, and the family of the deceased weep for him. In the Confucian ceremony for the deceased only males are allowed to participate, but both men and women participate in the *kut* ceremony.

Finally, a seance, the *nŏkchŏng-gŏri* (invocation of spirits) is performed (see figure 9.4). The shaman, wearing a paper image of a spirit on her head, invokes the spirit of the deceased by singing an invocation chant in time to shamanistic music; and while dancing wildly, the entranced shaman becomes possessed by the spirit of the deceased. At that moment, tinkling her bells, she begins to recite a mournful message from the deceased. In this way the shaman becomes the deceased. Shrieking "Oh! How awful!" or "Aaah! How awful!" she weeps over death and falls into a faint. Supported and awakened by the family of the deceased, she (the deceased) grasps his wife, sympathizes with her by saying "What will become of you alone in the future?" and consoles the widow in her sorrow. At the same time the widow weeps bitterly, grasping the deceased. And then the mournful message continues as follows: "I haven't benefitted from my parents and tried hard to make a living and so we had little leisure time." In response to the message, the widow irritably screams: "Don't you remember what I said? I said I wanted to die first. Why did you die first?" Again the message: "Well, a widow's better than a widower. You, whelp, what made you so hot-tempered?" "Oh! this is the last time to get hot-tempered." As if the deceased were living, a quarrel between the couple takes place. They are then parted, drink together, and smoking cigarettes, are reconciled with each other. Turning to his daughters-in-law, the deceased says, "Live your lives happily. You sisters-in-law, have affection for each other." And then turning to his wife again, "Please take good care of the housekeeping in my absence." Hearing the message, the family of the deceased embrace each other and weep.

Next the deceased claims his possessions (his watch, his hat, and clothes) but is irritated by the fact that the clothes are winter clothes stuffed with cotton, and not summer clothes. The deceased cries, "Where can I go on this sultry summer day with these cotton clothes on?" Then a comic skit with the clothes takes place. At last, he asks for a digestive aid for his stomach pain. His wife answers, "You've already died. Isn't that enough? Why do you, a dead person, want medicine?" The relatives ask the deceased to leave, saying "Why don't you stop complaining, rather than commenting on the diseases of your wife?" "Please give help to your son and daughters," and "Please stop grieving your family and fly away without any lingering attachment." In response to that, the deceased says "I'll give you no more grief," "Don't worry [about me], but take good care of your lives," and, "Now I'm leaving." The shaman again dances to the shamanistic music, and the *nŏkchŏngbae-gŏri* is completed.

The major part of the *chinogwi-kut* has now been completed. Finally, the *kut* ends with a *tuijŏn-gŏri* (feeding miscellaneous spirits and sending them away).

The above paragraphs have given a brief explanation of how one might deal with many dangerous spirits which haunt a family caught in a lingering attachment to the dead person. On the other hand, it has also been shown how the deceased can be made to join the ranks of helpful ancestral spirits through the processes of a shamanistic rite, the *chinogwi-kut*. These ancestral spirits will help protect the family's posterity. And the survivors, through participation in the dramatic process, come to believe in the deceased's entry into the blissful other-world and are thereby relieved of bitter grief.

A second type of role playing involving trance possession is carried out by the hereditary shamans, or *tangol mudang*, along the eastern coast of southern Korea. In some cases, one of the family members of the deceased, usually a wife, mother, or sister, holding a spirit basket, is possessed by the deceased. The shaman addresses various statements or questions to the deceased, and the deceased (a possessed member of his family) responds by causing the basket to shake if the particular statement is correct or if the answer to the question is affirmative. In other cases the deceased expresses his sorrowful message in words.

Role playing also occurs in *sumangogu-kut* (the shaman ritual for drowned fishermen), the second type of trance possession described here.

This particular *sumangogu-kut* was performed as a joint memorial service for eight young fishermen at a small fishing village of two hundred households and a population of about one thousand of Taebyŏn-ri, Kijang-myŏn, Yangsan-gun in Kyŏngsangnam-do for two days, 12–13 December 1981. The young fishermen were fishing for anchovies on a small, (thirteen ton) fishing boat named Tae-hwan in the Kampo sea when they met a sudden gust of wind on the first day of November. Except for the captain who rescued himself by swimming to shore, all of the crew were drowned. The villagers couldn't find their corpses.

Accidents like this happen from time to time in the villages of Korea's east coast. About one hundred fishermen drown or disappear every year. Whenever an accident takes place, the villagers perform a *kut* for the deceased spirits.

The ages of the eight men varied from nineteen to twenty-five. All of them were bachelors except for Ch'angsu Kang, aged twenty-five, who had a wife and children. Because it is believed that people who die in an accident, especially if they are bachelors, may cause their families to suffer misfortunes, a shamanistic ritual for the deceased must be performed whenever a fatal accident occurs.

The *sumangogu-kut* described below was performed by Sŏk-chul Kim, his wife, and ten members of his own *kut* party. It consisted of twelve rites. The first seance, *honkŏnjigi-kut* (salvaging or beckoning the drowned spirits) was held at ten in the morning at sea where the young fishermen were drowned. Four male shamans and one female shaman, carried in a boat eight spirit poles, offerings, and eight bowls, which had been used by the drowned, containing their name plates, paper images of spirit and rice. They perform the first rite of the *kut* with the families of the drowned men in attendance (see figure 9.5). After arranging the dishes of food for the dead and lighting candles on the boat, a female shaman bows down in four directions while male shamans play shamanistic music with a *changgo* and gongs. Then the shaman throws into the sea the spirit bowl tied to the ankle of a living hen (when the dead are women, they use a cock). These are also connected by a cord with the spirit pole on which they attach the name of the drowned victim written on a piece of paper. The shaman has a member of the family grip the cord, connected with the bowls tied with a hen and the pole, in one hand and shake the underwear of the dead in the other hand.

Each of the mothers, sisters, or brothers shaking the underwear, cries out to the dead to come back. The shaman asks the Dragon King of the Sea to return the spirits of the dead, praying, "Dragon King! With your mercy help the dead to return to the road to earth!" After this prayer, a male shaman hauls the

Figure 9.5 *Honkŏnjigi-kut* from *sumangogu-kut* where a group of shamans beckon the drowned spirits to return from the sea.

bowl and hen into the boat. (It is believed that the spirits of the dead stick to the feathers of a hen, which guides them to earth) while he calls out the names of the dead one after another. As the last item of this rite, the shaman throws the offerings wrapped in a piece of white paper and pours wine into the sea. This symbolizes offerings to the Dragon King. Then the participants return to the village from the sea, believing the spirits of the dead come back with them.

The second rite, *yŏngwang-kut* (prayer to the Dragon King for the peace of the drowned) is performed after the spirits of the drowned fishermen are transferred to the earth. Eight tables for the Dragon King are set up on the seashore; and with the participation of the families of the deceased, a shaman named Yusŏn Kim prays for the Dragon King to bring the young fishermen's spirits back to the earth by dint of the Dragon King's power and to send them away to paradise (see figure 9.6).

The shaman, performing the third seance, *kolmaegi-kut* (prayer to the guardian deity of the village for the peace of the drowned), prays for *Kolmaegi Sŏnangnim* (the guardian deity of village) to allow the spirits to go to the lotus blossom peaks of the Ten Kings in the other-world. When the *Chŏnwang* (the King of Heaven) pole is brought in after the *ch'ŏngbae-ga* (invocation of spirits song), the families of the deceased tie some money and cloths on the string of the Heaven King's pole. In the meantime the female shaman dances and prays, carrying with her a dragon-shaped boat.

Next, the fourth rite, *mun-kut* (ritual for passing through the gate of the other-world) is begun with mortuary tablets, portraits of the drowned

Figure 9.6 *Yŏngwang-kut* from *sumangogu-kut*. The female
shaman prays to the Dragon King for peace for the drowned.

persons, and spirit bowls placed on the table for the rite at the gate of the village
hall. After the *ch'ŏngbae* song is sung, both shamans, a male and a female,
playing shamanistic music, come in through the gate from the outside and
dance in a circle.

The later rites of the *sumangogu-kut* symbolize the act of opening the gate
for the performance of a rite for the deceased spirits. When the *mun-kut* is
completed, the shamans and the family move the mortuary tablets, the spirit
bowls, and the underwear to the altar in the village hall for a joint rite for the
drowned. On the altar there is a memorial table decorated with nine kinds of
artificial flowers (including lotus flowers which symbolize paradise). On this
altar are placed dishes of food offerings, eight spirit baskets in which paper
images of the spirits are put, and eight dragon-shaped ships. (It is believed that
the drowned men voyage to the other-world aboard the dragon-shaped ships.)
There are also eight rolls of hemp cloth, several *ch'orong* (silk-covered
lanterns), and several lighted candles in candle holders on the table.

After six in the evening, in front of the altar, the fifth rite, *ch'omangja-kut* (invocation of the drowned) is performed by a shaman named Sŏknam Sin. Singing the chăngbae song, the shaman calls out the names of the eight drowned young men. Holding the spirit baskets of each of them and twisting them above the families' heads she moves the families of the drowned to tears by making a statement in behalf of the deceased spirits. Most of the two hundred members of the families are women: mothers, wives, and sisters. The sound of their plaintive crying spreads out over the sea. The scene indicates how the various steps of the *kut* are needed to relieve their grief and suffering.

The next morning, the sixth, *palwŏn-kut* (prayer to the gods for the resurrection of the drowned) being completed, the seventh *pangogu-kut* (chamber rite to guide the spirit of the drowned), which is considered the climax of the entire *sumangogu-kut* (shaman ritual for drowned fishermen) begins. A well-known, old, and experienced shaman, Yu-sŏn Kim, takes charge of this rite. The shaman chants the *peridegi* (a variation of *pari-kongju*) song for three-and-a-half hours (see figure 9.7).

It should be noted that the *pari-kongju* song of central Korea is recited monotonously: the shamans merely sit and recite it. *Peridegi*, on the other hand, is a dramatic combination of song, narration, dance, and action, not unlike *pansori* (an indigenous theatrical performance of Korea). The theme of *peridegi* is similar to the motif of *pari-kongju*, however. The shaman says, "We perform this *sumangogu-kut* hoping the drowned can enter heaven where they can live long, as in *peridegi*. *Peridegi* gets medical water from the other-world and brings her father back to life when he fell sick and died."

Here is the last part of the long *peridegi* shaman song: "You! You eight spirits are now friends. God bless you! We hope you go to heaven, the best world, not to the hell, not to the bad place. We also hope you bequeath your remaining lives and happiness, which you can't enjoy any more in this world, to your family. We hope again you go to the lotus blossom peak in heaven. *Namu amita bul!*" (a Buddhist prayer).

After finishing the *peridegi* song at two in the afternoon, the shaman builds up eight *yŏngdūngmalgi* (abodes of the drowned spirits), one for each of the drowned men, and induces the families to hold the spirit baskets and become possessed. For the first three drowned spirits, their mothers hold the spirit baskets. When they become possessed by the spirits of their sons, they don't speak but give answers to the shaman's questions by shaking the spirit baskets.

After the family members sit down with the spirit baskets in their hands, the shaman sits beside them and invokes the spirits by calling out their names. She also chants an incantation while beating a drum. As the shaman keeps beating this drum, the atmosphere around the village hall reaches a climax. One mother who holds a spirit basket becomes possessed with excitement and answers the shaman's questions by shaking the basket violently. The shaman says, "You came! If you have anything to hope for, tell everything to your

Figure 9.7 Shaman Yu-sŏn Kim chants the *peridegi* song for three-and-a-half hours.

family. Are you leaving forever without saying a word?" And the bereaved family members calling out the name of the drowned cry out impatiently, "Hello, Ch'angsu (name of one victim)! Why don't you speak?" In response to these questions, the mother only shakes the basket. When the shaman makes the final statement, that the drowned man can go into the better world by virtue of the *sumangogu-kut*, for which he is indebted to his family, she again shakes the basket up and down in response. The sight touches the family, who, thinking the spirit will go forever to the other-world, wail for him.

From the family of the fourth victim, Yŏngdal Jo (aged 23), members possessed by the spirits, begin to reveal the emotions of the dead by speaking (see figure 9.8). In the case of Yŏngdal Jo, his father holds the spirit basket first but doesn't become possessed. His mother comes to hold the basket. Holding the basket, she becomes possessed. Shouting "Father was not fair to me!" she beats the father with the spirit basket. (The father had been stern with the drowned man.) The father answers, "I am sorry. But I was stern to you so that you should become a good man." The mother in the place of the dead son says "I went out to sea in order to make a fortune and then the accident occurred!" Then she picks up a guitar from the memorial table (the guitar was a great favorite of the drowned man). She plays the guitar and dances.

The mother of the fifth victim, Kyŏngsu Cho, possessed by his spirit, goes around asking the leading people of the village for travel money for his journey to the other-world. She takes this money and puts it in the spirit basket. She (the spirit) expresses her thanks: "I'm grateful to you all for the *sumangogu-kut.*"

An elder sister of the sixth victim, Sudong Park, is possessed by her brother's spirit. He says, "My elder sister helped me to go to school with hard-earned money. She had plenty of hardships without parents to support our family. I'm really sorry I can't help her anymore." He finishes his utterance wishing the family every happiness and good luck.

In this way, *taenaerigi* (being possessed by the spirits), which was begun at two in the afternoon, goes on deep into the night in the midst of the night in the midst of the bereaved families' weeping.

The next morning, two more rites (8–9), *suri-kut* (exorcizing the evil spirits from the house) and *chiokt'anil-kut* (prayer to the Ten Kings of the other-world) are performed.

The tenth rite is *yŏngsanmaji-kut* (shaman rite of cleaning the spirits). The shaman puts the paper images of the spirits on a piece of white paper and scoops them up with an artificial lotus flower. After the shaman puts the images into the spirit bowls, she takes a broom in her right hand and an artificial flower in her left hand. Then she begins to sweep the spirit bowls with the broom drenched in water scented with Chinese juniper, mugwort, and pure water. She prays for the drowned men to go to heaven where they will live forever. The act of sweeping the spirit bowls, in which the paper images are placed, with the broom symbolizes the cleansing of the pollution of death from the drowned. The process is similar to that found in the *ssikim-kut* (shaman rite of bone washing) performed in the southern part of Korea.

As the next item of this rite, the shaman takes the washed spirit images out of the bowls and lays them down on a spirit basket. Dancing with the basket in her hand the shaman sings a song for the drowned. Later the shaman makes a cloth bridge with about twenty meters of white cotton in order to perform the tenth rite. She puts the spirit basket, in which the paper images and mortuary tablets of the spirits are laid, on the bridge and pushes it up to the top side, while singing a *yongsŏn-ga* (a shaman song to make the drowned men get on a dragon-shaped ship and go to the other-world.

Next is the eleventh rite, *kkotnori-kut* (celebration with flowers of the resurrection of the drowned spirits). The female shamans pull out the artificial flowers from the memorial table, dance around, and sing a song to the accompaniment of shamanistic music. They finish the *sumangogu-kut* by performing the twelfth rite, *sisŏk-kut* (offering to the miscellaneous spirits). This is the equivalent of the *tuijon-gŏri* in the *chinogwi-kut.*[4]

The third type of trance possession is found in *mugam.* This term designates very vigorous dancing by the client of a *naerim mudang* (possessed or charismatic shaman) during the course of a rite. Here the client puts on the shaman's special costume and dances to the drum. When the body governing spirit (*momju*) possesses her, the dancing client begins to jump rapidly up and down to the drum. The *mugam* is a trance dance.[5]

Figure 9.8 Members of Yŏngdal Jo's family possessed by spirits. This is called *taenaerigi*.

We have till now observed three kinds of trance possession: *chinogwi-kut*, *sumangogu-kut*, and *mugam* dancing. A *naerim mudang* becomes a medium of the deceased principally in the seance of *nŏk-chŏngbae-goi* (the penultimate part of a *chinogwi-kut*) when the deceased speaks directly with his family through the mouth of the shaman.

It should be noted that this kind of shaman overcomes *sinbyŏng* (possession sickness) during her or his initiation and repeats this experience of healing in the process of performing a *chinogwi-kut*. This matches Eliade's statement: "the shaman is not only a sick man; he is above all, a sick man who has been cured, who has succeeded in curing himself." (Eliade 1964: 27).

A *tangol mudang* (hereditary shaman), on the other hand, does not undergo possession sickness when she apprentices herself to the job. Instead, she becomes a shaman by being born into a shaman's family. She can't become a medium of the deceased or possessed by a spirit but helps the family of the dead to be possessed by means of chanting an incantation and beating a drum continuously in the process of *taenaerigi* in the *sumangogu-kut*. As in the case of the shamans of Cheju Island, a *tangol mudang* experiences a professional, self-conscious pseudo-possession. The hereditary shamans do not have an unconscious genuine possession, which women of the deceased's family, such as wives, daughters, or daughters-in-law, can undergo.

Many anthropological reports say that shamanistic trance possession occurs most readily among the underprivileged lower classes with repressed social desires (Harris 1957: 1054). Lewis (1971: 112–13) similarly notes that possession (ecstatic cults) has always attracted followers among the weak and oppressed, and particularly among women in male-dominant societies. In Korea too, possession phenomena take place among the common people, especially among women of the dead man's family. The people of the lower classes, especially poor women, in shamanizing for the dead who meet a violent death, participate in the rite and act as performers – not as an audience – with the shamans. An old Korean proverb says, "Although the mother-in-law wants the shaman to come and dance, she does not like to see her eldest daughter-in-law dance." A severe mother-in-law usually doesn't want her daughters-in-law to take part in *kut* because they can easily enjoy themselves in *mugam* dancing with excitement like a shaman, and the mother-in-law can't prevent them from dancing. This also shows that the daughters-in-law lighten their pent-up feelings of oppression and console themselves with the *kut*. One of the specialists concerned insists, "Divine possession occurs at the moment when the resentment of the poor and the oppressed are suddenly given vent." (Kim, Yeol-kyu 1980: 63). In the entire process of participation, they, being possessed by the spirit and communicating with the dead, come to believe that the dead man enters heaven and thereby relieve themselves of sorrow.

As can be seen from the above, each type of trance possession in Korean shamanism not only involves role playing or the assumption of a particular identity, but also has the functions of religious salvation and the reduction of social tensions.

Notes

1. A good deal of research has been devoted to the symptoms of *sinbyŏng*, the possession sickness which is necessary for becoming a *naerim mudang*, a possessed or charismatic shaman. Taegon Kim gives brief accounts of the onset of this initiatory illness and analyzes twenty cases for consistencies in symptoms and precipitating events. He describes the symptoms of the destined shamans as: "persistent illness for no apparent reasons, appetite loss, unwillingness to eat meat and fish, craving for cold water, weakness or pain in the limbs, hallucination, and crazed wanderings." These symptoms can be cured only when the afflicted becomes a shaman through a specific experience of trance state. He notes that "similar experiences mark the would-be shaman in Siberia, the Americas, Africa, and Australia" (Kim Taegon, 1970: 91–132). In light of this *sinbyŏng* phenomenon, Korean shamans appear to have a close relationship with Siberian shamans and Northern Asian shamans, especially Tungus shamans, in their individual conditions for becoming shamans and recognition and election of a new shaman (Shirokogoroff 1935: 344–51).

   On the other hand, Kwang-Iel Kim, a psychoanalytically oriented psychiatrist, divides the *sinbyŏng* syndrome into two phases: a "prodromal phase" and "a depersonalization phase." In the prodromal phase, the destined shaman exhibits, ". . . hysterical or psychosomatic symptoms such as anorexia, weakness, insomnia, indigestion and/or functional paralysis of extremities." In the depersonalization phase, "symptoms are aggravated" and "hallucinatory experiences, dreams of revelation or prophecy, confusion, with/or psychomotor excitement are common additional symptoms." He concludes that "Consequently, 'sinbyŏng' can be understood not only as a psychopathological manifestation in that would-be shamans project their long standing inner conflicts unto the shamanistic complex, but also as a manifestation of an unconscious trial for resolving their conflicts by way of projection unto the shamanistic value system." (Kim Kwang-Iel 1972: 223–34).

Bou-Yong Rhi, another psychiatrist but of Jungian orientation, has also done considerable research on Korean shamanism. He says that shamans are recovered neurotics or psychotics. Both Kim, K.-I. (1972) and Rhi (1970) reached similar conclusions from their independent studies perceiving Korean shamanism as an institutionalized system of sublimation, with both positive and negative effects.

From W.G. Bogoras, and M.A. Czaplicka in the early second decade of the twentieth century to A. Ohlmarks, the last investigator who favors explaining shamanism by "arctic hysteria," Siberian shamanism has been studied especially as a psychopathological phenomenon. Devereux (1961) "characterizes the shaman as a severe neurotic or psychotic who serves his society as a deputy lunatic" (cited here from Harvey 1979: 242).

S.M. Shirokogoroff expressed the opinion that a shaman has a normal personality (1923: 248–49). And U. Harva seconds his point in noting that though there is no satisfactory explanation of symptoms of possession sickness, well-reputed Siberian shamans must not be considered as lunatics (1971, Japanese edition: 411). H. Findeisen says that the possession sickness which a novice must undergo in order to become a shaman is generally believed to be an uneasiness or mental affliction; Nobody can explain the true mental disorder of this kind, but as soon as the shaman, selected by the spirits, holds a shaman drum stick, he is believed to be free from the sickness forever, and he never suffers from the sickness again (1957: 51).

In relation to the opinions of these researchers, the Korean folk view of shamans can be summed up as follows: 1) the experience of disorder of some form is an essential feature in the recruitment of a shaman; 2) afflictions alone do not automatically make a shaman of the victim, who must overcome the illness; and 3) the relationship between a shaman and possessing spirits are mutually binding, as in a marriage (Harvey 1979: 251).

2. Y.K. Harvey outlines the personal attributes of a *naerim mudang*: 1) a high level of intelligence; 2) above average capacity for creative improvization (imaginative and capable of improvizing verbally, behaviorally, and in the use of available resources); 3) above average verbal fluency and persuasiveness; 4) strong goal orientation (they tend to be willful, self-centered, self-reliant, and self-directed); 5) keen sensitivity to intuitive cues of others; 6) calculating and manipulative interpersonal skills which enables them to manage social situations strategically; 7) a sharp sense of justice in terms of their own standards; and 8) an above average repertory of aptitudinal and/or achieved dramatic and artistic attributes such as singing and dancing (Harvey 1979: 235–36).

3. Other research has found that the Goldi tribe or Tungus tribe in Siberia express both the road of spirits and the road of the shaman by using a cord, string, or rope. (Harva 1938: *passim*).

4. "After the shamanizing, when the members of the audience recollect the various moments of the performance, their great psychophysiological emotion and the hallucinations of sight and hearing, they have a deep satisfaction, incomparatively

greater than that from the emotion produced by theatrical and musical performances, literature and general artistic phenomena of the European complex, because
in shamanizing the audience consists at the same time of actors and participants."
(Shirokogoroff 1935: 331).

5. The following is a comparison of ritual and theatre made by Schechner (1977: 75).

EFFICACY	ENTERTAINMENT
(Ritual)	(Theatre)
results	fun
link to an absent Other	only for those here
abolishes time, symbolic time	emphasizes now
brings Other here	audience is the Other
performer possessed, in trance	performer know what he's doing
audience participates	audience watches
audience believes	audience appreciates
criticism is forbidden	criticism is encouraged
collective creativity	individual creativity

10.
The practice of noh theatre

MONICA BETHE AND KAREN BRAZELL

Dance, music, poetry, costumes, and masks combine in the noh theatre to create a performance which can be aesthetically impressive and emotionally profound. How is this art nurtured? What enables the beauty of noh to flower on the stage in a particular performance? What motivates the actors to devote their lives to nourishing a traditional art form? Are there new species of noh growing out of the old? And finally can noh, or aspects of noh be successfully transplanted to a climate as unfamiliar as that of the modern Western world? These are the questions we explore here.

Noh is today practiced in Japan by several hundred highly trained professionals, both actors and musicians. As a traditional performance system passed down in an unbroken line from generation to generation of practitioners since the fourteenth century, every aspect – text, melody, instrumentation, choreography, and costuming – has become codified. The current repertory is essentially the same as that performed in the sixteenth century, and today's performers are responsible for mastering its two hundred plays.

The phenomenal memorization that this mastery implies is aided by the structure of noh, for it is an art based on the manipulation of fixed modules of performance combined according to underlying principles. Although the basic vocabulary is limited, the variations are endless, so that each play, indeed each performance of a given play, offers fresh vision, new insights. The underlying rules may never be explicitly stated or taught, but they are subconsciously internalized during the course of training.

The training of the performer is the first topic in our essay, a discussion which includes recognition of the delicate balance between learning and teaching. Secondly, we describe the intimate relationship between practice and performance and the particular preparations necessary for a perform-ance. After that we step back to look at what the practice of noh means as a way of life. We explore the ideas held by the father and son Kannami (1333–84) and Zeami (1363–1443), who are credited with perfecting noh, and show that, while these ideas continue to fulfill some present-day performers, others are attempting to stretch the bounds of their traditional art. Finally,

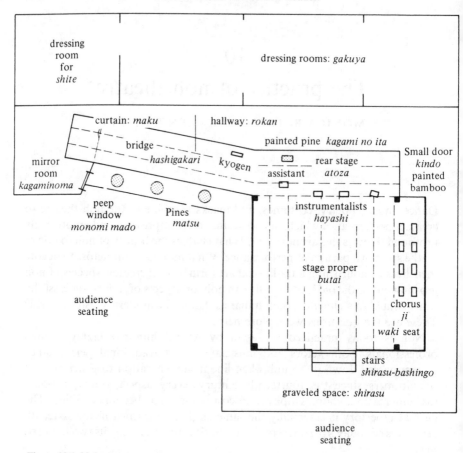

Figure 10.1 Noh stage.

parallel to these developments are the experiments of some modern artists, both Japanese and Western, who attempt to transfer aspects of the practice of noh to other theatrical forms.

Practice as training: learning and teaching

Like many theatrical genres with settled performance texts, noh emphasizes training. However, while for many other performance arts, this emphasis grows out of a need for traditionalism, in noh the essential role of training was recognized even in the formative period. Zeami's treatises, written before there were fixed performance texts and intended to instruct his descendants in the essence of his art, already concentrate on training. As Zeami perceived it, training lasts a lifetime; it develops the person as well as the performer, giving him a level of discipline, concentration and mastery which improves his soul as

Figure 10.2 Learning a piece by dancing side by side with a teacher. Takabayashi Kōji and his son Shinji.

well as his art. By mastering his art, the actor develops his "self," his understanding of life and his ability to deal with it.

The training of a noh actor traditionally begins before he enters school. As Zeami decreed centuries ago and is still true today, early practice centers on the essential arts of song and dance.[1] Typically the young boy begins training with his father. The first step is to learn, piece by piece, in bits and parts, the main plays of the standard repertory. The emphasis is on ingrained, intimate knowledge, the child internalizes the song and dance before he understands them intellectually.[2]

In the early stages of training, the child actor learns through imitation and repetition (see figure 10.2). The father dances sections from a play with the child; the father singing the words while child struggles to imitate his motions. Frequently the father manipulates the child's limbs, accustoming them to the proper positions. The training is adjusted to the temperament of the child, involving him as naturally as possible in the world of noh, attempting to spark his interest. Song is also learned by repeated imitation. Formal vocal training often begins later than dance training, although Kongō Iwao describes having some training in both when he was six (Kongō 1984: 76). In all of his lessons the child learns parts of plays, never isolated movements or scales. With each piece of added difficulty the child must bring into play greater control of detail. While at first he only strives to get through a piece without mistakes, later being in the right place at the right time becomes a minor aspect of mastery.

After the young actor has mastered a certain number of pieces and reached some degree of proficiency, the father begins to demonstrate less and to require the older child to study more. In addition to learning by imitating his father, the older child is told to study such and such a piece by reading chant and dance books. As Kongō Iwao recalls: "By the time I was in junior high I was expected to spend time practicing by myself, and to watch practices and study the instruments of the ensemble. Often my father would give me instruction just two weeks before a performance" (1984: 76). Memorizing a vast amount of text and technical detail becomes an ingrained habit which proves useful throughout a performer's life. Once the youth has learned a piece on his own, he performs it for his father at the next lesson. His mistakes are then corrected.

This learning process is possible because in the performance system of noh all plays have a similar underlying structure. The section labelled the *kuse* scene, for example, has a recognizable poetic, melodic, instrumental, and kinetic structure (Bethe and Brazell 1978, 1982–83). Once one has learned enough of these scenes to have internalized the underlying models and to have experienced the major variations, it is not difficult to learn the *kuse* from a new play very quickly. The teacher need point out only the variations specific to the piece.

Actual stage experience from an early age is considered a necessary adjunct to training. The noh repertory includes numerous roles for child actors. In fact, the typical actor may have already appeared on stage in a role designed for a child actor (*kokata*), before his regular, formal training begins.[3] The child's earliest roles are merely walk-ons, but as he continues his training, he will be given child's roles which involve song and even dance.[4] As Zeami first emphasized, the attributes of an actor's age should be capitalized upon: the childishness of a boy who can barely hold still, the high-pitched chant of a young boy, and the blossoming of a youth should all be exploited as part of their charm. This helps to create the flower (*hana*) of their performances (Rimer and Yamazaki 1984: 4–9). It was indeed the young Zeami's boyish charm as much as his father Kannami's talent that caught the attention and earned the patronage of noh by the military ruler of Japan, Yoshimitsu, in 1374.

Some plays are also appropriate for child-performance versions, particularly warrior plays, because they contain relatively active parts, which are considered easier for children.[5] Such plays are performed by children in costume, but without masks, and may be done in rather informal circumstances, or they may appear as part of a professional program of plays.

The second major stage of the training process most often begins when the youth has completed the equivalent of junior high and he becomes a live-in disciple (*uchideshi*) to a master actor, usually the head of his school of actors. Noh performers are divided into schools of performers, each school having a head (*iemoto*) who oversees the training of all the members. In larger schools there are several theatres which serve as centers for training; in smaller schools all disciples can study directly under the head of the school. The timing and length of live-in training varies considerably, but the practice is common to all groups of noh performers, instrumentalists as well as actors. This rather traditional apprentice role requires that the young actor do menial tasks for the master teacher, and he may spend more time scrubbing the stage than performing on it. The discipline is typically very strict. During this period the young actor learns to perform wearing a mask, usually beginning when he "comes of age." Kanze Hisao, recalling the first time he wore a mask in the title role of *Tomoe* at age fifteen, remembered that he was overjoyed when his grandfather said, as he handed him the mask, "You are full-grown now, so you must wear a mask" (Kanze 1984: 66). The teenaged actor may also appear on stage in *tsure* (secondary actor) roles. After his voice has changed, he will also start participating in professional performances as a member of the chorus.

Once the master teacher has certified that a young actor has attained sufficient professional proficiency, most commonly when he is in his mid-twenties, he may move out of the master teacher's house and begin to train students himself.[6] As a young professional he will still, however, continue training with a master actor, though on a less intensive level than before.

Both live-in disciples and young professionals can participate in youth training groups (*yōseikai*) which generally consist of all the young performers in a geographical area who are aspiring to become senior professionals. These groups put on regular full noh performances after which they critique each others' performances and are also critiqued by senior professionals associated with the group. These performances are not generally open to the public, but are an extremely important part of training and mutual support system for young performers. This system is supported by the national and prefectural governments and by professional noh actors resident in the area. After five years in the youth training group, the young actor may join one of a variety of more loosely structured study groups which provide him with continued opportunities for partially supervised performance. At the same time the young actors will be called upon to participate in fully professional performances as chorus members, *tsure*, junior stage attendants (*kōken*) and increasingly as *shite* (main characters).

The role of stage attendant is an important one which requires some explanation. The stage attendant sits at the back of stage right near the bridge from the time the *shite* enters until his exit. A seeming non-participant except when he adjusts the *shite*'s garments, sets out or removes a prop, or performs an on-stage costume change, the stage attendant in fact has the responsibility for making sure that all the details of the performance proceed smoothly, so that the main actor is entirely free of any worries and can concentrate on his role. Should the *shite* forget a line, the stage attendant serves as prompter, and should the *shite* become incapacitated in any way, the stage attendant steps in as understudy. The role is considered so important that the stage main attendant generally is an actor of equal or superior ability to the *shite*.

In contemporary performance practice there are often two stage attendants. The senior attendant is ultimately responsible for the performance, and, although he may sit immobile throughout the performance, he is constantly aware of what is happening and ready to respond to any emergency. The junior stage attendant performs the regular chores such as placing and removing props and obeys the slightest signal from his senior colleague. Serving as junior stage attendant is an important part of the training process.

The plays in the noh repertory are ranked according to difficulty, and an actor must have the permission of the head of the school to perform certain plays. This permission is granted when the head of the school deems the actor skilled and experienced enough to perform the role. The particular plays which serve as landmarks of development vary somewhat from school to school, but the four plays which most often serve this function are *Shakkyō*, *Midare*, *Okina*, and *Dōjōji* (see figure 10.3). The last is most often performed when the actor is in his late twenties to mid-thirties. The Kanze school actor Tsumura Reijirō claims: "For a Noh actor this play [*Dōjōji*] represents the single most important barrier to be overcome in order to be accepted as a fully qualified member of his profession. The critical evaluation of this first performance is of such importance that it can dominate the course of his professional life." (1984: 105)

In addition to learning his own part, each noh performer is also trained in most of the other roles necessary to produce a play. *Shite* or main actors memorize entire plays, learning to sing all the roles except that of the kyōgen, which is not considered part of the play proper. They also learn to beat at least two of the three drums and frequently to play the flute. Kyōgen actors, who, in addition to performing in the comic plays (called kyōgen) between noh plays, also perform the interlude scene between acts of a noh play and sometimes have minor roles within a noh play, usually learn something of all the arts, although the music for the independent kyōgen plays is much simpler than for noh. The training for *waki* or secondary actors emphasizes rhythm and song, and instrumentalists all study the other instruments and the chant, although few learn much dance. An actor often starts to learn the instruments before he is ten years old by studying with professional instrumentalists. As a child he will typically begin with the stick drum, because it does not require that the performer has memorized the texts. Then he will learn the hand drums and finally the flute. Thus by the time the actor is a young professional he will not only have learned to chant and dance all the plays in the repertory, but he will also know, at an advanced amateur level, how to play the instrumental parts. We discuss the ramifications of this training in the section on practice and performance below.

Another route is open to young people who want to become professionals, but who did not receive childhood training. They typically become interested

Figure 10.3 *Shōjō Midare*, often performed as a
"graduation piece." The sea elf offers some wine of long
life. *Shite*: Izumi Yoshi. 1964.

in noh in their teens or early twenties, usually through amateur lessons, often
through noh clubs at colleges and universities.[7] When they decide to turn
professional, they must be accepted as live-in disciples by a certified master
and belatedly learn all the arts of noh performance.

An even more radical experiment began in the summer of 1984. The
National Noh Theater in Tokyo, built by the government and opened in
September 1983, has established a program to train twenty students to become
instrumentalists, kyōgen, and *waki* actors, as it was felt that the numbers of
these performers is not equal to the demand. *Shite* actors will continue to be
trained in the traditional manner, although the National Noh Theater will
also help to encourage their training. Students in the National Noh Theater
program, who must have graduated from middle school and be less than

twenty-five years old, will be trained for three years in all aspects of noh, with most of the classes, including the practice of instrumental music and chanting, conducted in groups (Goff 1984: 449–50).

In addition to the many practical problems facing this program (the recruiting of good students, continual and adequate funding, etc.), there is always the question as to whether this type of training begun so late in life will succeed in producing first-rate performers. Though performers trained in a non-traditional fashion are accepted within the noh world, it is too soon to tell if any person who began his training so late will ever become a great performer. Most noh performers insist that these "newcomers" will always lack a certain something in their performance; this "something" is identified as that which is attained unconsciously and viscerally through the traditional, early childhood training and which does not rely in any way on intellectualization.

At every level of training, teaching concentrates on form, even though the art of a performer is judged by his expressive intensity. While learning the form, the young performer is expected to make it his own and fill it with meaning. This process is regarded as too personal, too individualized to teach overtly. Yet it is exactly this which constitutes the secret art and which the observant student hopes to gain from a master. The observant master in turn nurtures the spiritual growth of his trainee by ignoring it, so as not to encourage self-conscious manipulation. (Rimer and Yamazaki 1984: 4)

During the long years of intensive training, slow painstaking work on a single piece goes hand in hand with rapid memorization of new pieces from the repertory. The aim of this two-sided process is to increase the young performer's capacities for concentrating on several levels simultaneously and to develop a respect for fundamentals. A young performer may spend months preparing for a stage appearance, practicing and being corrected until he develops ever finer sensitivity to detail, and at the same time be asked to prepare a new piece for each lesson. The pieces are graded by level of difficulty, although the level may vary according to which art is being practiced. For example *Bashō* is considered an easy piece for chanting, but a more advanced piece for dance.

Noh performers constantly return to pieces they have already learned. This return to "easy" pieces is an integral part of the system and occurs in several ways. For example, when an actor learns the hand drums, he must review the texts of plays he has learned to sing and dance, this time with the added dimension of rhythmic give and take. He may be asked (with no advance notice) to chant a passage at his drum lesson to accompany another student or to sing while his father teaches an amateur. Also, in his training as an actor he will keep returning to earlier pieces. After learning complex pieces, the very simplicity of the early pieces leads to the discovery of new levels of difficulty. The performer is suddenly face to face with unadorned, naked simplicity whose ultimate expression cannot, he now understands, depend on technical virtuosity. Even when, as a mature actor, he reaches a point where the control of nuances is as much an element of technique as pitch or gesture, he increasingly relies on the fundamentals like stance and walk and breath. Zeami expressed the importance of returning to the basics with the admonition, "Do not forget the beginner's heart." (Nearman 1982a: 68)

The very simplicity of the form of noh makes its mastery extremely difficult. The emphasis on an intensity which, though centered in the individual, reaches out to encompass the entire performance, requires a very delicate balance of parts. Each performer must develop a concentrated sensitivity which picks up, responds to and adjusts to all the other performers on stage during the actual performance. The drummers, for example, may signal other performers through the quality of their calls. These calls regularly mark the eight beats of the measure. The shoulder drum player usually quickens the pace at the end of each measure by clipping short his calls before beats 7 and 8. However, if he wishes to suggest to the other performers that they are rushing, he may not accelerate in this manner or he may even deliberately lengthen his calls to alter the mood to one of greater dignity. If the main actor feels that the drummers' tone is too light, he can communicate this by filling out his syllables thus signalling the drummers to slow down and fill out their own calls. The ability to maintain such give and take within a set format comes only after broad training in all the arts of noh and extensive performance experience; it is partially for this reason that a noh actor is not generally considered fully developed until he is in his mid-forties.

The later stages of training, which to a large extent are accomplished through the self-examination of the performer as he practices, work towards a highly sophisticated art of stage presence.[8] To attain this, the performer must constantly reevaluate and rethink. Kongō Iwao claims, "Discerning [fine] points is really a matter of practice and experience. The secret is to learn from a performance so you do not repeat mistakes" (1984: 81). In his search to develop as he practices, the performer watches other performers with an eye to finding the key to their art. He may ask himself, "How does that actor express that so effectively? What is the basis of his timing? What is the secret to his sliding walk." Continued growth requires that a performer believe in his own ability and also that he have total humility, acknowledging that what he has achieved is not the full capacity of what noh can be.

Though the noh performer continues to learn throughout his life, he also teaches for much of it. Teaching is a form of practice. During lessons, as he sings, dances, beats out drum parts, and sings the flute solmization for his students, he reinforces memorized patterns for himself as well. Lesson time is always serious. The teacher brings to bear all the concentration he has developed in his own training and which now is a part of his unconscious attitude. Even if he knows the student will not notice three-quarters of what he is putting into the demonstration, he still performs seriously. This is partly because the unteachable aspects of noh are considered most important and therefore should always be there in case the student can pick them up, either consciously or unwittingly. It is also because seriousness of attitude towards the piece is as much a part of teaching and training as it is a part of performance.

Training professionals and amateurs is integral to the noh world; it is the system by which noh propagates itself, maintains a discriminating audience, and keeps up its artistic standards. Amateur students may be housewives, retired people, college students, foreigners, anyone who wants to pursue the singing and/or dancing of noh or the playing of one of the instruments as a hobby. There are thousands such people in Japan today. In fact many performers are financially more dependent on lesson fees paid by amateurs than on the proceeds from performances. Amateur students also provide an educated audience trained to pick up on the subtler aspects of performance and therefore to provide the discriminating evaluation which spurs performers to greater proficiency. Both critics and scholars of noh have also often had some training in noh practice, and a few of them are good amateur performers.

The importance of amateurs in supporting noh is not a recent phenomenon. Already in Zeami's time there were interested non-professionals studying from noh actors. A contemporary diary documents noh performances by warriors in 1432 and 1433, and by 1450 such performances had become commonplace (Raz 1983: 117). By the end of the sixteenth century even the military leaders Toyotomi Hideyoshi, his son Hidetsugu, and Tokugawa Ieyasu actively performed noh (126–27). This practice continued among the feudal lords of the Edo period, who competed in collecting costumes and masks both for their own use and for the use of their privately maintained noh troupes (Masuda 1984a: 2–3, 185; 1984b: 186–87). Amateur women's troupes also flourished until 1629 when women were prohibited from appearing on the stage all together. However private lessons for women did continue, and in the nineteenth century it was not uncommon to find wives of high ranking officials studying noh chanting or drumming.

Practice and performance

One salient characteristic of noh is that the training of the performers cannot be clearly separated from preparations for the performance. There are no drills to prepare the voice or the body, no scales to run through or warming up exercises, no role playing or breathing exercises, no exercises to improve concentration or rhythm; there is only performance. Practice is always performing bits of a play and is usually done without interruption. The teacher forces the student to struggle through the entire section, correcting him only after he has completed the piece. In this sense practice is performance; all that changes are the number and type of other performers who participate and the nature of the audience. When an actor practices by himself, he performs for himself, with as much concentration and self-projection as if he were on stage before an audience, although he may skip over purely formulaic parts.

An actor rarely practices with all of the instrumentalists and chorus members accompanying him. Some of the simplified types of practice are also done as stage performances. The simplest is unaccompanied chant (*suutai*) in which one or more performers sing the text.[9] Such performances can be heard on the radio and are published as records and audio cassettes. An actor may also perform a selected danced section of the text to vocal music (*shimai*), or he may perform a somewhat longer section to both vocal and instrumental accompaniment (*maibayashi*), or sing such a section without dance (*banbayashi*). These abbreviated performances, all done without costumes or masks, may occur as independent recitals, or they may be done between fully performed noh plays in a day's program. Such events may be seen as either practice or performance; the distinction is largely irrelevant.

Because of this elaborate practice/performance system and because each individual performer knows most or all of the parts for each play in the repertory, it is possible for a professional group to get together and perform a play without any rehearsals. This was standard before the recent past. Nowadays before a full noh performance the participants normally only get together once to listen briefly to the main actor's comments about his interpretation and run through the parts of the play which are important, difficult or require unusual timing or coordination.

It is not only all-round training and continual practice that makes single rehearsals a possibility; the structure of noh itself does much to aid memorization and to allow for mutual adjustment in actual performance. A noh play is constructed of building blocks or performance modules which are combined in predictable ways. Each specific play is a modification of a basic, underlying model. Although the various schools of performers may use different musical or movement patterns in a given play, the well-trained performer is aware of these differences as variations on the model. The more experienced the performers on stage are, the more freely they can adjust to differences in detail, even unexpected or previously unexperienced differences. This is because they have mastered the overall picture.

As a result, performers have different attitudes towards rehearsal. Young performers who do not have the breadth of experience to adjust almost automatically to unexpected situations and who still have to reassure themselves about how all the parts fit together can find repeated rehearsals very useful. This is a major purpose of the young actors' groups mentioned earlier. More experienced performers also benefit from several rehearsals when they have to prepare particularly difficult pieces which require sensitive and subtle responses to the rhythms of others on stage.[10] On the other hand, when experienced performers are doing an often-performed piece, they prefer not to over-rehearse because it takes the surprise out of the actual performance.

A noh play is a "one time event." That is to say a play is normally produced only once by the same ensemble.[11] Although an actor may perform a popular play numerous times in his life (especially if he gives performances for the public schools), he will normally do it with a different group of performers each time. There is usually only one chance for any group to create their version of a given play. This is an important element in the aesthetics and psychology of performance. If everyone on stage knows exactly what everyone else is going to do, the play is likely to become an empty exercise no matter how good the technique of the participants. Consequently when circumstances, such as a foreign tour, require the same group to play the same piece repeatedly, they face a challenge which is alleviated mainly by the change of theatre and audience, though in some groups the actors will change roles.

At the opposite end of the scale, when performers get together to do "misordered" noh (rannō), a performance in which everyone takes a role other than his professional role (i.e. drummers dance, kyōgen players sing noh, etc.), they capitalize on the unexpected adjustments required in order to create amusement. Such performances, sometimes done as end-of-the-year parties, add considerably to the performers store of experience.

The actor Izumi Yoshio explains the pitfalls of over-rehearsal using the following metaphor. Imagine a line with a circle moving back and forth on it in uneven rhythm. If your goal is to hit the center of the circle and you can accomplish that each time you try, the "game" soon becomes boring. This is what happens when noh performers become too accustomed to the rhythms and nuances of the others on stage. However, if you hit within the circle, now to the upper right, now towards the middle left, now almost on the edge, the pattern remains intact and your interest in the act increases. In noh performance this "almost, but not quite" hitting dead center increases the creative tension among the performers on stage. Each has to adjust slightly to the actions of another to keep the performance within the circle, for if the circle is missed all together the beauty of the pattern is destroyed. The necessity for constant adjustment sparks the performers' interest, deepens their concentration, and thereby intensifies the expression of the entire play.

A performance in the making

With the intensive, continual training a noh performer receives, he is capable of performing almost any play on a day's notice. This is rarely necessary, however. More commonly the actor performing the main role (shite) knows that he will do a certain play six months to a year in advance of the performance. Once the date is set the play is always in his mind, his mental vision of it slowly evolving as he makes practical preparations for the performance (Tsumura 1984: 109). The *shite* is generally responsible for choosing the other performers and for selecting the stage effects: the masks and costumes he and the *tsure* will wear, and the specifics of the props if there are any. Within the limitations of a set tradition, he chooses from the available store those people and items which will most adequately reflect his interpretation of the play[12]. In effect the *shite* takes the role of producer, director, costumer, and set designer, although each of these roles is extremely limited compared to its modern western counterpart because the actor is guided by established traditions for all aspects of the performance.

The choice of performers depends on the occasion of the performance as well as on the producing actor's interpretation of the play. For the regular monthly performances (*teiki nō*) each actor in the group plays the *shite* role at least once a year and participates in most of the other performances in a supporting role: *tsure*, head of chorus, chorus member, or stage attendant.[13] Each senior professional will also put on one or more private performances a year, arranging for everything himself, paying every other person who participates, and taking the box office proceeds or losses as they come. For such private performances the choice of supporting performers is both freer and more carefully considered than for the monthly performances, and fees paid to the performers are also greater. Noh performances given in commemoration of special events, the anniversary of one's father's death, for example, are considered especially sacrosanct, and for them extra care is given to making each selection as perfect as possible by gathering respected masters. Tickets are twice the normal price; so is the cost to the producing performer. Usually difficult or celebratory pieces are chosen (i.e. *Dōjōji, Shakkyō, Obasute*), so that much is also demanded of the performers. In addition to actors, other groups or institutions also produce noh plays: groups of musicians, municipalities, Shinto shrines, Buddhist temples, public schools, broadcasting companies, business organizations, etc. On these occasions the *shite* may have less control of the design of the performance, but he generally is also paid.[14]

Although the financial framework of a performance does much to dictate the age and proficiency of the invited performers, the actor producing a play also attempts to choose performers whom he feels will support and enrich his particular interpretation of the play. Sometimes he will choose one outstanding musician who he hopes can lead other, less experienced (and hence less expensive) musicians in playing beyond their normal capacity. Among the supporting actors, his most careful consideration will be given to selecting the leader of the chorus, who has the main responsibility for tying the musical fiber of the play together, particularly during dramatic highlights where the main actor is dancing to the chanting. A good chorus lies at the core of a good play: the dancer cannot fully express the subtleties of his interpretation without the support of well-atuned words and melody evoking the atmosphere of the play, nor can the drummers create the rhythmic tensions that drive the play forward without a distinct rhythmic context from the chanting. An equally important supporting actor is the stage attendant whose responsibility for the performance was described earlier.

Since noh is performed without sets and with few props, the costumes and masks are major vehicles for creating visual atmosphere. The mask embodies the personality of the character and must be chosen with special care.[15] Often this is the starting point for an actor's decisions about his interpretation for a specific performance.[16] In some cases tradition allows for a choice of several similar but distinct types of masks, but often the actor is restricted to selecting from among several artists' renditions of masks bearing the same name and expressing essentially the same personality. The distinctions between one and another are only in subtle nuances which reflect the art and sensitivity of the carver.[17] The actor will choose a mask not only for the appropriateness of its expression and its ability to come alive on stage, but also for its level of "dignity," making sure that the mask's sophistication is in line with his own ability. An inexperienced actor would not dream of wearing a highly esteemed, old mask. As Kanze Hisao has explained: "During a performance, the actor and the mask are in a state of confrontation, working to create art in a constant struggle to subjugate each other. It is for this reason that the true value of a superior mask is brought to its full realization only when it is worn by a superior actor" (1984: 71–72).

The costume not only creates atmosphere through its color combinations and designs, but also clearly indicates the social status, profession, and dignity of the character. The audience is trained in reading both costume and masks for interpretation. Although appropriateness is the most important criterion for a costume, rarity is also valued. Actors like to store up their own unusual costume pieces for special performances, but few can afford the expense. Most actors are largely dependant on the general store of costumes and masks owned by the head of their school or theatre group. Members of the group rent from these stores with the head's permission.

Private preparations for a performance vary greatly according to the actor. At an early stage in his preparation an actor will go over all the notes he has taken from his lessons, from his previous performances of the play, from peformances in which he has participated in a supporting role, and from performances by great masters. If he has questions about the details, he will take them to a master actor. A young actor may spend months going over the piece and practicing it privately. On the other hand, because of the many obligations and busy schedules of most professionals, a senior actor may never physically practice the entire piece, although he will run through it many times in his mind imagining his own figure on stage, seeing the piece through mental projection from inside and outside at once.[18] A day or two before the performance, he holds the general rehearsal.

The performance day

A modern noh program continues for around five hours and includes a number of plays and shorter pieces. The length of a program has gradually been reduced. In medieval Japan it appears to have taken the better part of a day; by pre-modern times a formal program consisted of the play *Okina*, five noh plays and four comic kyōgen plays. This formal program is still presented a few times a year and takes about ten hours. Regular performances now are usually held on Saturday, Sunday or holiday afternoons and rarely include more than three noh plays plus one or two kyōgen, and sung or danced recital pieces. In some cities, Osaka for example, short evening performances centering around one noh play are gaining popularity. The National Noh Theater in Tokyo also schedules single plays.

The performers arrive in good time for their parts and leave after finishing all their duties. Usually only the person who arranged for the performance stays for the entire day. From the time they start packing the costumes and instruments to take to the theatre, they begin to concentrate on their duties for the day. In one day most performers will appear on stage more than once. An actor may play the *shite* in one play and sing in the chorus in another, or he may serve as stage attendant in one play, perform a short dance without costume between plays, and sing in the chorus in yet another play.

Rooms backstage are set aside for depositing paraphernalia, dressing, and sitting and chatting when not on stage. Generally these are allotted to performance groups: one for *shite* actors (chorus, *tsure*, etc.), one or two for *waki* and kyōgen actors, and one for instrumentalists. A special room close to the stage is reserved for the elaborate costuming of the actors for the main roles (see figure 10.4). The costumes for each of the plays to be performed are laid out in separate piles.

Some twenty or thirty minutes before a play is to begin the *shite*, clad in white, padded underwear, appears in his special dressing room. Although this actor has been in charge of all the arrangements before the performance day, once he is ready to be costumed, he need no longer be concerned with anything except his own role. The senior stage attendant takes over all other responsibilities. He is in charge of dressing the *shite*, draping and tying each layer of garment according to tradition. The actor has only to stand and occasionally comment on whether a knot is pulled tightly enough. In the final stage of dressing, he goes to an area just outside the curtain, where, seated before a large mirror, he salutes the mask, and then holds it in place to his face (see figure 10.5).[19] Once it is secured, he sits and waits, concentrating on his image in the mirror until he is lead by the stage attendant to the curtain at the end of the bridge (see figure 10.6). At the moment he wishes the curtain to be raised, he grunts the word *maku* (curtain), indicating by his intonation the manner in which he wants it lifted. A quiet prolonged grunt sounding a bit like

Figure 10.4 Dressing the *shite* actor. Izumi Yoshio
playing lady Rokujo in *Nonomiya*. 1986.

"moo" is an order for a slow, smooth lifting of the curtain, while a sharp, clipped rendition demands a swift, sharp pulling back of the curtain.[20]

The *shite* is never the first performer on the stage, and usually enters only after supporting actors have played a brief scene or two. The preparation of other performers is a ritualization of necessary actions. *Waki* and kyōgen actors help each other dress in their appointed rooms. The musicians must prepare their instruments; all the drums must be assembled, and the hip drum must be dried over a charcoal fire for over an hour. Just before each play begins the instrumentalists gather behind the curtain and play a brief, formalized warm-up (*oshirabe*) (see figure 10.7). This is an opportunity to make sure the timbre of the instruments is correct and also a notification to the

Figure 10.5 Saluting the mask before donning it in the
mirror room. *Nonomiya*.

audience that the play is about to begin. The passage played for the warm-up is
fixed and is the same passage the student plays before each lesson, indicating
again the lack of distinction between practice and performance. Once the brief
warm-up is over, the instrumentalists line up to go down the bridge and take
their places in the extreme upstage area. As each instrumentalist passes by the
curtain which has been half pulled aside for him, he puts on his stage "mask":
his eyes are fixed straight ahead and his features loose all expressions except
concentration. The performance has begun.

At the end of the play, the *shite* is usually the first actor to leave, although
his exit is normally preceded by the exit of the stage attendants through the
small door at upstage left. The attendants remove the *shite*'s mask and wipe
the sweat from his face. He then sits in the area behind the curtain and awaits
the exits of the other actors and instrumentalists. As each comes off stage he
bows to the *shite* and takes his place till they are all seated in the area. The
members of the group thank each other with set words and a bow, then
disperse (see figure 10.8). This final greeting is an integral part of the etiquette
of the play and expresses the mutual interdependence of all on stage. (A
similar expression of thanks is performed after lessons. Even a father teaching
his six-year-old son insists on formal thanks after every lesson.) After this
exchange each person is free to leave if his duties for the day are over.
Occasionally the entire troupe of performers is invited to a party after the

Figure 10.6 *Shite* actor contemplating his image in the
mirror before going on stage. Izumi Yoshio playing the
Heavenly Maiden in *Hagoomo*.

performance. This tends to center on eating and small talk, though in some
groups the opportunity is used for more organized mutual critique.

The practice of noh as a way of life

The performance of noh as we see it today and as we have been describing it
has, of course, evolved over time. Each new generation has added its stamp,
interpreting traditional practices in a new light. Still the ideals and goals of
Kannami, Zeami, and Zenchiku, Zeami's son-in-law and inheritor of some of
his treatises, remain apt today. Their writings still speak to the modern actor.
To understand the world of noh today, one must reach back to its medieval
heritage, to some of the prevailing ideas of the thirteenth and fourteenth
centuries.

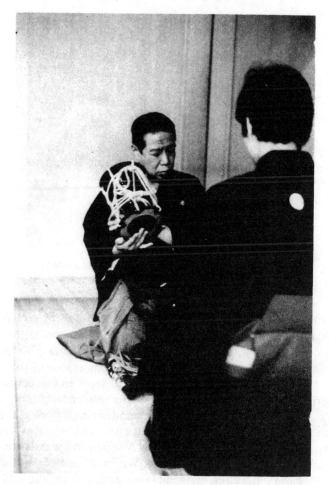

Figure 10.7 A drummer playing the warm-up (*oshirabe*)
just off stage before the performance begins. A young
disciple sits in front of him.

The concept of a way or path (*michi*, also pronounced *dō*) was central to the
culture of that period (Konishi 1975, 1985; Pilgrim 1972; Nearman 1980). To
follow a way is to immerse oneself in an activity, to practice it until one attains
mastery. What one masters is not as important as the process of mastering.
Anyone who attains true mastery, even in a humble art, enters a sphere of
consciousness unknown to the average person. This consciousness might be
defined as enlightenment or as art, for the dichotomy between the sacred and
the profane has never been as well-defined in Japan as in the West, and
aesthetic values have had as much force as moral ones.

Mastery in noh was seen by Zeami in his treatise *Kyūi* as spanning nine
levels from "the way of crudeness and leadenness" to "the art of the flower of

Figure 10.8 After performing *Hagoromo* Izumi Yoshio
exchanges a thank you bow with each of the other
performers.

peerless charm" (Rimer and Yamazaki 1984: 120–23). In explaining these
types of mastery, and indeed in developing many aspects of the aesthetic-
religious way of noh, Zeami draws on concepts from Shinto, Taoism,
Confucianism, and Buddhism. Esoteric Buddhism, especially the thought of
Kūkai (774–835) who systematized the secret rites of Indian origin which he
had learned in China, provided some important underlying concepts for
Zeami's art. Kūkai held that the universe manifests itself through art, and that
artistic activity leads the mind to identification with universal truth. Each
human possesses three mysteries in which all secrets reside and through which
enlightenment can be attained: 1) the mysteries of the body including hand
gestures (*mudra*), postures of meditation, and manipulation of religious
implements, 2) the mysteries of speech including true words (*shingon*) and
secret formulae (*mantra* and *darani*), 3) the mysteries of the mind, methods of
perceiving truth which often include the use of *mandala*, graphic representations of the cosmos (Tsunoda 1958: 137–75, and Ochi 1984: 3–91).

Just as these three mysteries include the body, speech, and the mind, so a
knowledge of noh is only possible through somatic, oral, and psychic
immersion in the art. To practice noh, to know noh, is to have it ingrained in
body and psyche. Thomas Kasulis uses the term "intimate knowledge" to
describe knowledge that is based on somatic mastery, such as the art of riding
a bicycle, and yet goes beyond it (1983). Mind and body function as one;
intellectual understanding is fused with visceral knowledge.[21]

As we have seen, the training of a noh performer aims at such knowledge
and its results can be seen on many levels. A simple example is that a noh actor
does not memorize a text as a string of words or a series of thoughts, but rather

as a song to be sung. If you ask an actor about a particular line of text, he will immediately know what play it comes from and begin singing the appropriate section of the play in a low voice until he comes to the passage in question. Similarly, movements are not learned through verbal instructions or diagrams, but rather by the student dancing side by side with his teacher miming the dance until it becomes ingrained.[22]

Another aspect of esoteric Buddhism which is of special importance to the practice of noh is the concept of secret transmission. The mysteries of esoteric Buddhism were transmitted orally from master to disciple, a relationship which was consequently extremely close. The innermost secrets were often transmitted only to a single outstanding disciple. This practice was adopted by various medieval Japanese arts including noh. The actors regard certain refinements of their art as secrets to be carefully guarded, to be passed on only to the initiated.

The head of each school will choose one of his disciples, most often his son, to be his successor and hence to become the guardian of the secret arts of the school. He will train this heir with special care and pass on to him certain secret instructions which other disciples are never taught. This method of transmission was extremely important to Zeami and was part of the reason that he was unwilling to pass on his secrets to his nephew, even though this refusal may have led to Zeami's exile. It is also the reason that the writings of Zeami, many of which were secret teachings, were not published until this century. Although there is much more openness in the noh world today, heads of school and some other master actors with long family traditions in noh, still transmit the secret refinements of their art only to their chosen successors. Kongō Iwao, current head of the Kongō school, discusses how he inherited the school's secret manuscripts at the unusually young age of twenty-seven when his father died. These manuscripts, compiled in 1716, contain all the plays and their standard variations (*kogaki*). However,

> the language is obscure and meant to be understood intuitively. It reflects the writer's own feelings and struggle with the role and must have been very difficult to write. Often there is no explanation, but only the indication that a certain place in the plays is of importance – that is all that is written. (Kongō 1984: 80–81).

The actor explains that he can only understand the commentary after having studied the plays carefully and experienced them in performance.

There are other levels at which secrets play an integral role in the life and training of a noh performer. Each step in the refinement of an actor's art is seen as the possession of a further secret. Performers are taught only as much as they can understand at their current level of skill. When they have developed sufficiently to go on to the next level, they may be told a secret which, since they have virtually come to it through their own experience, they are now able to comprehend. Indeed, for the uninitiated or unskilled the significance of a "secret" would not be apparent. Kongō Iwao has not yet shown his school's secrets to his son because, "he would not be able to understand anything. It would be of no value to him; rather, it would more likely to impede and confuse his studies" (Kongō 1984: 81). This is why the noh teacher will often explain to the novice, "those patterns are exactly the same," while to the more experienced student the same two things might be described as "completely different."

The medieval way of noh has been gradually transformed into a more modern concept of the profession of noh, but a dedication to and an understanding of the aesthetic-religious aspects of this art is found to a greater or lesser degree among all contemporary performers.[23] Most professional noh performers give their entire lives to the practice of noh and continue to transmit their art to their sons and disciples. Noh performers are not actors in the sense that a Western actor is, performing Greek tragedy today, Shakespeare, Chekhov or Sam Shepard tomorrow, and soap opera whenever the need or opportunity arises. Noh actors are noh actors. They normally spend their lives immersed in the noh tradition, thoroughly trained to perform the classical repertory, and sincerely concerned with transmitting it intact. This way of life satisfies most contemporary noh actors; however, as we shall see in the following section, a few attempt to go beyond the restrictions of tradition.

The practice of noh and transferability

Noh has been successfully transferred across six centuries and through a great amount of cultural and societal change. Although there were brief periods, most notably in the late fifteenth and late nineteenth centuries, when its popularity and patronage declined significantly, it has maintained an unbroken performance tradition. There are several factors that have made this possible. First is the strong tendency in Japanese culture for old forms (whether aesthetic, political or economic) to persist. Instead of being discarded, they are simply put on a side track and left to proceed in their own ways while new forms develop on parallel tracks. As is true of most Japanese arts, once noh was "perfected," noh performers felt it should be preserved rather than developed into new forms. Other performers created new theatres, such as the puppet theatre, kabuki, and various modern forms, which continue to exist alongside noh. These later arts drew on noh structures, techniques, and texts, but they did not destroy noh in the process.

Second, the support of the Tokugawa government (1603–1868), which used noh as a ritual in official functions and retained it as the theatre of the ruling warrior class, did much to preserve noh. Third, the emphasis on training as a life-time activity and the continuity between practice and performance and between learning and teaching have helped to maintain orthodox forms. Fourth, the identification of the sacred and the secular in the idea of noh as a way (*michi*) and the concordant practice of secret transmission meant that noh was painstakingly passed down among people who had dedicated their lives to the art.

Today the concept of noh as a way of life still fulfills many noh actors, but is found confining by others. Some young men trained by their fathers from childhood leave noh to follow other, more "modern" professions. This is particularly true in families where there are several sons; when one shows special interest or talent, the others may feel freer to leave the profession. Some who decide to quit noh disappear completely from the profession, others return to the fold, like Ōkura Shōnosuke, a shoulder-drum player who changed to the hip drum. Still others, such as Komparu Kunio, who was born to a family of stick drum players, became a critic of architecture, and then wrote a book on noh (Komparu 1983), linger on the fringes of the world of noh.

Among professional noh actors there are quite a number who, while remaining committed to the traditional repertory of noh, also try to reach beyond it. Experimentation includes the reconstruction of old plays whose performance traditions have been lost but whose texts remain. A successful example is the play *Motomezuka* which was active in the repertories of the Hōshō and Kita schools, but not in the others. In 1931 the Kongō school reconstructed a performance version; the Kanze school did the same in 1951 (Koyama, Satō and Satō 1975: 174). Another old play, *Matsuura Sayohime*, which had disappeared from the active repertories of all the schools, but was preserved in Zeami's holograph by the Kanze family, was staged in 1963 by Yamamoto Yoshihisa as part of a celebration marking the 600th year since Zeami's birth. It was performed again, in a somewhat different form, by Ōtsuki Bunzō in the spring of 1984. In the same year Umewaka Toshiteru staged *Daihannya*, another "lost" play for which there was an extant mask. In creating the melody, instrumentation, and choreography for old texts, the performers use what evidence is available about old performance practice and then draw on their knowledge of the noh system to flesh out the framework, modifying standard performance modules to fit the specific text. The result is a performance which grows out of the underlying model of noh.

Going one step further in their experimentation are performers who participate in productions of plays outside the noh tradition. One of the most successful plays in the modern Japanese theatre, for example, is Kinoshita Junji's *Yūzuru* (Twilight Crane), a story based on a popular folktale. In the mid 1950s it was produced by Takechi Tetsuji with the noh player Kitayama Hirotarō playing the leading role of the crane-turned-wife while the kyōgen actor Nomura Mansaku played the husband. The performance style was a blend of various traditional and modern forms (Beichman n.d.: 14–15). In the 1980s the kyōgen actors Shigeyama Akira and Maruishi Yasushi have been performing versions of the plays of Beckett and Yeats along with traditional kyōgen in both Japan and the West.

In the last century noh has also left its mark on Western artists and theatre. Although they never saw noh performed, Ezra Pound, T.S. Eliot and W.B. Yeats all admired the use of imagery in noh and Yeats made use of Fenollosa and Pound's noh translations to create his own plays for dancers. Bertolt Brecht made a translation of the noh play *Tanikō* his basic text for *Der Ja Sager* and *Der Nein Sager*, (*The Yea Sayer* and *The Nay Sayer*) and was inspired by various eastern theatrical forms in developing this theory of alienation (*verfundung*). Benjamin Britten, who saw two performances of the noh play *Sumidagawa* during a visit to Japan in 1956, used it as the basis for his and William Plomer's church parable *Curlew River*. Mishima Yukio's psychologically oriented, modern noh plays are often performed in translation in Europe and North America, and noh troupes have performed traditional noh to acclaim in many countries.

The complexity of the interaction between noh and modern theatre is particularly evident in two series of experiments. The earlier of these began with the creation of Yeat's *At the Hawk's Well* (1915–16), which seems to have been inspired by Fenollosa's translation of the noh play *Yōrō*. This play was later adapted by Yokomichi Mario, a musicologist and student of noh, as *Taka no Izumi* and first performed by the noh actor Kita Minoru in 1949. In 1967 Yokomichi retranslated the play as *Takahime*, making it closer to noh in structure. This version was first staged by Kanze Hisao with the assistance of Nomura Mansaku, a kyōgen performer, and has been performed several times since (Beichman, n.d.: 13). Another play with a similar history is *La femme et son Ombre* written by Paul Claudel who, as the French ambassador to Japan in the 1920s, saw various forms of Japanese traditional theatre and drew upon them in creating this play. It was performed in a Kabuki theatre in Tokyo in 1923 and again in 1929, both times in Japanese translation (Beichman n.d.: 8). Izumi Yoshio and Kimura Tarō transformed the play into a more noh-like piece with the Japanese title *Onna to Kage* and performed it 1968 and 1972 in Japan and in Europe (see figure 10.9).

Such exchanges of materials has been paralleled by interactions among noh performers and western actors. Jean-Louis Barrault, director of the Theatre de France, saw his first noh performance in Paris in 1957. Later (in 1960 and again in 1977) he went to Japan and exchanged ideas and techniques with Kanze Hisao and Nomura Mansaku. In between these visits Kanze Hisao spent six months of 1962 studying in Paris. Hisao's interest in contemporary forms never took him completely from traditional noh, and when he died in 1978 at fifty-three he was considered one of the best noh actors of his day (Tessenkai, 1979). His younger brother, Hideo, left the Kanze school to study in the Kita school, then spent several years studying with Jerzy Grotowski and Suzuki Tadashi. Later he returned to the Kanze school. As a consequence of his experience, he gives the plays he performs a rather more dramatic interpretation than is traditional.

Productions and experiments involving Western actors in noh practice also

Figure 10.9 1972 performance in Nagoya of Paul Claudel's *La Femme et Son Ombre* by Izumi Yoshio and Izumi Yasutake.

abound. The noh play *Ikkaku Sennin* (One Horned Hermit) was performed by American actors under the direction of Kita Sadayo at IASTA (Institute for Advanced Studies in the Theater Arts) in 1964. More recently Matsui Akira, a young actor from the Kita school, trained American students to perform *Funa Benkei* at the Universities of Wisconsin and Michigan State in English and Japanese respectively, and produced the play *Kiyotsune* with Australian students at Sydney University.

Finally, there is a growing group of foreigners who live in Japan and are becoming increasingly proficient in traditional noh performance. For example, Monica Bethe, David Crandall, Richard Emmert, Willi Flindt, and Rebecca Teele have all received long years of training not only in acting but also in the instruments. Although no foreigner has yet been completely accepted as a noh performer, some of these people work regularly with professionals in various ways. They also perform traditional noh plays themselves and are involved in experiments with various aspects of noh practice. Richard Emmert wrote noh music which was played by professionals for an English language performance of *At The Hawk's Well* in Tokyo in 1982. In 1983 David Crandall composed the words and music and Monica Bethe did the choreography for and performed in a modern play entitled *Crazy Jane* which was inspired by Yeats' Crazy Jane poems and combined the aesthetic principles of noh with a Western musical idiom. In 1985 and again in 1986 a new noh play in English called *Drifting Fires*, written by noh scholar and translator Janine Beichman with music by Richard Emmert, was performed by the noh actor Umewaka Naohiko.

Thus it is clear that noh is attractive to a large number of artists, Japanese and foreign alike. The traditional theatre remains healthy in Japan and noh troupes increasingly travel abroad. Experiments with noh practices and noh texts occur in many countries with and without the involvement of professional noh performers. Many aspects of noh have not only proven to be cross-culturally transferable, but also to have potentials for development that go far beyond the traditional bounds of noh. There remains, however, the question of just what one can and should label "noh." The noh system is a totality of and in itself. Every element contains the essence and reflects the whole, but none constitutes noh itself unless it appears in its proper place within the entire system of noh practice.

Notes

1. In his *Kadensho* Zeami states that training should begin at age seven, six by western count. Instrumentalists often follow the tradition of giving their sons their first lessons on the sixth day of the sixth month of their sixth year.
2. This idea of learning is discussed below, pages 186–87.
3. For example, Izumi Yoshio appeared in *Kashiwazaki* at age four, and Takabayashi Kōji performed in *Sakuragawa* at age four. On the other hand, Kongō Iwao didn't play his first child role, the emperor in *Kuzu*, until age seven. He describes how he appeared on stage without any previous practice; the stage attendant told him what to do as the time came (Kongō 1984: 76).
4. For example, the child roles in the plays *Kantan* and *Mochizuki* require solo dances, in *Funa Benkei*, sword play, and in *Kurama Tengu*, extensive chant and acting as well as a complex fighting scene.
5. The short and relatively easy piece *Tsunemasa* is an example. *Shunzei Tadnori*, *Ikuta Atsumori*, and *Kagetsu* are others. The play *Sagi* is, by stipulation, performed only by young boys and old men who, it is thought, can return to the transparent simplicity of a child's acting. In some cases children's performances have complete child casts, including musicians; in others adult performers play supporting roles.
6. The grading, testing and labelling of levels of proficiency vary considerably from school to school, but each school does have a clear hierarchy for ranking both its professionals and its amateurs.
7. Mikata Ken, Tsumura Reijirō, and Yamamoto Masahito are examples of actors who began as amateurs and turned professional.
8. Zeami discusses the pitfalls of over-confidence as well as outlining the ideals of art to strive for in his *Fushikaden, Kakyō*, and *Shikadō*. A good survey of his ideas can be found in Nearman 1981. Interesting comments on how his personal experience may have influenced these ideas appear in Hare 1986.
9. Practice, like performance, is usually done on a noh stage, either a public one or a stage in the actor's studio. These areas are reserved exclusively for noh and its sister art kyōgen.
10. The prime example is the play *Dōjōji* where the difficult rhythms of the *ranbyōshi* dance usually require extended rehearsals between the dummer and the dancer, and the tricky timing necessary for the raising and lowering of the bell usually requires that the entire company practice these sections several times. Tsumura

Reijirō (1984: 104–13) discusses how he prepared for two separate performances of *Dōjōji*.

11. This practice is not limited to noh, but is true of various medieval performing arts such as the tea ceremony and linked verse. It emphasizes the moment of creating the performance. Zeami in *Kyakuraika* discusses the advanced art of creating the once in a lifetime effect (Nearman 1980: 170–73).

12. The choices made by actors Takabayashi Kōji and Izumi Yoshio for 1982 performances of the play *Kiyotsune* are described in Bethe (1984: 149–50).

13. In the case of smaller schools such as the Kita and Kongō the school sponsors monthly performances. In larger schools, especially the largest Kanze school, each theatre has one or more groups of actors associated with it who hold regularly scheduled performances.

14. The performers are not necessarily paid when they participate in shrine or temple festivals. Although the instrumentalists all belong to a union which sets the prices according to the rank of the performer and the type of performance, the actors are not unionized and pay each other according to what they feel is appropriate with the funds available. There is quite a range of fees.

15. Zeami has surprisingly little to say about noh masks; his nephew Zenchiku is a bit more forthcoming on the subject. See Nearman (1984: esp. pp. 43–44).

16. Kongō Iwao describes how the interpretation of *Sumidagawa* differs when different masks are chosen (1984: 89–90).

17. The mask carver Kitazawa Ichinen elaborates on the subtle variations in the expression of two famous young woman (*ko-omote*) masks (1984: 125–29).

18. Zeami discussed how the actor must be able to visualize himself not only in practice, but while actually performing (Nearman 1982a: 372). Kongō Iwao also deals with the problem in discussing expression: "One thing the actor must do . . . is to keep in mind the concept of *riken*, or of watching himself from a distance . . . The actor must keep seeing himself from an objective point of view" (1984: 84).

19. To compare the attitude of a noh and a kyōgen actor towards donning the mask see Kanze (1984: 70) and Nomura (1984: 180). Takabayashi Kōji explains the difference between the *Okina* mask which he calls a symbol and other noh masks which he says are faces (1984: 98–100).

20. The curtain is a piece of stripped cloth which has two bamboo poles attached to its bottom corners. The stage attendants lift the poles raising the curtain up and inward away from the stage so that it is parallel to the ceiling. This lifting of the curtain is done only for the *shite*, *waki*, and *tsure* actors; for other performers (kyōgen, musicians) the far edge of the curtain is pulled aside. Special curtain effects include raising it only halfway and then lowering it again before the actual entrance.

21. Phillip Zarrilli, dealing with another Asian tradition, talks about a similar phenomenon as "in-body" knowledge and training (1984b).

22. However, the various noh schools today publish dance books for amateurs which give diagrams and explanations for the most commonly learned dances. Some schools have also created videotapes for students. We have provided similar guides in our analysis of noh dance (1982–83). These aides, however, are useful only to the extent that they enforce what has already been learned directly from a teacher.

23. For example, Kanze Hisao described the "realm of mindlessness" or the "condition of 'nothingness'" which one must have to perform noh (1984: 69–72), and Takabayashi Kōji describes his feelings about the play *Okina* as "the spiritual core of Nō," and "ones whole life ought to be in accordance with the spirit of performing *Okina*" (1984: 95–98).

11.
The profanation of the sacred in circus clown performances

PAUL BOUISSAC

The notion of ritual has been put to great use during the last few decades in the disciplines which are founded on the observation of social behavior, both in humans and animals. Ethologists, sociobiologists, sociologists, cultural anthropologists, semioticians and a few others, have found it useful to thus characterize some patterned behavior in face-to-face interactions as well as collective actions. This phenomenon has expectedly generated a certain conceptual confusion in spite of some attempts at integrating these various uses, including the original religious one, within a unified framework in order to establish *a posteriori* the scientific or philosophical validity of the extension of this notion (e.g., Douglas 1973; d'Aquili 1979). I.M. Lewis (1976: 129–44) has concisely retraced the migrations of this concept first from the domain of religion to ethology, then from ethology to the social sciences in a way which accounts for its current fuzziness if not inconsistency. In addition to the classical definitions propounded by the sociologists of religion (Nisbet 1967: 216–63), we have indeed, at one extreme, the ethologists' technical definition of ritualization as "the process by which non-communicative behavior patterns evolve into communicative ones." (Eibl-Eibesfeldt 1979: 14); on the other end of the spectrum, the term is used by some anthropologists of theological inclination with a value close to its primitive religious origins (e.g., Douglas 1973; Turner 1974). In between, it is found to mean for some: stylized, repetitive sequences regulating social interaction; but for others it is a way of focusing on the existential efficacy of collective events characterized by the deep involvement of the participants (e.g., Schechner 1977). In this latter sense, it can be considered as an effort to carry forward religious values in a desacralized world or to identify the particular intensity of some collective secular experiences as a re-emergence of the sacred in the Western cultures. On the conceptual level, still more confusion is introduced by the superposition to these various uses of the long-standing controversy in cultural anthropology, between those who claim that rituals basically are re-enactments of myths and those who emphasize their cathartic function.

In this context, for the sake of clarity, it is of utmost importance that everybody using the term "ritual" spells out – however tentatively it may be – the sense in which s/he takes it. The minimal definition given by Schwimmer in his lucid account of "Religion in Culture" will serve as a point of departure for this chapter: "A ritual is a traditional patterned action that may be either demonstrative or transformative" (1980: 513). Circus clowns will be considered as engaging in such traditional patterned actions. These actions clearly seem to be of the demonstrative kind inasmuch as these performances consist in representing some rules of the contextual culture and in performing some particular operations on these rules as I have shown in previous papers (Bouissac 1978, 1979, 1982). The nature of these operations, which amount to an acted meta-discourse on the tacit rules shaping the culture concerned, is usually characterized as being transgressive or subversive and, as such, are contained within strict boundaries, both in time and space. It is suggested in this paper that circus clown performances demonstrate the basic but unwritten rules on which our construction of a culturally bound meaningful universe rests. "Demonstrating" should be understood here not as simply "illustrating" but rather as "fully enacting," "making some sense explicit through various formal manipulations." If something concurrently happens in the audience as a result of such "demonstrations" it has to be on the cognitive level, within the limits defined by a playful context, but cannot be considered a transformation of the kind that transformative rituals achieve as in a change of status for instance. However it seems likely that performing such demonstrative rituals entails a permanent transformation of the performers themselves as social beings. Western circus audiences do not spontaneously consider clowns as actors, performers, professionals of some skill but as clowns, i.e., as individuals defined by a permanent special status, both feared and cherished. The general attitude is well documented in today's world. On the one hand the clown is exalted as a children's hero, a benevolent figure, the true giver of joys and toys; on the other hand he is stigmatized: the word "clown" can be used as a verbal abuse; a persistent literary theme concurs with all sorts of folk traditions to classify the clown as an outcast; it is noticeable that in American circus films he is more often than not the unsuspected murderer or a criminal in hiding; there are also many signs of a rampant feeling that professional clowns are morally depraved or that being circus clowns is the outcome of some misfortune. Is it not indeed generally assumed that clowns are the saddest of people under the deceitful merry expressions of their painted masks: What have they done to deserve that unique treatment?

The focus of this paper is on special kinds of operations performed by circus clowns, whose characteristics may account for this state of affairs. Not all clown gags have the same metacultural value. Some demonstrations are gentle and benign. Others address very sensitive areas in our cultural system. I would like to contend that some particular gags or scenarios which are a part of regular repertoires amount to ritualistic profanations of the sacred and that is what accounts for the stigmatized social status of the clown. But introducing the terms "sacred" and "profane" raises new problems. In spite of the fact that they have gained currency in the technical vocabulary of cultural anthropology, they are far from offering the conceptual clarity that would seem to be desirable in using them as descriptive tools. Can we afford, in this endeavor, to take the sacred for granted? There is not much to be learned from the circular definitions according to which the sacred is what is not profane and *vice versa*. Even a bad hypothesis would be preferable.

Approaching this problem through an examination of the concept of profanation may be more productive than remaining hypnotized by the concept of sacred because one crucial characteristic of the sacred is: "what can be profanated." Profanation is interesting for our purpose because it refers to a category of actions which is well documented in our culture, as it perhaps is in any culture in mythical or historical forms. For instance, we have an exemplary profanator in the person of Don Juan; but there are quite a few others, from the medieval profanators of the Holy Host to the Dadaists. In view of these data, a tentative and elementary morphology of profanation could include the following:

1   a particular object assigned to a certain place or position is moved to and placed in an inappropriate place or position,

2   an object that should be manipulated in a certain manner (or simply be seen) by a particular person or class of persons, is manipulated in this manner (or is seen) by an unqualified person, or is manipulated in an inappropriate manner,

3   a patterned behavior that should be performed in the presence of an object or person is performed in the presence of an inappropriate object or person,

4   a patterned behavior that is prescribed in a specific context is performed in another context or is not performed in the prescribed context,

5   a word or text to which a prescribed interpretation is attached, is interpreted in another manner or, still worse, the consequences of this new interpretation are actually implemented.

Naturally there can be several degrees of profanation because there is a whole range of prohibitions concerning what we have called "other," "different" and "inappropriate," from mere difference to diametrical opposition of the sort that cultures usually provide with respect to social functions, space and time structures, or animal categorizations, for instance.

Let me take a personal example to illustrate this: As a child brought up in pre-conciliar Catholicism, I was taught that eating meat on Fridays was a sin but that it was still a greater – in fact an unthinkable one – to do so on Good Friday. Literally only God knew what could have happened as a result of such an act. Of course, no reasons for this were given. Now, in this French Catholic worldview of the time, the arch enemy of the Church was considered to be the Free Masons, and as a proof that they were Evil itself, I was told that they used to meet secretly each year on Good Friday in order to feast on a roast leg of lamb. Naturally the selection of lamb as the alleged instrument of the profanation was not gratuitous because of the established association between Christ and the sacrificial lamb. The Church iconography as well as the hymns were then full of lambs. Note on the other hand that roast lamb was a must on Easter Sunday. The reason for which one should not eat meat on the day of the crucifixion and why one should eat plenty of it, preferably lamb, on the day of the resurrection may be justified by theologians, historians or structural anthropologists. This is not the point here. This personal example has been introduced because it brings together in an instance of ritualistic behavior the sacred and its profanation in a typical everyday life circumstance. The alleged profanations consisted in performing a patterned behavior (the consumption of a certain meat) normally prescribed in a certain context (Easter Sunday), in another context viewed as a qualitative opposite to the prescribed context.

One striking aspect of profanation in general is that it entails no drastic consequences whatsoever, either natural or supernatural. Eating meat on Good Friday does not cause instant earthquakes. Only in theatrical plays does the commander's statue come to life in order to punish the profanator Don Juan. Of course some legal systems may construe profanation as a major crime and put profanators to death if only to prevent the sacred from losing face. But this requires a massive consensus that complex societies do not usually provide. Profanation is not so much the breaking of a rule made explicit in a legal code as the exposure of the rule of the rules, the principle or principles that are so fundamental for the holding together of the regulative system that they cannot be formulated. For instance to make explicit and to publicize the following rule, "it is forbidden to British subjects to sneak into the Queen's bedroom unannounced at dawn," is unthinkable, in terms of the system, because it would imply that this action is indeed a possibility. There are countless other rules which are derived from the implications of this impossibility. The symbolic stature of an hereditary queen, in the name of whom justice is rendered, cannot need such rules which would obviously expose her nakedness, so to speak. This is undoubtedly the deep reason for which the British government decided not to prosecute the intruder to whom I was just alluding. The system could not admit the conceptual shock of seeing someone who logically should be put to death in order to restore the integrity of the sacred, being fined for trespassing. There is of course a way out of the dilemma, which is to disqualify the profanator by presenting him as an insane person, i.e., by excluding him from the system that his action jeopardized.

Therefore it seems obvious that the nature of the rule transgressed, not the quantity of the transgressions, distinguishes profanation from simple rule breaking. It is as if a cultural system with all the prescriptive and prohibitive rules which form its body were actually relying on a few crucial but unformulatable rules, some sort of culturally tacit axioms or silent dogmas from which all the other rules are derived and justified but which are themselves undemonstrable, unjustifiable and ultimately impotent. This necessary arbitrariness on which meaningful behavior and motivated regulations rest could then define what the sacred ultimately is. This is at least an hypothesis. From this point of view, the relative seclusion of clowns from "normal" society would be explained by the fact that they "demonstrate" these cultural axioms in the sense that they reveal their arbitrariness and impotency by manipulating the rules that are derived from them. In a way we could say, metaphorically, that every morning a clown sits on the Queen's bed, at the risk of losing his passport.

Thus, the sacred cannot be equated with explicit religious dogmas or rituals. A secular democratic society which admits as part of its system many various cults whose dogmas conflict, is no less grounded on a few fundamental dogmas itself. Religious freedom is usually qualified by some restrictions which are taken for granted. The cults' activities must not for instance infringe upon the Law or the Constitution. Founding rules cannot be justified by the rules they generate. In this sense, any society hangs from an unsupported hook. Mary Douglas has interestingly reported her frustration when trying to form a clear mental representation of the cognitive system on which the Lele's symbolic ritual treatment of animals rested:

> Although I could never get a direct answer that satisfied me as to why the pangolin should be the object of a fertility cult, I kept receiving odd scraps of disconnected information about it and about other animals in different religious and secular contexts. Gradually I was able to relate these ideas within a broad framework of assumptions about animals and humans. These assumptions are so fundamental to Lele thought that one could almost describe them as unformulated categories through which they unconsciously organize their experience. They could never emerge in reply to direct questions because it was impossible for Lele to suppose that the questioner might take his standpoint on another set of assumptions. Only when I was able to appreciate the kind of implicit connections they made between one set of facts and another, did a framework of metaphysical ideas emerge (1975: 28).

As Tocqueville remarked in connection with our culture:

> In order that society exist and, *a fortiori*, that a society should prosper, it is necessary that the minds of all the citizens should be rallied and held together by certain predominant ideas; and this cannot be the case unless each of them sometimes draws his opinions from the common source and consents to accept certain matters of belief already formed . . . If man were forced to demonstrate for himself all the truths of which he makes daily use, his talk would never end. He would exhaust his strength in preparatory demonstration without ever advancing beyond them . . . There is no philosopher in the world so great but that he believes a million things of the faiths of other people and accepts a great many more truths than he demonstrates (1945: II, 8).

Obviously the reference by Tocqueville to available time and energy as the limits making this task impossible should be understood as a figure of absolute impossibility of the type that some philosophers have conceived in terms of logical paradoxes. I would like to lay down for discussion the claim that profanation denotes a class of actions which question these tacit principles through the selective transgression of some of the rules that are derived from them or by exhibiting some behavior which implies a system of rules that would be derived from the negation of these cultural axioms; circus clowns would then specialize in such demonstrative actions performed in the ritualistic mode which is the only way in which the unthinkable and unspeakable can be actualized within the system. This, of course, raises the issue of whether such rituals are devised by society as cathartic outlets, as collective dreams of the cultural unconscious, or whether there is in all social systems a built-in irrepressible cognitive drive toward a representation of the system itself, or whether any other better explanations can be found. This question, which, after all, may be truly unanswerable, will not be dealt with in the limits of this chapter. We shall focus instead on an easier task: the description and analysis of a few clown acts in view of our hypothesis regarding their function as ritualistic profanators.

As mentioned earlier, previous investigations of clown performances (Bouissac 1972, 1977) seem to indicate that not all clown acts qualify as direct and major profanations. They often operate symbolically on minor cultural rules. Moreover a certain amount of censorship is exercised on the clowns' creativity for the sake of "good taste" or "good business"; this may cause at times some "displacements" in their meta-cultural operations. However there are quite a few scenarios that address head-on some of the great themes upon which most if not all societies focus their rituals, namely: birth, matrimonial alliances, and death. Even in a complex or "desacralized" society these socio-existential themes are articulated through institutions and legislations that are anchored in some implicit cultural axioms. Questions concerning the border-line which distinguishes humans from animals, or the precise moments when human life starts and is terminated, or the structure of identities, are questions which call for answers necessarily involving some amount of arbitrariness; but how could a society acknowledge it while edifying a self assumed system of meaning if not in a very special manner?

The first example I will introduce is a brief but very effective clown act that belongs to the regular repertoire of European clowns. But before describing it, let me remind you that European clowns traditionally work in pairs: the White-face clown who emphatically embodies all the characteristics of culture (artistic competence, sophisticated appearance, social prominence, etc.) and August, an exaggerated tramp-like figure in which all the features of the former are inverted. As I have shown elsewhere (1979) this pair must be interpreted as a semiotic matrix and not as a personalized one-way relationship between a persecutor and his victim. This chapter will provide some further examples of this important, indeed crucial aspect that is all too often forgotten. In the following act, only the August is involved and when it happens that the White-face clown takes part in the act, he does so marginally as an intrigued spectator, and intervenes only at the end to chase his partner out of the ring while expressing his angry disapproval.

Basically the act unfolds as follows: The August, who has donned grotesque female attire with a false and abundant bosom, enters the ring pushing a baby carriage of the type used for very young infants. He behaves as a mother or a nanny would do if a baby was resting in it. Suddenly loud and shrieking cries are heard, coming from the perambulator and the August asks the circus hands to go and fetch some milk. They soon return with a huge bottle (or a glass tank) full of a white liquid. The end of a rubber pipe which is connected to the container is put into the carriage, supposedly into the baby's mouth. The milk level gets lower and lower at a fast rate and the bottle is soon empty. As the "child" starts crying again the August picks it up, and the audience suddenly discovers that the "child" actually is a piglet wrapped in cloths. This revelation forms the punch line, so to speak, of the gag and this is when the White-face clown intervenes. Sometimes the act is expanded in the following manner: the August attends the "baby's" well being but either because it keeps shrieking or because the August wants to engage in some other temporary action, he trusts his charge to a "spectator" or a circus hand. Then the piglet abundantly "urinates" on its new guardian and is carried away, still dripping, from the ring, accompanied by the unfailing laughter of the audience.

The operation performed in this act consists first of substituting a piglet for a human infant, or, rather treating the former as if it were the latter. Two powerful cultural themes are thus brought together: on the one hand the care that humans have to take of their offspring as a prerequisite for the survival of the species and the ensuing sacralization of infants; on the other hand, an animal species, the pig, which is the focus of intense cultural attention in many parts of the world, including ours; second, if we take into account the expanded version of the act, a third important theme has to be added: urine and its polluting effect as excreta. In brief, the clown performs a conjunction which amounts to positing an equation and this operation causes as a result his expulsion from the ring. Given the nature of the two main themes involved, the operation is of considerable magnitude.

The pig is not indeed just any animal. In some cultures pigs are considered to be the abomination of creation and the object of strict taboos; Douglas (1966), Harris (1977: 31–48) and others have dealt extensively with this problem. It is doubtful that this clown act could be safely performed in those cultures. There are also cultures which traditionally rely on pig breeding for their protein intake and in which pigs are no less the object of rules and rituals. The intimacy of pigs and humans in some tribes of New Guinea (Rappaport 1968) is an extreme example, but the obsessive attention it seems to receive from (Western) anthropologists is truly fascinating. There is indeed little chance that the pangolin, in spite of its rich mythology and ritual, will ever enjoy a comparable popularity. This of course could be construed as a symptom of the fact that our culture is also traditionally pig centered and remains so in many direct and indirect ways. This is crucial for the understanding of the meaning effect of this clown act in the cultural context in which it is observed. In a little book on French carnivals (Gaignebet 1979: 57–64) both the economical and mythical importance of pigs in traditional European culture are emphasized. Many features indeed contribute to endowing this animal with a special status, something which was also under-lined by Leach in his important article on animal categories and verbal abuse (1964) in which he shows that the pig is loaded with taboo values. Many characteristics both anatomical and ecological concur to situate the pig in the immediate proximity of humans: the pigmentation of its skin; the unusually light body hair which makes it appear almost naked; the relative expressivity of its face which lends itself so well to anthropomorphization; the fact that in traditional subsistance farming it is kept closer to human habitations than the other domestic animals and is fed in a human way with leftovers and with specially prepared cooked food; the rumor that nothing tastes more like pork than human flesh. The ritual of killing pigs at dawn before the sun rises, with its murderous or sacrificial overtones, and the fact that this event was an occasion of reinforcing neighborhood bonds, confirms its unique status among the domestic animals, actually its place on the border line of the pet sphere. Incidentally, one should not forget that in the Middle Ages at a time when the Church conducted trials of animals suspected of evil behavior, pigs were accused of crimes more often than any other animal. The closely intertwined lives of pigs and men lead to the necessity of strongly disjuncting them from each other on the cognitive or symbolic levels. Both in English and French, and undoubtedly in the other European languages, being accused of behaving like a pig or of being a pig amounts to being excluded from mankind. No other animal seems to have provided such a wealth of insults as the pig has. In fact, it embodies the very essense of animality with its "vices": gluttony, selfishness, immodesty, lewdness, etc. A French saying claims that "a pig sleeps in every man's heart" and, in English, one can "make a pig of oneself." The list would be endless.

Returning now to the human infant, it would seem that its behavior is strikingly close to a pig's, in particular with respect to dirt, abundantly produced at the two ends of the digestive tract, and with respect to sound. This is a time in human life when the borderline between humanity and animality is particularly blurred because the human in-fant, as its name indicates, does not yet give that criterial sign: speech. But, at the same time, society takes great care to assert the human nature of infants by socializing them symbolically through all sorts of rituals. The identity of infants' behavior with animals' is emphatically denied in spite of much contrary evidence.

The statement produced by the clown confuses two categories whose disjunction belongs to the few sacred principles upon which culture is edified, namely human versus animal; but, the profanation is all the more serious as the "terms" involved are actually situated in the fuzzy liminal region in which the objective differences between the two categories are not clearly obvious, and the disjunction has to be sustained and constantly reinforced by all sorts of cultural devices. Moreover the severity of the sacrilegious confusion is still enhanced by the fact that the pig is the most edible animal as it is raised for this sole purpose and as, according to a French saying: "in the pig everything is good, from the head to the feet," whereas babies are definitely defined as not edible in spite of the obsessive theme that recurs in folktales concerning children who fall prey to cannibalistic witches and even to pork butchers, as in the old French song telling the sad story of the three toddlers who were killed and put into a pork barrel until a saint came by and resuscitated them. Note on the other hand that in the saying quoted above the expression "from head to feet" is an obvious anthropomorphization as it implies an upright, not a horizontal position.

A more detailed analysis of the act would deal with the quantity of "milk" and the rapidity with which it is consumed, undoubtedly an emphasis on the similarity between raising a pig and raising a child, as well as with the costume and mimic of the August. For the purpose of this chapter it will suffice to note in conclusion the outcome of the operation i.e., the expulsion of the profanator which is sometimes underlined by the pollution (urine) that a transgressive operation such as the one he has performed normally should entail, system-wise. It is symptomatic that, according to my observations so far, the pollution crisis occurs only when the categorical confusion spreads, so to speak, in the social group since it follows someone else's agreement to enter the August's game by accepting to look after the "baby."

Another area of great cultural sensitivity is the set of rules that governs matrimonial alliances. It is generally acknowledged that cultures express themselves in this domain with a high degree of sophisticated arbitrariness that is often legitimized by fragile ideologies. The scenario that will be analyzed now as a representative example of the treatment of our own system of matrimonial alliances by clowns is a part of the basic repertoire of European circuses. It is considered to be a sure winner with any European audience and the fact that no spoken dialog is necessary for performing it makes it an easy task for the clowns when they travel to countries whose language they do not speak. The following description is based on observations and recordings made in the summer of 1981 in Denmark at the Schumann Circus.

The traditional title of this act is "The Nightingales"; it unfolds as follows: The White-face clown enters the ring whistling like a nightingale (he uses an invisible apparatus placed in his mouth) and broadcasting his loving calls to whom it may concern. After a few seconds one hears loud cheeping coming from behind the curtain of the ring entrances, obviously a reply to his calls.

The August enters the ring dressed as a grotesque woman: gaudy pink skirt, large blue bow on a prominent bosom, flowery hat and purse. "She" looks at him in a bovine manner, and he immediately "falls in love" with "her," kneels down at "her" feet and takes "her" hand while lovingly whistling. "She" brutally withdraws her hand, makes a sign that he should keep his distance and shows "her" fingers, pointing out that "she" has no wedding band, with a mimicry indicating that "she" is a respectable girl who does not listen to just anyone.

The White-face clown moves back a few steps and displays his physical strength by showing off his biceps and throwing out his chest. "She" reacts by mockingly laughing through the whistle and contemptuously spits in his eye. This first failure notwithstanding, the male resumes his courtship with passionate melodies and gestures. But "she" ridicules him by mimicking his behavior and reaffirms by her posture that "she" is not so easily impressed.

The White-face clown then produces a bunch of roses that he offers to "her." "She" rushes toward the flowers with a greedy expression and impatient cheeping. But he withdraws the roses and indicates by signs that "she" must kiss him first if "she" wants them. "She" looks incredulous, turns towards the public and makes a gesture signifying that he is completely crazy and violently snatches the bouquet, smells it, makes a face of disgust as if they stank, and throws them on the ground in his direction. As a result, he feels offended and walks towards the audience, starting again his loving calls to whom it may concern. Suddenly he stops in front of a lady spectator and engages in a new courtship. The abandoned clown looks furious, rushes at him, hits him with "her" purse, and threatens "her" rival.

When they are both back in the center of the ring, the White-face clown expresses still more passionate feelings, and even sheds a tear. "She" shows some interest, kisses him on the forehead but immediately takes again her distance. He then extracts a golden bracelet from his pocket and presents her with it. "She" snatches it from his hands, examines it, and puts it into her purse. Now, "she" lets him get closer and he caresses "her" throat; "she" expresses contentment by emitting ecstatic cheeps, and when he stops "she" makes a sign ordering him to continue, but soon goes back to "her" previous position and attitude.

The White-face clown displays his wealth, shows off the bank notes he has in his pocket and, after this, mimes the following statement: "We are going to build a nest and we shall sleep together in it." "She" answers in the same way: "Sure we are going to do that, then as a consequence I will become pregnant and I will have many children." (The latter fact is expressed by putting "her" hand at various levels as if "she" were counting children of decreasing heights); in conclusion she emphatically makes a vulgar gesture meaning "no way!"

The White-face clown gives her a fistful of bank-notes, but "she" wants more, and still more. "She" literally empties his pockets, and, at last, signals that "she" accepts his proposal. Overcome with joy, he extracts from his vest a large heart made of red velvet and gives it to her, but "she" kicks him, then kisses him and they leave the ring somewhat ceremoniously, while the orchestra plays the Mendelssohn wedding march.

From this verbal transcription, it is possible to set forth some categories of patterned social behavior related to courtship, seduction, and marriage. The "male" displays in succession: the quest for a mate, love at first-sight, the seductive demonstration of his physical qualities, symbolical gift giving progressing from flowers to jewels, then to money, and eventually a proposal to copulate; his strategy makes use of jealousy, pity, touching, submission. The concluding nuptial march suggests a formal wedding as the outcome of his endeavor. On the part of the "female" several phases of stereotyped behavior can also be identified: acceptance of the courtship, outburst of jealousy when the male shows interest in another female, but, above all, the setting up of some tests, sanctioned by graduated rewards, and deliberate strategy aimed at establishing the relationship on a serious economic basis.

However, the morphology of this particular matrimonial transaction is more complex than a mere listing of the stereotyped actions it displays would suggest. This act forms a very sophisticated comment on the system of matrimonial alliances that is at work in the contextual culture. The tacit principles which articulate "normal" behavior are "demonstrated" by the two clowns in a way which amounts to producing a sociological or anthropological theory. But like the specialists who express themselves in a descriptive meta-language which prevents their endeavor from interfering with the functioning of the system, the clowns take two measures which may be prerequisites for engaging in their demonstrative ritual: First they pretend they are birds, second they do not use explicit verbal language but expressive whistling whose referential function is minimal. Both measures are remarkably appropriate; the former because, as Levi-Strauss (1962: 270) pointed out, birds provide felicitous metaphorizations for human social relationships in European traditional society; the latter because of the prominent role played by whistling in the seductive behavior of some of these cultures. Moreover, among the birds, nightingales are those which are the most commonly associated with love both as romantic passion and erotic theme in the cultural area where this performance has been observed. On the one hand European folklores provide indeed many examples in which the nightingale's song represents illegitimate sexual attraction, on the other hand it is, since the troubadours, the symbol of pure passionate love. Thus, through the redundancies introduced in the meta-language used, this scenario is firmly rooted in the institutions that regulate sexuality and procreation.

With this in mind, let us now return to the description of the act and try to translate it into more general terms: the male engages in natural seduction; the female's response invokes the cultural law referring to the wedding band. The male emphasizes successively his physical strength in a display of exhibitionism, his verbal, or rather vocal charisma, the technical competence of his caresses. The female consistently denies the validity of those feelings, moods, drives, maneuvers and systematically translates each phase of the courtship process into terms of economic transactions. She takes the proposal seriously only when she starts receiving valuable gifts. Indeed she does reject the flowers, an eminently perishable produce of nature that decays so fast that, as a gift in this context, it "stinks." Once the prospective alliance has been established upon a firm economic basis, she agrees to copulate within the institution's framework, something that the wedding march underlines. At this point the male whose passion has reached its paroxysm "gives her his heart" and is kicked in return, a final sign that the matrimonial transaction was based on two different systems of values.

Thus, as this scenario definitely does not depict the psychological particularities of the two individuals involved and as it is performed repeatedly over a large cultural area with constant success, it seems obvious that the "drama" being enacted has a general social reference; it formulates a cultural problem and resolves it in its own way. The two clowns indeed whose status as White-face clown and August remains evident throughout the entire act contrast with blinding clarity two conceptions of a matrimonial alliance: on the one hand a view of weddings as the consequence of mutual love i.e., an individual and selective feeling; on the other hand an economic transaction, a regulated exchange governed by institutional rules in which individual feeling has little part, if any at all.

Contemporary Western society entertains the idea that all matrimonial alliances are, or should be based on free choice motivated by love and that economic or social considerations that may play some part in the decision of getting married are a perversion of the institution. However ethnologists and sociologists who have investigated this domain have generally discovered a system that regulates most of the alliances, whose constraints are social and economic (e.g., Winch 1958; Winch, McGinnis and Barringer 1962; De Heusch 1971). The historical and cultural character of "love" as an institutionalized feeling has been indeed often underlined by historians of culture and sociologists. In his study of the family in American society, Goode (1964) notes that "love is viewed as a threat to the stratification system in many societies, and elders warn against using love as the basis for mate selection," and he suggests that the fact that "the child is socialized to fall in love," amounts to a form of conditioning, substituting itself for parental authority, since the selection criterion operates within the limits of homogamy. One could add that American literature and cinema obviously find a crisis caused by "exogamy + love" more "interesting" than one arising from "homogamy − love." Implicit constraints are indeed at work outlining in advance for each individual a possible and even probable kind of alliance. But at the same time, our culture mystifies itself by obsessively celebrating love as a determining and often sacred force. "The Nightingales" consists of the transformation of an elective theory of marriage into the restrictive theory that spells out the "truth" of our system. The tacit principles that provide the meaning of this crucial social behavior are laid bare and the vacuity of the ideology which masks these principles is exposed. The nuptial march concluding the transaction clearly indicates that we were not given to witness an instance of commercial sex, but a regular, normal, institutional matrimonial alliance.

But this is not all. This transformation is operated by the couple White-face clown/August in which the opposition culture/nature is exemplified. It may seem surprising that the White-face clown who embodies all hyper-cultural values should be the champion of a "natural feeling" and that the August who personifies the denial of culture should be the one who promotes the cultural law. However this is congruent with our analysis because the distribution of the roles denounces by itself the ideological character of the elective theory and the cultural nature of "love" as opposed to a system of constraints whose fundamental character makes it seem to be more natural by contrast inasmuch as it spells out the social nature of the system involved.

Naturally, the pig act and the birds act do not exhaust the repertoire of the gags and scenarios dealing with the implicit axiomatic rules through which birth and the socialization of infants, and matrimonial alliances are construed as meaningful articulations of the social universe of Western culture. On the other hand these two crucial stages in human life do not monopolize the sacred; death naturally also provides the clowns with an important theme of profanation. Traditional gags like the "dead" clown who "floats" his way out of the ring, or scenarios like "the haunted house" could be shown to operate on cultural axioms as well. But there are many other "sacred" themes such as the structure of identities, the nature of contracts, the specialization of functions, the work ethic or the transcendental value of art which are currently dealt with by circus clowns. For the purpose of this chapter, the two acts that have been described and analysed can be considered sufficiently illustrative. To conclude, I wish to raise a few issues in the light of these examples and in relation to the general theme of this book.

The first issue is the nature of ritual. Does Victor Turner's model of social drama as a universal form which is the "raw material from which many genres of esthetic cultural performance have been derived" (1982: 1) apply to these examples? Or, more importantly does it help in understanding them? Undoubtedly the pig act can be read as a breach of the regular continuity of ordinary life which shows in the expanded version a certain amount of contagiousness before a redress occurs in the form of the expulsion of the clown from the ring. But the bird act would seem less easily amenable to this structure, unless, at the cost of a drastic reduction, one sees the male as the transgressor who wants to seduce a female outside of the matrimonial bond and is eventually redressed by the female. But does not that sort of net let the bigger fish slip through? As all the syntactic models, Greimas' narrative grammar for instance, Turner's model leaves out the semantic or cognitive dimension and overlooks the great variety of syntactic strategies (for example the morphology of profanation) considered as irrelevant variations, or superficial realizations. Furthermore does not this Heraclitean vision of society as continuous tensions, conflicts and change preclude any possibility of knowing anything about anything? Two arguments could be raised against this general approach: *First*, it is not too difficult to show that in some respects a large number of social processes have a few things in common; true enough, the perception of similarities in objects otherwise different from each other is a crucial phase of scientific inquiry. But is it not equally important to account for their differences as well? In fact is not the explanation of details the real challenge of a science of social processes? In principle a valid general law should indeed account for all the observables that belong to its domain. But the "social drama" concept does little more than translate into theatrical and moral terms the concepts of homeostasis and catastrophe which apply to such a vast domain that in the end one cannot distinguish between a religious ritual, a circus act, a ceremonial, the level of a lake, the population of a group of mice, the founding of a new bee colony, the variation of body temperature and a heart attack, to mention only a very few relevant instances.

Secondly, observations that tensions, conflicts, and change occur in society – something that nobody could deny – do not necessarily lead to the conclusion that society is essentially "a process of movement" (1982: 1). Turner's ontological assertion does not take into consideration the fact that all social organizations are precisely attempts to overcome the destructive passing of time. This, of course, implies a constant fight and the devising of means of control in order to prevent or delay the natural dissociation of dislocation of social institutions. It is precisely these relatively stable cultural constructions that form the primary object of a science of human cultures. Levi-Strauss, in his Parmenidean vision claims that myths are machines made to stop time. Could not this be said of culture in general? The domestication of time is indeed a prerequisite for the edification of culture. The possible objection that the stability of a system is a fiction is certainly valid, but the point is that it is obviously a collective fiction which lasts long enough, by human standards, to make it an interesting object of study. The concept of synchronicity is not a mere methodological convenience; it could be used, it seems, as a synonym for society. The vast cognitive organizations that characterize societies enjoy a remarkable stability. In our culture even a creationist and an evolutionist share a great deal of cultural assumptions, in spite of their apparently irreconcilable points of view, which makes it more than likely that they would partake in the understanding and enjoyment of both the pig and the bird acts. Moreover, being traditionally patterned behavior, rituals are, so to speak, the mirrors of synchronicity which reflect and give some enduring materiality to the cognitive organizations through which a society makes sense of itself and its environment. Even when rituals provide some means for a society to reflect upon itself, through a meta-language which makes it possible to cognitively manipulate the tacit axioms in a relatively safe manner, the stability of the system is not actually jeopardized. Thus, rather than focusing on the movement or the process at the risk of losing sight of what changes it seems that attempting to describe the system or the structure as if it were out of time makes more sense if we want to understand ritual and theatre . . . and the circus.

12.

Ethnographic notes on sacred and profane performance

JAMES L. PEACOCK

How does a performance relate to life? One may speak of a performance as condensed, distilled, concentrated life – an occasion when one's energies are intensely focused. One may also speak of performances as set apart, marked by various signals as distinct from ordinary routines of living. And one must speak of performances as embodying meaning. A performance is not necessarily more meaningful than other events in one's life, but it is more deliberately so; a performance is, among other things, a deliberate effort to represent, to say something about something.

If a performance is an action which attempts to communicate meaning, then it is never purely "form." As I write (which is one kind of performance), I do not merely typewrite; if I did so, I could attend to form rather than meaning, as a typist could do in perfectly replicating a manuscript in a foreign language the typist does not understand. But as a would-be writer, I must struggle to ignite form with meaning, which is writing as opposed to typewriting.

These commonplace observations about the necessity of uniting form and meaning in a performance – exemplified here by the event at hand, writing, but normally by the more public performances, such as plays, rituals, concerts, and the like – leads us to our comparison of sacred and profane performances. Granted that this distinction – like that of form and meaning – is problematical if treated as a rigid dichotomy, it can be fruitful if treated as a guide to perceiving experiential aspects the dialectical interplay of which is central to the experience in question. Take the notion of a "sacred performance." The term is an oxymoron. Sacrality implies, at least in the salvation religions dominant in Western and Near Eastern history, a meaning rooted in a cosmic frame that transcends any immediate sensed form. The sacred cannot, therefore, be "performed." Any reduction of meaning to form deprives that form of meaning; to perform the "sacred" necessarily is to profane it. Yet the sacred becomes real only as embodied in form. Such a dialectical tension between the sacred locus of meaning and the profaning form is widely recognized in the history of culture. The dialectical pair separates into mysticism on the one hand and secular art on the other – sacrality without form versus form without sacrality – but power inheres where the two tendencies struggle without splintering.

Broadening our gaze beyond the performance as such, we realize that the tension between form and meaning pervades the entire life of the performer, not just the moments on stage or in the temple. How is routine life connected to that intensified union of form and meaning which constitutes performance? The distinction between sacred and profane suggests patterns. To the extent that performance is profane, the pattern would seem to emphasize separation of the performance from the rest of one's life, while sacred performances accord with a pattern emphasizing unity of performance with the rest of one's life. This distinction follows logically, although empirical variation may be complex. The logic is that as a performance is regarded as more nearly "form," then the umbrella of meaning is not felt to cover so much of one's non-performing life; officially, at least, a film star can do as she wishes. Conversely, so long as a performance is sacred, meaning is more prominent, and this meaning, by definition, transcends the immediate form hence pervades and constrains the rest of one's life; officially, at least, the priest is not free away from the altar.

Whether tending toward sacred or profane prototype all performers face the problem of connecting their performances with the rest of their existence. To do so, they employ some kind of mediating process. "Rehearsal" would seem conventionally associated with profane performances, rites of passage with sacred performances. What is the difference? Consonant with the argument that the sacred is more embedded in wider existence, rites of passage would be regarded as more a part of community life – spatially set apart to be sure, but obligatory, dictated by social norms shared by everyone in the community. Rehearsal, in contrast, is voluntary training pursued by specialists in performances. Here as in other typologies, the mixed cases such as the ritualized preparation of the noh actor (where rehearsal is ritual), the wedding "rehearsal" in Christianity (where ritual is rehearsed) and many others are suggestive for sharpening our sense of the permutations generated from an initially simple distinction such as sacred and profane. Our purpose here is simply to raise questions about the patterning of human experience which we can then explore more concretely through ethnographic fieldwork.

I am writing this paper in the midst of fieldwork among Primitive Baptists in the Blue Ridge Mountains of North Carolina and Virginia. I shall describe some features of their sacred performances – thunderous sermons, moving acts of communion, hard lives – which I am currently witnessing, in this way endeavoring to suggest some features of sacred performances in general. In order to compare these sacred performances (which we might as well term "ritual") to profane ones (which some might term "theatre"), I shall occasionally refer also to previous fieldwork, which was among the Javanese of Indonesia who performed a play they called ludruk (see Peacock 1968). The jumps between cultures as well as genres may jar, but are legitimate for the purpose at hand.

My focus is on the difference in relationship between form and experience associated with the two kinds of performance: sacred and profane.

Roots and resurrection

The evening service in the old log church of the St. Clair Bottom Primitive Baptist Association in Southwestern Virginia is opened by the moderator, who refers to "my old step-daddy" who had just died at an age over one-hundred years. The moderator is followed by Elder C. who in the prayer refers to his father, once an elder of this church; C. describes how his father would press against the thick chestnut logs of the church in order to draw strength. Then the first preacher of the evening, a visiting Kentuckian who has a church in Michigan, refers in his sermon to the unmarked graves of his grandfather and grandmother back in Kentucky.

Several hours later, the service comes toward a close as the second preacher, M. chants a vision of resurrection. Among other things, he depicts how dead ancestors, at least those who have been saved, will be reunited in the "home in heaven." This preaching evokes from several women (no men) shouts and a Pentecostal-like act of "praising God" with raised hands.

Here, the theme of resurrection is linked to the kinship network of the participants. Reference is made to "old daddies" and other ancestors or relatives of the preachers and by implication members of the congregation. Resurrection is thus rendered locally specific, but it also remains a category within the Calvinistic theology fundamental to the Primitive Baptist faith. Resurrection is given both a local and universal referent.

The ludruk plays are performed primarily in the large port city of Surabaya, Java. The plays are written, acted, and watched by the working class. They are staged mainly in commercial settings, such as the noisy, dirty bamboo shed in the People's Amusement Park. In these settings, admission is by purchase of a ticket. Actors and spectators come from throughout the city and are not bound together by kinship, residence, political party, religious sect or other corporate group membership. Though they are nominal Muslims, they are not pious and do not belong to the Muslim sects and organizations; in this lack of sect identity they differ from the Primitive Baptists.

A typical ludruk play lasts approximately four hours – from 8 p.m. to midnight. It opens with a dance, proceeds to a song and prologue by a clown, who laments the terrible economic conditions of the day, then moves into a skit in which two or three clowns play some prank on a scapegoat; the scapegoat is always old and established in a *kampong* (slum neighborhood) while the pranksters are young reprobates. After a song and dance by a transvestite, the main story begins, which, punctuated by transvestite dance/songs between scenes, lasts until the end of the show at midnight.

The stories are of three types: *tjerita rumahtangga* (stories about domestic matters), *tjerita pahlawan* (stories about legendary heroes), and *tjerita revolusi* (stories about the Indonesian Revolution of 1945–50). The majority of the eighty-two plays which I saw were of the domestic type. They largely turn around the conflict between the lower and upper classes and the younger and older generations.

In the ludruk plays, reference to ancestry or kinship is rare, and those made are general rather than specific to persons present, whether actors or audience. Such allusions are also satirical, poking fun at reverence for ancestry. An aristocrat asks his servant (played by a clown), "What does Semar come from?" (Semar is the clown-god revered by classical Javanese puppet plays, the *wayang kulit*, and elaborated in Javanese mythology). "God," replies the clown. (Sang Hjang Tunggal, the One God, is Semar's father.) "And what does Bagong (Semar's son) come from?" "Cowhide" replies the clown. (The puppet Bagong is made from cowhide.) Here the elaborate and revered genealogy of Javanese mythology, a symbol of sacred spirituality, is reduced to a lowly material substance: cowhide. In a similar joke, the punchline is "Old man Mangun"; the origin of the sacred figure is the laborer, signified by the lowly name "Mangun," who does the hand work to make the puppet. Again sacred geneology is profaned.

The setting of the ludruk is sufficient to explain its attitude toward ancestry and kinship. A commercial working class drama, situated in locales outside the family-oriented residential neighborhoods, ludruk is emancipated from family values, a stance it signals in its prologue when it makes the representative of such values its scapegoat. Ludruk denigrates roots and ancestry, parents and elders. It is a free aesthetic form, set apart from those group memberships and social contexts in which such values are affirmed.

This contrast between the Primitive Baptist and ludruk exemplifies one way in which a sacred performance grounds the aesthetic form in the experience of the participants – their roots, their kinfolk, and their resurrection seen in part as family reunion – while the secular performance in this instance denigrates this link to experience. The lack of reference to the familial pasts and futures of the ludruk participants themselves, the satire of ancestry, and the displacement of imagery toward fictional characters is one of many ways that ludruk states its theatricality, that it is a passing theatrical moment, free in some ways from entanglement in participants' experiences outside the theatre.

Chant, tongues, form, meaning

Primitive Baptist preachers often move from a spoken to a chanted, or as they put it, "sung" sermon. Moving melodically and repetitively up and down the scale back to a dominant tone, the chanter often achieves great volume and speed of speech. Not only is scripture quoted but also a message is preached, composed while chanting. As he preaches, the chanting preacher moves about rhythmically, shaking hands with other elders and perhaps others. (Example: a black Primitive Baptist preacher walks around shaking hands with women members while chanting to them the message that women may not hold any office in the church.)

Why does spoken sermon become chant, yet chant not become speaking in tongues (as among Pentecostals)? Speech, chant, and tongues constitute a gradient based on a ratio of form to meaning. A spoken sermon gives the greatest emphasis to meaning or message, while tongues elevates form over meaning to the extent that no meaning at all is conveyed except to special persons who, in Pentecostal churches, act as interpreters. The chant assumes the middle position, achieving a certain balance between form and meaning.

In other ways, too, Primitive Baptists strive to prevent the elevation of form over meaning yet to recognize the power of form. They do not permit musical instruments and in the most traditional churches, they sing songs from books which have only the song-texts, not notes. They do not permit preachers to prepare sermons by writing out or otherwise formulating any script or outline. They justify their taboo on instruments by saying that instruments stimulate only the flesh, while a song may express the "inner man," and they speak of song texts as little sermons. (One may see this as an avowal of forms that carry verbal and therefore spiritual meaning – the word – while rejecting forms that do not carry verbal meaning and therefore express sensuality – the flesh.) They explain that preachers should not prepare sermons, so that they remain open to inspiration from God at the instant when they mount the stand: Elder D. emphasized that to mount the stand and fail to be inspired (inspirited) served to prove that you were a "preacher instead of an actor" – that you depend on the spirit instead of learning lines like a performer. In short, spirit should energize form, rather than the reverse. The primitive Baptist attitudes, then, illustrate the struggle of a particular faith to keep sacred performances sacred while recognizing that they are performances: to sustain a balance between religion and aesthetics, meaning and form.

The contrasting tendency could be illustrated by secular theatre deliberately and artfully drawing attention to the form through reminding the audience that it is a form, and that the appearance of reality is illusion. An example is the noh play mask which covers only part of the face. The transvestite ludruk actor who deliberately reminds audience that he is a man displaying the illusion of a woman is perhaps parallel

Meler is funny looking – high waist, scrawny short arms, big flabby buttocks, no neck, big head. He acts very nervous, alternately smiling and grimacing, saying nothing, pointing first to himself, then to the audience. Finally he clears his throat in a deep bass. Listeners laugh loudly. Another series of screams, smiles and grimaces, then another throat-clearing, followed by laughter. Now Meler sings a refined introduction: "Be comfortable everybody . . ." and concludes by shrilling, "allow me to introduce myself. I am Meler from Tambakredia (a red-light district)." This evokes a shout: "Hey Meler – you whore!" Meler retorts, "Can you pay the price?" A man screams back, "You ask for the sword (ngedjak anggar)!" (Peacock 1968: 201).

By clearing his throat in a bass voice, Meler reminds his audience that he is not a true female, but an illusion of femininity. Their response is raucous insult, which is typical: a favorite shout when a transvestite punctures the feminine illusion by revealing a masculine trait is "He's a piece of shit, old, and about to die!" Culture, we are reminded, is grounded in nature.

The ludruk transvestite is, as Javanese themselves say, a fantasy (*chayal*). At a psychological level, the transvestite symbolizes a counterpoint to the conventional adult status. As an illusory woman rather than one capable of giving birth, he implies sexuality without procreation and the responsibility of children; oral rather than genital sex; and, as suggested by erotic dreams and fantasies recounted by some ludruk participants, an imagery of adolescence now lost through age and adulthood (see Peacock 1968: 198–99). At a cultural level, the transvestite sums up the nature of illusion, the suspended disbelief that is the basis of art itself. He manifests the symbolism of feminity but he is not female; he is a "fantasy." This symbolization of fantasy is signaled by the placement of the transvestite singer in the performance: in front of sets depicting other-worldly, legendary scenes, such as mythic palaces. His songs have dreamy musical accompaniment, high language, and poetic imagery (including the fantasy propaganda of the Sukarnoist regime, which was always given to the transvestite to sing). He is imputed magical powers, and he retains a somewhat tarnished glow of cosmic power associated with androgyny in Indonesian tribal myth.

The transvestite fascinates the ludruk participants not simply because of his identity with fantasy and illusion, but because he manifests tension between that illusion and reality. Meler's clearing his throat is one example. Ludruk goers enjoy constantly reminding themselves that the feminine illusion onstage was actually a man. "He is really a man," they would remark repeatedly. The transvestite gave a naughty thrill, not just of illicit sexuality but of art. In art, reality is cheated. Constructing women from men through padding and wigs, culture conquers nature.

Primitive Baptists do not relish this kind of aesthetic kick. They emphasize, instead, the Protestant value of "meaning it," that one means what one says, that the form represents reality. They are alert to deception, for this world is beset by such snares on every hand, but their objective is not to revel in illusion but to show "evidence" of the truth, which comes from God.

Victimage: mystical and theatrical

Primitive Baptist worship draws on the paradigm of Christ: His birth, crucifixion, resurrection, and salvation of all humankind from eternal damnation. This paradigm, though a narrative, is embedded in non-narrative paradigms, such as doctrine and typology.

Primitive Baptists profess to a doctrine of "universal and particular election": God's choice of who is to be saved and who is to be damned applies to every one, and this choice was made before the "foundation of the world." Christ's act of sacrifice is subsumed under this doctrinal frame.

Primitive Baptist preachers treat Christ explicitly as a "type" (their term) and speak of "symbols" (also their term) which express this type. Elder E. preached a sermon which can be summarized as follows. E. begins with the biblical reference to a skin covering Adam and Eve. He argues that this is not, as some have claimed, simply their human skin; it is an animal skin; but what animal? The lamb. E. then quotes scriptural references to humans covered with the cloak of righteousness, hence cleansed of their sins. He observes that man attempted to cover his nakedness (sinfulness) with vegetable matter (Adam's and Eve's leaves) but failed; God, however, succeeded by covering man with animal matter, the skin of the lamb, which was the cloak of righteousness: the purity brought by Christ through grace. In preaching this sermon, Elder E. (who, though a stone mason with only an elementary school education, is a gifted poet, preacher, and thinker, a scholarly man whose favorite reading matter, aside from the King James Bible, is the works of John Bunyan and John Gill) explicitly refers to Christ as the "type" of which the other items, such as cloak, lamb, etc. are "symbols." By what E. himself terms "typology," the narrative of Christ, though powerfully evoked, is embedded in a broader pattern which unites Old and New Testaments in order to reveal Christ as foreshadowed in the creation and history of the world prior to His coming.

Where the Primitive Baptists are positioned in their treatment of victimage as narrative (specifically, Christ as victim) is suggested by some comparisons to the *ludruk*.

The ludruk plays perform victimage of several types. One is the prologue, where an old established person is victimized by young reprobates. A moral admonition is sometimes tacked on to such pranks, but hardly noticed amidst the glee of the victimage. A second is the hero story, which ends "tragically" (we might say; the Javanese don't) when the people's champion, the hero, is captured and killed. The third is in domestic stories, stories about families.

The domestic stories divide into two sub-types. Type A, in a traditional Javanese setting, takes twenty-five years or so (fictional time) to unfold, and ends with a working class person failing in her effort to marry into the upper class. Type B, which was increasing in popularity while A was dying out, is in a modern setting, takes only a few months to unfold, and ends with a working class person succeeding in marrying up. Both types entail a victimage, which is associated with the type of social mobility. In A, it is the heroine herself who is a victim, spurned and destroyed by the upper class males who exploit her, leaving behind a child, who is a second victim. In B, it is a relative of the heroine who is the victim, always suffering some violent end precisely at the point when the heroine achieves her happy marriage with a higher class male. Emotions elicited by the two kinds of victimage differed. In Type A, it is not the loss of the heroine but the abandonment of her child as she is destroyed which evokes comment. This image of the abandoned child is virtually the only ludruk victimage which elicits explicit sadness. Introspective comments by spectators connect the emotion to their own experience of being separated from a parent, which is common in Java owing to a divorce rate of more than 50 per cent, or to other sad and lonely times. One spectator says, for example

> This reminds me of the time when I had just married, having been forced by parents to do so. I stole for the sake of the household. Then I roamed, seeking understanding. I always faced the trials and suffering of roaming with patience . . . Then my mother died.

The violent victimage in Type B evoked a different emotion. When two bad characters crawl in the gutter, begging at the door of the happily married hero and heroine whom they had previously spurned, a spectator cries "Great! This is revenge! Just silent (the couple do not speak to the beggars). Not even a sneeze!"

Both aesthetic and social logic motivate the victimages. In the A-type, the plot moves calmly through twenty-five years of upholding the status quo, and the sadness for the abandoned child is part of a general tone of sad acceptance of a social order in which the status quo reigns while its lower class victims suffer. In the B-type, the imagery moves through scenes of beating, destroying, grabbing, spitting, and killing, toward a savage victimage which is necessary to shake the old order and to break the bond of the heroine with her class of origin so that she can move up. The relationship between these two plots and the ambiguities and tensions of working class people in a society in transition between closed and open class structures is fairly obvious, though many subtleties are noted elsewhere (Peacock 1968).

The difference between this kind of victimage and that of the Primitive Baptist is that while both display aesthetic and social logic, the ludruk eschews any explicit religious interpretation. The villain's eventual punishment in B-plots, for example, is not explicitly linked to any cosmic process that rewards evil with suffering. The Javanese ludruk goers do vaguely believe that bad action today will some day cause the actor to be "struck by" ill fortune, but they do not designate any agent or agency to do the striking. They are not keen believers in Muslim theology, and though they may inherit some sentiments from Buddhism, they do not explicitly profess belief in *karma* or a like mechanism. In the plays themselves, no allusions at all are made to a supernatural cause of the plot's outcome or to other religious meanings. Certainly the victimage is not seen as having any direct mystical effect on participants' lives as in the Primitive Baptist belief that Christ was crucified to save man from eternal suffering.

This difference in worldview relates in turn to a performative contrast. Ludruk simply narrates the victimage, while the Primitive Baptist insists on containing the narrative, within non-narrative paradigms: theologies, typologies, family networks, even – and here is an important grounding – the environment: thunders an Elder, "I preach the God of these hills!" Such explicit framing is the bane of secular theatre, the basis of sacred ritual.

Emotional response and personal history

The usual response of ludruk audience is laughter, raucous and continuous, in this play dominated by clowns. As noted, there are sad stories, as in the victimages. But of the types of victimage, the only one that evokes explicit sadness is the abandoned child, and this is brief and episodic – never the final culmination of a play.

Primitive Baptists are solemn during services. Sermonic jokes are rare, as are smiles and laughter (the only frequent smiles I have seen were exhibited by one retarded man and another with an apparent nervous disorder). They sing mournfully and reflectively; such songs are "Mixtures of Joys and Sorrows," and they weep silently, usually when there is a reference to those who have gone before, hope of life beyond, or to God's grace, or when they extend to each other the hand of fellowship or wash each other's feet. One elder described the feeling during weeping as one of gratitude, that one is unworthy but potentially a recipient of grace.

Life histories of the ludruk participants were usually nostalgic, looking back to some frustrated, now-lost-love of youth: a plot parallel to many of the ludruk. Life history narrations of the Primitive Baptists fall broadly between the subjectivism and sentimentality of the ludruk narrations and the objectivism and legalism of some creeds. Frequently, the Primitive Baptists will tell of a spiritual experience which led to conversion, joining the church, and being ordained to preach. This spiritual experience, in which God "impresses" one, evokes powerful emotions, and hard men may choke up as they tell it. At the same time, the Primitive Baptist culture imposes severe constraints that prevent a Pentecostal-like subjectivism. Elder E. begins his account of his "life and experience" for example, with the caution: "If I have not been deceived" for it is to be expected that humans, who are sinners and depraved, will see crookedly instead of straight. And when E. tells of first sensing his calling, he describes it thus:

> During my early teens as I followed a yoke of oxen to a plow or harrow, I would sing some of the old songs of Zion . . . such as
>> Guide me, O Thou great Jehovah!
>> Pilgrim through this barren land;
>> I am weak, but Thou art mighty,
>> Hold me with Thy pow'rful hand.

As I would sing these old hymns, a sad lonely feeling would come over me that someday I would have to preach, but when or how I didn't know.

The point to note is the containing of subjective experience within public form, a remembered hymn, which preaches the subordination of self to God. Emotion is strong and deep, but rendered monumentally objective by firm doctrine (which includes distrust of human emotion), formal language, and collective forms. Experience is thus sacralized.

Just as the inner life is subsumed to the objective, so it is taken to *be* objective, if it bears a sacral stamp. Later in his autobiography, E. tells of a dream, part of which depicted him taking the stand at a church to preach, finishing his sermon, then *dying* on the stand

Just as I closed my discourse, the chill of death struck me in my feet and began to come up my legs and over my body. When it had enveloped me completely, I fell dead.

At this time, E. was elder in a Union Baptist Church, but he had concluded that he could not accept any longer the Union doctrine of salvation. After the dream he vowed to God to preach the scripturally correct doctrine even though believing to do so would, as in the dream, result in his death. On the appointed day, he walked the fifteen miles or so to the church, at every step burdened by the certainty that he was walking to his death. At the church, every feature was identical to the scene of his dream, but he mounted the stand and preached as never before, believing "this was my last and final message." Everything happened as in the dream, except that he did not die. Finally he concluded that the dream meant he would die to the "fellowship and love" of his church. Years later, after declaring his conviction and requesting his release, he left this Union Baptist Church, and was baptized in icy November waters into the Primitive Baptist Church, in which he soon became an elder.

In order to underline the epistemology that underlies this dream and E.'s interpretation of it, consider an alternative one offered by the Javanese. This can be illustrated by a session of Sumarah, a meditation group to which some of us were asked to recount our own dreams. I mentioned a dream showing a friend, who is in fact dead but appeared in the dream as alive. The Sumarah teacher responded: "that is all right, provided you realized, at the time you were dreaming, that he is in fact dead and only *appearing* to be alive." In other words, one should treat the experience as symbolic even while having the experience.

A parallel worldview is expressed in this conversation overheard at ludruk: A woman forgot herself when a son (on-stage) was killing his father. She screamed, "Waduh, Allah! The father is being choked!" Her husband reminded her, "It is only a character in a story, a performance." In accord with this view of ludruk as a performance, spectators comment on technical aspects as the play is going on: his voice is good, he is handsome, he is ugly, he is like so-and-so (another actor). Ludruk goers stand aloof from the form, reminding themselves it is fiction (recall here, also, their attitude about the transvestite).

E. treated his dream as real while having it, and interpreted the prediction of his death as symbolic only after reality had contradicted the literal interpretation. The Primitive Baptist treatment of dream in this case would seem better to accord with its sacralizing tradition, the Javanese Sumarah one with a theatrical tradition that accentuates the illusory character of experience even as it is experienced. On the other hand, the Primitive Baptist also has the Calvinist empiricist skepticism about human perception of experience: "If I have not been deceived."

The hearing of sermons in the context of experience

The great preachers of the Primitive Baptists are powerful personages. Elder R., though nearly eighty, stands erect, with piercing eyes and measured, cogent language. Elder E. is a gifted, scintillating poetic weaver of images and analyst of meanings. Elder Y. is ruddy-cheeked, jut-jawed, with bull-like shoulders, resonant voice, and strong convictions. Elder X. is small, soft spoken, and inhibited, not so obviously charismatic as the others.

Yet X. is seen as having the gift to preach; he was ordained without question, he has been called to several churches, and he has six months of invitations to visit churches around the country.

To understand X., one must broaden the context. He was suffering from a blood disease when he was called, after twenty years of refusing to accept the call. He rose from his bed and began years of hard manual labor, devoted pastoral service, and preaching.

X's hearers know this life, they know him, and one may assume that his sermons, which are what we record on our tapes, are not what they hear; they hear *him*. Even more, they hear that wider reality which he represents and in which they participate but in which, unfortunately, we do not.

A sacred performance is not simply a performance.

Whereas the Primitive Baptist ritual projects a religious personality, rather than just the forms and performance of the preacher, ludruk minimizes that larger framework and emphasizes the performance itself. In the stories, characters have fictional names, and those of the actors are rarely known. The clowns do retain their own names in the performance, but they are known only in their capacity as clowns; their daily lives are unknown to spectators, for they have not entered the domain of popular media which entertain readers with gossip about the lives of the stars, and few spectators seem interested in this kind of knowledge. The ludruk players are actors, playing roles, appreciated for their ability to assume a mask. At midnight, when they finish a performance, they are not the center of attention by the media or adoring fans; they vanish into the crowds of departing audiences.

Performance and daily life

The daily lives of Primitive Baptist, *ludruk*, and the other performers entail many levels from public to private, not all of which are accessible to the fieldworker.

At a formal, public level, the religious performers differ from the ludruk performers in their greater official stature. Ludruk actors, being of the working class and often of suspect political and sexual inclination, are rarely given much respect off-stage even when their artistic talent on-stage is appreciated. Within their respective sects, and to some extent in wider society, the Primitive Baptist preachers are treated with considerable respect; this is partly because they are not only performers but usually leaders as well, so that their "off-stage" lives are woven into routines of administrative and ceremonial obligation, whereas the ludruk actors have no public lives off-stage.

At an informal, personal level, the religious and secular performers seem rather similar. Away from the stand or stage, they seem to sink into a lull or low, perhaps even a mild depression, except when work and ritual obligations draw them into daily routines which have their own complementary power in relation to the "high" of performance. In providing such obligatory structures, Primitive Baptists exceed the ludruk. For ludruk actors, there is no doctrine, no well-established organizational or institutional structure to govern daily life experience; they are part of an animistically-grounded Javanese complex of ritual and social life, but this complex is rather loosely integrated in the urban slums where the ludruk players live, and their daily lives are anomic. Tradition and doctrine instruct the Primitive Baptists. They expect to work hard, often at physical labor, then to spend spare moments in meditation, prayer, or study of scripture and theological texts. They also expect to reflect on spiritual matters while at work, as Elder E. illustrates by this story of singing while plowing. They do not expect to devote time to formal preparation for a performance, as in writing a sermon, for this is forbidden. Instead, they should live their lives in a proper spiritual state, in which case spirituality will automatically be manifested when it is time to preach, sing, or otherwise perform. A spirit-filled life should ideally provide the kind of peaceful fullness that assures both proper daily behavior and superior performance on climatic occasions; such an ideal, coupled with the refusal to define obligatory routines and the necessary limits of the flesh (especially as vitality declines with age) does, of course, impose demands on the individual which, when not fulfilled, breed feelings of guilt and depression, but the arrangement is sufficient to provide considerable unity and balance in their lives of those who both exist and perform.

Within this general pattern, certain particular kinds of experiences warrant special note. One of these is travel. Travel is isomorphic with performance in that it separates one's life from normal routine and concentrates energies in a particular direction. Owing, perhaps, to this isomorphism, travel combined with performance seems to entail special excitement and also special tension among the performers, whereas travel without performance or performance without travel are both less exciting and less tense. Primitive Baptists narrating their autobiographies mark the rhythm of their lives by the preaching-tours. They describe such preaching-tours as periods of intensity and adventure. They speak of being carried away on the stand by some particularly ecstatic or eloquent sermon or speech. Times on the road but off the stand are described retrospectively as exciting, too, entailing all-night theological arguments, clever retorts in debate, humorous misadventures. In fact, when the elders are observed on the road, they often seem at loose ends – lacking their normal work routine, confined to someone's house, prisoners of their hosts; but laity describing the visits of elders in their homes characterize the elders as "having a good time."

Ludruk actors riding together on the back of a truck or sitting in a hut together while waiting to go on-stage in a village showed similar sentiments, though lacking the element of religious calling and the structure of religious obligations (such as prayer, reading the Bible or Qur'ān, and simply "being spiritual") that provide a constancy for the religious performer and sustain him as he travels on the road.

Conclusion

To symbolize is human, and to symbolize entails separating (and therefore struggling to reunite) form, meaning, and context. While all humans endeavor to arrange some kind of integration among these elements, the endeavor is perhaps most challenging for those who, as history evolves toward differentiation and complexity, are distinguished as "performers," and, therefore, must relate their "performances" to the rest of their existence; for them, the universal task of integrating form, meaning, and context becomes the personal task of rendering form meaningful while performing then subsuming this intensely concentrated unity of form and meaning within a wider unity which is life. The question posed in this paper is whether sacralization of performance makes a difference in this endeavor. Comparison of two varieties of performance experience drawn from fieldwork suggests that sacralization does make a difference. In comparison to the ludruk theatre, the Primitive Baptists interweave performance with kinship relationships, life history, doctrine, and other frameworks to contain form within meaning.

13.

The spatial sense of the sacred in Spanish America and the American South and its tie with performance

MILES RICHARDSON

Working with the same script, so to speak, and indeed, sharing many words in common, participants in two Christian faiths, the Catholics of Spanish America and the Baptists of the American South, put together action and artifact to construct two distinct senses of the sacred. The sense that the Spanish American Catholics have is that the sacred lies outside the person of the worshiper, while the Southern Baptists, in contrast, locate the sacred inside that person. In one, the communicant reaches out; in the other, the believer listens within.

To achieve their external sense of the sacred the Spanish Americans approach the sacred as individuals approaching factual objects. Conversely, to achieve their interior sense, the Baptists join together as a group. In addition, the individual in the Spanish American *iglesia* reaches out for the sacred in the context of a hierarchical structure at whose apex resides the Pope in Rome. The Baptists, in contrast, turn inward to feel the sacred's presence in the context of an egalitarian structure that proclaims the independence of each democratically constituted church.

Methodological note

"Spanish American Catholicism" here refers to the worship participated in by those Spanish speaking citizens of Latin America whose cultural heritage took shape during Spain's conquest of the New World. Excluded are the forms of Catholicism that include many American Indian or African elements and also excluded are the forms of modern worship that reflect contemporary, intellectual trends, such as liberation theology. The Baptists of the American South are a more recent version of Christianity, but who, since the American Civil War, have become so numerous among the white population as to epitomize the religious fervor of the region. The overwhelming majority of white Baptist churches are members of the Southern Baptist Convention.

Thus, for convenience, if not for absolute accuracy, "Baptists of the American South" and "Southern Baptists" are here synonyms.

Every ethnographer works with biases, some self-imposed, other unconscious. I am confident I have plenty of both. The ethnographic trick is not to factor out the biases, for that would factor out the ethnographer; rather the best strategy is not only to be aware of the biases but to utilize them in the research.

Since my first fieldwork in Colombia in 1962, when my informant explained that Christ died so that we too might die, I have been attempting, at times struggling, to understand Spanish American Catholicism, first in Colombia, later in Costa Rica, and more recently in Guatemala and Mexico. The effort has been sporadic, and my comprehension, obviously incomplete, comes more from what Spanish American Catholics do in their *iglesias* and less from how they interpret their religion to themselves.

For the Baptist, the situation is more complicated, and more painful. I was raised in a God-fearing family. One of my brothers was a Baptist preacher, and my sister, a devout person in her own right, married another. For reasons having to do with my life and with Baptist beliefs, I switched from being a Baptist to being an anthropologist – a change comparable in my case to a Shiite becoming a Quaker. Yet I became an anthropologist so that I might find out why people believe what they do, Baptists included. Once in Spanish America, I began to see that a comparison between the Catholics of that region and the Baptist of the South might provide an understanding of both and of the larger question. Realizing that from an ethnographic perspective, I had considerable familiarity with how Baptists interpret their faith but also recognizing that the experience was both highly personal and out of date, I attended, as an ethnographer, Baptist services during these last several years, principally, in Baton Rouge where I live. I believe I am now in the position to suggest how these two religions construct their sense of the sacred (Richardson 1986).

Material setting

In Spanish America, immense structures – the basilica, cathedral, and even parish *iglesia* – dominate the skyline of all but the largest of cities. In the South, despite Baptist disclaimers that works lead not to salvation, the First Baptist Church in any city may approximate the county courthouse in size if not in opulence. Size alone, however, is no measure of the significance of the settings in the construction of the sense of the sacred. We clearly see this as we enter one and then the other place of worship.

When we step from the street through the large portals into the Spanish American *iglesia*, we can distinguish in the gloom figures standing in ornately framed niches on either side of the aisles. In the flickering of the candles all share the same melancholy stare, the same frozen agony. As we approach the niches, and as we deepen our understanding, however, each figure becomes a distinct personage. Over there, if we are in Mexico, stands the Virgin of Guadalupe, her figure etched for eternity on the blanket of roses; or if we are in Costa Rica, the Virgin of the Angels, brown like Guadalupe, but tiny, doll-like, almost lost in her golden apparel. Over here, we see St. Peter, St. Paul, and the black saint of Latin America, St. Martin of Porras. Everywhere, we see the Son of God: as the Divine Infant, asleep on a pillow or cradled in his mother's arms; as Jesus the Nazarene, dressed in a purple robe, his hands tied; as Christ on the cross, his thorn-crowned head slumped to one side, his side pierced and bleeding; as Christ in the sepulcher, his body at rest, his face pale in death.

When we cross the parking lot, climb the steps, and enter the doors of the Southern Baptist church, we see, at first, nothing, for not a single figure peers down at us and, frequently, not even a plain cross adorns the wall. As we walk down the center aisle, we see an auditorium focused on a speaker's platform. On the platform stands the largest object in the church, the pulpit. On the pulpit, or on a plain table below the platform, is an opened book, the Bible. Above the pulpit, where in Spanish America Christ hangs forever in agony, there is apparently nothing.

What are we to make of the contrast between these settings? In answer, let us suspend our knowledge of both mass and sermon and consider the settings as such.

In both *iglesia* and church, we note a large section devoted to the audience headed by a much smaller portion of space for those who address the audience. Yet in the *iglesia*, the single focus of this arrangement is challenged by the figures in their separate spaces along the sides and in the larger *iglesias* by the chapels – nearly miniature *iglesias* in themselves – leading off the main structure. In the church, no separate niches break the plane of the sides. Even the windows, which are generally not stained and which in any case are usually narrow and curtained to conserve the air-conditioned climate, provide no distraction from the exclusive focus on the pulpit. Furthermore, the choir, which in the *iglesia* may be above and behind the audience, in the church is positioned directly behind the pulpit and thus reinforces the audience's concentration on the platform.

In both *iglesia* and church the dress of priest and of the preacher harmonize with the respective organizations. The priestly vestments of cope, alb, and surplice separate the office from the everyday, and often humble, dress of the parishioners. The preacher's suit, on the other hand, while at times more flashy and at others more subdued, is barely distinguishable from the suits in the congregation. Furthermore, preachers, during the heat of a particularly impassioned sermon, have been known to throw off their coats and loosen their ties to demonstrate solidarity, through the physical labor of the sermon, with working men. An equally clear connection between setting and organization in Catholicism is the ranking of structures from parish *iglesia*, to cathedral, to basilica, and, of course, to the Holy See in Rome. Among the Baptists, while structures range from mobile homes with instant steeples to the First Baptist Church in Dallas, which occupies a city block or more, there are no cathedrals, basilicas, or Holy Sees – unless the church in Dallas be so designated.

In the Spanish American *iglesia*, we are overwhelmed with a sense of presence. Everywhere we look, a figure, eyes alight in the candle's glow, looks back. In the Southern Baptist church, no matter how tasteful the decor, no matter how handsome the pulpit, we sense an emptiness, and when we look about, we see nothing.

Religious behavior

Although the material setting, in and of itself, provides important clues as to the composure of the sense of sacred, the full meaning of the setting awaits the participation of the worshiper.

The mass and the sermon differ in that the mass approximates what both anthropological and conventional wisdom define as ritual: a tightly organized, prescribed sequence of events whose outcome transforms a profane reality into a sacred one. The sermon, while certainly ritualistic in its repetitive organization, resembles a secular, albeit impassionate, lecture, as much as it does ritual. Yet, the sermon, like the mass, seeks to transform a profane state of being into a sacred one. The difference between the two stems essentially from the location of the sense of the sacred. A comparison of the eucharist of the mass and the invitation of the sermon will clarify the distinction.

The eucharist versus the invitation

The liturgy of the eucharist comes after the liturgy of the word, and depending if the mass is a shortened version said during the weekday or a longer version sung on Sunday, it appears roughly midway in the mass during the week and toward the end on Sunday. We might divide it into two main parts: *la oración eucarística*, (the eucharistic prayer) and *el rito de comunión* (the rite of communion).

The two segments together form layers of condensed symbolic action (Turner 1967) that recapitulate the Biblical account of the last meal Jesus and his disciplines shared shortly before his death. In addition, the segments allude to Jesus' crucifixion and to his sacrifice by God for the deliverance of believers from the certainty of death. During the *oración eucarística*, the priest, acting in the role of both the priest of the church and of Christ, the sacrificial victim, elevates above the altar and in front of the parishioners the thin wafer of unleavened bread and commands in the words of Christ

Tomad y comed todos de el
porque esto es mi cuerpo,
que será entregado por vosotros.

Take and eat this all of you,
for this is my body
which will be given up for you.[1]

The wafer, already a symbol of bread, becomes through the ritual, the body of Christ. The priest repeats the same movements with the chalice containing wine, and commands again in Christ's words

Tomad y bebed de el,
porque este es el caliz de mi sangre,
sangre de la alianza nueva y eterna,
que será derramada por vosotros
y por todos los hombres
para el perdón de los pecados.
Haced esto en conmemoración mia.

Take and drink this, all of you,
for this is the cup of my blood,
the blood of the new and everlasting covenant.
It will be shed for you
and for all men
so that sins may be forgiven.
Do this in the memory of me.

The ritual effects a transformation of wine into the blood of Christ.

The *oración eucarística* establishes the objective, material presence of the sacred outside the subjective interior of the worshiper and independent of the worshiper's private feelings. The ritual, in both dogma and behavior, is clearly the most important constellation of symbolic action in the mass. In its dogma, Catholicism teaches through the doctrine of transubstantiation that Christ becomes physically present in both wafer and wine. In their behavior, the parishioners likewise demonstrate the solemnity of the event. During other parts of the mass, for example, during the preceding homily, a discourse by the priest, which, in fact, is omitted during the weekday masses, the parishioners are frequently more attentive to their own spiritual preoccupations than to the mere words of the priest. Throughout the *oración*, in contrast, they kneel and cross themselves with concentration and dispatch.

Once the objective presence of the sacred is established in the wafer and wine, the second segment of the liturgy of eucharist, the *rito de comunión*, completes the reinactment of the last meal and of Christ's sacrifice. The priest, in his dual role of the church and of Christ, holds aloft the wafer once more and announces

> *Este es el cordero de Dios,*
> *que quita el pecado del mundo.*
> *Dichosos los invitados a la cena*
> *del Senor.*
>
> This is the Lamb of God
> who takes away the sins of the world.
> Happy are those who are called to the Lord's supper.

Those worshippers who are eligible, that is, those by virtue of the ritual of confession have been spiritually cleaned, reenact the role of the disciples at the last supper and kneel in front of the altar, the banquet table. Holding the ciborium containing the wafers that are now the body of Christ, the priest passes from one individual worshiper to another, and from the ciborium he takes a wafer and places it on the tongue of the person, saying *"El cuerpo de Cristo,"* The body of Christ. With the wafer melting in their mouths, with the external sacred now internalized, the communicants return to their seats.

The invitation is the fulfillment of the Southern Baptist evangelical commitment to "bring Christ to a lost and dying world" and consequently the occasion for the transformation of an individual from the state of profane human despair to the sacred bliss of salvation. In its construction of a sense of the sacred, it is the Baptist equivalent to the liturgy of the eucharist.

The invitation comes at the end of an hour-long service composed of an introductory segment of singing and announcements and the main segment, the sermon. The sermon concluded, the minister announces from the pulpit.

> While the choir sings the invitational hymn, 'Just as I Am,' if there is someone here today who is without Christ, let him come and accept Jesus as his personal Savior. If he will but come, if he will but confess his sins, if he will but surrender to Jesus, the Lord will forgive him. Come now, while the choir sings.

The minister steps down from the platform to a position in front and at the level of the congregation. There, particularly in the more conservative churches, he raises his hands and beseeches.

> Don't want. Don't wait. Don't wait until it is too late. No man knows when the hour is at hand. Don't be caught without Christ. Come now, while the choir sings the second verse.

After an additional verse, and even without a conversion, some ministers will bring the service to an end. Others will extend invitation.

> Let every head be bowed. Let every eye be closed. Come now. Come and put your trust in Jesus. Just say, 'I surrender all. I'm lost, dear Jesus, save me.' Now while the choir sings softly.

Should a person leave the congregation and walk down the aisle toward the minister, the minister will take a few steps toward him, with his right hand ready to grasp the other's and his left held high to embrace the person's shoulder. The two stand in an embrace in front of the congregation, while the minister whispers, "Do you accept Jesus as your personal Savior," and then in reply to the affirmation, says "Bless you, Bless you," and escorts the person to an empty seat at a front pew. The minister, turning back toward the congregation, proclaims, "Praise God! Praise God! Now is there another? Another lost sheep?"

Whilst the invitation continues, a deacon will sit beside the person and take his name and address on a card. At the close of the invitation, the two stand, and the deacon announces, "Paul Hewes, of 2415 Iberville, Baton Rouge, comes before us today to accept Jesus as his personal Savior and asks to be admitted into the fellowship of our church." The minister asks "All those in favor please raise your hand. All those opposed, and I am sure there is none." Following the closing prayer, members of the congregation come to the front to shake Paul's hand and welcome him into the congregation.

Like the liturgy of the eucharist, the invitation effects a change from the profane to the sacred. What is achieved, however, is not the "miracle of transubstantiation" but the "salvation of a sinner." The invitation attempts the transformation outside of the more strictly prescribed movements of the liturgy. Baptists speak proudly of this difference and lay claim to a more genuine, spiritual exercise. In actuality, the invitation is quite formalized and varies little from one occasion to another and even from one church to another. Furthermore, Paul Hewes, far from being a hopeless depraved drunk, may well be the twelve year old son of the choir leader who has attended church since the day his mother carried him into the nursery. Nonetheless, the invitation, as with the liturgy, is constituted of several symbolic layers.

One of the symbolic layers is the position and attitude of the minister. During the sermon, he stands behind the pulpit, separated from and above the congregation. Here he delivers a scathing attack not only upon the world at large but also upon the members of his own church and charges them with the false pride of putting self and family ahead of God. During the invitation, he comes down from the pulpit, and stands at the level of the congregation. Here, instead of haranguing, he pleads, and instead of pounding his fist on the pulpit, he holds out his arms in an embrace.

The change in the location and attitude of the minister parallels the movement of the confessing individual. He steps from his position among the congregation to a position apart and in front of them. He then puts himself within the embrace of the minister and confesses he is a sinner. He describes himself as surrendering to Jesus. At the same time, he is taking the first step to becoming a member of the church. Baptists insist that the conversion experience can occur away from the church, and indeed, ministers fill their sermons with accounts of the lost sinner struck down by the glory of the Lord in the most unlikely places. Yet most Baptists, I believe, would agree that the public confession marks the effective change from being lost to being found, from being a sinner to becoming a Christian, and from being outside the church to becoming a member of that particular congregation. Only baptism by immersion awaits the person's full participation. Thus, in a most forthright Durkheimian fashion (Durkheim 1947), the conversion experience and the public confession, the movement from the profane to the sacred, symbolically captures the existential movement from being outside to being inside the congregation. Furthermore, being inside the congregation parallels the location of the sense of the sacred inside the person of the believer. This is not to say that by simply becoming a member of a congregation, the person undergoes the internal transformation from the profane to the sacred that the Baptists describe as being saved. Yet, I doubt that being saved in its fullest sense can occur apart from being a member, in its fullest sense, of a congregation.

Let us now summarize the contrast between the Spanish American Catholic eucharist and the Southern Baptist invitation.

In both, the participants – the priest, the minister, and the worshipers – attempt to transform the sense of the profane and everyday into a sense of the sacred. The liturgy of the eucharist is a ritual in the more conventional concept where the wafer becomes the body and the wine the blood of Christ, as the priest reenacts both the last supper and Christ's sacrifice. By eating the wafer, the communicant reenacts the disciples and incorporates – embodies – the sacred. In the invitation, a less prescribed, but nonetheless repetitive movement, the internal state of the lost, profane person is transformed into a found, sacred one. The sinner, by first separating himself from the congregation, standing before it in a confessional pose, and then surrendering to it, embodies the symbolic states of being lost and then being found. By making a public confession that he now accepts Christ as his personal savior, the individual receives the joys of salvation and enters into the embrace of the minister and of the congregation.

Thus, the Spanish American Catholic, in the context of a rigid hierarchical organization, reflected in such diverse aspects as the regal apparel of the priest and the ranking of structures, approaches the sacred as an individual – properly cleansed by the private ritual of confession. He kneels at the altar, the banquet table, to partake of the body of Christ. The presence of the body of Christ, the transformation of the profane wafer into a sacred object, is in front and outside of him, independent of any subjective feelings he may have. The Southern Baptists, in the context of an egalitarian organization, reflected in both in the equality of clothing and structures, await the lost person to confess publicly before them that he surrenders to Jesus. Upon his acceptance of Christ, the sinner is infused, inside of himself, with the joys of salvation. In sharp contrast with the liturgy of the eucharist, the transformation of the profane into the sacred in the invitation rest on the subjective feelings of the participant and the congregation's acceptance of that feeling as genuine. While the effectiveness of the mass depends on the prescribed role-playing of the priest, the effectiveness of the invitation depends on the very absence of formalized roles.

Catholic *promesas* and Baptist visitors

Beyond the liturgy of the eucharist and the evangelism of the invitation, other attributes of these two Christian forms of worship may be contrasted to underscore the distinctiveness of each. Two particularly expressive ones are for the Spanish American Catholics, the contract of a *promesa*, and for the Southern Baptists, the treatment of visitors.

In the *iglesia*, and at nearly any time during the day and into the night, an individual may approach one of the holy figures in its niche along the walls, kneel before it, cross himself, pray, cross himself again, and rise. If the statue is sufficiently low, the person touches the statue's feet and then his own face, if the statue is encased in glass, such as the figure of Christ in the Sepulcher, the person wipes the glass and then himself.

This exchange between the worshiper and the figure may occur at a moment's thought, or even during mass. If the exchange occurs in an *iglesia* that is the home of particularly miraculous image, then it is likely that exchange is the fulfillment of a *promesa*.

Spanish American culture, as Foster (1961) has noted, is replete with dyadic contracts, arrangements made between two people, sometimes of equal rank, as between *amigos íntimos* (intimate friends) but frequently between a more powerful *patrón* and a less powerful person. In the religious contexts, the contract is a *promesa*. A *promesa* is a promise or a vow that an individual makes to a particular holy figure, that person's favorite saint, a national figure, such as the Virgin of Guadalupe, or a more local figure, with a reputation for miracles, such as the Virgin of Pueblito, the patroness of the city of Querétaro, Mexico.

If the individual finds himself in a circumstance that is especially worrisome and troubling, a mother with a sick child, for example, she will pray that if the figure will cure her child (or more technically, if the figure will in turn intercede with God on the child's behalf) then she will travel to the figure's *iglesia* and light a candle in the figure's honor. If the child is cured, then the individual honors the commitment. If, on the other hand, the figure does not agree, or fails in the attempt, and the child worsens and dies, then the mother is under no obligation to fulfill the contract.

The relationship between the two parties of the contract, the individual and the saint, is personal, that is, the relationship is an agreement between two and requires no action on the part of anyone else, certainly not the priest, and the relationship is face-to-face, that is, it is a voluntary, objective arrangement.

The distinctive personal, external quality of the *promesa* appears in the notes of appreciation dedicated to a miraculous image. In a small alcove near the entrance of the church of the Virgin of Pueblito, the patroness of *Ouerétaro*, for example, one note from a relieved mother thanks the Virgin for assistance in getting all three sons finally married; another is grateful for her help in getting the writer's father out of jail, and still another, with a hand drawn picture of a truck hurling down the highway, thanks her for setting the driver free from a legal infraction, which was, after all, the results of an accident. (See also Turner and Turner 1978).

Throughout the week, during mass and before and after, people cross the portals of the *iglesia* to complete their private exchanges with one of the figures along the sides. Tourists, both national and foreign, enter to admire and at times to photograph the ornate holiness. Strangers from far and distant lands, such as the anthropologist, may enter any *iglesia*, participate in the mass, and remain perfectly anonymous.

Southern Baptists both vigorously welcome and rigorously control who enters their churches. Fellowship begins at the outskirts of town where the traveler reads "The First Baptist Church Welcomes You." Should the traveler, however, approach the church during the week, he finds the doors locked. Why should he want to enter? There is nothing to see except an empty auditorium. Only of such landmarks as the First Baptist Church in Dallas, a unique edifice styled in American Gothic, would he care to take photographs.

On Sunday morning, however, and again, in a smaller way, on Sunday night, the traveler, if he is white, will be made welcome in the most literal sense of the word. If the traveler is black, the welcoming in many would be restrained; in others, absent; and in not a few, hostile. In the foyer, a deacon greets the traveler with a handshake and a pamphlet on which is listed the order of service. Along with the handshake, the deacon says, "We are pleased to have you. My name is Miller," and awaits for the traveler to respond with his own name. Seated, the traveler may be approached by others, and again there is the open hand. The choir leader, who as the minister of music, conducts the first half of the service, proceeds until he arrives at the point described in the order of service, "Welcoming of Visitors." With the now familiar, enthusiastic smile, he announces, "We want to welcome all of our visitors. We are a family-centered church, and we want you to feel right at home. Will you please stand?"

The traveler stands amidst a congregation of 100, 200, 300, or more faces, all friendly. A deacon, perhaps Mr. Miller himself, comes with a card and an attached ballpoint pen. The choir leader directs, "We ask you to fill out the card and drop it into the collection plate." The card reads:

Welcome!!

Mr.
Mrs.
Miss _____
Address _____ Phone _____
Are you a Christian? _____ Church Member? _____
If so, what church? _____ Where? _____
I am interested in:
_____ Knowing more about your church
_____ Becoming a Christian
_____ A visit from the Pastor

In their passion for welcoming the stranger, the Southern Baptists are doing more than maximizing the region's reputation for hospitality. They are using the cultural norm to fulfill the evangelical command "to bring Christ to a lost and dying world." The traveler may be without the Savior, and let not the door be closed to him who knocks. Consequently, instead of the individual, private but objective solace of the Spanish American *iglesia*, at the First Baptist in the American South, the stranger finds the firm hand of congregational fellowship.

Clarification

Cultural phenomena as complex as Spanish American Catholicism and the Southern Baptist faith resist neat summaries. The generalizations that the Catholics in Spanish America have an objective, individual sense of the sacred and the Baptists of the American South, a subjective, congregational sense require the following clarifications.

Supplemental to the objective, external location of the sacred, many Spanish American Catholics offer the concept of having faith (*tener fe*). From 1962 in Columbia when a small businessman explained his relationship to the Virgin of Carmen to 1985 in Mexico City when a taxi driver, on his way with me to the airport, lauded the miraculous nature of the Virgin of Guadalupe, I have heard time and again that in the interaction between an individual and the sacred, it is faith that has worth, *es la fe que vale*.

Faith is an attribute, almost a thing, that a person has inside of him, that allows him to activate the sacred. Without his faith, nothing will happen: the holy water will not protect, the pilgrimage will be wasted, and the Virgin will remain unmoved. Faith is worth more than going to mass. Some even say, in a manner a good Baptist would recognize, that with faith a person can be a better Christian and not go to mass than those who go everyday but do so without faith. So in the end, in this lay interpretation, it is not the liturgy of the eucharist that transforms the bread into the body of Christ, it is the personal faith that one has.

Under the leadership of a vigorous priest, parishioners on occasion may switch from individuals mumbling more or less the same lines to uniting in a truly group response. The same vigorous priest may deliver a homily that approximates if not matches a Baptist sermon. The clearest expression of unity I have heard was in June 1984, and again in 1985, during the Virgin of Pueblito's round of visits to the *iglesias* of Querétaro. On this particular occasion, she was arriving on the shoulder of her followers to spend several days at the *iglesia* of St. Anthony of Padua. As she appeared around the corner, the brass ensemble struck up a rousing march, and as she passed through the entrance, a rain of confetti fell upon her. Once inside and placed in the sanctuary, the crowd clapped even more enthusiastically. The priest shouted, *"Viva La Virgen!"* and all the individuals standing in the church, including the anthropologist, responded, *"Viva!"*

The Baptists define their church as a band of baptized believers, as a social group, but they also insist that Christ speaks to each, alone, in the stillness of the night. As with the Spanish American mother, so too a Baptist mother calls upon Jesus (but never Mary or one of the disciples) to return her child to good health. The relationship between the mother and God is a personal one, but it is one freed of the objective assurances found in the dyadic contract of the Catholic mother and her saint, and consequently, it is a relationship at the mercy of the Baptist mother's interpretation. The only way she knows that God loves her is that she knows, in the secret recesses of her heart. If the Lord in his wisdom decides that her child will recover, then the child will; if the Lord does not, then all the mother can do is to continue to place her trust in Jesus.

Such a relation lacks the factual, face-to-face contractual characteristic of the Spanish American dyad, and in the absence of that facticity, the relation grows anxious, even fearful, and this anxiety is the source of constant stories told in numerous sermons about God's mercy, a mercy that may or may not be bestowed upon the grieving and the ill.

The one objective fact in the Baptist sense of the sacred is the Bible. The physical book is not sacred, although the family Bible is a treasured inventory of marriages and deaths; what is sacred are the words within. Many Baptists, perhaps the majority, continue to believe that the Bible is the literal voice of God. Each word is divinely inspired. Consequently, each word has the same objective sense of the sacred found in the Spanish American Christ. Accordingly, Baptists approach the Bible not as a scholar pondering the intricacies of a text, but in the same manner that the Spanish American communicant accepts the eucharist wafer, a sacred object not to be tampered with.

The tie with performance

In this essay I have attempted to explicate, that is, to extract from the flow of events, those factors of location, mode of worship, and structure of organization whose intersection brings about a sense of the sacred in two Christian faiths. For the Spanish American Catholic, worshiping as an individual in the context of a hierarchical structure, the sacred lies outside of his person. For the Baptists, joined together as a group in the context of egalitarianism, the sacred lies within.

How might these two opposing senses of the sacred relate to performance? Performance, of course, is not religion, but, to quote Erving Goffman on the distinction between the stage and everyday life, "the crucial ways in which it isn't are not easy to specify" (Goffmann 1959: 72). More specifically, how might the location of the sacred connect to the presentation of a performing self?

Because the liturgy of the eucharist is a ritual in the narrow, conventional sense, the tie between Spanish American Catholicism and performance seems evident. Catholicism has a rich history of possessions and pageants, and its connection to the origins of European drama, through the medieval morality plays, is well known. It is the location of the sacred external to the worshiper that places Catholicism parallel to performance. To perform, the actor has to construct a self other than the everyday self the performer ordinarily claims as her or his own. The actor must become that other, theatrical self to the extent that it is credited as having life. The magic of the moment, so to speak, is when the performance achieves a reality of its own. For the performing self to be credited as real it must be an objective, external self so that others, actors and audience, may respond to it. To worship, the believer must construct a sense of the sacred that becomes real. In Spanish American Catholicism that sense of the sacred lies external to the interior, profane self. In her or his behavior, then, the worshiper must mold that external sense so as to construct an objective self that the worshiper now is. Thus, the *iglesia* becomes peopled with selves embodied in statues that portray scenes of agony, despair, and occasionally, bliss; these are performances frozen at the moment of their most intense reality. Corresponding to the acts in ceramics are the flesh and blood performances of the priest and the communicants. At the altar, the priest must prepare the sacrifice of and as Christ and at the altar rail the communicants must kneel as the disciples for the liturgy of the eucharist to achieve its reality and for the profane wafer to become sacred body.

In sharp contrast, here, as elsewhere, the tie between Baptist religious behavior and theatre seem far less clear, and indeed, antithetical. Music is much more welcome than theatre. A history of pageantry and possession is noticeably absent among the Baptist and their plain folk tradition. In Baton Rouge the nearest approximation to passion dramas is an occasional skit or a larger play written and performed by church members.[2] During Christmas, some churches have live manger scenes, with church members costumed as Mary, Joseph, the Three Wise Men, and Shepherds.

The antipathy of the Baptist toward possessions and pageantry springs from interior location of the sacred. In the absence of any external, objective presence of the sacred, the worshiper must perform as himself. If he genuinely confesses to God his sins, then, but only then, he is saved. And the only way he knows he is saved is that he knows. Thus, the self he plays must constantly be his own. Furthermore, since the sense of the sacred lies within him, all else, save the Bible, is "symbolic." The grape juice and crackers served during the Lord's Supper, which occurs not more than once a month, are "only symbols." The water used during baptism is "only water," and the ritual of baptism itself is "only symbolic" of the death and resurrection of Christ. Truth, then, lies not in the external surface but inside, in feelings and in the case of the Bible, in the words. In contrast, performance, by its very nature, stresses the exterior, not the interior; not the real person, but the act.

Yet, there is a tie between the Baptist service and performance; rather there is a tie between attending church and going to the theatre. Both are occasions distinct from everyday; both require, at least, in the culture of the South, that those attending dress appropriately, a suit for men, stockings for women; both are rigorously scheduled; both have signs outside that announce the title of play or the name of the sermon; both have a program and ushers to seat the audience; and finally, both start on time.

With the exception of the first half of the service, during which the audience rises to join in the singing, when the main event comes, the audience in the church, like the audience in a theatre, sits and watches, while on the stage and on the platform the show and the sermon transpire. Here, however, especially for the conservative churches, the tie between attending the theatre and going to church breaks. On stage the actors perform; on his platform, behind the pulpit, the minister preaches. During his preaching, he may be and frequently is, theatrical, but what he must be is be sincere. If his voice breaks, it must be that he is truly overwhelmed; if he cries, the tears must be real; when he pleads for the sinner to come forth, the plea must be from the heart. He must play himself without letting anyone suspect, least of all, God, that he is acting.

Conclusion

At its best, like the performing arts, religion creates a sense of reality that transforms the profane self into a sacred self, a self that transcends the loneliness of being human. Like performance, too, the sacred, more than once, falls flat; its sense disappears, and the body of Christ is nothing but a thin wafer; the invitation a tedious, overly acted commonplace. Yet, like performance again, so strong is the urge to transcend, to break through the barriers of solitude, that the worshipers, like actors, gather for another effort, an effort seemingly futile, but genuinely heroic.

Notes

1. The wording, both Spanish and English, is taken directly from the officially authorized missals. The careful reader will note the differences between the two translations of the Latin text.
2. During Easter 1981, one Baton Rouge church presented a three act play, "The Rock," which told the story of Simon Peter, "who yearns to better his station in life and ends up realizing he is the rock that will support the church on earth built by Jesus" (*State-Times*, 18 April 1981: 6-A).

14.
Space and context

YI-FU TUAN

Culture viewed as speech, gesture, and action is performance; and performance not only requires but commands its own kind of space. I should like to
discuss this theme under two headings: 1) precultural or unrehearsed acts and
2) rehearsed acts, as well as a sample of those acts that fall between these two
extremes.

Unrehearsed acts

Infants do not perform. Their self-consciousness and consciousness of others
are minimally developed. The space they occupy is small; likewise the world
they perceive. As they grow older they gain greater mobility, acquire more
control over space, and become more aware of the expectation and critical
appraisal of others. They have fallen from innocence into culture – into a life
of performance. Older children and adults are subject to attacks of shyness
and even stage fright. On important occasions people rehearse the gestures
and words that they may be called upon to present. Even in casual talk among
friends, there are those moments when the voices of others are tuned out as an
individual prepares the words that s/he hopes to contribute, words with
accompanying gestures that will raise her in the esteem of others. The shyness
and self-consciousness come out of the premonition that the rehearsal may be
inadequate, or that it may not produce the desired result. Worse is the feeling
that one's posture, motions, and words may transmit messages that are not
part of one's intention: this is the actor's fear of inducing laughter at the wrong
places. Normally, social exchange is not so dire. Friends appear to be paying
attention. When this happens, space expands and resonates as in a music hall
with perfect acoustics. Friends, however, can look distracted and yet say,
unconvincingly, "Go on, we are listening." Space then turns cold and dead;
one's voice begins to sound tinselly and disembodied (Barthes 1978: 167).

   Under what conditions do we adults shed our status as cultural beings? I
was going to say, "while we perform our natural functions in the privacy of the
bathroom." Perform? The word sounds right. We remain actors. After all, as

236

toddlers we perform on the pot to the applause of our parents. Perhaps we are truly natural beings at the moment before we fall asleep. The status of the sleeping body is curious. On the one hand, it seems a mere object vulnerable to the predatory gaze of others. It is an object that occupies space but does not command it. On the other hand, a sleeping body can emanate a sense of power. People may gaze but not too close. Any time the eyes may open and in a flash destroy a relationship of inferiority and superiority. An aura of drama can surround a sleeping body – the drama of its imminent repossession of a world.

Someone has a heart attack and collapses on the floor. Such a sudden and dramatic movement is yet not a performance. Witnesses become frantic and calm down only after they have straightened the body, placed the arms in repose across the breast, and pulled a sheet over the face. The contorted body, even though it is known to be dead, cannot be left in the natural – that is, unlearned and undeliberated – posture of collapse. An onlooker instinctively feels that the contorted posture cannot be maintained. The corpse may spring back to life in protest. An electric tension fills the space surrounding the body until it is laid out like an effigy over a tomb and the eyelids are closed (Maurois 1960: 76).

The following story comes out of the death camp at Treblinka. A dancer stands naked in line waiting for her turn to enter the gas chamber. We see a human being with its natural power to command space reduced to a body taking up space, passively submitting to the prospect of death. A guard tells her to step out of line and dance. She does, and carried away by her authoritative action and by her repossession of a self and a world she dances up to the guard – now within the compass of *her* space – takes his gun and shoots him. What a surprise to the guard that a zombie-like creature can spring back to life by means of performance! (Hallie 1969: 46).

The desperately sick and the dying in a hospital have withdrawn from the field of action. They submit to nature. Yet how strong is the call upon them to perform – to die with dignity or peacefully, and perhaps with a gesture or words that reassure the living. The hospital, unless one is inured to its ambience, is a dramatic place. To people who work there, it can seem a life-enhancing place where babies are born, and the sick and the old die. Birth, pain, and death give focus to life. Someone like Walt Whitman, who volunteered service in a hospital, would have appreciated the quickening of the senses in a world where the senses are *in extremis* (Hyde 1983: 206).

The hospital as theatre? That would seem to be a frivolous idea. Yet the operating room is often called the theater. Space there is charged with tension and high drama. Who are the spectators and who the actors? In a teaching hospital, the medical students are the spectators; they are seated on rising tiers of benches that overlook the operating table in center stage. The doctors and nurses are the actors, but also spectators when they are not actively engaged. What about the anesthetized patient? All he has to do is to lie still and breathe.

Yet his is the cynosure of attention. Isn't this an actor's ideal – to sway multitudes without seeming to act at all?

Anthropologists like Erving Goffman have familiarized us with the idea that in almost any social setting we not only act but put on an act whether we know it or not (Goffman 1974). But from the viewpoint of the participants this "not knowing" makes a crucial difference. It is what makes life seem normal and sane albeit also somewhat boring. After prolonged submersion in this normal life, we wish an opportunity to put on an act, to dramatize ourselves and our world; we wish for a quickened sense of life, which can also be got vicariously by watching a performance – sports, plays, and even a car accident. Normal, ordinary routines are themselves not worth watching. Yet this is not quite correct. The sort of things that people do every day *are* worth watching, provided we can look without being looked at. Hence the popularity of side walk cafés where one can sit and watch the street scene. Hence also the peculiar fascination of catching glimpses of ordinary life behind the illuminated windows of tenement houses which may happen when, in the early hours of the evening, we ride on an elevated train back to our suburban home. We see a family having supper and then, through another window, a man scratching his armpit or watching TV. Because they cannot see us, we who can see them feel like the gods; and what lie open to our gaze are the unguarded and unrehearsed – hence vulnerable and genuine – moments in people's lives (Wittgenstein 1980: 4–5).

Conscious performance

In ordinary activities, we are conscious of space and time and make calculations concerning them out of practical needs. We are not, however, usually aware of how our bodies form patterns and rhythms, or of how our bodies command space. In ritual and theatre, people are of course far more conscious of their relations. A choreographer or (for that matter) a football coach may well think of human bodies as merely devices for defining space and time. The different ways that people can be aware of space or try to create spectral realms and spatial sculptures by means of bodily movements and gestures are almost infinite. Here are a few.

A human figures sits on the ground, legs crossed Buddha-fashion. Calm space surrounds it. The figure stands. It stays still and yet projects a sense of imminent action, charging the space ahead with tense potency. As the figure moves, space takes on a fluid and dynamic character. To the individual in action, space is primarily a kinesthetic feeling – a feeling that reaches well beyond the body. To the spectator, space is kinesthetic feeling to the extent that he is able to identify with the performer. But to the spectator, space is also a visual pattern "out there" – a pattern woven by the performing figure. Where several figures appear, their positions and motions define space. Again, compared with performers, spectators are more fully conscious of the overall visual pattern of space: the space of spectators – even while it visibly changes before their eyes – is less packed with tingling energy than the space experienced by performers.

Although space and time can be separated for purposes of analytical efficiency, in most of life's activities and in performance they cannot. A still figure is as much an image of time as of space. A figure that moves swiftly and fluidly across the stage represents quite a different image of time from one that moves slowly or jerkily. When we look at the face of a clock we see "time" rather than "space." When we watch performing figures, do we say to ourselves, "spatial patterns" or "temporal rhythms?" The answer may be neither, because in experience space and time are inseparable.

Consider a procession. A 4th of July parade may begin at the fire station and end at the post office. These points have no particular significance. The movement is linear and directional, but it is pseudo-directional because the goal does not matter. What counts is the movement itself. Questions of "where to" and "what for" are barely raised. By contrast, a religious procession has a goal which is the sacred circuit or center. Space-time, aptly represented by an arrow, *is* directional. This sense of linearity and direction weakens, however, if many pauses occur along the way. It also weakens if processioners depart freely from the moving stream to mix with the spectators. When this happens, the distinction between route and place, procession and *in situ* festival becomes fuzzy.

Light affects the character of space. In total darkness, space acquires tangibility. We move hesitantly in it as though we expect material resistance. Of course, no performance occurs in total darkness. In semi-darkness, space can still seem an enveloping medium, like mist. Some tribes in Africa dance only at night, around the camp fire. The dancers sometimes go into trance. It may be easier to go into a trance or enter a mystical state when the normal landmarks of common-day reality are invisible and when space is concentrated around the camp fire with the circumambient darkness serving almost as a tangible wall. Are outdoor performances ever given deliberately at high noon? The sun shining high in the sky bleaches out space. Space seems to lack depth. Time seems to stand still. By contrast, twilight gives space the feel of depth and of movement. Shadows, we say, move, lengthen, or crawl. How important is lighting and control over the quality of light to ritual and theatre? Are there cross-cultural studies of this topic?

Sound, it goes without saying, affects the character of space. The picture that we look at is always "out there," although we can enter it imaginatively. The music that we hear comes from a definite source, which we may be able to see, but the sound itself is less localized. The degree of localization depends on the frequency of the sound waves. Bass sound of low frequency has the power to "touch" and surround the listener; it has a dark, directionless quality. The listener does not face the sound but rather feels immersed in it. High notes, by contrast, appear to be bright, sharp, and more precisely located in space. Can the audience be immersed in throbbing bass sounds and still attuned to delicate visual details – such as the shape of the actress's hand – out there? (Schafer 1977: 115–19).

The space of a traditional festival is hard to describe because it is heterogeneous, multilocal, and shifting. Neither space nor time is likely to be sharply defined. A festival may last several days. It begins when people start to drift in, a few performers set up their stalls and try out an act or two, and it ends as loosely and informally as it starts. The space of the festival is the space of these movements and activities. There are a few physical markers: the market square itself, a tent here and there, some benches and stage props. But these physical markers do not by any means define and exhaust the experience of space and place. The events are heterogeneous and may occur simultaneously. Performers are also spectators and vice versa. People may pay little attention to the formal events. They go there to gawk, eat, drink, chat, and flirt. They go to immerse themselves in *life* – that is, a confusion of sounds, colors, and movements that nevertheless are undergirded by a sense of order and common purpose. No one can have or would want to have a bird's-eye view of the festival as a whole. To do so would require the sort of distancing that is antithetical to the celebration of life.

Theatre, insofar as it grew out of religious festivals and performances, is necessarily a mixed genre. A theatrical occasion may last many hours, filled with heterogeneous events. Again people may go in and out, eat and drink, talk with each other and with performers. Performing space may be fluid, hard to separate at times from spectator space. How many of us are old enough to remember the afternoon matinee at the neighborhood movie house? A show there still retains a bit of the air of a festival. Children run in and out to buy ice cream and soda pop. They shout their encouragement to the hero crushed by a falling skyscraper at the end of a serial. The show itself is a mixed genre of newsreel, cartoon, serial, supporting feature, and main feature. Nowadays, when we go to an arts cinema, we are likely to be confronted by *Wild Strawberries* with no dressing or sweeteners whatsoever. A critical distinction between "traditional" and "modern" theatre is that whereas the former is a celebration of life, the latter is a criticism – a deconstruction? – of life and a cold look at death.

Let us now take a closer look at the physical characteristics of the stage and of the theatre. "Space" and "scene" describe the premodern stage. The performing area may simply be a piece of available open space – public square or dining hall. In it are stage scenes or props. These are separate entities or places where actions occur: they do not cohere into "landscape" or "scenery," which are modern concepts and constructions. Actors, having played their parts at one scene in the performing area, may stand aside and merge with the spectators to watch what goes on at the next scene. The space between the scenes (or props) is neutral. It does not signify anything in itself but can, however, come to life should action – a march or a battle, for instance – take place in it. In this type of theatre, the attention of the spectators shifts from one locality to another. It is not directed to the performing area as a whole. There is no special advantage in having a bird's-eye view of the entire stage.

The individual scenes or props in the performing area do not attempt to simulate real geographical localities. They are symbolic places. Thus a tree is not merely something that provides shade but also (in the contest of a Christian morality play) the Tree of Life. A bridge, in another theatrical tradition, is not merely a pleasing architectural prop but may also symbolize "passage" – the passage from one life to another. In contrast to these scenes and props is *scenery*. In scenery, the parts are subordinate to the whole: a tree here and a house there are elements of a total picture. The scenery, in the Vitruvian tradition, may not simulate any particular geographical locality such as Rome or the Tuscan countryside. It is a type or a standard set. Each type or set suggests a special class of play: thus a set consisting of palaces and temples is suitable for tragedy and a set consisting of ordinary houses and a common street is suitable for comedy. A characteristic of the modern stage set of scenery is that it is unique to a particular play. The scenery, in the social dramas of modern times, is an extension of and a reflection of the distinctive (unique?) personalities of the characters. Another difference between scene and scenery is this. Scenery is illusionary space – an illusion of depth, for instance, created by perspective. This illusionary space is best appreciated at a privileged location in the hall. Modern drama presumes the privileged individual spectator. Historically, this is the prince who alone on his elevated seat in the court theatre sees the total picture; nowadays it is (in principle) every theatre goer ensconced in his padded seat in a darkened hall wherein he could believe himself to be the sole spectator.

In some rituals and theatrical performances, all the senses are involved and stimulated. Each sensory mode calls forth its own space. For this reason alone, any attempt to describe *the* space ends in hopeless abstraction. Other rituals and performances are deliberately austere. They appear inevitably later in time, and are the result of a deliberate thinning process. Fewer and fewer senses are involved until in the extreme case the appeal is made only to the inner ear or eye. The space may be a sparsely furnished room or an empty sky arching over an empty beach (Burns 1972).[1]

Participation and space

Performance presupposes the spectator. Even when we perform alone, a part of the self stands aside, appreciating and evaluating what we do. Or the lone performer is conscious of the eye of God. In ordinary social life, we are performers one moment and spectators the next. A similar fluidity of roles exists in a festival: having done one's act as juggler one may stand aside and watch someone else's show. Festivals celebrate life. Hence everyone wants to participate, to join actively in the happy motions of celebrations. Space is kaleidoscopic, rarely well defined – a reflection of the surging, shifting, inchoate character of life. Popular theatre exhibits some of the traits of a village festival. Chinese opera, for instance, has never become a solemn High Art for the elite: people who attend it drink tea, crack watermelon seeds, shout approval at their favorite arias, walk about and visit with friends as they see fit. Comedies, in general, have this informal festive character. The audience laughs and laughter is active participation: what barrier may exist between performing space and spectator space is thus breached. Nothing truly threatening or awesome occurs in a social comedy. The audience does not feel the need to maintain a protective or deferential distance.

Ritual is different. Officiants at a ritual transform rather than perform. A priest by his gestures and incantations acts on reality as an architect-builder may be said to act on it. Is Pope John Paul II acting? Note how ambiguous that word is – and disturbing to those who want their sacerdotal figures to act but not to put on an act. Ritual places people in contact with reality – with divine potency. Hence the moments of danger from which only the consecrated and those who know precisely what to do are protected. Ordinary people do well to maintain a distance. But they are not there merely to look. They kneel, stand, or join in prayers. They participate as members of a congregation, whose lives will be affected by how the ritual is conducted. Insofar as ritual celebrates a success – important birth or harvest – it has some of the informal attributes of a festival. But to the degree that it claims to uphold a world, a certain seriousness and compulsion for precision prevails.

Comedies do not generally present human situations so extreme and painful that we would want to keep our distance. Tragedies do – and we respond by being spectators (Langer 1982: 109–10). A person can "enjoy" a tragedy by sitting somewhere apart and watching. How resentful and utterly repelled a spectator would feel if King Lear moved across the footlights, grabbed him by the lapels and started to howl, spitting into his face! We have here the old ethical problem of the amorality of the eye. Lucretius noted, "What joy it is, when out at sea the storm-winds are lashing the waters, to gaze from the shore at the heavy stress some other man is enduring! Not that anyone's afflictions are in themselves a source of delight; but to realize from what troubles you yourself are free is joy indeed" (1951: 60).

In a festival, everyone is involved, plunged in the midst of a world of exciting color, sound, and movement. In sharp contrast is the bystander in a glassed-in world of his own. But what does "involvement" mean? Surely it means more than just physical contact – touching and being touched. An anthropologist who coolly observes a festival from the sidelines is, we rightly say, minimally involved. But what about Lucretius, or a modern bystander who watches a car accident? He enjoys the safety of physical and emotional distance, and yet he is enthralled, riveted in place. A part of the spectator is engaged – a part that we call curiosity, and there is something reprehensible in being merely or idly curious, in not making a move when some action seems clearly called for.

What constitutes participation in a classroom? The instructor speaks. Although he speaks with vigor what he says is barely coherent. Students break in constantly to ask questions and to offer opinions of their own. We have here much participation and involvement: hands wave, and words are shouted back and forth. In another classroom, students sit in rapt attention. They participate by *listening*, which is a difficult and specialized act. To attend properly and over a period of time, one must make an effort – often an exhausting effort. Yet, one cannot *will* attention by knitting one's eyebrows or sitting up straight. Such muscular exertion can produce the opposite effect. One must forget oneself and try to be actively receptive. This contradictory state of being both active and passive accounts for the difficulty of paying attention.

Involvement may mean: two wrestlers in a body lock; two persons animately exchanging gossip; one man speaks – perhaps trying to articulate a personal problem – and a friend listens intently. Involvement may also mean: submergence in the sensuous ambience of a festival; cheering one's team in the football stadium; listening to a Beethoven quartet with such disembodied concentration that a cough or rustling of paper is taken as a distressing fall back to earth; watching two men on a bare stage waiting for Godot. Human isolation can be overcome in a number of ways. Farthest removed from the common experiences of day-to-day life is the bridging of interpersonal distance by means of attention.

How would we characterize the space of each type of involvement? In a festival, we may speak perhaps of interpenetrating spaces – a reflection of the heterogeneity of the events, of the people who attend (from young children to the aged and all social classes), and the absence of any sharp distinction between performers and spectators. In a football stadium, playing field and spectator area are clearly demarcated. Nevertheless, the boundary between them is easily transgressed. Excited fans may rush across it at the end of the game and even in the middle of the game when emotion runs uncontainably high. The ball sometimes flies out of the field into the spectators' seats, and spectators often try to breach their designated space with shouts and waving arms. In a physical-emotional way, spectators participate as much as they can. They are intensely – though not, perhaps, deeply – involved. At the other extreme, consider what transpires in a symphony hall or in a proscenium-stage theatre. The sharpness of the separation between performance and audience space is emphasized by the use of foot- and ceiling lights and by the darkening of the hall. During a performance, take a glance at the sea of silent faces submerged in semi-darkness. They look blank as though the souls behind them had departed to mingle with the music or with the stage drama. When the music stops or when the curtain falls there is a moment of silence during

which the spectators wait for their souls to return. Separated physically from
the object of attention, audience involvement can nevertheless be total, which
should encourage us to reevaluate the insight that separation is a precondition
for becoming deeply absorbed.

Notes

1. I have discussed this theme at greater length in *Segmented Worlds and Self* (Tuan
   1982: 86–113).

15.

The transformation of consciousness in ritual performances: some thoughts and questions

BARBARA MYERHOFF

What do we mean by transformation in consciousness?

Everyday usage suggests a transformation is a major and lasting change: in structure, appearance, character or function. One becomes something else, and since we are emphasizing consciousness, we must add, one has an altered state of consciousness, a new perception of oneself or one's socio/physical world, a conversion in awareness, belief, sentiment, knowledge, understanding; a revised and enduring emergent state of mind and emotion.

The term *consciousness* focuses us on an individual, subjective state, rather than that of a collectivity or sociological relationship, which may of course also be transformed. In short, we are brought into an area where anthropology is traditionally weak and vague: the examination of subjective experiences, psychological states, non-normative and often unconscious information where maximum sensitivity, subtlety, inference and courage are required of an ethnographer, not to mention psychological sophistication and depth of experience in and knowledge of the language and culture in which observations are being made. Many anthropologists have followed Max Gluckman's admonition and considered the psychological domain simply off-limits, a form of esoteric knowledge not within the expertise of anthropology. But there are other reasons that may prevent the anthropologist from clarifying the change in consciousness that transformation implies. The more powerful altered states: trance, ecstasy, possession, obsession, conversion, and the like, are often regarded as ineffable. In part this may be an "emic" categorization. For example, the Huichol Indians are forbidden to discuss their peyote-induced religious visions because they are personal to each individual, and in that sense esoteric. But recently, physiological studies of ritual have suggested that the ineffability of intense emotional, transformative states may be due to the dominance of right brain activity. These states, like dreams, are fundamentally non-linear, non-discursive, non-linguistic and are

245

distorted beyond recognition when rendered in collective, verbal, conscious categories. The "oh wow" descriptions of these states are not simply self-indulgence or cultural protection, then. How are we to describe them if this is the case? New techniques, perhaps drawing or performing them, as is often done with dreams, may be required to study them.

Transformation has been usefully described in several places. Langer refers to it as occurring when symbol and object seem to fuse and are experienced as a perfectly undifferentiated whole. In this case, symbols fire the imagination, and insight, belief and emotion are called into play, "altering our conceptions [. . .] at a stroke." In such cases, the invisible referents or realities to which ritual symbols point become our experience and the subject may have the sense of glimpsing, or more accurately, *knowing* the essential, accurate patterns of human life, in relation to the natural and cosmic order. This reminds us of Geertz' comment that rituals have the effect of fusing the dreamed-of and the lived-in order. Thus transformation is a multidimensional alteration of the ordinary state of mind, overcoming barriers between thought, action, knowledge, and emotion. The invisible world referred to in ritual is made manifest and the subject placed within it. But such experiences cannot be compelled, only invited and sought. Hence transformation is seldom made the explicit goal of a ritual, on whose appearance success is thought to depend. Rituals may dependably succeed on a sociological level, effectively transforming jural relationships or social status, without involving transformation of individual consciousness. Rituals are communicative performances that always provide a sense of continuity and predictability. They must be reasonably convincing, rhetorically sound, and well-crafted, but do not require an alteration in individual belief at the deepest level, though that is often highly desired. Even rites of passage in which individuals are re-made or religious vows in which they may be thought of as re-born do not require transformations. Perhaps it is the unusual, ad hoc, volitional ritual performances – pilgrimages, conversions, healings and the like – which we should look at in considering where transformation of consciousness is an essential ingredient.

Schechner differentiates "transformation" from "transportation" in discussing performances. He views both as "twice-behaved behavior," versus "free and easy" spontaneous emergent conduct. Though such behaviors are rule-generated, known and/or practiced and rehearsed, they must be absorbing – for performers and witnesses. It is essential that the performer maintains a measure of control and awareness, is not utterly "lost" in his/her own portrayal or obliterated by it. Most acting, Schechner notes, involves temporary transformation; the actor(s) return to the beginning point. The same is usually true for audiences, though little systematic examination has been done, to my knowledge, of lasting, profound changes induced in audiences by witnessing performances. In personal rites of passage, the performer is permanently changed, transformed, rather than transported from Point A to Point B and back again. In part this may be because in religious rituals the line between "performative world" and "ordinary mundane world" is fine or non-existent. The actions of the performer change the state of the deities, or the natural world: an associative or even causal relationship is posited where the individual is a microcosmic expression of the macrocosm, and conduct in one alters the other. But, Schechner correctly notes, even transformative performances have limits and the two realms of experience are never identical; "all transformations are incomplete," however richly layered and interpenetrating macrocosmic/microcosmic formulations may be.

Some germane discussions concerning the degree to which the individual is lost and carried away in performance versus conscious, controlled, and aware have been conducted in various disciplines. Csikszentmihalyi has described "flow" as the state where action and awareness merge, destroying a dualistic perspective; a performer becomes "aware of his actions but not of the awareness itself." Heightened concentration and focus on a delimited aspect of reality has the effect of excluding all but the central experience; this obliterates ordinary consciousness: critical, cognitive, perhaps even cynical and solipsistic – the very attitudes that destroy the possibility of belief. Thus it has been suggested that the attitude of "flow" is the opposite of reflexive awareness. But this leads us into a paradox: many rituals induce reflexive awareness just as they invite the fullest participation and concentration that brings about flow. Rituals' perpetual play with mirrors and masks, with borders and transitions, make self-reflection nearly inevitable, telling the individual what s/he is and is not at once. Another state may come about: transcendence, where one is aware simultaneously of being in flow as well as aware of his/her actions. This may result in the generation of new possibilities of many kinds; in liminality, the generative and emerging states of mind that Turner has often pointed out are implicit in in-between states. A dichotomy between flow and awareness may be misleading, then, for surely they are in a complex dialectic relationship. Eliade too, has suggested this by discussing shamanic trance as an "archaic technique of controlled ecstasy," stressing the shaman's training in conscious manipulation of transformational states, whose voluntariness and predictability in no way destroy or render them inauthentic.

On another tact, Rappaport has stressed the irrelevance of "authentic" experience in rituals. Lying he points out, is common and permissible. Ritual is a performative genre; one performs a statement of belief through a gesture. That is all that is socially required and all that is of interest to the society. Personal feelings are irrelevant; genuflection is all. Indeed, he suggests, all ritual is a kind of lie, the lie of "as if" which Goffman and Bateson refer to as "the frame," which Langer calls with more kindness a sort of virtual magic, which in theatre is simply the willing suspension of disbelief, which as experimental, ludic creatures by evolution, we all know as "Let's pretend."

Do we forget ourselves, forget we are pretending? There are those who would say the forgetting is the very hallmark of rapture, the height of human imagination, and those who warn us of the madness, the dangers of forgetting that we are always in a play of our own construction.

Turner is one of the eloquent writers on states of consciousness in performances – in the context of his discussions of the experience of liminal beings and states in general, and in particularly the phenomenological precision in his discussions of the state of communitas, the "Zwischen-menschlicheit" of role less cameraderie that may come about temporarily between fellow liminals. His description suggests the intensity of subjective states that is part of "transformation." It also includes the collective dimension (which few writers do), indicating that profound, subjunctive experiences may occur not only within isolated individuals but may be expanded to involve small groups and even communities. Turner is accurate and courageous in pointing out the "dark side" of communitas and shared raptures involving self-loss and conversion. Jonestown, some political rallies and demonstrations, revival meetings are upsurgings that absorb critical consciousness along with loneliness and responsibility. They share certain properties, and remind us always of the need for close examination of the ominous as well as enviable aspects of transformational experiences.

States of religious ecstasy, prayer, meditation, and ecstasy accompanying spontaneous, drug-induced, or ritual-induced mystical experiences are pertinent to the question of transformation during performance, but too broad to be included here. Still, specialists would find mines of information in phenomenological classics by poets and scholars such as Blake, William James, Abraham Maslow, Ruth Underhill, Alan Watt, and Aldous Huxley.

One of the intriguing questions of belief, absorption, conviction, and transformation involved in performance circles around the problem of secular and emergent rituals that do not cluster about a set of shared, powerful, and axiomatic symbols. Myerhoff has examined so called nonce-rituals, and the processes whereby a community propels itself into conviction about the truth of its invisible kingdom: an invented, recent culture that is an adaption to contemporary circumstances. In that the work, the persuasive, performative dimension of ritual is seen as highly significant in allowing individuals collectively to experience, perceive and portray their invented common, fictive reality, to themselves and witnesses. Here "doing is believing," and members of the new culture perform: to behold themselves, finally becoming what they behold. For the same reason, Eliade reminds us, a dancer may put an eagle feather in his hair, thus becoming a bird that flies, incarnating his own wish and intention, transformed imaginatively into what he desires and displays.

It should be noted here that our emphasis on "transformation" in ritual performances inclines us toward emotionally intense and absorbing rituals, thus precludes us from attending to one of the major functions of ritual performances: that of establishing a distance from a situation or emotion.

Rituals are reenactments, not original occurrences, and they are repetitive and highly stylized. These features control and delimit as well as inspire and arouse strong subjective states. Freud, Malinowski, and others have stressed ritual performances as coming into play during crises and times of distress to provide distance and control. Goffman stresses the highly non-transformative nature of many rituals, their very perfunctory, conventionalized character that allows the individual to disappear underneath them. And Geertz treats rituals as performances that create pervasive and ephemeral moods that have little direction, duration or power. Scheff also discusses the issue of distancing in and by ritual, and sets forth the notion that the blandness of contemporary mass media entertainment removes us rather than engages us in their substance. Neither catharsis nor transformation can occur, so diffuse and inauthentic are the ways mass entertainment genres handle distress. The re-experiencing, not merely the re-performing of the original source of distress, is essential for catharsis to occur, according to Scheff, in a properly distanced fashion.

Kapferer too has considered the problem of establishing proper distance in rituals, in particular in demonic possession during rites in Sri Lanka. His intense interest in the reported experiences of those possessed is unusual in the available ethnographic reports at least, which so often confine themselves to what is externally observable. The release from possession often occurs, he reports, when a ludic element has appeared. The patient is transported back to the normal world, released from the grip of the demon, with the reappearance of the ridiculous, which, in my interpretation, is an expression of the patient's freedom, individuality, ordinariness, and separateness. As we are often told in fairy tales, and in politics, laughter breaks the spell and rights the world.

Perhaps on this note, I may conclude. It is the ludic element that is at the basis of all these questions, the play frame that embraces all performances, whether imitative, representational, transformational, whether grim or light, whether cosmic or mundane, enduring or fleeting, personal or collective, whether we snicker or are terrified, indifferent or carried away. The ludic is neither true nor false, nor does it suggest a specific emotional state – pleasure or pain. It simply points us to the power, the inevitability of our imaginative activities in which we have the opportunity to inscribe our fates, our desires, our stories in the air, and partly believe (to some degree) in their reality; ritual performances are testaments to our capacity to endlessly bring new possibilities into being without entirely relinquishing the old, prior understandings that have given rise to them; we make magic, believe in it and do not, at once, we make ourselves anew, yet remain familiar to ourselves, are capable of being carried away, changed, yet know fully and freely exactly what we are doing and why.

16.
Universals of performance; or amortizing play

HERBERT BLAU

Henry James, whose struggle with the theatre left performative traces in the consciousness of his prose, wrote succinctly in one of his prefaces of the drama as an *ado*. There is in the brevity of the word an almost molecular view of performance, like the Freudian *fort/da*, the child's game of disappearance and return, played with a spool, in which by the repetitive deferral of pleasure the reality principle is enjoyed. According to Freud, the disappearance which is being performed is the departure of the child's mother. The *fort/da* is an ado which pivots on an absence. We know from Shakespeare that it is possible to make, in theatre, much ado about nothing; and we know from Beckett, and Zeami, that it is possible to perform the seeming absence of an ado as a precise nothing to be done.

Nothing may come of nothing, but it would also be precise to think of that replicated nothing as a substantive ado. For there is a crucial particle of difference – especially where nothing is concerned – between that and just doing, between just breathing eating sleeping loving and *performing* those functions of just living; that is, with more or less deliberation, doing the *act* of breathing, eating, sleeping, loving, like Didi/Gogo *do* the tree in *Godot*. It is a difference as distinct as the presence or absence of punctuation in the previous sentence. The most minimal performance is a differentiating act: *fort* (gone)/*da* (there). It is an act which introduces (or is introduced by) an element of consciousness in the function, like "the *economic* motive" – the yield of pleasure in the anxiety – of the apparently gratuitous play of Freud's grandson rehearsing the two-act drama of his wooden reel: the representation of a lack which is the recovery of a loss (Freud 1961: 8–9).

What is universal in performance – aside from the ambiguity as to which comes first – are the marks of punctuation which are inflections (or economic indices) of *consciousness* even in performance which, like autistic play, speaking in tongues, or Sufi whirling, seems to occur without it. In those performances which seem more like a raga than a drama, where the "story" behind it is dispersed, attenuated, or "musicated," like the compositions of

Steve Reich or Charlemagne Palestine, or extended over many years like a tribal cycle, you may have to wait longer to discern it. There seems to me, however, no point in talking about performance, no less universals of performance, unless you discern it, although *who* exactly is doing the discerning – and whether inside or outside – is so critical an issue *in performance* that the problem itself can be considered a universal. To what degree and when the members of a tribe are aware, in the absence of anthropologists, of the performative nature of the long space of living between the sacraments, is a case in point; but we can also see the problem in the most minimal performance. When, say, Chris Burden announced that he was going to disappear, and then disappeared, it would have been a quite different performance if, with no further ado, he simply disappeared without the announcement, whether or not he returned.

The difference between the ado and just doing would appear to be self-evident except for the current discourse on performance which, now refusing, now accepting, more or less obscures the ontological gap between the actuality of everyday life and the actuality of a performance, between the ongoing processes of a culture and – with symptoms of ergotropic behavior: quickened pulse, flaring nostrils, sweat secretion, eye dilation – the emergence of "dramatic time" (Turner 1982b: 8–9). The discourse is inseparable from the praxis of recent performance which has widened its parameters to include the activities of everyday life, even while aware of an opposing tendency: a narrowing asepsis of performance which, by burning away the signs of ordinary life, seems to widen the ontological gap. Sometimes the two tendencies are encouraged simultaneously with no sense of contradiction. We have seen in the strategies of performance which aspire to Total Theatre the desire for *more* theatre and the desire for *less* theatre, with more or less theatricalized permutations on the theme of less is more. There appears to be, for instance, in the new paratheatrical enterprise of Grotowski – what he calls a Theatre of Sources – the somewhat utopian desire to replace the illusion of Total Theatre with the promise of Total Life. Whatever the ontological status of that quest, we have become attentive in recent years to modes of performance which involve transformations and exchanges in the here-and-now, more or less ritualized, more or less participatory, more or less risky and irreversible, more or less "actuals," (Schechner 1977: 3–35), where the doings are ados. In the study of aboriginal cultures, we have been made aware of the accretions of everyday life which become, with inflexions of ceremony but no clear demarcation from just living, occasions of performance.

Conversely, there are accretions of everyday life which are still – in theatre and other cultural practices – felt as impediments to performance. That accounts in part for the stagings of initiation in ritual process and, in the marriage of acting craft and spiritual exercises, the stress on *de*conditioning, getting rid of the habits, down to the most rudimentary basis of our actual living. I can hardly think of a technique of performance, even the most naturalistic, which doesn't reconceive of the breathing we take for granted as a bodily process to be explored or a spiritual discipline to be aquired. "Kill the breathing! Kill the rhythm!" repeats the dancing master – whether Azuma or Merce Cunningham – trying to break the reflexive attachment of the rhythm of respiration, and thus the movement of the dance, to the measure of the music.[1] Whether synchronous or ruptured, the universal movement of performance is through an equivocating cadence of more or less performance. If movement, according to *The Secret of the Golden Flower*, "is only another name for mastery" (Jung 1958: 332), there is nothing named performance which is not, at the last declension of a shadow's breath, concerned with the degree of mastery in the movement, and the degree of measure as well.

The Japanese noh drama, the Tai Chi Ch'uan, the *Hevehe* cycle of the Elema in New Guinea, Richard Wagner's or Robert Wilson's operas, a voodoo ritual or a High Mass seem to require time as the condition for forgetting it. But how much time, O Lord, with timeliness? Take *time*, says the director to the actor in a realistic play being rehearsed under an Equity contract; *take* time, says the therapist to the patient in an analytical session which costs sixty dollars an hour. The protraction of time is in every case, real or illusory, a mode of deconditioning, bringing performance back to "life." The question always remains, however, as to how *much* performance and how *long* and, in performance as in life, how much *life* – and how much apparent or disguised agitation over the temporality. If you think for an instant about timing in acting, you will eventually be caught up in a metaphysic. Whether prescribed or felt out, the determining of time is a universal of performance. It determines in turn the relations between what seems then familiar and what strange, the artificial and the natural, the sense of just being or being some*one*, the presentation of a self, a service in time or time-serving, whether measured by a clock, hypocrisy (the actor's duplicity), or the scruple on the price of a ticket. That is not only true of theatrical performance. One may look, as I used to do, upon a baseball game as the Japanese noh drama of American culture. I remember the long summer afternoons with the Bushwicks and the House of David which, even before floodlights came into the ballpark, seemed hardly subject to time. But once the networks took over the game, there were two dimensions of time: one orchestrated with breaks for commercials and the other, when electronic scoreboards came into the ballpark, a collateral entertainment – with fireworks, waterfalls, more commercials, and instant replays on the scene – which is always filling up time.

Sometimes the accretions of time in everyday life are the accretion of technique. Aside from the natural tendency to breathe in time to the music, dancers who had been studying ballet since next to infancy need to be, when they come to modern dance, saved from the perils of the barre. Cunningham has always said that he didn't want "steps" in his technique; Stanislavski did, and didn't. Cunningham, for all his openness, always shows traces of ballet in his own movement; and Stanislavski, who was trained in opera at a time when singers were in peril if they moved, could not entirely have escaped certain reflexes which were, no doubt, compensated for in the emotional memories of his method. They were both seeking, through the exactions of technique, forms of *natural* movement. It is the distinction, however, between just doing and performing the doing that made it possible for Stanislavski to say that the hardest thing for an actor to do on stage, though he has been doing it all his life, is to walk. It took him time to teach his actors to walk but when they were deconditioned and started to walk again, he wanted it to seem as if they were doing it as they had always done.

Doing it as it has always been done seems to be, whether sacred or profane, a universal of performance, even when it appears to be done as if for the first time. There has been a serious effort over the last generation to eliminate the *as if*, to return performance to *unmediated* experience, as with The Living Theatre, but with whatever measure of "truth" or "authenticity" it is at best only appearance. There is nothing more illusory in performance than the illusion of the unmediated. It can be a very powerful illusion in the theatre, but it *is* theatre, and it is *theatre*, the truth of illusion, which haunts *all* performance whether or not it occurs in the theatre, where it is more than doubled over. It is, actually, the unavoidable *doubling* in life, in a feedback circuit with theatre, that has induced Richard Schechner, after much experiment with actuals that attempted (more or less) unmediated activity with an emphasis on the here-and-now, to accede to the "restoration of behavior," which he now distinguishes as "the main characteristic of performance," from shamanism and therapy to social drama and aesthetic theatre (1985). What distinguishes the performative ethos and the postmodern – in a time of recuperation from the illusions of theatre-as-life – is not only redoubled awareness of what is being restored, but an exponential play around the combinatory sets of stored or past experience which is, since there is utterly no assurance of an uninterrupted present, all we can make of a dubious future.

There has been, then, a chastening accession of belatedness in the dialectic of appearances. And it points to the almost undeniable remembrance of history that *there is something in the nature of theatre which from the very beginning of theatre has always resisted being theatre.* Or "always already" resisted, as Jacques Derrida might say, if there were no beginning of theatre, and thus no nature but a trace. It is, indeed, the inevitable *reappearance of history* in performance which corrects the illusion of performance that refuses the future of illusion – the reign of representation – and insists that the theatre *is* life or, if not yet so, that it must be so. That this insistence can be a historical illusion of apocalyptic dimensions we have seen in Artaud and can still see in Derrida's essay on Artaud, "The Theater of Cruelty and the Closure of Representation."[2] If we can imagine, however, a state which is the becoming of theatre or all theatre or beyond theatre, we can also imagine a state before theatre which would appear to be something other than theatre, what we have sometimes *named* life, which could not possibly *be* theatre.

For like the sign in a hypothetical simple state, as idea or image or perception, the theatrical *gestus*, the signifying element *of* theatre "can become a sign," as Foucault says, "only on condition that it manifests, in addition, the relation that links it to what it signifies. It must represent; but that representation, in turn, must also be represented within it. That is a condition indispensable to the binary organization of the sign [. . .] The signifying idea becomes double, since superimposed upon the idea that is replacing another [the representation within] is also the idea of its representative power" (1973: 64). Derrida himself has elsewhere pointed out, in the denial of origins, the origin of doubling: "Representation mingles with what it represents, to the point where one speaks as one writes, one thinks as if the represented were nothing more than the shadow or reflection of the representer." Then, in the high melodrama of post-structuralist theory, which resembles the anxiety over perception in the Jacobean theatre, he speaks of the "dangerous promiscuity and [. . .] nefarious complicity between the reflection and the reflected which lets itself be seduced narcissistically. In this play of representation, the point of origin becomes ungraspable [. . .] For what is reflected is split *in itself* and not only as an addition to itself of its image. The reflection, the image, the double, splits what it doubles. The origin of the speculation becomes a difference. What can look at itself is not one; and the law of the addition of the origin to its representation, of the thing to its image, is that one plus one makes at least three" (1976: 36). Which is, at the logocentric impasse of the Western metaphysical tradition, like performing the Tai Chi or repeating the Tao which "begot one./ One begot two. Two begot three" – out of which arises the created universe, the "ten thousand things" with their ceaseless play of difference in the exchanges of *yin* and *yang* (Tsu 1972: 36), as if reality were a performance.

The *substance* of the theatrical in the idea of performance is the critical question in the act of performance. Nor is it merely a question of the succession of theatrical forms or modes of performance within those forms. It has rather to do with the radical critique of representation and, in the animus of recent thought, an intense distrust of the almost lethal legacy of a savage god who never meant the theatre to reveal itself as such, nor for representation to show its duplicitous face. The central figure in this critique, as in the most important theatrical experiment of the last generation, is Artaud, whose Theatre of Cruelty is not a form of New Theatre waiting to be born, but a primordial and juridical power whose urge, as Derrida shows, is the abolition of representation, which seals off the division between theatre and life as it separates birth from death. "The void, the place that is empty and waiting for this theatre which has not [as we say] 'begun to exist'," writes Derrida, "thus measures only the strange distance which separates us from implacable necessity, from the *present* (or rather the contemporary, *active*) affirmation." Artaud's theatre is not a representation. To the degree that life is unrepresentable, it is meant to be the *equal* of life, "the nonrepresentable origin of representation" (1978: 8).

In this mission, the enemy is mimesis, which breeds the lie of humanism, with its myth of individuation. What we see rather in the image of man is the grotesque offspring of the theatre's self-perpetuating enormity: ego, self, personality, a mere reproductive subject, slave to the ideological apparatus of reproduction, who must learn to free himself from false acting by true performance (thus, too, the distinction between the actor and the performer which has turned up in recent years). So far as the *institution* of theatre is concerned, if it is ever to be anything except a part of the apparatus, it must become the designated site of the extermination of the mimetic. In various zealous, adulterate, radically innocent, or depleted versions of this thought, innovation and renovation in the contemporary theatre has proceeded. It can obviously be nothing less than a falling away of thought from the affirmation which, despite itself, lets itself be evacuated by the doubling and redoubling of a negation in performance, as if the neutral force of representation were itself the indemnifying Plague. It is the problem that Artaud himself was never able to resolve, what drove him mad, though he seemed to come at the finest filament of his nerve-wracked thought as close as humanly possible to the nonrepresentable origin of performance where "the true theater [. . .] is born out of a kind of organized anarchy after philosophical battles which are the passionate aspect of [. . .] primitive unifications" (1958: 51).

As we become enamored of the unifications which we project upon "primitive" cultures, we tend to forget that even performances which are presumed to be outside representations exist within its enclosure. Without the enclosure, we would find ourselves, so to speak, within a performance that, whatever it may continue in an uninterrupted present, had never really begun, since it would only continue as *seeming*, like a dream. Denying the enclosure, the "stage edge" of the *mise en scène* of the unconscious, is to find yourself in Artaud's position, crying out in dreams, knowing you're dreaming and exerting the will to the point of madness, whipping your "innateness" so that it might prevail, as Artaud claimed for himself, on both sides of the dream. It is a noble if manic ambition. None of us, however, has ever seen a performance which, in the revulsion against the mimetic, the desire to banish seeming, has not (the more effective it is) radically increased the quotient of *pre*tense, the disruption of time by seeming – *especially if we have seen it*. As we understand more acutely from the interpretation of dreams, with their decoys of displacement and secondary revision, it is of the nature of performance to *be seen*. (I remember a moment in the presentation of a Yaqui ritual by the tribal chief – *his* interpretation of the Christo Rey ceremony – when he was explaining the origin of the *tampaleo*, the ritual drum. It was part of the saga of his personal creation myth, and he was very conscious of being studied by those who were there [all of whom he took to be anthropologists] as he told the story: a tree was cut, the wood was soaked, and then bent, and soaked some more, the ends joined. When the drum was sealed, a hole was bored in the side so the sound could escape, and then another for the emission of a longer sound and – just as we were forgetting that this version *was* a performance – he lifted the drum and looked at us through one of the holes, demonstrating how the drum might be used as a fixating instrument of the cruel performing eye. In that look we passed from a reconstruction of the spirit-world of the *huya aniya* to the solipsistic world of post-Genetic performance, where the watchers are watching the watchers watch . . .). The boundary of performance is a *specular* boundary, marked by speculation, the *idea* of a boundary. So, too, the boundary of a dream is the condition of the dreamer in the enclosure of sleep which, admittedly, may blur into the semblance of a waking dream, like the *huya aniya* of the Yacquis or like the somnambulistic ambition in the oneiric performances of Robert Wilson.

So long, however, as there is a performance to be referred to *as such* it occurs within a circumference of representation with its tangential, ecliptic, and encyclical lines of power. What blurs in the immanence of seeming are the features of that power, which needs to be taken into account in the current speculation on the state of performance in art and culture. It is not so much a matter of formalist experiment or behavioral innovation or ethnological renewal – all of which is taking place – but a breaking down of the structure of belonging which is, at the same time, inscribed in the becoming of representations which are, through the acceleration of cultural exchange, accumulating in a repertoire which is worldwide. If there is an infusion of energy as cultures cross, it is always competing with the universal extension of the apparatus of reproduction. Even as the imagery appears to change, the image-making systems appear to reflect the implacable and unchangeable image of an imageless and invisible power. This was a prospect which the theatre always foresaw, from the hallucinations of Cassandra to the fantasies of Genet, since it was its living, interminable, and recurring image.

As we think, then, about the future of performance, the questions are simultaneously technological and metaphysical. It makes no difference that some performance is far from conceptual and some of it, experimenting with the abolition of mimesis, next to brainless. The metaphysics comes in, as Artaud and Nietzsche thought, but not always as they wished, through the skin, into the muscles epistemically. We know that Artaud's critique of occidental theatre was part of a grander design for a Final Solution. He wanted to pulverize the contaminated structure of Western understanding, a contamination which has unfortunately spread at an alarming rate as we exchange, with whatever benefits, conceptual disease with other parts of the world. Most ambitions in the theatre itself, or in other Performance Art, are neither so rabid nor all-consuming, so venereal as Artaud's. But they are, if tentative or partial, responses to the same disturbance, at least those that have any cultural weight. Another villain of the piece, a blood relation of mimesis, is *speech*, mark of a theological space of performance where the primacy of the Logos continues to prevail. It prevails, despite the antiverbal experiments of the sixties, not merely in the proliferation of born-again Christians but in the ramified disguises of the Author-Text, that overpowering absence which unceasingly "regulates the time or the meaning of representation" (Derrida 1978: 9), not in the intrinsic purity of the actor's desire but according to the wishes and authority of that anterior force. The picture has been extensively painted in critical theory, perhaps over-painted: the idea that we are all in servitude to an interpretation which gives the illusion of an acting freedom but really comes from elsewhere, so that what is being performed is, in Artaud's view, the excrement of another mind.

Any way you look at it – which may be the price of looking – the theatre is the place where nothing is being transacted except what has been imposed on the disfigured body of thought of an infinite chain of representation. The missing links of this chain, its *structure of disappearance*, wind through the body politic and are strengthened, as Genet suggested in *The Balcony*, by the delusions of revolution, which maintains the chain of servitude intact. We felt something like that after the sixties (when "the whole world" was "watching") and it appears to be no different after every insurrection around the globe. On the stage as we normally know it, long after the prompter's box disappeared from view, we still felt a suspect and filthy breath, a vitiating whisper in the vomitorium. Or there was something in the cellarage or the wings or muffled in the teasers and tormentors, prescribing the words to be spoken or the figures of the dance or – even with the representation musicated or masticated in a participatory theatre where dinner is served – still cooking the stew or calling the tune, like the rather deranged figure in a theatrework of my own, *The Donner Party, Its Crossing* (about cannibalism), where the square dance kept turning and turning in the exhaustive pursuit of a vanishing power. It is against this power that performance continues to struggle, always coming round, with no higher aspiration than another reversal of history in the play of appearances: the liberation of the performer as an *actor* who, laminated with appearance, struggles *to appear*.

By whatever means the actor achieves autonomy – whether through charisma or flagrancy or transgression of the Text or by sheer power of apparent understanding (the rarest presence) – the machinery of the theatre quickly disables the appearance and marshals itself around a space of subversion, so long as there *is* a performance. No seeming self-denial on the part of an actor, no pretense of immediacy, however momentarily powerful or time-effacing, can amplify the privileged instant, for it is only for the instant timeless – and once again the theatre suffuses the truth with its presence, the only *presence* which is there. It is then that we realize that approval has been, in our very assent to the transgression of performance, institutionalized, historicized, *on borrowed time*. The theatre is a space of amortization. The interest is in the performance, and there is no performance without interest on a loan that can never be paid.

What is true of the actor is also true of the regenerative illusion of an *empty space* (Peter Brook's term) in which the actor has been seeking immediacy, usually missing its point. This is all the more true when the actor goes halfway across the world and rolls out a carpet in an aboriginal village, presumably to start from scratch, improvisationally, with elemental stories or something like pure play. No sooner is it looked at with anything like performance in mind, the empty space is a space of consciousness, also subject to time, and to the attritions of time, as if there were nothing but history in the nap. What is thought of as a space of risk or danger has a relapsable or collapsable edge. The collapse is, if first into the abyss of wonder (or the exotic), then into the trough of the commonplace. Even the astonishing quickly becomes – especially in the world of publicity, adjunct of the image-system (*is* there another world?) – a household word.

It is the momentary usurpation of "reality" by the truth of performance that, like the (*Fr., cliché*) photographic memory it soon becomes, validates the usurped system theoretically. And it is the system, with *its* sense of time (linear or synchronous) which is really the subject of play. It determines the steps or their apparent absence in the dance. It allows for the propriety of the event, however disturbing or obscene (against the scene) it may appear to be. The more it appears so by unavoidable reproduction, the more tautologically assured is the validation. Common sense tells us that what we experience at a play or other performance is not so tortuously deceptive as all this, but it is the purpose of common sense to overcome the real insidiousness of epistemological deceits lest, in reproducing them mentally – as Hamlet did, or Artaud – we may go mad. It is the power of Derrida's critique of Foucault on madness that he demonstrates how even the performance of madness, and its valorizing discourse, can never move outside the system of speech because "madness is indeed, especially and generally, silence, stifled speech, within a caesura and a wound that *open up* life as *historicity in general*" (1978: 54), which prevents madness – the limit of the unmediated – from ever being mad enough, as we can also see persuasively in *King Lear*.

To recapitulate: what seems to be confirmed by the pursuit of unmediated experience through performance is that there is something in the very nature of performance which, like the repeating spool of the *fort/da* (Krapp's extrapolated sp*ooo*l), implies *no first time*, no origin, but only recurrence and reproduction, whether improvised or ritualized, rehearsed or aleatoric, whether the performance is meant to give the impression of an unviolated naturalness or the dutiful and hieratic obedience to a code. That is why a performance seems *written* even if there is no Text, for the writing seems imbedded in the conservatism of the instincts and the linguistic operations of the unconscious. It seems, moreover, corporeally inscribed, even when there's a performance without any body, nothing but an absence, like the graffiti on the once-smooth body of the only too palpable Ghost.

With all the actable and unactable intricacies of the play within the play – that palimpsest of performance which breaks down the text in the image of the Text – *Hamlet* seems to affirm more than any other play in the canon that *what is universal in performance is the consciousness of performance.* That is nowhere more palpable than at those moments of negative capability when, after all the rationalizing intemperateness of the performance, there appears to be a (re)*lapse* of consciousness and – as if there were a cultural transference, a metathesis, a genetic crossing of East and West – there is some respite from the splitting infinitives of representation (to be or not to be) and only the *letting be.* When I speak, therefore, of the consciousness of performance, I am stressing the consciousness in the grain of performance – no outside no inside – which in certain kinds of performance may appear not to be there but, as in a topological warp, is there in its appearance, appearing not-to-be.

Even in the resistance to appearance, as in the *Verfremdungseffekt* derived by Brecht from Chinese acting, appearance is universal to performance. What makes it so? Thinking makes it so. Which is to say: consciousness *of* performance. A baby may be performing without consciousness, or so it appears (Marx insists that the whole history of the world is in the sensory expression of any moment, and Freud reminds us that the unconscious is our oldest *mental* faculty), but what would we know of performance if the world were full of babies. As with the disenchantments of the world, so with other states of elapsed consciousness. It's the falling away from trance, or its doubling in split consciousness, that makes us aware of trance as perform-ance, as well as the possibility – engrailed in the most skeptical thought of performance, in performance as a thinking body – that the world may be entranced.

"What, has this thing appeared again tonight?" (*Hamlet*, I.i.21). Obviously, if it appears there's going to be trouble for the performance. But if it doesn't appear there will be no performance, or not much worth mentioning if there is a performance. And that's true I would suppose, East or West, or at whatever meridian of performance anywhere in the world. The thing seems to suggest the almost unnameable form of some ancestral figure, not only the Hamletic ghost, but the Japanese *shite*, the Balinese *patih*, the *shave* of the Shona in East-Central Africa, or the God of Abraham in the Oberammagau Passion Play. Coleridge spoke of the credibilizing power of the omnibus word *thing.* Whatever the power is behind that power – like the power which summons away the Ghost which came in the Name of the Father – the thing is sufficiently indeterminate that one feels it has to do with more than the mere physical presence of a probably improbable ghost, or from what terrestrial direction the appearance occurs (although in some cultures, true, it won't appear unless it comes from the right direction, like "The Older Father" entering the ramada of the Yaquis). What we are anticipating, rather, in the goings and comings of these ghosts is the *ghostliness* that moves the performance. That is universal. Over the long history of performance it has moved by many names: as Destiny, Providence, Eternal Return, Oedipal Complex or Viconian Gyre: or as an inspiriting force or *influence*, often associated with the breath, such as *pneuma, taksu, shakti, ki*; or as some dematerialization of the Text into a fusion of vapor and power, like the fiery white letters of the Kabbalah or the smoke from the *shabbāth* candles that my grandmother, hooded by a napkin, wafted up her nose in one of the lovelier performances of my childhood; or as the "complete, sonorous, streaming naked realization" (1958: 52) which was, if Artaud's vision is true, the Orphic writing on the wall behind the Mysteries of Plato's Cave.

It is to the writing on the wall that, if there is an Eternal Return, the performance always returns. If it's never quite the same, that's because there is something mortifying in the mystery. Think again of the space of amortization. As with the economics of the psyche, it is half in love with death. Whatever the ghostly thing, there is an abrasion in performance (the "rub"), some interior resistance to the aboriginal romance of a pure libidinal flow. That is the real substance of the representational split which doubles over and over. The splitting occurs, as Freud discerned, not within the libido alone but, with a kind of activating *rigor mortis*, between the libido and death, which solicits and subverts and precludes representation. It is exactly what goes out of sight that we most desperately want to see. That's why we find ourselves, at the uttermost consummation of performance, in the uncanny position of *spectators*. It is uncanny because, in some inexplicable way (though Freud comes uncannily close to explaining it), *we are seeing what we saw before*. And that is true not only for those who attend upon the event, spectators at the start, but for those who become, through the event, participants, and for those who began as performers, in a kind of reversal of roles. It is as if, as Artaud says of the power of "true illusion," we are situated "magically, in *real terms* [. . .] between dream and events" (1958: 93) – his alternative to Aristotle's situation of tragedy between philosophy and history. If repetition is fundamental to performance, it is – after all or to begin with – death which rejects pure presence and dooms us to repetition. For Freud, the performance is always already scored in the irreducible dualism of the performance, although he also saw what Euripides foresaw in *The Bacchae*, that presence is not forbidden by some Apollonian power with whom Dionysus must make his peace; it is always already forbidden in the Dionysian power itself.

There are two realities meeting, then, at a single vanishing point, life and death, art and life, the thing itself and its double, which prepares the ground for performance. I don't want to rehearse all the reasons why we might think of it as sacred ground, except to say that it is inherent in the memory imbedded in the ground, like "the uncontrollable mystery on the bestial floor" in Yeats' poem or the Funeral Studio in the brain cell of Genet's Brothel. Once we think of death as already "at the origin of a life which can defend itself against death only through an *economy* of death, through deferment, repetition, reserve," we may realize how powerful a force memory is in the life of performance with its intrinsic *secondariness*, as it sustains the enigma of a *first time*. As Derrida explains in his account of memory as the constituting principle of the psyche in Freud, it is in the first time – which can only be *thought of* as a trace of originary violence and pain, in the contact of life and death – that repetition has already begun. It was there in the beginning which is always beginning again.

Whatever course the history of the theatre takes afterward, the condition of theatre is an *initiatory breach* which remembers the primal violence. That is why Freud – like tragic drama and, so far as I can see, every major form of theatre, with more or less memory of the tragic – "accords a privilege to pain" (Derrida 1978: 202). What we once thought of as catharsis is an equivocal aversion to an excess of pain which, lest it ruin the psychical organization, must be deferred, like death, even by those cultures which extend the deferral through stages (or stagings) of death. We may defer it by laughter or meditation or random play or trance, or by the dream of an actual which is a perpetual present, but "Life is already threatened by the origin of the memory which constitutes it, and by the breaching which it resists, the effraction which it can contain only by repeating it" (Derrida 1978: 202). What is being repeated in the tautological cycle of performance – replay, reenactment, restoration, the play within the play within – is the memory of the origin of the memory which is being solicited and resisted. It is in this recursive way that performance is a testament to a life which seems to look like death because it is always being left behind.

There are, of course, ceremonial occasions which are joyous, but if there is in the disappearing space of performance something of a cemetery too, the wonder is that this world of the dead can tell us as much as it does about the living. The reason is that it is only in terms of the living that we imagine the world of the dead. Yet there is a sense in which the performer is always imagining his own death. He may project it into the future as another deferral, but it seems to come like memory from behind, as if it had already happened. That's why, too, there is always the residue of a lie or a self-deception in the claim of the actor or shaman or hungan that he is wholly (self)possessed and does not see himself performing. Shakespeare dwells upon this evasion in the sonnets – a virtual manual of performance which is sonorously intimate with possession. The self-observing voice of the sonnets speaks explicitly at one point of the "unperfect actor on the stage,/Who with his fear is put *besides* his part" (23.1–2, emphasis mine). There are glimpses of a perfect actor, but he might as well be an effigy for, "moving others," he is himself "as stone," pure influence, but subject of an invisible power (94.1–4). If the actor does not see himself performing, he is nonetheless a spectator because of this duplicity in the presence of the Other, the familiar, the double, the formerly buried avatar of a constantly duplicating self. In a culture which appears to have no such concept as the self, that (un)consecrated victim of the Word, the repressed appearance will be an ancestral *figure* which, whatever case you want to make for the spirit-world, is just as likely to be a figure of speech.

It is, however, in the presence of the seemingly dead that we can see – as we have come to see in recent years – that the archaic ceremonies from which the theatre was presumably born did not preclude theatre; that is, ritual has no priority. It might indeed have *followed* theatre in the instituting trace, although the institutions of ritual and theatre are coextensive in time, mirroring and mirrored in the same mystery. If we were rummaging, though, in the long history of anthropological guesses as to which ritual form – year-gods, vegetation ceremonies, shamanism, etc. – tells us most about the emergence of theatre from whatever was not-theatre (assuming there was an emergence and it was not forever there), my inclination would be to focus, as Genet so acutely did, on some death-rite or funeral ceremony as primal, a rite of *separation* rather than a rite of incorporation (van Gennep's terms), which would seem to come after the more primordial fact – just as the cosmic marriage ceremony and the hymeneal feast came rather arbitrarily not only after the tragic drama but after the disruptions of comedy as well, as in the betrothal of the old fart Pisthetairos to the young beauty Basileia, Miss Universe, like some *deus-ex* ingenuity to heal an irreparable breach. The point is, again that there is no performance without separation or division, though the nature of performance may preserve, more or less reverently or irreverently, the memory of a time – the now-famous *illud tempus* – when there was *no* separation. That is another way of describing the recurring aspiration of performance to efface itself or – in the irresistible shading of performance into theatre, theatre into performance – whatever it is that is *theatrical*, the substance of all divisions, in performance, especially if the ritual is sacred. (I remember being present at a Eucharist, as an observer, when the communicants went up to receive the wafer and the wine, and the priest reciting the liturgy reversed the order of the offering in the repetition of the words. I believe I was the only one who heard it, maybe not even the priest and the woman before him when it happened, who was going to be ordained and with whom, I had reason to suspect, he was having an affair. It is interesting to speculate about the nature of that performance if I hadn't been there and – in what appeared to be a "perfect ceremony of love's rite" (Shakespeare's Sonnets, 23.6) – nobody had heard it, though my separating presence might have induced it by already theatricalizing the event). Even in shamanism, there is an *aftering* effect that comes of separation. The spirit-ancestor, at some indeterminate space of being or non-being, perhaps among the dead, teaches the shaman to dance and sing. Then there is a synapse where the shamanic soul is released by ancestral powers and, as if awaking from a dream, remembers what he has been taught. The dance and song are efforts to rehearse back the hereditary world from which the shaman is separated. Sometimes the shaman forgets and, as if some punitive expedition has been ordered from the underworld, spirits appear and in another separation tear his body apart so he may the better remember.

In the modern theatre, the rites of separation came out of an "ethos of suspicion" (Ricoeur) as a heuristic strategy, as if separation were reflecting on separation. It is probably just as well, in the gullible order of things, that there is now and then an intelligence like Brecht's which tries to dispel the mystery in performance by looking at it from a distance, while not at all depreciating just how stubborn the mystery is. What is, I think, still incisive about Brecht's theory of Alienation is that it distrusts not only the illusions of performance that sponsor a repressive oedipal force in the infrastructure of our culture, but the anti-oedipal enchantment as well, fortified now by the impact of other cultures. If one reads carefully the essay on Chinese acting, it is clear that it is not the arcanities that attract him, no more than an unrestricted subconscious in the actor. And if we think through the charges of the "Short Organum" against the obfuscating agencies of bourgeois theatre, we may also be reminded that the empowering forces or creative energies of non-western cultures, those I've already named, as well as *shun toeng, prāna, kokoro*, and the metamorphosing versions of *ki*, are not necessarily divine emanations but as much historical constructs as sexuality, gender, race, and class, with all the liabilities of such constructs in the social and political world. If we furthermore think for a moment about history, we may recall just how empowering they can also be. Like the creative energies, they have been attached to spiritual disciplines, more or less efficacious (and more or less destructive), as performance must be, whatever the unnameable force that through the green fuse drives the appearance.

Brecht preferred to stress in performance not the intangible power but the *structure* of appearances and the historical *gestus*: *what*'s happening and *why* and who is paying for it at one end or the other of a scale of victimization, which is another measure of performance, including as it does the status of the performer and the social cost of a mystifying energy which pays tribute to other unmoved movers, maybe more crippling forms of absent power, like *dharma*. I am not trying to deflate the alluring and truly creative traditions behind such concepts, which I don't pretend to understand, though I've spent years studying certain spiritual techniques and ritual processes as an extension of the art of acting. What I am trying to do is suggest that there is in any performance the universal question, spoken or unspoken, of *what are we performing for?* (This became a serious issue in my own theatrework with KRAKEN when, for instance, we decided to do, in the evolution of a technique [called *ghosting*], the Tai Chi Ch'uan rather than Yoga or Aikido or any other of the martial arts. Why one rather than another? Why a martial art? Why, in fact, among all the conceivable forms an actor might study, any particular choice in the definition of a method? Even among Western techniques of, say, modern dance or mime – whose dance? whose mime? in respect to what? what for? and what, even in the generation of a "universal" technique like Grotowski's, what does *it* preclude?)

We can see in the politics of older cultures that they are also dealing with the return of the repressed. If we've screened them out, they've screened us out. To younger people in those cultures, struggling to retain perhaps (some not) what is generic and life-giving in the long deformities of traditional order, that may also mean the recognition, as on the other side of a mutual dream, of creative energies which we are, in the post-industrial world, only too swiftly dismissing, like the life-giving power of another historical construct, quite visible in Brecht, the indignant brainpower of the rational mind. Which is not what they mean – in the cybernetic universe which seems to resemble those other, earlier, or remoter worlds – by software.

In any case, what Brecht asked us to do, confronted with any play of appearances, is to observe critically, with a reserve of consciousness *outside* performance, though he was early on aware that both the instruments of perception and the ideological structure of perception alter the appearance of what is seen. He would have been unpersuaded, surely, by the new doxology of play which suggests, as I have done myself, that it may be impossible to get outside performance in the illusory structure of World-Play. Brecht readily knew, moreover, that there was a necessary pretense in an apparently legible structure which may certainly have, as in his stagings of his own plays, a misleading enchantment. But what was always important in Brecht – who after all started his career inspired by Rimbaud, worshipping Baal, going to non-theatrical performances, and anticipating Genet – was the tireless effort, not often conspicuous in the solipsism and domesticated shamanism of postmodern performance, to navigate the fine line between the visible appearance and the invisible happening, the dream and the event, the doing and the ado, keeping his eye on the actual in the most empirical sense, as a distinct matter of historical perception.

On that empirical basis, all performance moves between expectancy and observance, between attentiveness to what happens and astonishment at what appears. The performances of a given culture may stress one more than the other, but no performance is either all happening or all appearance. And there is no way of resolving which comes first, the happening or the appearance, no more than there is of performing some gesture of the Tai Chi and determining as it is performed whether the *chi* flowed so that the sparrow's tail could be grasped or whether, in grasping the sparrow's tail, and only then, illusory as it seems, the *chi* flowed, like the *lightness* which Brecht wanted from his actors when they left East Germany to play in London. I can't imagine a cultural form which really has anything conclusive to say about the fugitive relationship between the premonitory act and the actualization, the incipience and the immanence, whether you make the gesture in order to have the vision or have the vision so the gesture may be made. And that applies to other kinds of performance which seem, at first sight, to have little to do with these subtleties of appearance with their patina of theatricality. I am thinking, for example, of Lynn Swann running patterns of a passing route or Nadia Comaneci on a vaulting horse or Philippe Petit on a highwire between the towers of the World Trade Center or, mixing virtuosity and appearance in the most self-conscious of performances, Muhammad Ali in that once audacious ado, dancing like a butterfly and stinging like a bee. I am not sure, all nuances considered, that there is any kind of performance that is non-mimetic, since what is being performed is – the more perilous the performance, like Swann's patterns or Ali's shuffle – an image of perfection in the head.

But returning from such marvels of performance to the theatricalizing of everyday life, not only the appearance of the actual but, nowadays, the supplement of reflexive consciousness about that appearance: if there is no performance without consciousness, there is also the exercise of consciousness in watching a performance in which those who seem to be performing are under the illusion that they are merely living. I say under the illusion because, were they to think about it at all, that first reflection, they would be susceptible to the vice of performative consciousness which theatricalizes everything it looks upon, seeing the living as nothing but performance. As for those who know they're performing, they may call attention to it, but we know there are also techniques of performance, not only the Method, designed to make them forget it. Whether or not the consciousness of performance is to be forgotten is perhaps the major issue of the history of performance, as it certainly is of postmodernism. It does not, however, appear to be the same problem for those cultures which are taken as models of performative consciousness without *self*-consciousness *about* performance, because they are still perhaps on the aboriginal margins of history.

But, as everybody knows, not for long. It is a curious thing, too, to be thinking about universals of performance at a time when performance itself seems to be universal. As we widened the scope of performance to include not only theatre events in theatres or environments or other dispersed places, we have also had to consider a variety of hybrid happenings and conceptual events, as well as sports, games, circuses, rituals, politics, fashion, therapies, sexual practices, private fantasies and illicit ceremonies, informal gatherings or rehearsed stagings, with or without texts, virtuals or actuals, plays not only without plot or character but with or without people – not to mention those more or less elusive shadows of the performing self which by disappearing accretions of performance eventually refuse the concepts we associate with people: personality or presence or a self. We have come to admit within the field of performance not only behavior(s) in everyday life but what used to be the disciplines by means of which we approached an understanding of behavior, what the French call the Human Sciences: philosophy, linguistics, anthropology, and psychoanalysis, with conceptual crossovers into the biological domain of genetics, ethology, and brain science. All this gestation of performance in non-theatrical disciplines has been summoned up and perhaps summarized in the performance virtuosity of our literature, particularly literary theory.

Along with the valorization of play in the postmodern, we have taken with considerable seriousness the theatrical notion that all the space of the world is a stage or, with varying magnitudes and commutations of illusion, a cosmic manifestation of a universe of play. The play within the play occurs – more or less "framed," as well as "written" – at every level of the great chain of being or, in the unchained signifiers of a polysemous discourse, some recursive or reptilian equivalent. The uroboric play includes forms of behavior and irruptions of play not dreamable in our philosophy or studied in the fieldwork of ethnographers or yet available for deconstruction in our theory. As our view of performance expands almost galactically through the infinite space of thought, we find it curving back like the linguistic and historical constructs of a performative consciousness, to embrace, tautologically, the interminable play or chamber drama of the *mise en scène* of the unconscious.

Granted, then, the bewilde* ng plenitude of performance, if not its absoluteness, I have tried to pursue – in thinking about what is universal in performance – the thing which appears in that subjunctive moment when whatever was there before becomes a performance. Or, so far as it is imaginable, that which in performance is other than that which is *not* performance, the cipher which marks it off from, shall we say, life? or shall we say, death? There is, within the new dispensation of theatricalizing consciousness, a surfeit of performance that almost teases us out of thought. But what I've wanted to approach in this discourse on performance – and to perceive in the theatrework I have done – is what in performance can almost *not be seen because it is thought*. "Is this not something more than fantasy?" (*Hamlet*, I.i.4). We are not always sure. If it cannot be seen, it has nevertheless – like the flowers in Eliot's *Burnt Norton* or the Japanese *ikebena* (which makes flowers live) (Barba 1982: 19) – the look of something that is looked at. That is, as an aspect of thought, also universal in performance. There has always been – not only in Hamlet and Rousseau, but in other cultures – a dream of performance without theatre, nothing to see and nothing to show, like the Taoist mirror. What I have been trying to evoke is as delicate and fragile, perhaps, as the imagined performance of that dream, or like the curtain between the greenroom and the *hashigakari* in the noh theatre, that intimation of a diaphanous membrane between the world of spirits and the diurnal world or, for that matter, gravely, the equally fragile difference between the phantasmal noh and the present noh or between the dramatic noh and the refined noh, or the state of being in which the actor was *before* he appeared (who was he?) on the *hashigakari* carrying, as it appears (who is he now?), his ghostly space with him.

I think we are very close then to the most elemental consciousness of performance which *precipitated* performance, whatever else it becomes. That thing is universal in performance, in the ideographic noh and in the looser mimetic language of the most realistic of appearances. It has been said of Eleanora Duse that her subtlety was a secrecy, the absence of all rhetoric. She seemed exempt from the Logos even when speaking words. If legend can be believed, she allowed herself in the very act of performance to be *overlooked*. It was not simply humility, rather like a refusal to appear or to be discovered in performance. She seemed to do her acting on that selvedge of performance where performance with anything less would cease to exist. Yet it was not that coverup of performance in psychological acting which pretends that it is not performing. Moving others, she was not as stone, but what she was, materially, it was hard to say. I have always retained (from I know not where) an image of her in perfect stillness, then something passing over her face like the faintest show of thought, not the play of a nerve, *only thought*, and you would suddenly know she was dying. I mean dying right there, *actually*, articulating the dying, with a radiance of apprehension so breathtaking that, in the rhythm of your breathing, you could hardly escape your own death. Of course, you *are* dying too, actually, right there, in the play of thought, though it is overlooked, and it is likely to be missed if it is in the course of performance merely thought and not *shown* – unless you are a Duse, who seemed to show it by merely thought.

Someone is dying in front of your eyes. That is another universal of performance. There are, to be sure, a myriad of ways in which the history of performance has been able to disguise or displace that elemental fact. You can joke about it, you can laugh it off, you can perform great feats of physical skill, but the image of it is before your eyes all the more because you are looking, even if the space is empty. You can't escape that look even if you close your eyes. Every look is the Law, which kills, as Kafka knew, who wrote a doomsday book of performance.

Performance occurs in a middle region between the world of transparency and the world of opacity. There is an ideal vision, such as Rousseau's, of a fête or carnival in which all the obscurities cease and all of us are, because outside the realm of exchange and reproduction, no more than what we appear to be, and no less. We see that world in the wine harvest of *La Nouvelle Héloise*, the unperformed *claritas* of the open air, rustic and convivial, without boundaries, classless (or with all classes *participating*), a unison of reciprocity and shared being such as utopias have imagined and probably no culture, even the most rustic and convivial, has ever approached. It is a *mise en scène* without a gaze, everything seen and nothing to show. There is nothing remotely like the edge of a stage, as if repression had been lifted in the unconscious, where there is always a stage. As we understand from the operations of the unconscious, there is no way to eliminate the edge which is reconstituted "elsewhere" in the expenditure of the desire to eliminate it. There may be some approximation of a spectacle-without-looking in the case of an aboriginal ceremony or in what we think of as high ritual process like a Mass, where the spectator and the spectacle presumably merge. But then the coalescence occurs below the gaze of a god or a totem or, trying to determine the absence of a seeming in what only seems to be there, a visiting anthropologist, wavering in the pathos of his own performance, between presence and absence, visbility and invisibility; even with the end of imperialism, the incorrigible representative of an occupying power.

When the gaze returns to its source, from the invisible frontier of all desire, we are back to that other vision of performance, essentially theatrical, which is made of (dis)appearances and, with various illusions of other purpose, deploys appearance to no further end but its ceaseless reappearance. That process reflects a world which, so far as it can be distinguished, is as endlessly interpretable as a dream – and which is sometimes marvellously reinterpreted *by* appearance. All the varieties of performative experience move between the two imaginings of its real presence in whatever objective or symbolic forms. But even when appearance is imagined as absent, it is appearance that dominates the idea of performance, since it suggests what would not be there, in performance, if it were merely lived or experienced without distinction.

The ulterior motive, I would suppose, of the desire to identify universals of performance has been stated by Victor Turner in his *From Ritual to Theatre* (1982b). In concluding his introduction with "an appeal for global cultural understanding," he mentions the attempts "being made by a handful of anthropologists and theater scholars and practitioners to generate an anthropology and theater of experience" for the purpose of mutual understanding across cultures. "The ethnographies, literatures, ritual, and theatrical traditions of the world now lie open to us as the basis for a new transcultural communicative synthesis through performance. For the first time we may be moving towards a sharing of cultural experiences, the manifold 'forms of objectivated mind' restored through performance to something like their pristine effectual contouring" (1982b: 18–19).

I hesitate to be a spoilsport in this admirable mission, but if we are seeking to perceive universals of performance aside from their outer show – bodies, space, light, sound, gesture, motion, dress or undress, more or less dramatic content, coherent or scattered narrative, song and dance, masking and mimicry, exhibition of skills, shamanic or mimetic, and an auditory more or less specular or participatory, itself either gathered or dispersed – then we will inevitably come back to that suspended moment of a Duse or on the *hashigakari*, when the ghostly thing appears, the latent substance of performance which is divisive, solitary, alien, and apart. Whatever the appearance or actuality of communitas, performance is a testament to what separates. In the empty space, an empty solitude. I may be reflecting no more than the escalation of estrangement in our time, the doubling of separation, when I say *that* remains the thing which is most moving in performance, and always was: its essential aloneness. You can see it in the effectual contours of the most pristine forms of acting, as on the highwire with Philippe Petit. For what we think of as stage presence is related to that aloneness, the nature of the performer who, in a primordial substitution or displacement, is born on the site of the Other. It is the one thing which, if there is no communicative synthesis at all, nothing but a breach, also crosses cultures.

We can see it in the resemblance of Zeami's *yūgen*, whether as "transcendental phantasm" or "subtle fascination" (Nogami 1955: 51–61), to Stanislavski's Public Solitude, which is the rudimentary estrangement of what he elsewhere calls "charm." It is a substantiating presence which is just about as elusive as the "naked charm" and "strangeness" of subatomic physics. (As for the psychological acting associated with Stanislavski, I want to make amends for what I said somewhat invidiously before. I should add in all cultural equity that, while it has had a bad press in our experimental theatre, for its presumptions of ego, its techniques of concentration, focus, and centering are universal; and their generating sources – *emotional memory* and *sense memory* – are no more mystifying than and are equally evocative as their correlatives in the creative energies of other cultures. As for the ego, despite its bad press in the West, it is being widely adopted, or some self-reliable facsimile, by people in other cultures who have never had any social identity but dispossession. Psychological acting is of course also associated with the vices of the mimetic, but if there was something wanting in our experimental theatre – aside from a theoretical critique of the valorization of performance to the detriment of acting – it was the enviable meticulousness of histrionic skill required for an acute psychological portrayal of what we once thought of as character.) In considering the principle of *yūgen* recently, Eugenio Barba emphasized the property of fascination in the temperament of the performer, as a transition from his remarks on *prāna* or *ki-hai* ("profound agreement" of the spirit with the body) to his discussion of *shakti*, the creative energy which is genderless but represented in the image of a woman (1982: 28–29). It is the traditional dispossession of the woman which may account for this, her apartness which is encompassing, like the womb of the universe.

And indeed, if one traces it, *yūgen* was originally a poetic term which suggested a pensiveness arising from estrangement and loneliness, as in the following twelfth-century *haiku* of Saigyō: "Insensible as I am, I share/the loneliness of the autumn dusk/at the Swamp of the Solitary-snipe" (Nogami 1955: 51). By the close of the Kamakura period (1184–1335), *yūgen* came to signify a delicate brightness, like a moonray on a passing cloud or the subtle fascination of the glitter of snow falling. But the acquired brightness is still permeated by loneliness and pensive motion, as in the exquisite lines of Thomas Nashe about queens dying young and fair and brightness falling from the air. I believe that here both traditions touch upon that quality of the performer which is universal, the sense of removal or distance, however possessed, whether a virtuoso on a trapeze in a circus or, with all the illusions of choral unity, whatever it was that caused the first actor to separate himself from the communitarian pathos, knowing perhaps that even surrounded he was essentially alone, in the Public Solitude which is the precondition of his charm, his fascination, his representativeness, and his power. It is also the precondition, like some genetic repercussion in the form, of the appearance of the second actor, in Aeschylus, and the third actor, in Sophocles, those incremental separations that led from the seeming harmony of the Chorus to the equivocal catechism of the dialogue which, even in its dispersions and lapses through many actors, as in the silences of Chekhov's plays, eventually dominated the theatre, along with the hermeneutical Text, which we have been trying to dissolve back, via Artaud, into the naked sonorous streaming realization out of which the Chorus seemed to be born.

Performance may transform the one performing. That it has the capacity to transform seems to be universal. But at the level of community, whatever the powers of performances once were, they no longer are. For one thing, the performative instinct has been so distributed in art and thought and everyday life that we find it harder to discern the special value of performance *as* transformation, when transformation seems, moreover, in a culture of signs – with the supersaturation of images in the media – a universal way of life. It is also hard to think, as Plato did, of performance as something perilous because of the intensity of its imagining power. We simply do not take the powers of art and imagination as seriously as Plato did, or as seriously as they take poetry, say, in the Soviet Union. I suppose it takes some authoritarian political order to make it seem important, a matter of life and death. When you can go to jail for it, you will listen to it. The transformative threat of performance seems to require an agency of repression. That agency has certainly not disappeared, but its invisibility in a world of high visibility, that is, in a culture of signs, is a qualitatively different problem from that faced by performance before or elsewhere, say in the "empire of signs" (Barthes) that gives meaning to the Bunraku or the Japanese tea ceremony. I also suspect that's a threatened empire.

In any case, performance of that kind is not well served, it would seem, by the illusions of the democratic. We are still not sure that performance of any kind was really well served by the illusions of the sixties, which spread the desublimating gospel of performance and tried, more or less clumsily, to appropriate the media, the image-making apparatus, whose powers are vast and omniverous and inarguable. The outcome of all the subversion was a conspiracy with the invisible, all the more when the theatre went underground with the radical politics. What it succeeded in doing by making everything theatre was to thin the theatre out, so that it has had to learn again how to *be* theatre, in the right proportions with performance, I see no evidence that anything like that has been accomplished yet.

Where performance remains, in our society, most transformative, it is hardly an agency of communitas. Think, for instance, of the libertarian dissonance of rock that turned, in punk, into an anarchistic dispersion of music like the mimesis of primal violence. Which was, as with rock before it, appropriated by the invisible exchange of the trickle-down economy. There is also, inarguably, the transformative power of television. We have mixed feelings about that, as art, as community, since it debases its technical skills and seems to breed isolation in the home which is not exactly Public Solitude. It has, moreover, encouraged a mimetic violence among young people which, after many years of study of the self-evident, has been recently pretty much confirmed. Sports are also transformative for those who play and compete, and they still provide models of emulation for those who watch. We still have nothing in the theatre to correspond to the experience you have in a stadium during the play of a double reverse, not to mention the stupendous involvement of spectators all around the world in a championship soccer match. Yet the highest skills of athletics are also caught up in the new ruthlessness of entertainment, which is big business even without the drug traffic; and the community among the spectators is one which is – as with the patriotism of the halftime ceremonies or the violence of a football game during the Vietnam War – something more than suspect. There is an undeniable excitement at a ballgame as at Broadway musical, where even the most begrudging of us will admire the extraordinary abilities of the performers, but it is not exactly the communitas we have in mind.

We return, then, to the question raised before, about not only the means of performance, the technical skills or procedures which we can more or less exchange across cultures, but also the ends of performance: *what for?* As any good performer knows, that also determines the means. As Turner suggests, everything seems open and available to us now, things which were once in the realm of the arcane. But we inevitably have to ask just what the appropriation of any performance technique from an alien culture will mean, not only in the transformations of performance, but in the transformations of power by which all performance is known, even as it reveals that power. The critical question is, as I've remarked, universal in performance, although we are once again in a period where little resembling an answer, or even a possible response, has shown itself persuasively in performance – except for those modes of performance which may look upon the question as a non sequitur, like climbing Mount Everest, which you do because it is there.

That kind of performance, like orbiting in space, may have lost some of the aura of individual heroism, but it remains an exemplary model of teamwork or ensemble playing. Such teamwork is not necessarily a universal of performance, but that there is something exemplary in performance is still universal. The problem is that the example, today, may be read in competing ways. Landing on the moon or climbing Mount Everest may also suggest, though remote from the centers of power, the structure of power which supports the example, and of which we may not entirely approve. It appears to be the same structure in which – amidst the profusion of performances, casual or codified – performance is losing its force *as* example. We can of course hope that a transfusion of power from other cultures will reverse this tendency, but there is nothing so far as I can see which is universal about that. What we may also want to remember in view of that is that performance is the site-specific appearance of local initiative and – whatever it acquires as cultures cross in a worldwide network of appearances – still very much dependent on the discriminating perceptions of individual will, which may be trained to accuracy through performance. As for performing in general, Stanislavski and others have warned against that.

Notes

1. The line was actually spoken by Azuma to his pupil Katsuko Azuma; she took the master's name, according to tradition. Quoted by Eugenio Barba (1982).
2. The essay is also in Derrida, *Writing and Difference* (1978: 232–50).

Appendix

Participants in the Conference on Yaqui Ritual, 19–24 November 1981. Conference on Contemporary Japanese Theatre, 19–24 May 1982, and Symposium on Theatre and Ritual, 23 August–1 September 1982. An asterisk * signifies that the participant is a performer or director whose work was seen at one of the conferences; ** signifies artist-scholar whose work was seen at one of the conferences.

Name	Yaqui	Japan	Theatre and Ritual
Joanne Akalaitis		×	
Keith Basso	×		
Monica Bethe*			×
William O. Beeman		×	×
Herbert Blau	×		×
James Boon		×	×
Paul Bouissac			×
James Brandon		×	×
Karen Brazell**		×	×
Kenneth S. Brecher			×
Victoria Bricker			×
T.J. Chandrachudan			×
Eum-Jeon Choe*			×
Roberto da Matta			×
P.N. Girija Devi*			×
George DeVos		×	
Fred Eggan	×		
Joan Eggan	×		
Larry Evers	×		
Richard Emmert*			×
Jim Griffith	×		
Richard Haefer	×		
Frank Hoff		×	
Arata Isozaki		×	
Yoshio Izumi*			×
Clifford R. Jones			×
Taegon Kim			×
Theresa Ki-ja Kim		×	×
Keum-Hwa Kim*			×
Barbara Kirshenblatt-Gimblett			×
Anthony Heilbot			×

Name	Col 1	Col 2	Col 3
Ron Jenkins			×
Du-Hyun Lee			×
Alan Lomax	×		×
Ruth Maleczech			×
Brooks McNamara			×
Felipe Molina**	×		
Barbara Myerhoff		×	×
A.M. Narayanan Nambiar*			×
A.M. Sivan Nambudiri*			×
K. Vasudevan Nambudripad			×
Mansaku Nomura		×	
Ranjini Obeyesekere			×
James Peacock			×
K.P. Achunni Poduval*			×
C. Radhakrishnan*			×
K. Raman*			×
P.M. Ramamohonan*			×
Miles Richardson		×	×
Farley Richmond			×
Jerome Rothenberg	×		
P.S. Sathidevi*			×
Richard Schechner	×	×	×
Emory Sekaquaptewa	×		
Kayoko Shiraishi*		×	
C.K. Shylaja*			×
Edward Spicer	×		
Rosamond Spicer	×		
Tadashi Suzuki**		×	
Koji Takabayashi*			*
Shinji Takabayashi*			×
Yasunari Takahashi		*	
Barbara Tedlock	×		
Robert K. Thomas	×		
Yi-Fu Tuan		×	
Edith Turner	×	×	×
Victor Turner	×	×	×
P.V. Eswaran Unni*			×
Anselmo Valencia**	×		
William Wiggins			×
Masao Yamaguchi		×	
Masato Yamamoto*			×
Jeong-Hwa Yoon*			×
Phillip Zarrilli**	×	×	×

Bibliography

Akiba, Takashi. 1959   *A Field Study of Shamanism in Korea* (in Japanese). Nara, Japan: Yotokusha.

Armstrong, Robert Plant. 1981   *The Powers of Presence: Consciousness, Myth, and Affecting Presence.* Philadelphia: The University of Pennsylvania Press.

Artaud, Antonin. 1958   *The Theater and Its Double.* New York: Grove Press.

Ashley, Wayne. 1982   "Some Comparisons of the Stage Text in Three Productions of *The Golem*: From Purim-shpil to 'Experimental' Theatre," unpublished paper.

Barba, Eugenio. 1982   "Theater Anthropology," *TDR* 26, 2: 5–32.

Barthes, Roland. 1978   *A Lover's Discourse.* New York: Hill and Wang.

Beichman, Janine n.d.   "Drifting Fires: An English Nō and its Context," ms.

Belo, Jane. 1976   "Trance Experience in Bali,": 150–61 in *Ritual, Play and Performance*, Richard Schechner and Mady Schuman, eds. New York: Seabury Press.

Berberich, Junko Sakaba. 1984   "Some Observations on Movement in *Nō*," *Asian Theatre Journal* 1, 2: 207–16.

Bethe, Monica. 1984   "No Costume as Interpretation," *Mime Journal*: 148–55.

Bethe, Monica and Karen Brazell. 1978   *Nō as Performance: Analysis of the Kuse Scene of Yamamba*, East Asia Papers 16. Ithaca: Cornell University China–Japan University China–Japan Program.

1982–3   *Dance in the Noh Theater*, East Asia papers 24, 3 volumes. Ithaca: Cornell University China–Japan Program.

Birdwhistell, Ray. 1964   "Communication Without Words," manuscript supplied by the Eastern Pennsylvania Psychiatric Institute, Philadelphia.

1970   *Kinesics and Context.* Philadelphia: University of Pennsylvania Press.

Blacking, John. 1977   "Towards an Anthropology of the Body," in *The Anthropology of the Body.* London: Academic Press: 1–28.

Bogan, Phebe M. 1925   *Yaqui Easter Dances of Tucson, Arizona: an Account of the Ceremonial Dances of the Yaqui Indians at Pascua.* The Archeological Society, Tucson.

Bouissac, Paul. 1972   "Clown Performances as Meta-semiotic Texts," *Language Sciences* 19: 1–7.

1977   "From Joseph Grimaldi to Charlie Carioli: A Semiotic Approach to Humour" in *A Funny Thing, Humour*, A. Chapman and H. Foot, eds. London: Pergamon.

1978   "The Semiotics of Nonsense: Clowns and Limericks" in *Sight, Sounds, and Sense*, Thomas A. Sebeok, ed. Bloomington: Indiana University Press.

1979   "Le Cirque: operations et operateurs semiotiques" in *Sight, Sounds, and Sense*. T.A. Sebeok, ed. Bloomington: Indiana University Press.

1982   "The Meaning of Nonsense (Structural Analysis of Clown Performances and Limericks)" in *The Logic of Culture*, I. Rossi, ed. South Hadley, Massachusetts: Bergin & Garvey.

Brandon, James. 1982   "Notes on Audience Perceptions of Theatre in Asia and the West," paper prepared for Wenner-Gren Symposium 89, *Ritual and Theatre*.

Burns, Elizabeth. 1972   *Theatricality: A Study of Convention in the Theatre and in Social Life.* New York: Harper Torchbooks.

Carlson, Marvin. 1984   *Theories of the Theatre.* Ithaca: Cornell University Press.

Carnicke, Sharon Mari. 1984   *"An Actor Prepares/Rabota aktera nad soboĭ, Chast'I*: A Comparison of the English with the Russian Stanislavski," *Theatre Journal* 36, 4: 481–94.

Chapple, E.D. 1970   *Culture and Biological Man.* New York: Holt, Rinehart, and Winston.

Choe, Kil-song. 1982   "Community Ritual and Social Structure in Village Korea," *Asian Folklore Studies* 41: 39–48.

Cornford, Francis. 1914   *The Origin of Attic Comedy.* London: Edward Arnold.

Crapanzano, Vincent and Vivien Garrison. 1977   *Case Studies in Spirit Possession.* New York: John Wiley & Sons.

Csikszentmihalyi, Mihaly. 1975   *Beyond Boredom and Anxiety.* San Francisco: Jossey-Bass.

Czaplicka, M.A. 1914   *Aboriginal Siberia: A Study in Social Anthropology.* Oxford University Press.

Densmore, Frances. 1932   *Yuman and Yaqui Music.* Washington, D.C.: Smithsonian Institution, Bureau of American Ethnology, Government Printing Office, Bulletin 110.

d'Aquili, Eugene and Charles D. Laughlin, Jr. 1979   "The Neurobiology of Myth and Ritual" in *The Spectrum of Ritual*, eds. d'Aquili, Laughlin and McManus.

d'Aquili, Eugene, Charles D. Laughlin and John McManus. 1979   *The Spectrum of Ritual.* New York: Columbia University Press.

De Heusch, L. 1971   *Pourquois L'Epouser? Autres Essais.* Paris: Gallimard.

Derrida, Jacques. 1976   *Of Grammatology.* Baltimore: Johns Hopkins University Press.

1978   *Writing and Difference.* University of Chicago Press.

Devereux, George. 1961   *Mohave Ethnopsychiatry and Suicide.* Bureau of American Ethnology, Bulletin 175. Washington: Smithsonian Institution.

Dobkin, Toby Blum. 1979   "The Landsberg Carnival: Purim in a Displaced Persons' Center," in *Purim: The Face and the Mask*, Shifra Epstein, ed. New York: Yeshiva University Museum.

Douglas, Mary. 1966   *Purity and Danger: An Analysis of Concepts of Pollution and Taboo.* London: Routledge and Kegan Paul.

1973   *Natural Symbols.* London: Pelican Books.

1975   *Implicit Meanings.* London: Routledge and Kegan Paul.

Durkheim, Emile. 1947   *The Elementary Forms of Religious Life.* Glencoe: The Free Press.

Eck, Diana L. 1981   *Darśan: Seeing the Divine Image in India.* Chambersburg, Pennsylvania: Anima Publications.

Edwards, Christine. 1965   *The Stanislavski Heritage.* New York University Press.

Eibl-Eibesfeldt, Irenaus, 1979   "Ritual and Ritualization from a Biological Perspective" in *Human Ethnology*, von Cranach, M., K. Foppa, W. Lepenies, and D. Ploog, eds. Cambridge University Press.

Ekman, Paul. 1972   "Universal and Cultural Differences in Facial Expressions of Emotion" in *Nebraska Symposium on Motivation, 1971*; 207–83. Omhaha: University of Nebraska Press.

1983   "Autonomic Nervous System Activity Distinguishes Among Emotions," *Science* 221 (16 September): 1208–10.

Ekman, Paul, Wallace Friesen, and Phebe Ellsworth. 1972 *Emotion in the Human Face*. New York: Pergamon Press.

Eliade, Mircea. 1964 *Shamanism: Archaic Techniques of Ecstasy*. New York: Bollingen Foundation.

Eliot, T.S. 1953 *Selected Essays*. London: Faber and Faber.

Epstein, Shifra. 1979 "The Celebration of a Contemporary Purim in the Bobover Hasidic Community," unpublished Ph.D. dissertation, University of Texas, Austin.

Evers, Larry, ed. 1981 *The South Corner of Time: Hopi, Navajo, Papago, Yaqui Tribal Literature*. Tucson: University of Arizona Press.

Findeisen, Hans. 1957 *Schamanentum*. Zurich: Europa Verlag. (Japanese edition, 1977.)

Fischer, Roland. 1971 "A Cartography of the Ecstatic and Meditative States," *Science* 174 (26 November): 897–904.

Foster, George. 1961 "The Dyadic Contract: A Model for the Social Structure of a Mexican Peasant Village," *American Anthropologist* 63: 1173–92.

Foucault, Michel. 1973 *The Order of Things*. New York: Vintage.

Freud, Sigmund. 1961 *Beyond the Pleasure Principle*. New York: W.W. Norton.

Gaignebet, C. 1979 *Le Carneval*. Paris: Payot.

Geertz, Clifford. 1973 "Deep Play: Notes on the Balinese Cockfight," *Interpretation of Cultures*: 412–53. New York: Basic Books.

1980a "Blurred Genres: The Refiguration of Social Thought," *American Scholar* (Spring): 165–79.

1980b *Negara: The Theatre State in Nineteenth-Century Bali*. Princeton University Press.

1983 "From the Native's Point of View," in *Local Knowledge*: 55–70. New York: Basic Books.

Ghosh, Manomohan, ed. and translator. 1967 *Natyasastra* (ascribed to Bharat-Muni). Calcutta: Manisha Granthalaya.

Goff, Janet E. 1984 "The National Noh Theater," *Monumenta Nipponica* 39, 4: 445–52.

Goffman, Erving. 1959 *The Presentation of Self in Everyday Life*. Garden City: Doubleday.

1963 *Behavior in Public Places*. New York: Free Press of Glencoe.

1969a *Interaction Ritual*. Garden City: Doubleday.

1969b *Strategic Interaction*. Philadelphia: University of Pennsylvania Press.

1971 *Relations in Public*. New York: Basic Books.

1974 *Frame Analysis: An Essay on the Organization of Experience*. Cambridge: Harvard University Press.

Goode, W.J. 1964 *The Family*. Englewood Cliffs, NJ: Prentice Hall.

Goodman, Felicitas D., Jerannette H. Henney, and Esther Pressel. 1974 *Trance, Healing, and Hallucination*. New York: John Wiley & Sons.

Griffith, James S. and Molina, Felipe S. 1980 *Old Men of the Fiesta: An Introduction to the Pascola Arts*. Phoenix: The Heard Museum.

Grotowski, Jerzy. 1968 *Towards a Poor Theatre*. Holstebro, Denmark: Odin Teatrets Forlag.

Hallie, Philip P. 1969 *The Paradox of Cruelty*. Middletown: Wesleyan University Press.

Hanson, T. Allen. 1981 "The Semiotics of Religion," *Semiotica* 33, 1/2.

Hare, Thomas Blenman. 1986 *Zeami's Style: The Noh Plays of Zeami Motokiyo*. Stanford University Press.

Harris, Grace. 1957 "Possession 'Hysteria' in a Kenya Tribe, *American Anthropologist* 59: 1046–66.

Harris, Marvin. 1977 *Cows, Pigs, Wars, and Witches: The Riddles of Cultures.* Glasgow: Fontana/Collins.

Harrison, Jane Ellen. 1912 *Themis: A Study of the Social Origins of Greek Religion.* Cambridge University Press.

1913 *Ancient Art and Ritual.* New York: Henry Holt.

Harva, Uno. 1938. *Religiosen Vorstelungen der Altaischen Volker.* Helsinki. (Japanese edition, 1971).

Harvey, Youngsook Kim. 1979 *Six Korean Women: The Socialization of Shamans.* St. Paul: West Publishing Co.

Henney, Jeanette H. 1974 "Spirit-Possession Belief and Trance Behavior in Two Fundamentalist Groups in St. Vincent,": 1–111, in *Trance, Healing, and Hallucination,* Goodman, Felicitas D., Jeannette H. Henney, and Esther Pressel. New York: John Wiley & Sons.

Hochschild, Arlie Russel. 1983 *The Managed Heart.* Berkeley: University of California Press.

Hunt, Eva. 1977 *The Transformation of the Hummingbird: Cultural Roots of a Zinacantecan Mythical Poem.* Ithaca: Cornell University Press.

Hyde, Lewis. 1983 *The Gift: Imagination and the Erotic Life of Property.* New York: Random House.

Izutsu, Toshihiko and Toyo Izutsu. 1981 *The Theory of Beauty in the Classical Aesthetics of Japan.* Amsterdam: Martinus Nijhoff.

Jones, Betty True. 1983 "Kathakali Dance=Drama: An Historical Perspective," in *Performing Arts in India: Essays on Music, Dance, and Drama,* Bonnie C. Wade, ed. Berkeley: Center for South and Southeast Asian Studies.

Jones, J.J., translator and editor. 1949 *Mahavastu,* volume 1. London: Luzac and Co.

Jung, C.G. 1958 *Psyche and Symbol: A Selection from the Writings of C.G. Jung,* Violet de Laszlo, ed. Garden City: Doubleday Anchor.

Kanze, Hisao. 1984 "Life with the Nō Mask," *Mime Journal*: 65–73.

Kapferer, Bruce. 1975 "Form and Transformation in Ritual Performance," paper presented at the Annual meeting of the American Anthropological Association (unpublished).

1979 "Mind, Self, and Other in Demonic Illnesses: The Negation and Reconstruction of Self," *American Ethnologist* 6: 110–33.

1983 *A Celebration of Demons.* Bloomington: Indiana University Press.

Kaprow, Allan. 1983 "The Real Experiment," *Artforum* 22, 4: 36–43.

Kasulis, Thomas. 1983 "Intimacy: A Heuristic for Understanding Japanese Religious Thought," manuscript.

Kendall, Laurel M. 1977 "Mugam: The Dance in Shaman's Clothing," *Korea Journal* 17, 12: 38–44.

1979 *Restless Spirits: Shaman and Housewife in Korean Ritual Life.* Ph.D. dissertation, Columbia University.

Kim, Kwang-Iel. 1972 "Sin-Byung: a Culture-bound Depersonalization Syndrome," *Neuropsychiatry* 11, 4: 223–34.

Kim, Taegon. 1970 "A study of the Shaman's Mystic Illness During Initiation Process in Korea," *Journal of Asian Women* 9: 91–132. (In Korean, with English summary.)

1982 *A Study of Korean Shamanism.* Seoul: Jibmum-dang. (In Korean, with English abstract.)

Kim, Yeol-kyu. 1980 "Several Forms of Korean Folk Rituals, Including Shaman Rituals," *Customs and Manners in Korea*, Shin-Yong Chun, ed. Seoul: International Cultural Foundation.

Kirby, Ernest Theodore. 1975 *Ur Drama – The Origins of Theatre*. New York University Press.

Kirshenblatt-Gimblett, Barbara. 1980 "Contraband: Performance, Text, and Analysis of a Purim-shpil," *TDR* 24, 3: 5–16.

Kitazawa, Ichinen. 1984 "The Expression of Ko-Omote," *Mime Journal*: 125–29.

Komparu, Kunio. 1983 *The Noh Theater*. New York, Tokyo: Weatherhill/Tankosha.

Kongō, Iwao. 1984 "Recollections and Thoughts on Nō," *Mime Journal*: 74–92.

Konishi, Jin'ichi. 1975 *Michi: Chūsei no rinen*. Tokyo: Kodansha.

  1985 "Michi and Medieval Writing," in *Principles of Classical Japanese Literature*: 181–208, Earl Miner, ed. Princeton University Press.

Konner, Melvin. 1982 *The Tangled Wing*. New York: Holt, Rinehart, and Winston.

Koyama, Hioshi, Kikuo Satō, and Kenichirō Satō. 1975 *Yokyokushu* 2. Nihom koten bugku zenshu 34. Tokyo: Kodansha.

Langer, Susanne K. 1982 *Mind: An Essay on Human Feeling*, volume 3. Baltimore: The Johns Hopkins University Press.

Leach, Edmund. 1964 "Anthropological Aspects of Language: Animal Categories and Verbal Abuse" in *New Directions in the Study of Language*, E.H. Lennegerg, ed. Cambridge: MIT Press.

Levi-Strauss, Claude. 1962 *Le Pensee Sauvage*. Paris: Pion.

  1963 "The Sorcerer and His Magic" in *Structural Anthropology*: 167–85. New York: Basic Books.

Lewin, Tamar. 1984 "Ex-Stewardesses vs United," *New York Times*, 24 February, section D: 1, 15.

Lewis, I.M. 1971 *Ecstatic Religion: An Anthropological Study of Spirit Possession and Shamanism*. Middlesex, England: Penguin Books.

  1976 *Social Anthropology in Perspective*. New York: Penguin Books.

Lex, Barbara. 1979 "The Neurobiology of Ritual Trance" in *The Spectrum of Ritual*, d'Aquili, G. Eugene, Charles D. Laughlin, and John McManus. New York: Columbia University Press.

Lucretius. 1951 *On the Nature of Things*. London: Pengiun.

Marcus, George E. and Michael M.J. Fischer. 1986 *Anthropology as Cultural Critique*. University of Chicago Press.

Marriott, McKim. 1976 "Hindu Transactions: Diversity Without Dualism," in *Transaction and Meaning: Directions in the Anthropology of Exchange and Symbolic Behavior*, Bruce Kapferer, ed. Philadelphia: ISHI.

Masakazu, Yamazaki. 1984 "The Aesthetics of Ambiguity: The Artistic Theories of Zeami," in *On the Art of the Nō Drama, The Major Treatises of Zeami*, J. Thomas Rimer and Yamazaki Masakazu, translators. Princeton University Press.

Masuda, Shozō. 1984a *Iikei denrai nōmen kyaku sugata*. Tokyo: Heibonsha.

  1984b *Iikei denrai nō shozoku hyaku sugata*. Tokyo: Heibonsha.

Maurois, Andre. 1960 *Illusions*. New York: Columbia University Press.

McDermott, J.J., ed. 1981 *The Philosophy of John Dewey*. University of Chicago Press.

Merleau-Ponty, Maurice. 1962 *Phenomenology of Perception*. London: Routledge and Kegan Paul.

Monier-Williams, Sir Monier. 1984 *A Sanskrit–English Dictionary*. Delhi: Motilal Banarsidass. (Originally published 1899.)

Murray, Gilbert. 1912a *The Four Stages of Greek Religion.* Oxford University Press.
1921b "Excursus on the Ritual Forms Preserved in Greek Tragedy" in Jane Ellen Harrison, *Themis.* Cambridge University Press.
1925 *The Five Stages of Greek Religion.* Oxford University Press.
1961 "Foreword" to *Thespis,* Gaster, Theodor H. Garden City: Doubleday.
Myerhoff, Barbara. 1978 *Number Our Days.* New York: Dutton.
Nagasena. 1963 *The Questions of King Milinda,* parts 1 and 2. Translated by W. Rhys Davids. New York: Dover Publications.
Namboodiri, M.P. Sankaran. 1983 "Bhāva as Expressed Through the Presentational Techniques of Kathakali," *Dance as Cultural Heritage* volume 1. Betty True Jones, ed. New York: Congress on Research in Dance.
Nearman, Mark J. 1978 "Zeami's *Kyūi,* A Pedagogical Guide for Teacher's of Acting," *Monumenta Nipponica* 33, 3: 299–332.
1980 "*Kyakuraika* Zeami's Final Legacy for the Master Actor," *Monumenta Nipponica* 35, 2: 153–98.
1981 "Zeami on the Goals of the Professional Actor," in *Japanese Tradition: Search and Research:* 43–51. Los Angeles: University of California Asian Performing Arts Summer Institute.
1982a "*Kakyō* Zeami's Fundamental Principles of Acting," *Monumenta Nipponica* 37, 3: 333–74.
1982b "*Kakyō* Zeami's Fundamental Principles of Acting, Part Two," *Monumenta Nipponica* 37, 4: 459–96.
1983 "*Kakyō* Zeami's Fundamental Principles of Acting, Part Three," *Monumenta Nipponica* 38, 1: 49–70.
1984 "Behind the Mask of Noh," *Mime Journal:* 20–64.
Nisbet, Robert. 1967 Sociological Traditions. New York: Basic Books.
Nogami, Toyoichiro. 1955 *Zeami and his Theories on Noh.* Tokyo: Tsunetaro Hinoki, Hinoki Shoten.
Nomura, Manzo. 1984 "Mask Making," *Mime Journal:* 171–76.
Obeyesekere, Gananath. 1963 "The Great Tradition and the Little, in the Perspective of Sinhalese Buddhism," *Journal of Asian Studies,* 22, 2: 139–53.
1969 "The Ritual Drama of the Sanni Demons: Collective Representatives of Disease in Ceylon," *Comparative Studies in Society and History* 11, 2: 174–216.
Ochi, Reiko. 1984 *Buddism and Poetic Theory: An Analysis of Zeami's Higaki and Takasago.* Ph.D. dissertation, Cornell University.
Ortalani, Benito. 1972 "Zeami's Aesthetics of the Nō and Audience Participation," *Educational Theatre Journal* 24, 2: 109–17.
1983 "Spirituality for the Dancer-Actor in Zeami's and Zenchiku's Writings on the Nō," in *Dance as a Cultural Heritage* volume 1: 147–58, Betty True Jones, ed. New York: Congress on Research in Dance.
1984 "Shamanism in the Origins of Nō Theatre," *Asian Theatre Journal* 1, 2: 166–90.
Ortner, Sherry. 1978 *Sherpas through their Rituals.* Cambridge University Press.
Painter, Muriel Thayer. 1950 *A Yaqui Easter.* Tucson: University of Arizona Press.
1981 *With Good Heart.* Tucson: University of Arizona Press.
Peacock, James L. 1968 *Rites of Modernization: Symbolic and Social Aspects of Indonesian Proletarian Drama.* University of Chicago Press.
Pilgrim, Richard. 1972 "Zeami and the Way of Nō," *History of Religions* 12, 2: 136–48.
Rappaport, Roy. 1968 *Pigs for the Ancestors: Ritual in the Ecology of a New Guinea People.* New Haven: Yale University Press.

Raz, Jacob. 1983 *Audience and Actors: A Study of their Interaction in the Japanese Traditional Theatre*. Leiden: E.J. Brill.

Rhi, Bou-Yong. 1970 "Analytic-Psychological Study on Shamanistic Treatment of the dead Spirit in Korean Shamanism," *The New Medical Journal* 13, 1: 79–94. (In Korean with abstract in German.)

Rhys Davids, T.W., ed. 1921 *Dialogues of the Buddha*, Part III, volume 4. Humphrey Milford, Oxford University Press.

Rhys Davids, T.W. and C.A.F. 1938 *Dialogues of the Buddha*, part 2. London: Luzac and Co.

Rhys Davids, T.W. and William Stede. 1923 *The Pali English Dictionary*, part 5. London: *The Pali Text Society*, Routledge Keegan and Paul.

Rimer, J. Thomas and Yamazaki Masakazu, translators and eds. 1984 *On the Art of the Nō Drama: The Major Treatises of Zeami* Princeton University Press.

Richardson, Miles 1986 "Material Culture and Being-in-Christ in Spanish America and the American South." In *Architecture in Cultural Change: Essays in Built Form and Culture Research*. David G. Saile, ed. Lawrence, Kansas: School of Architecture and Urban Design, University of Kansas.

Rothenberg, Jerome and Diane Rothenberg, eds. 1983 *Symposium of the Whole*. Berkeley: University of California Press.

Sarachchandra, E.R. 1966 *The Folk Drama of Ceylon*. Colombo: Department of Cultural Affairs.

Schafer, R. Murray. 1977 *The Tuning of the World*. New York: Knopf.

Schechner, Richard. 1966 "Approaches to Theory/Criticism," *TDR* 10, 4: 20–53.
1977 *Essays on Performance Theory*. New York: Drama Books Specialists, Publishers. Second edition in press, Methuen, Inc.
1982 "Universals of Performance: Magnitudes of Performance," paper prepared for Wenner-Gren Symposium 89, *Theater and Ritual*.
1983 "Performers and Spectators Transported and Transformed," in *Peformative Circumstances: From the Avant Garde to Ramlila*: 90–123. Calcutta: Seagull Books.
1985 *Between Theater and Anthropology*. Philadelphia: University of Pennsylvania Press.
1986a "Victor Turner's Last Adventure," Introduction to *The Anthropology of Performance*, Victor Turner. New York: PAJ Publications.
1986b "Wrestling Against Time: The Performance Aspects of *Agni*," *Journal of Asian Studies* 45, 2: 359–64.
1987 "A 'Vedic Ritual' In Quotation Marks," *Journal of Essays on Performance Theory*, second edition. London and New York: Methuen.
1988 *Performance Theory* (second revised edition of *Essays on Performance Theory*). London and New York: Routledge.

Scheflen, Albert E. 1973 *How Behavior Means*. New York: Gordon and Breach.

Schwimmer, E. 1980 "Religion in Culture." In *People in Culture*. I. Rossi, ed. New York: Bergin & Garvey.

Scott, A.C. 1975 "Reflections on the Aesthetic Background of the Performing Arts of East Asia," *Asian Music* 6, 1–2: 207–16.

Shirokogoroff, S.M. 1923 "General Theory of Shamanism among the Tungus," *Journal of the Royal Asiatic Society, North China Branch* 54.
1935 *Psychomental Complex of the Tungus*. London: Kegan Paul, Trench, Trubner & Co.

Shuman, Amy. 1982 "Shalakh-mones: The Folklore of Reciprocity," unpublished paper.

Singer, Milton. 1972 *When a Great Tradition Modernizes: An Anthropological Approach to Indian Civilization.* New York: Praeger.

1984 *Man's Glassy Essence.* Bloomington: Indiana University Press.

Spicer, Edward H. 1940 *Pascua, A Yaqui Village in Arizona.* University of Chicago Press (1983 Tucson: University of Arizona Press).

1954 "Potam, A Yaqui Village in Sonora," *American Anthropological Association* 56, 4, part 2, Memoir no. 77, August.

1962 *Cycles of Conquest: The Impact of Spain, Mexico, and the United States on the Indians of the Southwest, 1533–1960.* Tucson: University of Arizona Press.

1980 *The Yaquis: A Cultural History.* Tucson: University of Arizona Press.

Spicer, Rosamond B. 1939 *The Easter Fiesta of the Yaqui Indians of Pascua, Arizona.* M.A. thesis, University of Chicago.

Staal, Frits. 1987 "Professor Schechner's Passion for Goats," *Journal of Asian Studies* 45, 1: 105–7.

Stebbins, Genevieve. 1977 *Delsarte System of Expression.* New York: Dance Horizons.

Takabayashi, Kōji. 1984 "Okina," *Mime Journal*: 93–103.

Tambiah, S.J. 1981 "A Performative Approach to Ritual," *Proceedings of the British Academy* 65 (1979): 113–69. London: Oxford University Press.

TDR *(Tulane Drama Review).* 1964 *Stanislavski in America* (special issues) 9, 1 and 2.

Tessenkai. 1979 *Kanze Hisao: Shika no fūshi.* Tokyo: Heibonsha.

Tocqueville, Alexis de. 1945 *Democracy in America*, P. Bradley, ed. New York: Alfred Knopf.

Tsu, Lao. 1972 *Tao Te Ching.* New York: Vintage.

Tsumura, Reijirō. 1984 "*Dōjōji*: Preparations for a Second Performance," *Mime Journal*: 104–13.

Tsunoda, Ryusaku, William de Bary, and Donald Keene, eds. 1958 *Sources of the Japanese Tradition.* New York: Columbia University Press.

Tuan, Yi Fu. 1982 *Segmented Worlds and Self.* Minneapolis: University of Minnesota Press.

Turner, Frederick. 1985 *Natural Classicism.* New York: Paragon House.

Turner, Victor W. 1967 *The Forest of Symbols.* Ithaca: Cornell University Press.

1969 *The Ritual Process.* Chicago: Aldine.

1974 *Dramas, Fields, and Metaphors.* Ithaca: Cornell University Press.

1982a "Are There Universals in Performance?" paper prepared for participants in Symposium 89, Wenner-Gren Foundation for Anthropological Research.

1982b *From Ritual to Theatre: The Human Seriousness of Play.* New York: Performing Arts Journal Press.

1983 "Body, Brain, and Culture," *Zygon* 18, 3 (September): 221–46.

1986a *On the Edge of the Bush.* Tucson: University of Arizona Press.

1986b *The Anthropology of Performance.* New York: PAJ Publications.

Turner, Victor W. and Edith Turner. 1978 *Image and Pilgrimage in Christian Culture.* New York: Columbia University Press.

Varenne, Jean. 1976 *Yoga and the Hindu Tradition.* University of Chicago Press.

Walens, Stanley. 1982 "The Weight of my Name is a Mountain of Blankets: Potlatch Ceremonies," in Victor Turner, ed., *Celebration: Studies in Festivity and Ritual.* Washington, D.C.: Smithsonian Institution Press.

Wilder, Carleton S. 1963 *The Yaqui Deer Dance: A Study in Cultural Change.* Washington, D.C.: Smithsonian Institution, Bureau of American Ethnology, Government Printing Office, Bulletin 186, Anthropological Papers, no. 66.

Winch, R. 1958 *Mate Selection.* New York: Harper & Row.
Winch, R., R. McGinnis, and H.R. Barringer. 1962 *Selected Studies in Marriage and the Family.* New York: Holt, Rinehard, and Winston.
Wirz, Paul. 1954 *Exorcism and the Art of Healing in Ceylon.* Leiden: E.J. Brill.
Wittgenstein, Ludwig. 1980 *Culture and Value.* University of Chicago Press.
Zarrilli, Philip. 1977 "Demystifying Kathakali," *Sangeet Natak* 43: 48–59.
    1978 Kalarippayatt and the Performing Artist, East and West." Ph.D. dissertation, University of Minnesota.
    1979 "Kalarippayatt, Martial Art of Kerala, *TDR* 23, 2: 113–24.
    1984a *The Kathakali Complex: Actor, Performance, Structure.* New Delhi: Abhinav.
    1984b "'Doing the Exercise': the In-body Transmission of Performance Knowledge in a Traditional Martial Art," *Asian Theatre Journal* 1, 2: 191–206.
    1984c "Tradition and Change in Kathakali Dance-Drama," manuscript in press.

Index